Critical Lessons

Critical Lessons concentrates on the critical, reflective thinking that should be encouraged in high schools. Taking seriously the Socratic advice "know thyself," it focuses on topics that will help students to understand the forces – good and bad – that work to socialize them. This book argues that critical thinking is necessary in both schools and society, and that it requires the discussion of controversial issues: how we learn, the psychology of war, what it means to make a home, advertising and propaganda, choosing an occupation, gender, and religion. Learning how to discuss such issues is vital for life in a liberal democracy.

Nel Noddings is Lee L. Jacks Professor of Education, Emerita, at Stanford University. She is past president of the Philosophy of Education Society and of the John Dewey Society. In addition to publishing fourteen books – among them are *Caring: A Feminine Approach to Ethics and Moral Education, Women and Evil, The Challenge to Care in Schools, Educating for Intelligent Belief or Unbelief,* and *Philosophy of Education* – she is the author of some 200 articles and chapters on various topics ranging from the ethics of care to mathematical problem solving. Her latest books are *Starting at Home: Caring and Social Policy, Educating Moral People: A Caring Alternative to Character Education,* and *Happiness and Education* (Cambridge University Press).

Noddings spent fifteen years as a teacher, administrator, and curriculum developer in public schools. She served as a mathematics department chairperson in New Jersey and as Director of the Laboratory Schools at the University of Chicago. At Stanford, she received the Award for Teaching Excellence three times, most recently in 1997. She also served as Associate Dean and as Acting Dean at Stanford University for four years.

Ah, what a dusty answer gets the soul
When hot for certainties in this our life!

George Meredith

Critical
Lessons

What Our Schools Should Teach

NEL NODDINGS

CAMBRIDGE UNIVERSITY PRESS
Cambridge, New York, Melbourne, Madrid, Cape Town, Singapore, São Paulo

Cambridge University Press
40 West 20th Street, New York, NY 10011-4211, USA

www.cambridge.org
Information on this title: www.cambridge.org/9780521851886

First published 2006

Printed in the United States of America

A catalog record for this publication is available from the British Library.

Library of Congress Cataloging in Publication Data

Noddings, Nel.
Critical lessons : what our schools should teach / Nel Noddings.
    p. cm.
Includes bibliographical references and index.
ISBN 0-521-85188-2 (hardback)
1. Critical thinking – Study and teaching (Secondary)   I. Title.
BF441.N63 2006
373.1102–dc22   2006004121

ISBN-13   978-0-521-85188-6 hardback
ISBN-10   0-521-85188-2 hardback

Contents

Acknowledgments • vii

Introduction • 1

1   Learning and Self-Understanding • 10

2   The Psychology of War • 36

3   House and Home • 64

4   Other People • 93

5   Parenting • 119

6   Animals and Nature • 147

7   Advertising and Propaganda • 170

8   Making a Living • 198

9   Gender • 224

10 Religion • 250

11 Preparing Our Schools • 282

Bibliography • 291

Index • 307

Acknowledgments

The writing of this book was aided greatly by ideas and feedback from lecture audiences at Rowan University, Richmond School District (Canada), the University of Rochester, Hobart William Smith College, the Norton Lecture at the University of Delaware, the East-West Philosophy Conference at the University of Hawaii, and Horace Mann School. Thanks, too, to the editors and readers of *Phi Delta Kappan* for comments on an early version of Chapter 2, "The Psychology of War."

For reading and commenting on several chapters or outlines, I thank Liora Bresler, Randall Curren, Harvey Siegel, and Steve Thornton. Conversations with Steve and with Lynda Stone were also helpful.

I also thank Philip Laughlin, Helen Greenberg, and Helen Wheeler at Cambridge University Press for their continued interest and admirable efficiency.

As usual – and always – thanks go to my students, children, grandchildren, and husband, from whom I continue to learn about issues on which our best critical thinking is required.

Introduction

> "It is not our business," he said, "to help students to think for them-
> selves. Surely this is the very last thing which one who wishes them
> well should encourage them to do. Our duty is to ensure that they
> shall think as we do, or at any rate, as we hold it expedient to say
> we do."
>
> The Professor of Worldly Wisdom in Samuel Butler, *Erewhon*

When the United States invaded Iraq in 2003, many public
school teachers were forbidden to discuss the war in their
classrooms. Such a restriction on free discussion seems outrageous
in a liberal democracy. But, although free debate is rarely so directly
forbidden, the suppression of discussion and critical thinking in our
educational system is widespread. Usually it is accomplished by defin-
ing the curriculum so narrowly and specifically that genuinely controversial issues simply do not arise. Without controversial issues,
critical thinking is nonexistent or, at best, weak. Students are encouraged now and then to exercise a bit of critical thinking in science or
mathematics as they try to solve word problems or think of alternative
hypotheses, but such exercises are usually constrained tightly by the
topic at hand and the limited knowledge of young students. Further,
this sort of critical thinking does not challenge deeply held beliefs or
ways of life.

In recent interactions with students at some of our finest universities and colleges, I've been amazed to learn that many of them have
never been asked in school to consider: that the story of Adam and
Eve is a myth, and that its status as a myth is part of its great power;
what it means to make a home; how their own minds work and what

1

motivates their thinking; that the drive for top-notch grades may actually reduce intrinsic motivation for learning; that joining the military and engaging in battle may cause the loss not only of life or limb, but of moral identity or soul; that some forms of parenting are more effective than others for life in liberal democracies; that it might not be true that most jobs in the near future will require a college education. This list presents just some of the topics, claims, and issues to which critical thinking should be applied, but they are rarely addressed in schools. Good teachers should not ask that students believe or disbelieve the ideas and claims involved in the topics just mentioned, but they should encourage students to think about them and discuss them.

The neglect of critical thinking is not limited to poor urban and rural schools. It is pervasive. Young people preparing to teach are not encouraged to challenge the slogan "All children can learn" or even to ask what it means. Some have told me, in amazement, that I was the first (respectable) person who had ever suggested to them that perhaps not all children need algebra and geometry. Again, some are aghast when I tell them honestly that I do not believe that "poor children can learn as well as rich children." They have never considered the possibility that, by advertising the success of some hard-working educators with poor children, we may be encouraging a mean-spirited public to suppose that it need do nothing about poverty and its attendant ills – lack of decent housing, medical insurance, safe streets, financial security, adequate diet, and sufficient time for a rich family life. Just expect more from poor children and their teachers!

The neglect of topics that call forth critical and reflective thinking pervades our system of education. Teachers study some psychology and are urged to use what they learn in classrooms. They use psychology *on* students but not *with* them. Teachers and students are rarely invited to turn a reflective eye on their own thought processes and work habits. In a passion to control students, parents and teachers often structure homework and study time, assign penalties for missing deadlines, and preach lessons on the value of hard, steady work. But teachers might instead encourage students to ask questions such as: When and under what conditions do I do my best work? Is it ever productive to stop thinking and just look or listen? Is it possible that a problem, topic, or potential product might "speak" to us or somehow reveal itself? Is it sometimes morally acceptable and creatively productive to do less than my best work? What does it mean, anyway, to be educated?

An exploration of such questions opens the door not only to reflective thinking about one's own work habits but also to a host of wonderful biographical accounts, psychological/historical studies, and the analysis of claims for the enhancement of creativity through religion, drugs, alcohol, exercise, meditation, and fasting. Why do we not teach critical lessons on these topics? One answer to this question is ignorance. People who have never explored these topics are unlikely to provide opportunities for others to do so; the notion never arises.

But fear may be an even greater impediment. What harm might we do to our students if we encourage them to think critically and reflectively? It is not only fictional characters like Butler's Professor of Worldly Wisdom and Dickens's Thomas Gradgrind who fear that real harm might be done to individuals or to the social fabric by promoting critical thinking. Edmund Burke expressed misgivings along these lines and, more recently, William Galston warned against encouraging students to question their own ways of life.[1] Burke and Galston feared that the social order itself might suffer if citizens were to exercise critical thinking. But there are other fears. If students hear about artists who have used drugs, might they decide to copy them? If they hear about people who dropped out of school and yet became highly successful, might they quit school then and there? If they learn that some religious revelations are the products of near starvation, might they either discount the revelations or starve themselves?

Fear of adverse effects also inhibits discussion of the psychology of war, religion, and even parenting. On the last, although every sensible person recognizes the importance of the topic, many fear that teaching about parenting in public schools may offend those who wish to keep public and private domains sharply separated, upset some minorities whose parenting styles may not be favored, and raise

---

[1] See Eamonn Callan, "Liberal Legitimacy, Justice, and Civic Education," *Ethics* 111, October 2000: 141–155; see also William Galston, *Liberal Purposes: Goods, Virtues and Diversity in the Liberal State* (Cambridge: Cambridge University Press, 1991); also Galston, "Two Concepts of Liberalism," *Ethics* 105(3), 1995: 516–534.

issues about gay/lesbian families. Why open ourselves to controversy when there are so many safe (if boring) topics to teach?

In this book, I consider an array of topics that demand critical thinking. In doing so, I use a broad definition of critical thinking, and I rarely differentiate it from reflective thinking. *Critical thinking* refers not only to the assessment of arguments (that will certainly be included) but also to the diligent and skillful use of reason on matters of moral/social importance – on personal decision making, conduct, and belief. By including its application to personal belief and decision making, we extend critical thinking to every domain of human interest. Mathematicians, health care professionals, artists, and farmers all properly use critical thinking in deciding what to believe and what to do in their professional lives. For present purposes, however, I have chosen topics that should be of crucial interest to everyone: teaching and learning, war, homemaking, parenting, advertising, making a living, relating to nonhuman animals, issues of gender, and religion. To neglect critical thinking on topics central to everyday life is to make the word *education* virtually meaningless.

Concentrating on the diligent and skillful use of reason does not imply that we will ignore emotion and feeling. With David Hume, I believe that human beings are mainly motivated by emotion or passion, but that belief does not entail that our emotions should not be carefully examined by reason. (There may be exceptions to this, as Freud has noted.) It is rarely helpful for others to tell us that we "shouldn't feel that way," but it can be enormously useful for us to ask ourselves, "Why am I feeling this way?" Nor will I argue that all of our commitments must be supported by rational argument. Some of our most important commitments are nonrational, but even these may be enriched by asking, Why? and accepting the reassuring inner answer that they are somehow final in themselves: She is my child, I love him, this is my country, God says. . . . Notice, however, that others may ask, Why? even though we are content with our nonrational commitment. When that happens, we should be willing to engage in a new round of critical thinking. However, caring and affect will always be factors in the application of critical thinking.

Almost all of the topics considered here might be explored from a civic perspective; that is, our main concerns might be directed at improving the communities in which we live. Such concerns will indeed arise, but their careful examination must await a future volume. Here the emphasis – not exclusive, of course – is on self-understanding and how critical thinking may be applied to our individual lives.

I start this book on critical lessons with the least controversial of the topics to be considered: learning. Why do I learn? What motivates me? Must I learn everything the teacher or expert sets out? Is it all right to do less than my best work? Under what conditions do I work best? Why do I work hard (or not work hard) in school? When we talk with students about these questions (and we rarely do – instead, we talk at them), we often propagandize. Without thinking critically ourselves, we simply pass on the party line: Work hard, get high marks, go to a good college, get a good job, make lots of money, and buy lots of stuff! Will this bring happiness? Is this what education is all about?

The second major topic for critical lessons is the psychology of war. Most of the young people who fill the enlisted ranks in our armed forces are not college graduates. They have had little exposure (perhaps none at all) to the literature on pacifism and opposition to war. They know, of course, that they might be injured or killed in battle, but they have not been encouraged to consider the horrible things that they might do as fighting rages. Atrocities? Those are committed by the enemy, by the bad guys. Our side stands for peace and freedom. We say that education should prepare young people for adult life. Can we claim to educate, then, if we do not prepare our students for the many possible soul-destroying effects of war? How does it happen that otherwise good people commit atrocious acts in war? How do some real heroes avoid moral degeneration?

American students study a lot about war in their social studies courses. Indeed, a year's course of study may be organized around war: "From the Revolution to the Civil War" or "The Civil War to World War I." They learn something about the political and economic causes of war, but they do not study the psychological causes of participation. What makes war so exciting? Why are so many people drawn to it? And why do educators accept texts and curricula that fail to address the psychology of war? As we explore this topic, we will see, too, that the psychology of the public response to war should be examined. Why are military personnel ignored or even denigrated in times of peace? How do they become, overnight, "our boys" and "heroes" in times of war?

The next several topics concentrate on everyday life. What does it mean to make a home? It may seem odd to consider critical thinking in connection with homemaking. What is there about making a home that requires critical thinking? The short answer to this question is, almost everything. For many of us, home is the major source of both sustenance and happiness; for others, it is a source of contention and misery. Today we insist that everyone (almost without exception) must study academic mathematics. Yet relatively few students will actually use this material in their adult lives. In contrast, all of us make a home of some sort. Why, then, does homemaking not appear as a serious and sustained subject in our schools? Among the questions we will consider are these: What is a home? What does our house, room, or corner say about us? What attitude might we take toward our possessions? What organic habits do we acquire in our childhood homes? Is it possible (or desirable) to enjoy household tasks? What role does conversation play in contributing to the growth of partners and children? What does ignorance or ineptitude on these topics contribute to present societal conditions? Are there people who want to maintain those conditions? Can it be that your ignorance might serve my purposes?

The next topic, other people, is one of primary interest to adolescents. How do we relate to other people? What do we need to learn about patterns of communication? Is it true that, as one of Sartre's characters lamented, "Hell is other people"? Or is our greatest happiness derived from relations with other people? In treating this topic, we will look at the relation between mother and child, between men and women, and the history of relations characterized by domination. Why have men insisted on dominating and controlling women, and what harm has been done by this longstanding pattern of domination? That question will be revisited in the chapter on gender.

In all of this discussion, topics will be suggested that might add greatly to the cultural literacy of students. Students cannot think critically without some knowledge of the topics under consideration, but it is a mistake to defer critical thinking indefinitely while we stuff information into our students. I hope to convince readers that much of the curriculum now taught in unmotivated fragments might better be introduced as material to trigger or facilitate critical thinking. Conversely, critical questions may well necessitate a search for knowledge.

Introduction

Many of the questions we consider will appear in several contexts and thus will be treated more than once. For example, in the discussion of male–female relations, I will raise the question of why so many theologians and preachers have preferred the creation story of Adam and Eve over the simpler one – "male and female created he them" – that also appears in Genesis. This question will arise again in the chapter on religion, but its treatment there will extend to a study of evil and its role in religion. Repetition of this sort – of topic, not of argument – can be taken as evidence for the centrality of certain issues in human life. Their frequent appearance makes us wonder even more why they are not addressed critically in schools.

Among our most important human relations is that of parent and child. Why is parenting not a central object of study in schools? Raising this question provides an opportunity to discuss the traditional liberal separation of public and private life and to ask who benefits and who is harmed by that separation. What arguments are made to support the separation? The study of parenting should also include open, sensitive examination of parenting styles and why it is now widely believed – at least in professional circles – that an authoritative style is more effective for life in a liberal democracy than either an authoritarian or a permissive style.[2] Not only would social studies and psychology courses be enriched by such study, but one can well imagine great interest being aroused by a semester's study of children's literature in English.

In addition to a host of critical questions on our relations with other human beings, many people today are concerned with our relations to nonhuman animals. The object of critical thinking in this area is neither to convert students to vegetarianism nor to debunk the work of those who insist on the ethical treatment of animals. The aim is to examine a host of questions concerning our love and care for pets, the treatment of animals raised for food, the harm done to the environment by some methods of animal farming, and the many dilemmas (both logical and moral) that arise as we try to work through these problems. Again, related topics will appear in more than one chapter.

[2] See Diana Baumrind, *Child Maltreatment and Optimal Caregiving in Social Contexts* (New York: Garland, 1995).

7

The emphasis in this book is on critical thinking for self-understanding, but the questions considered will lead us into social and philosophical problems as well. As we ask questions central to everyday life, we have to explore issues of social, moral, and cultural importance. When students are invited to think about how they will eventually make a living for themselves and their families, they should also be asked to reflect on the lives of others. In the best society, would anyone live in poverty? What have social thinkers said about this problem? What sort of work might I enjoy and why? What do I owe to those who do necessary work that I would hate to do?

Continuing a focus on everyday life, we will explore the topics of advertising and our lives as consumers. Math teachers often use ads to get students to do some consumer calculations. Which of two similar brands is the better buy? Sometimes teachers have students look for outright (or likely) lies in advertising. But we rarely ask students to consider how we are all manipulated by advertising. Why is it so profitable? If we were to ignore it – even defy it – would our economy collapse? Is the deliberate choice of a simple lifestyle unpatriotic? Is it ethical to work for a company that produces or advertises a harmful product? How should critical thinkers resist the manipulation of advertising?

In chapter 9, we'll return to topics treated earlier – now from the perspective of gender. Why are women paid less than men for the same work? Why are so many women, and so few men, employed in the so-called caring professions? Should girls be taught to avoid these fields? Are males and females genetically different psychologically and intellectually as well as anatomically? How has the topic of "woman" been treated in Western culture and by whom? What attitude should we take toward homosexuality? Some of the questions addressed here will lead logically to the following topic.

That topic – religion – is perhaps the most controversial of all. Dare we discuss religious questions in school? Young people who have the good fortune to attend fine universities or liberal arts colleges are introduced to powerful arguments for and against religion. We do not suppose that exposure to Augustine will convert our students to Catholicism or that reading Freud will make them atheists. Conscientious teachers approach questions of religion (and all other questions) nondogmatically. They search out and present the most powerful arguments on all sides and invite students to engage them critically. Students are not told what to believe. They learn what others have said and believed. Some of the world's most beautiful and engaging literature treats religious issues. It should not be reserved for elite college students. But I am not suggesting a mere survey course in which students are introduced to the world's great religions. When students read Augustine and Freud, they will encounter *arguments*, and this will invite critical thinking on the logic of certain religious doctrines. Although I believe this sort of examination should be conducted in secondary education, I am not at all sure that it can be done well. The alternative – to shield large numbers of people from knowledge and critical thinking on religion – is unattractive, but my suggested course of critical lessons is loaded with problems. I will leave it to readers to decide how much of what I suggest is feasible.

Finally, in a brief conclusion, I turn to the problems of teacher education. Most teachers are not critical thinkers because they have not been asked to think critically. They readily accept the propaganda put forth by their professional associations and professors, and then they pass much of it along to their students. How can we help those training to teach to become critical thinkers? Is it important that we do so? As we explore these questions, we will see that the massive structure of schooling as it is makes our task very difficult. Indeed, many of the great educational critics of the 1960s all but despaired in their efforts to move public schools toward the greater freedom and critical thinking required by democratic education.[3] Still, if only as a thought exercise, we should try again.

[3] See Ron Miller, *Free Schools, Free People: Education and Democracy After the 1960s* (Albany: State University of New York Press, 2002).

1

Learning and Self-Understanding

> What brains they must have in Christminster and the great schools, he presently thought, to learn words one by one up to tens of thousands!
>
> Thomas Hardy, *Jude the Obscure*

P ossibly no goal of education is more important – or more neglected – than self-understanding. Socrates advised us, "Know thyself," and he claimed that the unexamined life is not worth living. We may feel that Socrates went too far on this, thereby dismissing the lives of millions who have not had the opportunity to examine their lives. But when we claim to *educate*, we must take Socrates seriously. Unexamined lives may well be valuable and worth living, but an education that does not invite such examination may not be worthy of the label *education*.

In an important sense, this entire book is about self-understanding and an examination of how external and internal forces affect out lives. We need to ask not only what we believe but why we believe it. Similarly, we need to ask, What do I feel? Why? What am I doing? Why? And even, What am I saying? And, again, why?

The most fundamental expectation of schooling is that students will learn. If we want them to learn to use their minds well, it is reasonable to help them understand how their minds function, how and why they learn. What motivates us to learn? What habits are helpful? Why do I remember some things and forget so many others? Does the object of learning ever enter actively into the process? If so, how can I encourage it to speak to me?

Motivation

Every living human being is motivated. We are motivated to satisfy our felt needs. Psychologists and philosophers have argued about the meaning of *motivation* and how to distinguish motives from desires, impulses, instincts, and drives. I will not engage in this debate unless the topic under discussion demands it. Instead, I will mainly use *motive* and *motivation* because they appear so often and so prominently in the literature on pedagogy. A big question for educators is whether teachers should work with the motives that students bring to the classroom – trying, of course, to steer them toward worthwhile ends – or encourage new forms of motivation designed to satisfy needs of which students are not yet aware. In the latter case, it could be argued that teachers are simply using existing motives such as the desire for rewards to "motivate" students to learn history, math, and science. Both theories of motivation recognize inherent motivation, but the second is willing to manipulate motives thought not to be all that admirable toward new motives that will seek to satisfy the needs inferred by parents and teachers. The difference between the two theories is often expressed this way: Theory 1 claims that internal motivation and intrinsic interests, properly guided, are sufficient for learning whatever the student needs to learn; Theory 2 claims that external motivation must provide students with the incentive to learn what they should learn.

The theory of motivation embraced by teachers influences how they select subject matter and how they teach. Teachers in the Progressive tradition lean toward the first; that is, they believe that teachers should identify and work with (ethically acceptable) student motives.[1] Such teachers do not motivate. Rather, they work with existing intrinsic interests. In contrast, some teachers in the classical tradition believe that students do not know their real needs or what should interest them, and therefore it is the job of schools to motivate

---

[1] A large literature exists on this topic. Theory 1 is prominent in holistic education; for an analysis, see Scott Forbes, *Holistic Education: An Analysis of Its Ideas and Nature* (Brandon, VT: Foundation for Educational Renewal, 2003). It also appears in the progressive education of John Dewey and his followers. Dewey's analysis, however, places activity and natural impulse prior to motive, which he associates with judgment. See Dewey, *Human Nature and Conduct* (New York: Modern Library, 1930).

students to meet these real needs. From this perspective, students need academic mathematics, science, and foreign languages, and teachers should motivate their students to master these subjects. Behaviorist educators also take the view that needs (other than the obvious physical ones – some instincts and drives) are motivated externally through systems of natural and social conditioning.[2] Then there are educators who take an intermediate position, preferring the first theory for its generous acceptance of the variety of human interests but recognizing the power of external motivation in a complex world.[3] Even A. S. Neill, the most permissive of educators holding the first view, admitted that, unfortunately, human beings – like dogs – can be conditioned.[4] But good teachers, according to Neill, refuse to manipulate students in this way and encourage naturally good intrinsic interests.

For present purposes, the focus of attention is not on the selection of a theory of motivation but on sharing knowledge about theories of motivation and helping students to understand their own motives and how their society attempts to manipulate them. Suppose, to get the discussion started, a high school teacher were to ask her students: "How many of you would study this topic (or do this work) if I just left it up to you?" What sorts of answers might we hear? Some, of course, would be dishonest. This is especially likely when we initiate such a discussion with students who are conditioned to give a teacher what the teacher wants. But if we persevere openly and honestly, we are likely to hear any or all of the following:

1. I would. I really like this stuff.
2. I'm not crazy about it, but I know I'll need it to become a ———. So I'd do it.

---

[2] For the behaviorist position, see B. F. Skinner, *Science and Human Behavior* (New York: Free Press, 1953); also Skinner, *Beyond Freedom and Dignity* (New York: Vintage Books, 1972). For the position – very different in its psychology from behaviorism – that children must be strongly directed through prescribed studies, see Mortimer Adler, *The Paideia Proposal* (New York: Macmillan, 1982); also Robert Maynard Hutchins, *The Higher Learning in America* (New Haven, CT: Yale University Press, 1936).

[3] See my "Must We Motivate?" in *Teaching and Its Discontents*, ed. Nicholas Burbules and David Hansen (Boulder, CO: Westview Press, 1997), pp. 29–44. See also the statement of his own interactive position in Lee J. Cronbach, *Educational Psychology* (New York: Harcourt Brace Jovanovich, 1977).

[4] See A. S. Neill, *Summerhill* (New York: Hart, 1960).

3. My father would make me do it. I wouldn't even be in this class otherwise.
4. You've made it sound sort of interesting, so maybe I'd do it.
5. If I could, I'd quit this stuff right now. Up to me? I'm outta here!

The teacher might follow up with a hypothetical scenario, saying that she is seriously thinking about turning the class loose on the topic for two or three weeks. "I'll give you any help you request," she says, "and at the end of that time, we'll talk about what you've learned." The next student comment will almost certainly be, "And what'll we get?" What, indeed? Now teacher and students must face the facts of institutional demands for grading. Teachers are usually not free to let students pursue their own interests even on topics selected by the teacher. What the teacher does next probably depends on the theory of motivation she accepts. Perhaps the initial discussion could end with the teacher's suggestion to think about it: "What motivates you? Should I (the teacher) motivate you? How?"

Notice that this conversation could take place in any subject matter class, and it would be useful in all subjects. With a Theory 1 teacher of mathematics, for example, the conversation might end (temporarily) with recognition that the teacher cannot turn the students loose on the subject but that she will provide material suitable for the full range of stated motivations. There will be lots of mathematical puzzles and challenges for those intrinsically motivated, substantial preparation for those whose future occupations require mathematics, and a defensible minimum accompanied by genuine sympathy for those forced into mathematical study against their will.

Theory 2 teachers might conclude the initial discussion by pointing out to students that they do not yet understand their needs – that in fact it is in their best interests to increase their commitment to work hard. "I'll help!" can also be the attitude of these teachers, and students may then better understand why certain incentives are offered.

Notice that there are critical lessons here for teachers as well as students. Perhaps neither theory of motivation can hold up against all challenges. As a teacher, I have always favored Theory 1, but there are times when I have used practices more consonant with Theory 2. The structure of schooling forces this compromise on us. Further, students are not always aware of needs that will surely arise, and there are students so accustomed to external rewards that they cannot function without them. Should I abandon these students because they do not fit my theory of motivation? Moreover, careful study may reveal features of either theory that should be questioned by a critical thinker. For example, many advocates of Theory 1 believe that the child is born naturally good and has inherently good motives. I don't believe this. But neither do I believe that children are born evil and need to be saved or that they are inherently lazy and seek only pleasure. With Dewey, I believe that children (like all of us) have both good and bad desires – desires that we evaluate as good or bad motives.

There is a larger point here for teachers. A theory held stubbornly against every objection becomes an ideology, and as an ideology it loses some of its usefulness as a guide to practice. Instead, it becomes an end to itself and demands continual and vigorous defense. In later discussions, we'll meet several examples of this distortion of theory in teaching. Clinging to an ideology has the appearance (and many of the effects) of idolatry.

Whatever theory is held, teachers concerned with critical thinking should invite genuine reflection and further study. Further study, however, raises new problems. We might suggest that students interested in the motivation to learn read Ivan Illich's *Deschooling Society*, in which Illich claims that people would be motivated on their own to seek out mentors and instruction for skills and information they might need. We don't need compulsory schooling! They might read A. S. Neill's *Summerhill* and become interested in free schools or perhaps something by Abraham Maslow. (Any of these would be useful in supporting Theory 1.) They could also read something by B. F. Skinner (to support Theory 2) and perhaps Mortimer Adler's *Paideia Proposal* (to support Theory 2's claim that students do not know their own needs).[5] But where would they read such books? Clearly, we can and should talk about motivation in all of our classes, but can we assign or even strongly encourage the reading of, say, Skinner's *Walden Two* in math class? It is one thing to invite reflection, quite another to deepen that reflection with careful study and analysis. The system is not organized to encourage such study.

[5] See Ivan Illich, *Deschooling Society* (New York: Harper & Row, 1971); Abraham H. Maslow, *Motivation and Personality* (New York: Harper & Row, 1970), and Maslow, *The Farther Reaches of Human Nature* (New York: Viking Press, 1971).

Suppose for the moment that we could find a home in the curriculum for this interesting topic – without separating it off in a one-semester course in psychology. Suppose, for example, that a team of tenth- or eleventh-grade teachers got together and agreed to address the fascinating topic of motivation to learn. With this important step taken (and notice how unlikely it is that this will happen), what problems might be encountered as students read, say, Maslow? Almost certainly, many students will be attracted to his humanistic psychology – to the ideas of innate motivation, the basic goodness of human desires, self-actualization, and peak experiences. Will they also be attracted to his interest in psychedelic drugs as enhancers of religious and creative experience?[6] And if they are, where should the teacher steer them to get more balanced information? One can see why, instead of making a commitment to real education, educational policymakers usually decide that the discussions induced by reading Maslow (and others) should be deferred until university days.

But surely high school students should be involved in the study of what it means to be educated. Why should this question be shrouded in mystery for those compelled to submit to schooling for twelve or thirteen years? Reading Maslow, students may become aware of holistic education and want to read Carl Rogers, perhaps even Rousseau.[7] They might compare Socrates' claim that the unexamined life is not worth living with Maslow's that those who have lost the capacity for spontaneity are mere "human impersonators."[8] These people strive to be like those they admire but never accept themselves – thus failing to achieve authenticity. But must one engage in self-examination to be fully human? Must one be authentic, and what does this mean? Might concentration on finding oneself lead to selfishness and neglect of other members of the community? What do the subjects students

---

[6] See Maslow, *Farther Reaches*.

[7] Carl Rogers, *Freedom to Learn* (Columbus, OH: C. E. Merrill, 1969); this is easily accessible by high school students. Rousseau is more difficult, but see the account in Forbes, *Holistic Education*. If students do become interested in Rousseau, they should be introduced to the feminist critiques of Rousseau in Jane Roland Martin, *Reclaiming a Conversation* (New Haven, CT: Yale University Press, 1985), and Susan Moller Okin, *Women in Western Political Thought* (Princeton, NJ: Princeton University Press, 1979).

[8] Maslow, *Farther Reaches*, p. 132.

are forced to study have to do with self-actualization or, for that matter, with the sort of education envisioned by Socrates?

We could have used any of the writers mentioned earlier to outline rich critical lessons. If we had chosen Neill, we would have to anticipate that students might actually demand more freedom in their studies or even that they might claim their "right" not to study at all. If, following their expressed interests, we were to encourage them to read about holistic education and free schools, might they feel cheated by the education they are actually receiving? I chose Maslow to discuss illustratively mainly because his name is so often connected with Theory 1 but also because of his interest in spirituality and transcendence.

Some of those topics will be explored more deeply in the chapter on religion. One reason that young people are drawn to humanistic psychology and New Age material is that they are motivated not only to make something of their own lives (which many fear they will be unable to do) but also to connect with whatever lies beyond – the cosmos, God, or some form of ultimate concern. This is a motive of central importance in human life, but for now I want to concentrate on motivation to learn.

Psychologists have discussed something called *achievement motivation* or, sometimes, an *achievement ethic*.[9] The latter label suggests that human beings *ought* to be oriented toward achievement. Motivation Theory 1 says that people are naturally motivated to learn and to accomplish things and, if they are not corrupted by a bad or coercive upbringing, the things they strive to learn and accomplish will be good things. However, these good things may not be those that the school establishes as goals for achievement. Theory 2 warns that students will often avoid worthwhile learning and achievement. They must be externally motivated toward the good. Adler, in recommending the same course of study for all children through high school, even says that allowing elective choices "will always lead a certain number of students to voluntarily downgrade their own education."[10] Wise

---

[9] See Cronbach, *Educational Psychology*; also Nancy Cantor and Catherine A. Sanderson, "Life Task Participation and Well-Being: The Importance of Taking Part in Daily Life," in *Well-Being*, ed. Daniel Kahneman, Ed Diener, and Norbert Schwartz (New York: Russell Sage, 1999), pp. 230–243.

[10] Adler, *Paideia*, p. 21.

educators, Adler says, know what children really need, and it is their job to motivate students to learn the appropriate material.

Those who adopt a pragmatic, hybrid theory of motivation are not at all sure that all natural motivation is good, nor are they confident that adult inferences about children's needs are always right. They see decisions on which motivations to encourage as interactive. If the expressed need of the student is assessed as good, it should be guided toward worthwhile ends. If a student persistently ignores a need identified by adults as essential, teachers may well want to try some form of external motivation to get the student moving in the right direction.

Teachers from all three orientations should encourage students to ask questions. What is achievement motivation? Is it always a good thing? Does it matter what one is trying to achieve? Or how one goes about it? These questions are too seldom addressed. It is often assumed that students should strive almost indiscriminately for high grades in all of their courses. "Always do your best in everything" is a slogan urged upon children as early as first grade. But why should anyone attempt to do this? If you are vitally interested in mathematics, why should you "do your best" in art? In other discussions of this issue, I have suggested that living by this slogan puts one on an almost sure road to mediocrity.[11] Would we have wanted Beethoven or Mozart to do his best in algebra?

Students today need help in working through the meaning of achievement. Schools, with their system of competitive ranking, encourage students to think of success in terms of beating others out. Achievement, then, is defined as attaining a higher grade point average (GPA) than those with whom one is competing. Youngsters who buy into this system are often both "successful" and miserably unhappy.[12] There is a paragraph in John Knowles's *A Separate Peace* that illustrates my point vividly. I have used it in several other places, but it is worth repeating here. The book's narrator, Gene, has

---

[11] See my *Happiness and Education* (Cambridge: Cambridge University Press, 2003); also see my, "Caring as Relation and Virtue in Teaching," in *Working Virtue: Virtue Ethics and Contemporary Moral Problems*, ed. P. J. Ivanhoe and Rebecca Walker (Oxford: Oxford University Press, 2006).

[12] For an impressive set of case studies, see Denise Clark Pope, *"Doing School": How We Are Creating a Generation of Stressed Out, Materialistic, and Miseducated Students* (New Haven, CT: Yale University Press, 2001).

found a way to surpass his only academic rival, Chet, in the grading game:

> I began to see that Chet was weakened by the very genuineness of his interest in learning.... When we read *Candide* it opened up a new way of looking at the world to Chet, and he continued hungrily reading Voltaire, in French, while the class went on to other people. He was vulnerable there, because to me they were all pretty much alike – Voltaire and Molière and the laws of motion and the Magna Carta and the Pathetic Fallacy and Tess of the D'Urbervilles – and I worked indiscriminately on all of them.[13]

Was Gene blessed or cursed by his achievement motivation? Most high school students read *A Separate Peace*, but I wonder how many students are invited to participate in a critical discussion of this passage. Students should hear that a basic motivation – toward happiness – is most often satisfied by the pursuit of intrinsically valued, freely chosen goals.[14] If students believe this, will they neglect many of their required studies? Maybe. But perhaps they will learn to do a merely adequate job on all that is required and save their energy and passion for topics and tasks toward which they are intrinsically motivated.

There are biographical accounts that students might find helpful on this issue. Many highly successful creative people were mediocre students. Some even hated school. Einstein and Edison are well-known examples, but there are many others, among them Winston Churchill, George Orwell, Clarence Darrow, and Charles Darwin. Again, teachers might contribute their own stories to encourage reflection.

Under the pressure of current conditions of schooling, however, many students will ask how they can motivate themselves to do what the system demands. Can we answer this question honestly and helpfully? Theory 1 advocates are often reluctant to admit that most people are at the mercy of external motivation. They may even believe that these people (the vast majority) are human impersonators. Caring teachers – no matter the theory of motivation to which they subscribe – will not scorn the expressed needs of their students. If students want to succeed – even to succeed without real learning or self-understanding – these teachers will respond. How can they help?

---

[13] John Knowles, *A Separate Peace* (New York: Macmillan, 1960), p. 46.
[14] See again Cantor and Sanderson, "Life Participation," and Noddings, *Happiness and Education*.

Study Habits

The plaintive question of students who ask how they can motivate themselves throws further doubt on both theories. These students are, in effect, asking how they can use Theory 2 techniques to find the motivation promised by Theory 1. How can I get myself to do that which I do not want to do? This is a sad question. The only honest answer to it is, You must find something that you really do want that requires your doing this thing that you would prefer to avoid. In essence, the student must answer the question, Why do you want to motivate yourself? The search for an answer should induce reflection on the student's basic motivation. When a tentative answer has been found, the student must now ask whether the goal sought is something important and long-lasting or something trivial and short-lived. If the latter – some reward promised for an A in biology – what will the student do to motivate himself when that goal has been reached? If, for example, a boy is willing to work at biology or chemistry long enough to get a monetary reward from his parents, where will he turn after he has received the reward? Will his parents continue to offer him extrinsic rewards?

Students need to understand that even intrinsic motivation flags now and then. A lover of literature may have to force herself through a required book that she hates. A lover of math may have to struggle with a concept or skill she finds uninteresting and tedious. And, of course, a boring, inconsiderate teacher can reduce almost anyone's intrinsic motivation. Then one must take time out from the boring material and indulge in a topic or project that promises to restore her or his motivation. Becoming absorbed in such a topic, the student may respond with relief: Ah, this is why I love literature (or math, physics, etc.)!

Can we supply ourselves with motivational rewards if our basic motivation is weak? A discussion of this possibility could be very helpful, and teachers should not hesitate to share their own strategies. I can remember placing a cold Coke (or glass of white wine – dare I mention this?) just outside the kitchen when I was scrubbing the floor, and I worked quickly toward the reward. Even now, when I have a stack of clerical work and e-mail to get through, I often prod myself by saying, "Okay, do five of these, and then you can (in good conscience) read a chapter of the book you're enjoying." Later, I might do another five and then read another chapter. This is, of course, self-discipline, but what is self-discipline other than discovering and employing one's own motivation?

Under what conditions do I work best? This is another question that can be explored through biography as well as introspection. Sometimes reading or hearing about the working style of others triggers a desire to try something similar. Descartes, for example, did much of his best thinking while lying in bed mornings. (Understandably, this appeals to many students.) Some think best while soaking in a hot bath. Some need to pace to and fro. Some need silence; others need music. Physical exercise seems to stimulate some mental workers; others are exhausted by physical activity and must avoid it to think well.

Is order – that is, orderliness – important? Simone Weil put great emphasis on order – the orderliness of the universe and the importance of learning an appreciation of order. She suggested that the study of school subjects should, in addition to cultivating the habit of attention and an attitude of humility, encourage a love of order.[15] Yet, the need for order in the lives of creative people seems variable. Some must have it, while others can work in near chaos. Those who belong to the orderly group might as well resign themselves to tidying up before starting on homework. All sorts of idiosyncrasies should receive attention. I, for example, cannot work in the presence of a drooping plant, and it doesn't help to move to another room. The plant must be watered before I can work. How about food or drink? Is one's best work done on a full or empty stomach? At night or in the morning? A self-study of conditions under which good work is accomplished is well worth undertaking.

Copying others, however, is not usually helpful. Reading accounts of others' lives and habits may stimulate experimentation, but slavish imitation will likely be disappointing.[16] This is a good place, too, to remind students that those striving to become like people they take to be exemplars are more likely to become human impersonators.

---

[15] See Simone Weil, *Simone Weil Reader*, ed. George A. Panichas (Mt. Kisco, NY: Moyer Bell Ltd., 1977); see also Robert Coles, *Simone Weil: A Modern Pilgrimage* (Reading, MA: Addison-Wesley, 1987).

[16] For more on the effects of working conditions on learning, see Noddings and Shore, *Awakening the Inner Eye*.

Learning and Self-Understanding

Let's suppose that students can find reasons based on their own desires or motives to do the work assigned in school, and let's suppose that they begin to analyze the conditions under which they seem to work best. How should this "best" be described? What is going on while they "study" or do homework? Are they learning or just putting in time? Sometimes parents (and children, too) believe that students are working hard because they spend considerable time at a desk or with a book in hand. But much schoolwork can be done with half a mind, and little learning is then accomplished.

John Dewey devotes several pages to the importance of *single-mindedness* or mental integrity in thinking and learning. Students need to understand how their real underlying motives or interests can distort their professed intention to "learn this stuff." If the student's real motive is to satisfy his father or to get a better mark than John or to get finished with this and go on to something more pleasurable, his mind is likely to be divided. Dewey says that the result

> is a confused and divided state of interest [double-mindedness] in which one is fooled as to one's own real intent. One tries to serve two masters at once. Social instincts, the strong desire to please others and get their approval, social training, the general sense of duty and of authority, apprehension of penalty, all lead to a half-hearted effort to conform, to "pay attention to the lesson," or whatever the requirement is.[17]

The pages in which Dewey discusses single-mindedness and double-mindedness would make wonderful reading for high school students (and their teachers). He writes of the mind wandering, the loss of energy, the self-deception, and the confused sense of reality accompanying double-mindedness. He then reminds readers that school conditions often encourage this double-mindedness. Much that schools demand can be done with half a mind, and many school tasks are so dull that students need penalties and rewards to tackle them. Doing tasks in this way, however, may destroy the possibility of any intrinsic interest in the topics.

Should we, then, rethink the strategy explored earlier of providing ourselves with rewards when we must perform unwanted tasks? There seems to be no reason to reject that strategy, provided that we

[17] John Dewey, *Democracy and Education* (New York: Macmillan, 1916), p. 176.

21

are honest about what we are doing. For example, I am not in the least concerned that, by promising myself a cold drink for scrubbing the kitchen, I will lose intrinsic interest in that task. I can honestly say that the task holds no intrinsic interest for me. But if I had to force myself to complete a task that I believed should hold intrinsic interest for me, I might experience triple-mindedness![18] Not only would I be distracted from the task by my genuine desires (as in double-mindedness), but now I would also feel guilty for my lack of real interest. Thus, in one moment, I would apply myself to the task; in another, my mind would wander to my real interest; and, in the next, I would guiltily scold myself for lack of attention and interest. This is surely a familiar scenario to anyone who has experienced schooling for several years.

The remedy, I think, is the honesty that should result from critical thinking directed at one's own interests and work habits. Teachers can help by assuring students that they should not feel obliged to develop an intrinsic interest in everything that is taught. The message should be, "Look, it's okay not to like math. I'll help you all I can, and you have my sympathy. Just do an adequate job." Of course, good teachers do not want students to like a subject *less* because of them. Indeed, students who have always hated math sometimes warm a little to it when they know that their own interests (and lack of interest) are respected. Students can do an adequate job, even when double-minded, if they are not pretending to themselves that they are single-mindedly engaged with the material. Double-mindedness may even disappear when it is acknowledged. Without professing interest, one can turn one's energy single-mindedly to finishing the task in short order. My advice to students: Don't "do your best in everything." Do an adequate job on what is required and save your energy for that about which you are passionate. But teachers should help students connect their passions to what is taught whenever that is possible.

Freed from the expectation to be intrinsically motivated, students may become fairly efficient learners. But there is a downside to this, and students should be aware of it. The purpose for which I learn something seems to influence how I learn it. For example, if I learn something in order to pass a test, I will probably forget it quickly after

---

[18] On the deleterious effects of extrinsic rewards, see Alfie Kohn, *Punished by Rewards* (Boston: Houghton Mifflin, 1993).

the test, just as I forget the telephone number after connecting with the party I intend to reach.

This is one of the saddest features of contemporary education. Much of what is offered in schools is promptly forgotten, and this is true at every level. A course in literature or philosophy offered at the college level to "broaden" the minds of engineers presents material that is remembered until the term exam is over. In part, this is because the required courses are not designed to broaden anyone's interests but to provide another highly specialized view of a different discipline. The stated aim is highly desirable; the means chosen are not likely to achieve the aim. The same is true of the one-semester required math or science course for elementary school teachers. And, of course, the facts of American history that critics insist should be taught to high school students *are* taught, but they don't stick. Year after year, we hear critics wailing over the results of various surveys that show convincingly that high school graduates do not know the dates of the Civil War or who fought whom in World War II. *But we do teach these things.*

One response to this state of affairs is to press harder, retain children in grade 3 until they pass a standardized test (which some may never do), and refuse diplomas to high school students who cannot prove that they know what we take to be important facts. But even if test scores were to rise (and they might, minimally), the material would be mostly forgotten after the test. Thus, this is faulty response. Unfortunately, it is the one current policymakers have made.

Another response focuses on exposure as an aim of education. From this perspective, we do not expect people to remember the sorts of facts that usually appear on tests. We offer literature to engineers and science to elementary school teachers because these studies may open new and wonderful worlds to them. If they are taught well, new worlds may indeed open. But if this is our purpose, then we should find a different way of evaluating what we have accomplished. We should find a way to ask "What have you learned?" instead of "Have you learned X?"

There is an obvious exception to the rule that much of what is learned is quickly forgotten. When the material is basic to social life (like reading) or is cumulative and sequential, as it is in much of mathematics, the continual exercise of skills and use of concepts will likely prevent forgetting. Even then, however, if the material or skill is not used for several years, it will decay and sometimes disappear entirely.

Students should be invited to reflect on what they learn and how lasting it might be. It may not matter that much material is forgotten. If students honestly admit that they are working to satisfy requirements and not to learn, why should it matter that they forget many facts and details? They have learned what our society teaches best – how to satisfy the requirements of authority and acquire a credential. But it would be a shame if students never found a subject or topic that they could connect to their real interests. Both students and teachers should be constantly alert for this possibility.

Remembering

There are students who remember much of what they learn. Usually, these people have made connections to things that interest them, and this is, of course, the best way to learn and remember. When we are genuinely interested, we listen and read attentively, and we relate everything coming in to existing knowledge that acts as a scheme for categorizing and filing. There is no powerful substitute for real interest.

The worst possible way to go about remembering is to say to one-self, "I must remember this." Even those of us who remember volumes of material easily because we have intrinsic interest in it occasionally try the "I must remember" technique on bits that really don't interest us. The predictable (and highly irritating) result is that we forget. Annoyed with ourselves, we wonder how we could have forgotten something after we repeated "I must remember" three times and counseled ourselves to remember.

Some techniques do seem to help when the material itself does not interest us. Songs and rhymes help. Most of us learned "Thirty days hath September, April, June, and November . . ." and many of us learned the alphabet by singing our ABCs. We use "fall back, spring ahead" to remember what to do with our clocks in changing to and from standard time. Similarly, many music students learned to identify the spaces by F-A-C-E and the lines of the staff by "Every good boy deserves friends" (EGBDF). And we often recite to ourselves "i before e except after c" when we are trying to remember how to spell *sieve* or *receive*. I recall a beloved high school friend who remembered how to spell *accommodate* by using the initials of her name (Connie Carhart) and those of her grandmother (Molly Magee) – two Cs, two Ms. For quite a few years, when I had to spell *accommodate*, I found myself mumbling "Connie Carhart, Molly Magee." Readers can surely add to these examples. Students should be asked to consider the effective (and ineffective) techniques they use.

Schemes to help us remember are called *mnemonic devices*. Not long ago, while rereading parts of Lee Cronbach's *Educational Psychology*, I came across a mnemonic for the value of π: "See, I have a rhyme assisting my feeble brain its tasks ofttimes resisting." Count the number of letters in each word, and these numbers will give you Π to 13 digits: 3.141592653589. Aside from the fact that few of us feel the need to remember this, Cronbach asks us to consider whether remembering the mnemonic might be harder than simply memorizing the digits.[19] Reading this, I recalled a much easier mnemonic: "May I have a large container of coffee?" But that one yields only eight digits (still enough to astonish a class of sophomores). Then I remembered a better one but had to struggle with two of the words: "How I need a drink, alcoholic of course, after the ——— chapters ——— quantum mechanics." Using Cronbach's device, I knew that the first blank had to have five letters, and so I wrote "*tough*," but I knew that wasn't right. Why not? Well, because the original mnemonic (which finally popped up on its own) said "*heavy*." The temptation was to fill the second with *in* or *on*, but checking against Cronbach's device, I knew the word had to have nine letters. Ah! *Involving* was perfect. What we are doing in situations like this one is reconstructing our memories. Even a mnemonic – something designed as an aid to memory – may have to be reconstructed.

The discussion of mnemonic devices can be fun. It can also be historically informative and personally useful. Students may find the memory experiments William James performed on himself quite fascinating.[20] James found that no amount of "exercising" the memory increased its capacity. Brute memory remains brutish. However, there

---

[19] Cronbach, *Educational Psychology*, p. 471.
[20] See William James, *The Principles of Psychology* (New York: Dover, 1950); see also the accounts in Cronbach, *Educational Psychology*; and Donald A. Norman, *Memory and Attention: An Introduction to Human Information Processing* (New York: John Wiley & Sons, 1969), p. 8.

are aids that help, such as the rhymes, songs, and devices mentioned earlier. Ancient Greek orators made a practice of locating parts of their speeches in various rooms of a great, well-known building. In planning their speeches, they first determined a sequence of rooms – a tour of sorts – and then placed their topics (or paragraphs) in rooms connected along the tour. To retrieve each topic, they had only to follow a well-remembered path through the building. Students might be encouraged to try this technique in planning and presenting short talks.[21]

What stands out in this brief account of remembering is that we rely heavily on structure, and we are the ones who must create this structure. Textbook guides to reading may not be as useful as text writers suppose. Indeed, these guides to reading may prevent readers from becoming absorbed in the text and discourage them from creating their own structures to organize the material. There is some evidence that such guides are better given as aids to review *after* reading than as preliminary guides to reading. It might be even better to invite students to create their own review structure and then perhaps to compare it to one prepared by the text writer. (The text's guide should be hidden in an appendix!) The idea to get across is that nothing is more powerful in remembering than performing the cognitive acts that structure what one is trying to learn.[22]

If it is true that creating our own patterns of organization is fundamental for lasting learning, the present emphasis on behavioral objectives – telling students exactly what they must learn, exactly how they must respond to certain questions – may be an error. Skills required for further learning – sequential skills or concepts built into the next work – may profitably be learned this way, but most important topics require the work of individual construction.

There is no question but that we remember best the things in which we are interested. But we also pick up bits and pieces of information that somehow attract us. A story, poem, joke, or song may simply stick

---

[21] Students might also be interested in the famous mnemonic scheme "One is a bun, two is a shoe..." described by Galanter, Miller, and Pribram in Norman, *Memory and Attention*, p. 102.

[22] The classic work on this is Sir Frederick Bartlett, *Remembering* (Cambridge: Cambridge University Press, 1932).

with us, and then whatever facts it contains will also be retained. The source of information also plays a significant role. Somehow we remember all sorts of things better when we experience a strong affective response to the person who introduced us to them. A story told by a loved teacher may be remembered better than one told by someone to whom we are indifferent. (Unfortunately, the opposite extreme may also assist memory. We remember things said by people we hate or fear.) Finally, although students can be forgiven for doubting this, subject matter can sometimes cooperate in its own mastery. The subject may speak to those who listen. Our best students suspect this, but we rarely explore the possibility explicitly. We should.

The Object Speaks

There are wonderful stories to be told about the objects of study or contemplation speaking to the receptive student or would-be creator. It is said that Michelangelo saw the angel in the slab of marble from which he would create it; it was as though the angel spoke to the sculptor, asking to be liberated. The great mathematician Johann Gauss was often "seized by mathematics" and fell silent under its spell even in the presence of lively companions. The artist Joan Miro described himself as "like drunk" when an artistic image took possession of him.[23] The poet Paul Valery said that the first stage of artistic composition announces itself as a dazzling light, and Robert Frost said that a poem "finds its own name as it goes and discovers the best waiting for it in some final phrase at once wise and sad...."[24]

Perhaps the classic case is that of Mozart. He wrote that when he took quiet walks in the evening, melodies came to him and, as he listened attentively, the parts of all the instruments were added until the composition was complete in his head. The music seemed to have been dictated to him. Indeed, the music seemed to be so thoroughly in charge that Mozart even asked, "Now...how does it

---

[23] For more such examples, see Jacque Hadamard, *The Psychology of Invention in the Mathematical Field* (New York: Dover, 1954); also Noddings and Shore, *Awakening the Inner Eye*.

[24] Robert Frost, *Complete Poems* (New York: Henry Holt, 1949), p. vi.

happen that . . . my compositions assume the form or the style which characterize Mozart and are not like anybody else's?"[25]

Creative geniuses often describe incredible interactions with the objects of their artistry. However, many of us have such experiences occasionally. We say that an idea just popped into our mind, and we are all familiar with the depiction of such events in comic strips – the light bulb drawn over the head of one who suddenly gets an idea or sees the point.

Most of these events – while they retain a real mystery – are more obviously connected to the work and previous effort of the thinker than Mozart's story suggests. There are many stories, for example, of mathematicians working on unyielding problems until they simply had to give up for a while. Then, occupied by entirely different matters – usually simple daily affairs – the answer presented itself. The mathematician Henri Poincaré tells the story of his struggle with Fuchsian functions. Interrupted by the need to attend a geological excursion, he put all thought of mathematics aside. Nevertheless, he writes, "The instant I put my foot on the step [of the bus] the idea came to me,"[26] and that was not the only such event for Poincaré. He tells us of two more that followed some time later.

Poincaré attributed this sudden result to the continuing work of his subconscious. The psychologist Graham Wallas described the process in terms of three stages: preparation (the hard conscious work Poincaré had already done), incubation (the subconscious work still shrouded in mystery), and illumination (the point at which the light dawns). In talking with students about the wonders of incubation and illumination, teachers are often dismayed (and amused) by their students' expressed desire to skip the preparation stage and move enthusiastically to incubation and illumination. Caught napping when they are supposed to be solving word problems, students may say, "I'm incubating, I'm incubating!"

---

[25] See the account in Hadamard, *Psychology of Invention*, pp. 16–17. William Blake, too, insisted that lines were "dictated" to him. See Leopold Damrosch, Jr., *Symbol and Truth in Blake's Myth* (Princeton, NJ: Princeton University Press, 1980).

[26] The part quoted is from E. T. Bell, *Men of Mathematics* (New York: Simon & Schuster, 1965), pp. 550–551. Poincaré's essay, "Mathematical Creation," appears in *The World of Mathematics*, ed. J. R. Newman (New York: Simon & Schuster, 1956), pp. 2041–2050. It is also discussed in Hadamard, *Psychology of Invention*.

There are several important messages to extract from this conversation. First, not all mental work – even very good mental work – culminates in an answer or success. At least once in a while, teachers should ask students to tackle problems, issues, or projects without the expectation that correct, complete answers will result. Follow-up discussions could be rich as students recount what they tried, where they got stuck, what they learned, the resources they lacked, and so forth.

Second, it is sometimes better to stop thinking and just look at the object of study. Thinking can deteriorate to perseveration – a rigid process in which the thinker tries to force his or her method of choice on the problem over and over, despite the problem's reluctance to yield. Time to stop thinking, then, and just look. What is this thing I am struggling with? What methods can be used on things of this sort? The thinker becomes an acute observer, looking at the object from all angles; then he or she may become a tinkerer or inventor, trying this and that.

Third, an interest in the use of time may arise again. Earlier, I suggested that students should study their own work habits to see whether they are really engaging the material or just putting in time. When serious mental work is going on, however, time becomes almost irrelevant. For serious students, the discovery that they are spending hours on topics they really enjoy is confirmation of a genuine scholarly bent. Never mind the GPA or doing one's best in everything. Here is something that seizes me. One could not find a better motivation for study. Of course, students who have intensive interests still have to do an adequate job on the subjects that are required. On this, they should have both our sympathy and the realistic reminder that life is riddled with both necessary and unnecessary distractions. Even creative geniuses have to bathe, pay bills, and take out the garbage.

Closely related to the discussion of preparation, incubation, and illumination is one of energy cycles. Some creative artists (perhaps writers more than others) live in fear that the Muse will desert them. When the Muse departs, the object falls mute, and the writer experiences writer's block. How often this has happened to great writers is not clear, but it certainly happens to students at every level. Graduate students who have chosen a dissertation topic that seemed to interest them fall into periods when the subject fails to elicit even a flicker of motivation. Something is wrong here, but what? Perhaps the topic was never a passionate interest; doctoral students are

29

sometimes pushed into studies preferred by their advisors. In those cases, it is wise to invoke the adequate job strategy and get on with one's scholarly life. But for others, energy may just be flowing temporarily toward something else. Then the best advice may be to let it flow and wait for a turn in the cycle.

Carl Jung discussed a concept he called "enantiodromia."[27] In the simplest terms, it means a conversion of one attribute or desire into its opposite. By accepting opposites in ourselves (where they exist), we allow enantiodromia to bring us into internal harmony. When we resist what we take to be the dark (or unwanted) side of ourselves or strive mightily to emphasize the wanted side, enantiodromia occurs – sometimes with cataclysmic results. While we are denying our anger, sloth, or deceitfulness and masquerading as calm, industrious, and honest, energy is flowing toward the opposite pole. If this process continues for a long time or is exacerbated by ever greater efforts to deny the dark side, we can expect what Jung called an "enantiodromia in the grand style."[28] The worst features of the denied self burst forth in an explosion of energy. Thus, sometimes a quiet loner suddenly becomes violent or a conscientious worker finds herself unable to rise from bed in the morning.

The concept is far from perfect in its explanatory power, and we rarely hear it mentioned today. There are many other explanations for violent acts, and we rarely hear of cases in which energy flows from bad to good. Perhaps that is because almost all people want to think of themselves as good or striving for the good even when they are doing evil things. Ebenezer Scrooge is the only character I can think of whose determination to be nasty and stingy culminated in an outburst of generosity and goodness. But readers may think of other cases.

Without giving undue credit to the concept, then, a discussion of enantiodromia might help students to understand themselves better and to lead healthier emotional lives. An acceptance of polar opposites in oneself – provided that one does not act on the bad impulses – can contribute to inner harmony. Young children especially need to be assured that their bad thoughts do not cause harmful results. "But

---

[27] See Carl G. Jung, *Collected Works*, vol. 2, 2nd ed. (Princeton, NJ: Princeton University Press, 1958). See also Jung's references to Eastern philosophy.

[28] Jung applied this expression to the misplaced energies of Christianity, in *Collected Works*, p. 433.

I wished he would get hurt!" a young child may sob when her brother has been injured. Not only should children be reassured that wishes are not instrumental but, as they grow older, they should be encouraged to let bad thoughts run their course and wear themselves out. Repressing them almost certainly increases the energy flow that sustains them.

At a less serious level, we all undergo the ebb and flow of energy with respect to our interests. Even when we are usually interested in a topic, hobby, or project – even devoted to it – there are times when we just don't feel like engaging in it. If the general principle described in enantiodromia is right, we may make the situation worse by denying our flagging interest or fighting against it. Teachers can be helpful by admitting their own experience with energy flow. I have learned to let it be when one of my great interests – reading, gardening, cooking, writing – fades a bit. If one interest fades, another usually increases, and the one that has flagged will come back. And it always has. This discussion is obviously closely related to our earlier one on motivation. If it is possible (neither unethical nor selfish) to act on intrinsic motivation, it is better to do so than to force oneself into work one would prefer to avoid. It is especially important not to risk losing permanently a genuine interest that will return naturally if it is not coerced.

Finally, if we want the object of our study to speak to us, we must not only listen, we must also believe, at least temporarily.[29] Eventually, as critical thinkers, we may be bothered by something in what we read or hear, and then we should engage in analysis. However, it is usually better not to analyze at every step in a first reading. If you're tackling Dewey, Piaget, or Derrida, just read or listen in a believing mode. You may have to read three or more books by Dewey before you'll have a clear picture of what he's saying. Then you can engage in productive analysis. I have never understood why English teachers require students to read important books piecemeal, analyzing each bit before they read the next. One should read the whole thing, enjoy, and believe. It may be better to read everything this way – even the "heavy chapters involving quantum mechanics."

---

[29] For powerful suggestions along these lines, see Peter Elbow, *Embracing Contraries* (Oxford: Oxford University Press, 1993).

Thinking about Critical Thinking

So far, we've been considering topics that are critical to understanding how and why we learn. I have suggested that students best learn how to think critically by hearing, thinking, and talking about issues critical to their present or future lives. I defined critical thinking in this context as the "diligent and skillful use of reason on matters of moral/social importance – on personal decision making, conduct, and belief." Before tackling the next controversial topic – the psychology of war – I should say more about critical thinking and what research has had to say about the subject.

Philosophers and psychologists have told us much about critical thinking. Psychologists are usually concerned with critical thinking as a process or set of processes that they study and attempt to describe. Philosophers are more interested in critical thinking as a concept: What is its nature? How is it related to other concepts involving thinking? Under what conditions would we logically expect it to arise?[30] The definition generally accepted by other philosophers differs very little from mine. I have acknowledged that critical thinking – as the diligent and skillful use of reason – is and should be exercised in every domain of human activity, but in this book I have emphasized discussion of emotional/social issues not often discussed in schools.

Critical thinking often appears as an educational aim in school statements, and a number of competent writers have published work designed to help teachers guide, promote, and evaluate critical thinking in their students.[31] Books of this sort can be very useful when

---

[30] For a good introduction to and summary of the research, see Sharon Bailin and Harvey Siegel, "Critical Thinking," in *Philosophy of Education*, ed. Nigel Blake, Paul Smeyers, Richard Smith, and Paul Standish (Oxford: Blackwell, 2003), pp. 181–193; see also Nel Noddings, *Philosophy of Education* (Boulder, CO: Westview Press, 1995), ch. 5; and Harvey Siegel, *Educating Reason: Rationality, Critical Thinking and Education* (New York: Routledge, 1988).

[31] Some good examples of such books are Diane F. Halpern, *Thought and Knowledge* (Mahwah, NJ: Lawrence Erlbaum, 2003); Matthew Lipman, *Thinking in Education* (Cambridge: Cambridge University Press, 1991); Richard Paul, *Critical Thinking: What Every Person Needs to Survive in a Rapidly Changing World* (Rohnert Park, CA: Center for Critical Thinking and Moral Critique, 1990); Norman J. Unrau, *Thoughtful Teachers, Thoughtful Learners* (Scarborough, Ontario: Pippin, 1997). In mathematics, see Stephen I. Brown and Marion I. Walter, *The Art of Problem Posing* (Philadelphia: Franklin Institute Press, 1983); Arthur Whimbey and Jack Lockhead, *Problem Solving and Comprehension* (Philadelphia: Franklin Institute Press, 1982).

we want to encourage critical thinking in the standard school subjects. They help us to identify assumptions, pose problems, and assess claims and arguments.

Useful as these books are, however, there are some risks involved in trying to teach critical thinking skills directly. Some approaches are almost formulaic, and then critical thinking may become just another lesson – something to be gotten through and then put aside as having little to do with real life. If the approach is too rigid, creative thinking may suffer. Students may acquire some skill in criticizing the arguments of others but fail to engage in developing and supporting their own positions. Most dangerous of all is the possibility that students will content themselves with a destructive form of criticism and become skillful but unfeeling bystanders.[32] As educators, we should be very unhappy when our teaching results in cynicism or lack of commitment.

The critical lessons discussed in this book encourage passionate personal engagement as well as critical thinking. Such lessons should also help students to believe that critical thinking can profitably be used on matters central to their lives. When we refuse to discuss highly controversial subjects that affect the lives of our students, it is predictable that they will either dismiss critical thinking as just another, harder demand of schooling or dismiss us as hypocrites. Neither result is attractive. But what do students need to know in order to address controversial issues responsibly?

One important issue that philosophers have debated is whether or not critical thinking skills are generalizable.[33] Those who believe these skills are generalizable sometimes recommend teaching logic and general rules for the assessment of arguments. Those who deny such generalizability insist that students must be very knowledgeable in a particular subject before they can engage in critical thinking on that subject. Both sides make important points.

It seems obvious that there are certain attitudes and habits of mind that are generalizable. One is the habit of recognizing that we often

---

[32] See Jane Roland Martin, "Critical Thinking for a Humane World," in *The Generalizability of Critical Thinking*, ed. Stephen P. Norris (New York: Teachers College Press, 1992), pp. 163–180.

[33] For major arguments on both sides, see Robert Ennis, "A Concept of Critical Thinking," *Harvard Educational Review* 32(1), 1962: 83–111; John E. McPeck, *Critical Thinking and Education* (Oxford: Martin Robertson, 1981).

need more information before we can evaluate a claim or argument. In a sense, we bring a critical attitude to the task that precedes the particulars of critical thinking. Another generalizable way of approaching the critical task is to ask what sort of claim we are looking at. In the chapter on religion, this will be of first importance. Certain religious claims are not susceptible to scientific resolution. For example, we can't scientifically settle basic claims such as these: God exists; Jesus is divine; miracles occur. However, many derivative religious claims can be subjected to empirical or logical scrutiny. Even the Catholic Church submits every particular claim of a miracle to a meticulous test. (This is not to say that the tests applied by the church would satisfy scientists.) We can also examine clusters of religious claims for logical consistency, for example, the compound claim that God is all-good and that Hell exists; that belief in God is necessary for moral life; or that preferred interpretations of biblical material are sometimes politically motivated. In any discussion, on any topic, it is useful to ask what sort of claim we are facing before trying to defend or reject it.

I am less sure about the value of teaching formal logic as a set of generalizable thinking skills. I usually do so as part of my introductory course in philosophy of education because I'm interested in how students react to it. I try to make it fun, and I do not give tests on it. Students often say that it has changed their thinking for the better, but I'm not entirely convinced. As a former math teacher (working with high school students), I remember too many occasions on which otherwise intelligent students gave ridiculous responses after instruction in logic. In teaching the nature and use of the syllogism, for example, I (like all teachers) always emphasized the fact that if both major and minor premises are true *and* one's reasoning is correct, then the conclusion must be true. That's the way we prove things in geometry. However, consider how some of my students responded to this simple problem:

What conclusion can you draw from the following:

1. All fish can swim.
2. I can swim.
Therefore: ?

A surprising number concluded, "I am a fish." Somehow they had gotten the idea that formal logic is different from – and can even contradict – common sense. No student, before my logic instruction, would have claimed that he or she was a fish. Most students (I'm glad to report) answered correctly that no conclusion could be drawn, and they could have named and explained the error made by their fishy peers. I remain interested in but ambivalent about the claim that training in the basics of logic will contribute to critical thinking in general.

The people who insist that critical thinking is domain specific are probably not entirely right, but they have a point. We really can't think critically in an area about which we know little or nothing. For example, knowing in general how to use a taxonomy will be of little use to me in reading a botanical taxonomy unless I also know the relevant botanical vocabulary. But then, if this condition – sufficient knowledge of the topic – is added to the generalizability claim, we can speak with greater confidence about the transfer of skills from one domain of knowledge to another. We can also reaffirm a fundamental habit of mind associated with critical thinking – seeking sufficient knowledge to make our assessments credible.

It seems reasonable to suggest that all teachers point out the general rules of logic and careful thinking whenever the opportunity arises. But beyond that, we have to find ways to introduce vital topics that do not usually appear in the school curriculum. This is the point of critical lessons.

In this chapter, I have suggested several topics that might be used for critical discussion with high school students on the subject of their own learning: motivation, study habits, memory, and remaining sensitive to both the object of study and one's own energy flow. Clearly, there is much more we could do to help students achieve self-understanding concerning their patterns of learning, but even this much is usually absent from today's schools.

Understanding and accepting our own motives to learn are fundamental in attaining a measure of authenticity – in becoming real persons and not human impersonators. But in addition to the challenge to learn – one that faces every child throughout the schooling process – young people should be invited to think critically about large issues that will confront them as adults. One such issue that arises for many young people right out of high school is war. We turn to that topic next.

2

The Psychology of War

I sing of arms and the man....

Virgil, *The Aeneid*

Social studies and history text books are often organized around the topic of war, and students learn many facts about the dates, causes, outcomes, and leaders of war. However, despite the fact that few students who enter the military have even a smattering of college education, we seldom ask whether these youngsters can be given opportunities that will be enjoyed by some of their college-bound peers to learn something about the psychological aspects of war. Young enlistees know that they may be killed or injured in military service, but few have any idea that they might lose a cherished part of their moral identity. If we claim to educate, we must encourage young people to reflect on what war does and might do to the human beings engaged in it.

The Attractions of War

It is common for political leaders to declare that "no one wants war." They would have us believe that somehow, despite everyone's being against it, war is necessary. Critical thinkers should pause right here and ask whether it is true that no one wants war. It is not. There are people who want war for financial gain, national dominance, or personal glory. But, additionally, there are many who want war because their lives seem to be empty or meaningless without it. Chris Hedges writes:

> The enduring attraction of war is this: Even with its destruction and carnage it gives us what we all long for in life. It gives us purpose, meaning, a reason for living.[1]

This is a sad comment on average lives, and we should spend time discussing what it takes to find meaning in life. (This is a topic for another set of critical lessons.) But war has been and continues to be a quick road to purpose and meaning. Some young people look forward to the excitement of war, to the possibility of heroism, to the close-knit comradeship of warriors, to getting away from home, and even to giving up responsibility for their own actions. Without reflecting on it or admitting it, some even look forward to an excuse for breaking fundamental laws against killing and destroying property.

Anthony Swofford, writing of his experience as a young marine, goes so far as to say that many of the Vietnam films – supposedly antiwar – actually excite young men in the military. "Fight, rape, war, pillage, burn. Filmic images of death and carnage are pornography for the military man.... It doesn't matter how many Mr. and Mrs. Johnsons are antiwar – the actual killers who know how to use the weapons are not."[2]

There are many books on the political and economic causes of war and even quite a few studies of the psychology of wartime leaders.[3] In addition, there are anthropological studies that discuss the possibility that human beings are innately aggressive.[4] These are topics worth studying and discussing. However, in this book, the focus is on the individual and group psychology of ordinary people with respect to war. Why are so many men attracted to war? Why have so many women supported it? Why is hatred so easily aroused and sometimes

---

[1] Chris Hedges, "War Is a Force That Gives Us Meaning," *Amnesty Now*, Winter 2002: 10–13; see also Hedges, *War Is a Force That Gives Us Meaning* (New York: Public Affairs, 2002).

[2] Anthony Swofford, *Jarhead* (New York: Scribner, 2003), p. 7.

[3] See, for example, Greg Cashman, *What Causes War?* (New York: Macmillan/ Lexington, 1993); Ron Rosenbaum, *Explaining Hitler* (New York: HarperCollins, 1999).

[4] See, for example, Konrad Lorenz, *On Aggression* (New York: Bantam, 1966); Robert Ardrey, *The Territorial Imperative* (New York: Atheneum, 1966). For many more references on this topic, see Cashman, *What Causes War?*

so quickly forgotten? Why does the public so quickly change its attitude toward young military people when war occurs – from mere
tolerance to hero worship?

One element in the attraction to war is a long history of associating
masculinity with the warrior. Paul Tillich, whose work is important
for those who would construct critical lessons on finding meaning in
life, gives a brief history of *courage*, noting that the Greek word for
courage is synonymous with manliness.[5] The emphasis on bravery in
battle – the willingness to kill and be killed – has distorted the meaning
of courage, all but obliterating any consideration of what goals and
acts are worthy of courage. Courage is too often admired for itself.
Philosophers have debated the standing of courage in the hierarchy
of virtues, in particular whether courage should be subordinated to
wisdom or vice versa. But the more important question is this: to what
ends, with what care for the lives and well-being of others, should this
virtue be exercised? Indeed, we might ask: Is courage always a virtue?

Most high school students read at least part of the *Iliad*. From start
to finish, it is a story of rage, killing, and a pervasive fear of being
thought cowardly. Fear of the charge of cowardice overwhelms both
fear of death and fear of becoming cruel and merciless. Again and
again, young men who have sensibly fled from a powerful, vengeful
enemy turn back to the battle because they are even more afraid of
being called a coward. Not to exhibit a warrior's courage is to lose
one's manliness.

In her discussion of the *Iliad*, Simone Weil argues that *force* (or
"might") is the only hero of the story.[6] Before it, all men become
objects, things. Conqueror and vanquished alike are objects, under
the control of force. Some men, she comments, regain their humanity after the battles, but others never do. "These are another species,
a compromise between a man and a corpse."[7] From the perspective
of those like Weil who define humans as social and spiritual beings,
notes Seth Schein, the Trojans – because they are living in and defending their own community – are more fully human than the invading

---

[5] Paul Tillich, *The Courage to Be* (New Haven, CT: Yale University Press, 1952).

[6] Simone Weil, "The Poem of Might," in *Simone Weil Reader*, ed. George A.
Panichas (Mt. Kisco, NY: Moyer Bell Ltd., 1977), pp. 153–183. *Might* is often
translated as "force." For further comments on this essay, see Seth L. Schein,
The Mortal Hero (Berkeley: University of California Press, 1984).

[7] Weil, "The Poem of Might," p. 158.

Greeks. But from another perspective – one that defines human meaning in terms of the vigorous conduct of war – the Greeks are more human.[8] In Weil's view, both attackers and defenders are made into objects, pathetic half-humans. The more reprehensible party is the attacker who acts as a weapon of force to destroy the social fabric that might have nourished a full humanity.

Weil has been accused of using a modern perspective to condemn an ancient way of life.[9] But is the *Iliad* best described as an ancient way of life or as a prime example of human folly that has never lost its appeal? When J. G. Gray speaks of "the enduring appeals of battle" and "the delight of destruction,"[10] he expresses the attitude of many young men right down to the present day. Is there something wrong with these men, or are they the legitimate heirs of a great tradition?

Many good men and women have been torn between admiration for the virtues of warriors and horror at war's senseless destruction. William James, horrified by war, considered ways of life that might provide war's opportunities for the exercise of courage and stamina while avoiding the cruelty and destruction of war. He wrote:

> What we now need to discover in the social realm is the moral equivalent of war: something heroic that will speak to men as universally as war does, and yet will be as compatible with their spiritual selves as war has proved itself to be incompatible.[11]

But then he asked "whether this wholesale organization of irrationality and crime [war] [will] be our only bulwark against effeminacy...."[12]

And here we encounter a major problem for young people to consider: Must masculinity be defined in terms of the warrior

---

[8] See Schein, *Mortal Hero*, p. 82.

[9] See again Schein, *Mortal Hero*.

[10] Quoted in Schein, *Mortal Hero*, p. 84; on the attractions of war, see also J. G. Gray, *The Warriors: Reflections on Men in Battle* (New York: HarperCollins, 1977); Lawrence Le Shan, *The Psychology of War* (Chicago: Noble Press, 1992); James Tatum, *The Mourner's Song* (Chicago: University of Chicago Press, 2004); and Lorrie Goldensohn, *Dismantling Glory* (New York: Columbia University Press, 2003).

[11] William James, *The Varieties of Religious Experience* (New York: Modern Library, 1929), p. 359; see also James, "The Moral Equivalent of War," in *The Writings of William James*, ed. John J. McDermott (New York: Random House, 1967), pp. 660–671.

[12] James, *Varieties*, p. 359.

tradition? To be a real man, must one be willing to "fight, rape, war, pillage, burn" or at least be attracted to such activities? To be a real woman, must one encourage, admire, and perhaps even envy "real" men? Asked how we might avoid wars, Virginia Woolf said, "No I don't see what's to be done about war. It's manliness and manliness breeds womanliness – both so hateful."[13] Sara Ruddick also notes that although women have often opposed war – the destruction, literally, of the fruits of their labor – some have supported it enthusiastically.[14] Masculinity demands femininity, as Woolf said, and the result is a population that can easily be excited by the demands and exertions of war.

Many thoughtful women and men today are seeking to redefine what it means to be a man or woman in a just, caring society.[15] Why does the warrior model still captivate the human imagination? Part of the attraction is almost certainly a negative reaction to "effeminacy." Men feel superior to women. To feel superior is more attractive than feeling inferior; to identify with a dominant group is more satisfying than to be classed with a subordinate one. It has long been considered a terrible insult to call a man *womanish*, and soldiers in training have often been ridiculed for behaving *like girls*. Women themselves have been respected – at least treated with some deference – for behaving in ways that would bring scorn upon men. Feminine women have reaped some rewards for their cheerful submissiveness, and this has made it hard for women to break the pattern of masculinity/femininity. Indeed, the very traits so much admired in men have been castigated and mocked when they appear in women.[16] Assertive men are strong; assertive women are bitchy. Male intellectuals have been admired; female intellectuals have often been called *unnatural* women.

But the issue is complicated. Some men – some Christians and Buddhists, for example – have been staunch opponents of war, and

---

[13] Quoted in Sara Ruddick, *Maternal Thinking: Towards a Politics of Peace* (Boston: Beacon Press, 1989), p. 154. Ruddick cites Virginia Woolf, *Letters*, vol. 6, ed. Nigel Nicholson (London: Hogarth Press, 1980), p. 464.

[14] See Ruddick, *Maternal Thinking*; also Jean Bethke Elshtain, *Women and War* (New York: Basic Books, 1987).

[15] See Emilie Buchwald, Pamela R. Fletcher, and Martha Roth, eds., *Transforming a Rape Culture* (Minneapolis: Milkweed Editions, 1993).

[16] On the genderization of attributes, see Jane Roland Martin, *Reclaiming a Conversation* (New Haven, CT: Yale University Press, 1985).

many women, as already noted, have been strong supporters of war. Further, it is not only the desire to dominate others that attracts men to war. Nor is it merely the chance to prove one's ability to withstand miserable conditions. If it were this, James points out, men would be attracted to the ascetic life, but few are. Perhaps the hope of glory beckons. To be part of a victorious military force, perhaps even to achieve recognition as a hero, could be a powerful source of motivation – even if it is overtly denied. Movie scenes of Roman triumphal marches, of American liberators in France, of parades on the streets of New York City are all images that may excite and invite. The longing for meaning, to be part of something larger than the self, is again evident. And, again, we are led to ask why many lives are so meaningless that people should welcome war. High school students should have opportunities to explore this question in some depth.

We should not overlook the fact that many young men who go to war do so reluctantly. Many accounts of men who go because they love their country are available, and World War I poetry is eloquent in its depiction of both hatred of war and devotion to country. Wilfred Owen, for example, describes the horror of war vividly and decries the "old lie" that it is "sweet and seemly" to die for one's country. In contrast, Rupert Brooke composes a romantic message that, if he should die, there would be "some corner of a foreign field/ That is for ever England."[17] Brooke died early in the war; if he had lived longer, his message might have changed.

Critical lessons demand commitment to critical thinking on all sides of an issue. First, the critical thinker eliminates nonsense and whatever is clearly morally repugnant. Then she or he goes on to examine the arguments that remain. Students should certainly hear stories of genuine heroism in war. That such stories exist was recognized by James; if they did not, we would have no need to seek a moral equivalent of war. One high school text book includes the testimony of a young man who served in the Vietnam War. His story captures the ambivalence, confusion, and bravery exhibited by many:

Vietnam was my generation's adventure. I wanted to be part of that adventure and I believed that it was my duty as an American, both

---

[17] For the poetry of Owen and Brooke, see *Anthem for Doomed Youth*, ed. Lyn Macdonald (London: Folio Society, 2000). For a critique of World War I poetry, see Goldensohn, *Dismantling Glory*.

to serve my country and particularly not to stand by while someone else risked his life in my place. I do not regret my decision to go, but I learned in Vietnam not to confuse America with the politicians elected to administer America, and I have learned that I have a duty to myself and to my country to exercise my own judgment based upon my own conscience.[18]

In this voice, we hear an attraction to adventure, a sense of duty, and an awakening of critical thinking. Probably most young men go to war with mixed emotions – inwardly welcoming the excitement but outwardly denying it, fearing death but fearing the accusation of cowardice and loss of manliness more, determined to do their duty but unsure what that duty is, hoping for glory but quickly finding filth and tedium. A genuine education would at least prepare them for the psychological upheaval they may experience. It should include at least the matters briefly discussed here: the desire of some to fight and to engage in legal killing, the role of masculinity and femininity as social constructs, the genderization of virtues and attributes, the hope for glory, the search for meaning, and the honest dedication to duty.

Possibly the worst thing that may happen to young warriors is that they will lose their moral identity and commit acts that, before the battle, they thought could only be done by an evil enemy. I'll treat that theme in the last section of this chapter.

Rejecting War

There is no complete, sure-fire response to James's search for a moral equivalent of war. In particular, we will not find such an equivalent if we identify it with a bulwark against effeminacy. That identification is a big part of the problem, and we need to work on redefining what it means to be a man or woman. We need to explore the characteristics of good people and the goals they seek irrespective of traditional views of gender.

Pacifism and peace movements rarely appear as major topics in today's social studies text books. A critical thinker should ask why this is so. Might the historical study of pacifism work against patriotism

---

[18] Quoted in Gerald A. Danzer, J. Jorge Klor de Alva, Larry S. Krieger, Louis E. Wilson, and Nancy Woloch, *The Americans* (Evanston, IL: Houghton Mifflin, 2000), p. 907.

and leave us in a vulnerable position under attack? It might, of course, but that result is probably no more likely than having students turn to communism after reading Marx. That too has happened occasionally and could happen again. The antidote, however, is not to reject the study of Marx or pacifism (or any other historically significant topic) but to read widely, think critically, and discuss openly.

The history of pacifism is loaded with examples of courage and devotion that young people may find inspiring. There are strong pacifist traditions in some religions, particularly Christianity and Buddhism.[19] However, neither tradition is free of violence, and Christianity has often defined itself in terms of banners, battles, wars, and crusades. But the world's first conscientious objectors were Christians who refused to serve in the armies of Rome.[20] These Christians sometimes lost their lives by standing up for their belief in nonviolence.

As part of a set of critical lessons, the purpose of studying pacifism is not so much to inspire emulation as to reveal possibilities for thought and debate. What arguments have been advanced for pacifism? Is such a position at all practical? Are there variations on the theme of pacifism?

Nations at war have been forced to deal with pacifists in order to control conflict among their own people. In the United States, it was easiest to recognize the traditional peace churches – for example, Quakers and Mennonites – and to accept their members as conscientious objectors. But among these, some are willing to serve in noncombatant roles in the military, others will accept only civilian alternative service, and still others refuse to cooperate in any way with a government at war.[21] The last group has often suffered imprisonment, especially if their objection has included refusal to pay taxes.

The United States first faced the problems of conscientious objection in the Civil War when both the Union and the Confederacy

---

[19] See John Ferguson, *War and Peace in the World's Religions* (New York: Oxford University Press, 1978). For more on Buddhism, see David W. Chappell, ed., *Buddhist Peacework: Creating Cultures of Peace* (Boston: Wisdom, 1999); Daisaku Ikeda, *For the Sake of Peace: Seven Paths to Global Harmony* (Santa Monica, CA: Middleway Press, 2001); and Daniel L. Smith-Christopher, ed., *The Challenge of Nonviolence in Religious Traditions* (Maryknoll, NY: Orbis Books, 2002).

[20] See Charles C. Moskos and John Whiteclay Chambers II, eds., *The New Conscientious Objection* (Oxford: Oxford University Press, 1993), chapter 1.

[21] Ibid., p. 5.

employed conscription. Recognition of the historic peace churches seemed reasonable, but complications arose when conscripts were allowed to buy substitutes to serve in their stead. Students today learn that draft riots occurred during the Civil War, but they rarely hear what happened to conscientious objectors after that war. The memory of those protests prompted authorities in World War I to make the law governing conscientious objection more equitable in some ways. It recognized membership in existing religious organizations that forbade participation in war as grounds for conscientious objection, but it no longer allowed any form of buying off. But the World War I law did not allow exemption for personal belief, and it was not always easy for pacifists to convince boards of their sincere belief in pacifism.

When the law eventually made it legal for young men to give secular reasons for their moral objection to war, the number of conscientious objections rose dramatically. The exemption rates for conscientious objectors in World War I and World War II were .14 and .15, respectively. These rates rose drastically in the Vietnam War to an all-time high of 130.72 in 1972. That means that 130.72 men were exempted for every 100 inducted![22] The enormous protest against that war effectively ended Selective Service and established a voluntary military force.

Students should be aware that pacifism and nonviolence are much more acceptable to societies when war is neither underway nor threatened. Dorothy Day noted with some bewilderment that *The Catholic Worker* had been advocating pacifism for years without its readers recognizing the fact:

> But there were a very great many who had seemed to agree with us who did not realize for years that *The Catholic Worker* position implicated them; if they believed the things we wrote, they would be bound, sooner or later, to make decisions personally and to act upon them.[23]

This is hard. Few of us can embrace absolute pacifism. Is it right to refuse to fight when we are attacked? Might fighting today prevent

[22] Ibid., p. 42.
[23] Dorothy Day, *The Long Loneliness* (San Francisco: Harper & Row, 1952), p. 264.

many deaths tomorrow? Students should hear arguments on all sides of the issue.

In considering absolute pacifism, the story of Jeannette Rankin stands out. Rankin, the first woman elected to Congress (1916), had voted against World War I. Sentiment was against her, and she was not elected again until 1940. In 1941, after the Japanese bombed Pearl Harbor, she cast the only vote (388 to 1) against declaring war on Japan. This time her political career was finished. Almost no one defended her. However, a well-known editor, William Allen White, although he disagreed with her position, wrote, "But Lord, it was a brave thing."[24]

Rankin explained her position this way:

> I believe that the first vote I cast was the most significant vote and a most significant act on the part of women, because women are going to have to stop war. I felt at the time that the first woman [in Congress] should take the first stand, that the first time the first woman had a chance to say no war she should say it.[25]

Contrast Rankin's brave consistency with Woodrow Wilson's behavior. In campaigning for reelection in 1916, Wilson's supporters used the slogan "He kept us out of war." In 1917, he asked Congress for a declaration of war. Young students should probably not be asked who made the right decision on World War I; they almost certainly do not have enough information to use critical thinking well on this issue. Rankin's bravery is to be admired, but that doesn't make her decision right. Wilson's apparent abdication of the position that attracted voters to him may not have been wrong.

What students can and should consider are the motives and reasons that lead people to uphold their initial positions or to reject them. Harvey Siegel wants people to be moved by good reasons.[26] I doubt that people are often moved by reasons (as Hume insisted, we are moved by emotions), but I agree with him that reasons should be examined, and we should ask what motivates us to select and prioritize our reasons. Rankin made her decision on principle, even though

---

[24] Quoted in Gail Collins, *America's Women: 400 Years of Dolls, Drudges, Helpmates, and Heroines* (New York: HarperCollins, 2003), p. 373.

[25] Quoted in Danzer et al., *The Americans*, p. 554.

[26] See Harvey Siegel, *Educating Reason: Rationality, Critical Thinking, and Education* (New York: Routledge, 1988).

she knew that the decision would end her political life. Although it is still debated, Wilson's change of heart might also have been principled. Questions for students: Do you question your own motives? Do you follow the crowd? Can you be persuaded to change your mind? How do you defend a change of mind or a refusal to change it?

Rankin's statement that she was doing what women must do to stop war is important. Most of the feminists writing on war admit that many women have supported and continue to support war. But women have often been leaders in opposing war. Jane Addams, like Rankin, lost much of the public support she had previously enjoyed when she spoke out against World War I.[27] But she continued to speak out, not only against the war but against the mistreatment of immigrants in the United States and of conscientious objectors whose religious views were held in contempt by a war-fevered populace.[28] Although she had seconded the nomination of Theodore Roosevelt for the presidency in 1912, Roosevelt called her "the most dangerous woman in America" when she remained firm in her opposition to World War I.[29]

Accounts of female leadership in peace movements are powerful and important.[30] Not only do they provide counterexamples to the models of womanliness deplored by Woolf, but they also provide positive examples of the virtues that might well characterize those who seek a moral equivalent of war. Young women, as well as young men, need to be prepared for the psychological pressures that may lead

---

[27] See Jean Bethke Elshtain, *Jane Addams and the Dream of American Democracy* (New York: Basic Books, 2002).

[28] See Elshtain, *Jane Addams*, also Jane Addams, *Peace and Bread in Time of War* (New York: King's Crown Press, 1945); also John C. Farrell, *Beloved Lady: A History of Jane Addams's Ideas on Reform and Peace* (Baltimore: Johns Hopkins University Press, 1967). For an account of feminists against war, see Frances H. Early, *A World without War* (Syracuse, NY: Syracuse University Press, 1997).

[29] Quoted in Michael True, *An Energy Field More Intense Than War* (Syracuse, NY: Syracuse University Press, 1995), p. 14.

[30] In addition to the references already cited, see Elise Boulding, *One Small Plot of Heaven* (Wallingford, PA: Pendle Hill, 1989); Birgit Brock-Utne, *Educating for Peace: A Feminist Perspective* (New York: Pergamon, 1985); Margaret Crocco and O. L. Davis, eds., *"Bending the Future to Their Will": Civic Women, Social Education, and Democracy* (Lanham, MD: Rowman & Littlefield, 1999); and Betty A. Reardon, *Sexism and the War System* (New York: Teachers College Press, 1985).

them to support war. It is useful to know that we have had heroic foremothers in the struggle to end war.

The question still remains whether pacifism is always the right way to approach conflict. Martin Buber, who generally opposed the use of force or violence, admonished Gandhi when the latter suggested that Jews might have resisted the Nazis nonviolently. Buber pointed out that nonviolent resistance to people who intend to destroy you only helps them to accomplish their purpose. He said, too, "I do not want force. But if there is no other way of preventing the evil destroying the good, I trust I shall use force and give myself up into God's hands...."[31] Buber's point in reference to the Nazis and the Holocaust is persuasive. The same words from the mouths of others, in very different contexts, should cause us to reflect more deeply.

Not only women and religious groups have embraced pacifism. Members of the Pueblo tribes – the Hopi in particular – claimed and were granted conscientious objector status as pacifists in World War II.[32] Clark Wissler notes, ironically, that their pacifism reduced their status in American history:

> Probably because of their long passive resistance to white influence, they have few heroes known to history. Wars seem necessary to reveal greatness. Had the Pueblos terrorized the settlements, massacred women and children, left a trail of blood and destruction behind them, they would hold a high place in history, as we know it....[33]

This is another sad comment on the human condition and on how difficult it will be to find a moral equivalent of war.

Sometimes those who have fought in wars turn against warfare, but even this is not a universal reaction. Wilfred Owen and Rupert Brooke responded very differently to war as it was occurring. There are, however, many accounts in both biography and fiction of soldiers who felt as though they were in alien territory when they mingled with civilians during leaves. Having no idea what war is really like,

---

[31] See Martin Buber, *The Way of Response*, ed. Nahum N. Glatzer (New York: Schocken Books, 1966), p. 196; also Buber, *Pointing the Way*, trans. and ed. Maurice Friedman (New York: Schocken Books, 1957), p. 146.

[32] See Moskos and Chambers, *New Conscientious Objection*.

[33] Clark Wissler, *Indians of the United States* (New York: Anchor Books, 1989), p. 242. The Hopi are also mentioned but not discussed in Moskos and Chambers, *New Conscientious Objection*.

civilians have often been more warlike and ferocious in their hatred of enemies than the warriors who sometimes sympathized with their enemy peers.[34] In the 1930s, many young men, including thousands of Americans, signed the Oxford Pledge, vowing never to serve their country in war.[35] Yet when World War II arrived, many of those who were eligible put aside their vow and signed up to fight.

How can people be brought to reject war? Virginia Woolf explored the possibility that a broad education in the arts and literature of other nations might have an antiwar effect.[36] Yet she knew that British enthusiasm for the music of Beethoven, Mozart, and even Wagner had not fallen off during World War I. German culture was somehow neatly separated from German political views and the conduct of war. Woolf also thought that realistic art depicting the horrors of war might turn people against war. Revisiting Woolf's exploration, Susan Sontag comments:

> Not to be pained by these pictures, not to recoil from them, not to strive to abolish what causes this havoc, this carnage – these for Woolf, would be the reactions of a moral monster. And, she is saying, we are not monsters, we members of the educated class. Our failure is one of imagination, of empathy: we have failed to hold this reality in mind.[37]

But Sontag is not optimistic. She notes the dramatic difference noted earlier between those who have actually experienced war and those who have only looked at pictures. It is hopeless for the pictured dead and maimed to speak to us: "We don't get it. We truly can't imagine what it was like. . . . Can't understand, can't imagine."[38] Worse, there are those – like the marines described by Swofford – whose reactions are just the opposite of those anticipated by Woolf. These young men are not moral monsters, but they are deplorably ignorant and lacking in moral imagination.

---

[34] See, for example, Robert Graves, *Goodbye to All That* (London: Folio Society, 1981); also Erich Maria Remarque, *All Quiet on the Western Front*, trans. A. W. Wheen (New York: Fawcett Books, 1975).

[35] See Donald J. Eberly, "Alternative Service in a Future Draft," in Moskos and Chambers, *New Conscientious Objection*, p. 58.

[36] See Virginia Woolf, *Three Guineas* (New York: Harcourt Brace, 1966).

[37] Susan Sontag, *Regarding the Pain of Others* (New York: Farrar, Straus, and Giroux, 2003), p. 8. See also the discussion in Tatum, *Mourner's Song*.

[38] Ibid., pp. 125–126.

The Public Psyche

Self-understanding requires studying not only the self as an individual but also the self that belongs to various groups. As a group member, a person is likely to be persuaded more by group-think than by careful, critical thinking. For example, many of those who elected Woodrow Wilson to a second term as president because he had kept the United States out of World War I reacted with enthusiasm to that war just a year later. Those who had apparently never noticed that their champion for stronger unions and better working conditions – *The Catholic Worker* – held an unshakable pacifist position suddenly woke up and objected to its pacifism during the Korean War. Those who might have opposed the internment of Japanese Americans in World War II (and even knew in their hearts that it was wrong) kept silent. "To oppose what everyone else deems a necessary evil is to be a collaborationist."[39] Whenever the United States has gone to war, there have been substantial numbers of people willing to suspend the very liberties for which the country stands.

President Wilson contributed to the anti-immigrant feeling in World War I when he said in an address to Congress:

> There are citizens of the U.S., I blush to admit, born under other flags but welcomed under our generous naturalization laws to the full freedom and opportunity of America, who have poured the poison of disloyalty into the very arteries of our national life.... Such creatures of passion, disloyalty, and anarchy must be crushed out.... The hand of our power should close over them at once.[40]

Passions ran high against socialists, pacifists, Wobblies (members of the Industrial Workers of the World), and citizens of German ancestry. Lynchings and beatings occurred and were excused as errors of patriotic fervor. Schools gave up the teaching of German, and many German American families stopped speaking and teaching the language to their children. Germans became *Huns* whether they lived in Germany or the United States.

Jane Addams maintained her devotion to immigrants and to pacifism, and for this devotion she was publicly castigated. She lost much

---

[39] Richard Powers, *Prisoner's Dilemma* (New York: HarperCollins, 1988), p. 132.
[40] Quoted in Elshtain, *Jane Addams*, p. 207.

of her former support and public admiration. Other feminists and pacifists worked vigorously to help young men obtain conscientious objector status and to defend those wrongly accused of subversion.[41] It is important to study this period of U.S. history as an exercise in trying to understand what happens to people caught up in patriotic excitement. It is easy to look back at past patriotic hysteria and deplore it. It is much harder to ask: Could I be so swayed? What might do it? How could I resist it? It might help to read about those who have had the courage to resist patriotically driven cruelty and unfairness toward fellow citizens.

Propaganda has been used effectively throughout the past century. Jonathan Glover observes, "To resist propaganda, people need the ability to think critically,"[42] but schools do not cultivate this ability. Some may espouse critical thinking as an educational aim and sometimes require students to exercise it on historical issues long past, but there are people who oppose even this,[43] and they have a point, although it is not one I would endorse. The point I would acknowledge is that young people are sometimes asked to think critically on issues they are ill prepared to think about.[44] They do not have enough information to reason well and frequently do their "critical thinking" emotionally. The remedy, however, is not to abandon critical thinking but to provide *critical lessons* and encourage students to seek the information they need to reason well. Moreover, the titles of chapters in a recent book deploring the "failure" of social studies do little to encourage critical reasoning: "The Training of Idiots," "Garbage In, Garbage Out," "Ignorant Activists."[45] There is little critical thinking in any of these chapters. If the writers' reasoned objection is that critical thinking in our schools leans too much to the left, then the answer is to check that thinking for truth and to restore balance where truth requires it. The use of emotional rhetoric of scorn and contempt is a poor educational strategy.

---

[41] See Early, *A World without War*.

[42] Jonathan Glover, *Humanity: A Moral History of the 20th Century* (New Haven, CT: Yale University Press, 2000), p. 360.

[43] See James Leming, Lucien Ellington, and Kathleen Porter, eds., *Where Did Social Studies Go Wrong?* (Washington, DC: Thomas B. Fordham Foundation, 2003).

[44] Leming, "Ignorant Activists: Social Change, 'Higher Order Thinking,' and the Failure of Social Studies," in *Where Did Social Studies Go Wrong?* pp. 124–142.

[45] See Leming et al., *Where Did Social Studies Go Wrong?*

Glover points out that some people have "found it a relief not to think,"[46] and although Glover was here referring to a leading Nazi, Albert Speer, such statements can be found in the accounts of people all over the world. To submit to orders, to stop thinking for oneself, can be a relief; one is no longer responsible for one's moral conduct. Further, the civilian population seems sometimes to prefer not knowing the truth.[47] Community spirit, the feeling of unity, can be shaken by information that contradicts preferred beliefs. Brian Fogarty remarks: "The desire to believe a comfortable lie in the face of an uncomfortable truth is a powerful blinder, and it gives the official propaganda machine an enormous advantage."[48]

All sides try to seize this advantage. The Nazis used lies at first to cover and later to continue their program to exterminate Jews. The U.S. government used lies to hide the errors, accidents, and cruelties of the Vietnam War. In the first Gulf War, propaganda accused Iraqi soldiers of killing babies and destroying incubators; it wasn't true. Today, Islamist propaganda makes Americans into demons and America itself into the Great Satan.

The temptation to believe and the comfort of believing are increased by the pressure of others who, because their need to believe is so strong, see every attempt to rethink or advise caution as a sign of betrayal. Many people might act on their brief moments of doubt or reflection if it weren't for the constant accusations and threats of monitoring peers. The comrades of fearful Trojans and Greeks in the *Iliad*, the loud-mouthed audience at a lynching, the government officials who see all dissent as a lack of patriotism – these insecure but vocal people make it uncomfortable to put down the sword or rope or even to suggest that the present course of action is questionable.

Thoughtful, gentle people who refuse to participate in violence may nevertheless stand aside helplessly when their government commits reprehensible acts. We hear about fellow citizens of Arabic origins detained incommunicado, and we are disturbed. But suppose they are involved in terrorism? Doesn't the agency that picked them up know more than we do? Suppose that, in defending them, we are

---

[46] Glover, *Humanity*, p. 361.

[47] See Brian E. Fogarty, *War, Peace, and the Social Order* (Boulder, CO: Westview Press, 2000).

[48] Ibid., p. 214.

endangering innocent others? It may take some time and thought before we muster the strength to object and to support organizations that insist on maintaining the rights and liberties for which we are supposedly fighting.[49] And it might get more difficult to do even this. If terror strikes harder or closer to home, many of our fellow citizens may engage in the sort of deplorable behavior exhibited in previous wars.

Because of the lasting danger of behavior contrary to our finest ideals of justice, schools must include these episodes in social studies courses. There are those who, vaunting their own patriotism, blame the schools for focusing too long and too narrowly on the faults of our society. I agree that this fault-finding can become obsessive and have the effect of turning students into cynics. But the faults must be faced. Where possible, the fault should be held up against the ideal for criticism. In this way, examination of the fault enhances the ideal and calls forth new, better-informed commitment.

It will take courageous teachers to withstand the attacks now launched at them in the name of defending America and its history. The terrorist attacks of September 11, 2001, brought forth feelings of fear and outrage. Such destruction of innocent life, most of us agree, is inexcusable. Discussing how social studies educators responded to the attacks and to what to teach students about them (in the volume with the deplorable chapter titles mentioned earlier), Chester Finn writes:

> And the despicable answer, from many quarters of the social studies field in particular and the education establishment in general, was teach them to feel good about themselves, to forgive their trespassers, not to blame anyone (lest this lead to feelings of hatred or prejudice), to appreciate diversity, and to consider the likelihood that America was itself responsible for this great evil visited upon it.[50]

Finn quotes no one here, preferring to castigate the entire social studies field and education in general. He never pauses to consider that good teachers will certainly teach the ideals of America that

---

[49] See David Cole, *Enemy Aliens: Double Standards and Constitutional Freedoms in the War on Terrorism* (New York: New Press, 2003); see also Anthony Lewis, "Un-American Activities," *New York Review of Books*, Oct. 23, 2003: 16–19.

[50] Chester E. Finn, Jr., Foreword in *Where Did Social Studies Go Wrong?* ed. Leming et al., p. iii.

he defends in his next paragraph. At the same time, under such circumstances, thoughtful teachers will try to ease the pain and horror students are suffering (not simply "teach them to feel good about themselves"), and they might (if they dared to mention religion at all) remind them that there is a beautiful doctrine of forgiveness in the Judeo-Christian tradition. Most important of all, good teachers *will* want to prevent feelings of hatred and prejudice. This does not in any way imply reluctance to put blame on the perpetrators. Rather, it should help to protect those who bear a superficial resemblance to the perpetrators from unjust vengeance. And finally, while making it clear that terrorism is not to be defended or excused, teachers should help students understand that Americans might indeed examine their own behavior in the world to see if there are ways in which they are acting to invite enmity. It is just plain common sense to do this. Critical thinkers should, of course, condemn evil, but they should also want to prevent its growth and recurrence. Again, every fault admitted should be examined in light of the ideals of which we are rightly proud.

People are pressed to believe propaganda, but many want to believe. It seems plausible, too, that critical thinkers are sometimes slow to resist propaganda because their critical habits counsel them to examine all sides even when one side is almost certainly wrong. This is a worry mentioned earlier: critical thinking can lead to indecision and lack of commitment. It need not have this effect, but we have to be prepared for the possibility. Even after a commitment has been made, a critical thinker remains open to new evidence. Rigidity is anathema to critical thinking.

George Orwell remarked in 1940 on the rigidity of Adolf Hitler's thinking. Hitler had a mind closed on its own terrible vision. Yet Hitler was able to collect followers and promote his vision. People want to believe in something, and they often seek a strong leader to point them on the way. Glover quotes a Nazi concentration camp commander:

> I was full of gratitude to the SS for the intellectual guidance it gave me. We were all thankful. Many of us had been so bewildered before joining the organization. We did not understand what was happening around us, everything was so mixed up. The SS offered us a series of simple ideas that we could understand, and we believed in them.[51]

---

[51] Quoted in Glover, *Humanity*, pp. 361–362.

Someone, some group to follow, to believe in. The longing to believe and to follow is strong in most human beings. Thus, some immerse themselves in religion, some in political or ideological movements. Time, reflective modifications, and moral criticism transform some leader-dominant movements into institutions that provide reasonably safe and attractive shelters for believers. But students should be aware that religions begin with strong leaders, people who say "follow me" and promise great rewards to those who do so.

Followers are not necessarily cowardly – at least not in the physical sense of cowardice. It took great courage for the early followers of Jesus and Mohammed to express their beliefs and live by them in public. Nor are today's Islamic suicide bombers cowardly. But their physical bravery can hardly be called virtuous – not if we consider virtuous acts those that contribute to a better life for both self and others. The deliberate killing of people who do not want to die can never be considered virtuous.[52]

Glover reminds us that the appeal to sacrifice and community solidarity can be a powerful rallying message.[53] People are not always looking for security and comfort. He notes that Hitler urged people to join together for greater strength, to sacrifice, and to seek tribal glory. Indeed, Hitler wrote:

> This will to sacrifice in staking his personal labor and, if necessary, his own life for others, is most powerfully developed in the Aryan. He is greatest, not in his mental capacity *per se*, but in the extent to which he is ready to put all his abilities at the service of the community. With him the instinct of self-preservation has reached the most noble form, because he willingly subjects his own ego to the life of the community and, if the hour should require it, he also sacrifices it.[54]

Take out the word *Aryan* and substitute something else – *American, Englishman, Christian, Jew, Marine* – and many people will find the paragraph inspirational. Teachers might substitute *some individuals* for *Aryan* and ask students to guess at the author. Messages like Hitler's are especially appealing, as Glover observes, to those who have felt left out of things and desperately want to belong.

---

[52] See my argument in Noddings, *Starting at Home: Caring and Social Policy* (Berkeley: University of California Press, 2002).

[53] See Glover, *Humanity*, pp. 360–366.

[54] Adolf Hitler, *Mein Kampf* (New York: Reynal and Hitchcock, 1939), p. 408.

The search for a leader in whom to believe arises again and again. It arises with special force when discussion and critical thinking are discouraged. Günter Grass, in his novel *Crabwalk*, tells the story of a teenager in today's Germany who becomes obsessed with the World War II Russian sinking of the *Wilhelm Gustloff*, in which some, 9,000 people, many of them children, died. In part, because his teachers will not allow him to analyze or even to speak about the episode and the boy hears only a lopsided version of the story from his grandmother, who was a survivor of the disaster, he eventually decides to kill a young man he thinks is a Jew. His killing mimics the assassination of Wilhelm Gustloff, a minor Nazi official before World War II, and the reason he gives for the killing is an echo of the one given by Gustloff's killer. Frankfurter, the killer of Gustloff, had claimed that he killed the Nazi "because I am a Jew." Konny, the new killer, says, "I shot because I am a German."[55]

In prison, Konny seems to start on a recovery from his obsession, and his father begins to hope for his son's future. However, after one encouraging visit, the father browses the Internet, where Konny's troubles had blossomed, and he finds a website campaigning for his son:

> "We believe in you, we will wait for you, we will follow you ..." And so on and so forth. It doesn't end. Never will it end.[56]

Might the result have been different if Konny's teachers had encouraged discussion? Students also need to know that the rigidity of mind attributed to ideologues and followers is more than skin deep. Loyalties and enmities are not fixed to the present cast of characters. Rather, they illustrate and serve a deeper rigidity. It doesn't matter much to the lonely outsider who accepts him and demands his loyalty, just so long as *someone* does. Similarly, it doesn't matter whom he hates. It is the hatred itself that inspires him. Eric Hoffer comments:

> Passionate hatred can give meaning and purpose to an empty life. Thus people haunted by the purposelessness of their lives try to find a new content not only by dedicating themselves to a holy cause but

---

[55] Günter Grass, *Crabwalk*, trans. Krishna Winston (Orlando, FL: Harcourt, 2002), p. 204.
[56] Ibid., p. 234.

also by nursing a fanatical grievance. A mass movement offers them unlimited opportunities for both.[57]

But, lest students think that belonging to a group is necessarily bad, there should be study and discussion of the positive aspects of group membership. Hoffer points out that unscrupulous leaders have often achieved complete control by separating dissenters from the groups that might support them. He notes that the same Russians who cringed in fear of "Stalin's secret police displayed unsurpassed courage when facing . . . the invading Nazis."[58] To be part of a group gives us courage – sometimes to stand up for what is good, sometimes to perform atrocities. One test that critical thinkers must bring to their choice to belong or not to belong is whether the group under consideration will encourage them to continue to think critically. As Paul Tillich puts it, one must have the courage to be as a part and also the courage to be as an individual.[59]

Belonging to a "good" group, however, does not immunize us against hatred. The public psyche is quick to hate in times of war. The Germans were *Huns* in World War I, the Japanese *yellow monkeys* in World War II, the North Koreans and later the Vietnamese *slopes* and *gooks*. It is somehow easier to hate and to kill Huns and gooks than German and Vietnamese human beings. Sometimes hatred precedes war and violence, as it has in many cases of ethnic cleansing.[60] But for American students, it is more important to study and try to understand how the public – not only soldiers under fire – can be brought to hate in times of war.

In Richard Powers's *Prisoner's Dilemma*, there is a powerful fictitious conversation between Henry Stimson (secretary of war during World War II) and Walt Disney. The real Disney had been making films to promote the war effort. The fictional version of Disney is asked to "Make something that will last."[61] The fictional Stimson suggests that the present hatred of "Japs and Germans" will pass and new hatreds will have to be promoted – hence the request to make something

---

[57] Eric Hoffer, *The True Believer* (New York: Harper & Row, 1951), p. 92.

[58] Ibid., p. 63.

[59] See Tillich, *The Courage to Be*.

[60] See Norman M. Naimark, *Fires of Hatred: Ethnic Cleansing in Twentieth-Century Europe* (Cambridge, MA: Harvard University Press, 2002).

[61] Powers, *Prisoner's Dilemma*, p. 179.

that will last. What isn't clear is whether Disney is being asked to help maintain a "world of permanent threat" in which hatred can be quickly aroused and employed to settle political issues or to find a way to block this horrific future. The context leads us to believe that it is the former that Stimson requests. The fictional Disney knows that he must do something – something fictitious, make-believe – but he realizes that it may not matter which end he tries to satisfy. The world is already lost.

The public is fickle not only in its hatred of enemies but also in its attitude toward its own soldiers. Members of a voluntary military are rarely held in high esteem except in times of war. Rudyard Kipling dramatized this fickle attitude toward British soldiers in his poem "Tommy."[62] Tommy was despised or ignored as a loser during peacetime but extolled as a hero when war came. Even in the United States today we see that hypocritical attitude. The young people who staff our volunteer service are, for the most part, kids who have not done very well in school and sometimes seem to lack direction. They are rarely the kids who have brought joy to the hearts of their teachers. War comes, and they are now "our boys" and "our heroes." War passes, and too often they are again outsiders, forgotten. Their day as heroes is over, and the public will be ready to hate new enemies and cheer new temporary heroes.

The Loss of Moral Identity

Young people considering service in the military should be aware that combat sometimes induces the loss of moral identity. Good boys who would probably never hurt their neighbors commit monstrous acts. But the perpetrators are not monsters; they are "our boys."

The world was shocked when, during the Vietnam conflict, American troops massacred as many as 500 civilians in the village of My Lai. Although no one fired a shot at Charlie Company (the soldiers who attacked My Lai), this is what they did:

> They burnt down every house. They raped women and girls and then killed them. They stabbed some women in the vagina and disemboweled others, cut off their hands or scalps. Pregnant women had their

[62] See "Tommy" in Rudyard Kipling, *The Works of Kipling* (Roslyn, NY: Black's Readers Service, nd), pp. 84–85.

stomachs slashed open and were left to die. There were gang rapes and killings by shooting or with bayonets. There were mass executions. Dozens of people at a time, including old men, women and children, were machine-gunned in a ditch. In four hours nearly 500 villagers were killed.[63]

One American soldier, who had deliberately killed two young children, asked, "Why? Why did I do that? That is not me."[64] The soldier who did this had lost his moral identity – "that is not me." But the acts committed in war become part of the individuals who commit them. Ever after, what was done by this moral stranger *is* "me." Surely our young people should know of such horrendous possibilities before they leave high school.

Swofford describes an event that occurred during a bus parade for marines returning from victory after the first Gulf War. One marine helped a down-and-out Vietnam veteran onto the bus:

> The man had no shoes on his dirty feet and wore tattered jeans and a faded camouflage blouse of indeterminate origin. Tears fell from the man's eyes and rolled down his deeply wrinkled and hurt face . . . the man was somewhat drunk, but obviously less drunk than he was used to being. He steadied himself . . . , and he opened his dry mouth and licked his cracked lips and yelled to the bus, "Thank you, thank you, jarheads, for making them see we are not bad animals."[65]

What had this veteran gone through, what had he done, that made it impossible for him to return to productive civilian life? Was he, as Weil described such men, a "compromise between a man and a corpse"? Why did he need to believe that civilians no longer thought of warriors as "bad animals"? And will he ever stop thinking of himself as a bad animal?

Simone Weil told us that the only hero – indeed, the only subject in the *Iliad* – is force. All the human beings are mere objects, things used by force to accomplish the purposes of war. Swofford, who had

---

[63] Glover, *Humanity*, p. 58. For a full description of the events, the resulting trial, and public opinion, see Herbert. C. Kelman and V. Lee Hamilton, *Crimes of Obedience* (New Haven, CT: Yale University Press, 1989).

[64] Quoted in Glover, *Humanity*, p. 61.

[65] Swofford, *Jarhead*, p. 251.

joined the Marines eager for combat ("fight, rape, war, pillage, burn"), returned from war with a different view:

> I am entitled to despair over the likelihood of further atrocities. Indolence and cowardice do not drive me – despair drives me. I remade my war one word at a time, a foolish, desperate act. When I despair, I am alone, and I am often alone.…
> I am alone and full of despair – the same despair that impelled me to write this book, a quiet scream from within a buried coffin. Dead, dead, my scream.[66]

Grass said of the search for a strong leader willing to kill, "It doesn't end. Never will it end," and Swofford writes at the end of his memoir, "This will never end. Sorry."[67] Sorry indeed. It is parents and educators who should apologize for sending our kids into the military without telling them that they might lose their moral selves.

Stories of those who have resisted participation in atrocities must be heard. How do some young soldiers find the strength to refuse orders to kill noncombatants? The pressure of orders is increased by the conduct and verbal incitement of peers. Like the warriors of Troy and Greece who were accused of growing weak when they were frightened and sick of killing, soldiers in Vietnam were urged by their buddies to join in the killing. Probably the men who were already killing were seeking the familiar juvenile justification "everyone is doing it," and they would have felt better if in fact everyone had joined in. But not everyone did. Where did those who refused find the moral resources to do so? These are stories that should be told again and again.

All wars produce moral atrocities, and they are not confined to one side. The Japanese were guilty of great cruelty before and during World War II,[68] and American soldiers committed horrible acts against Japanese soldiers.[69] Horrors such as cutting off enemy ears and making necklaces of them were repeated in the Vietnam War.[70]

---

[66] Ibid., p. 254.
[67] Ibid., p. 255.
[68] See Glover, *Humanity*, pp. 94–95.
[69] See Peter Schrijvers, *The GI War Against Japan* (New York: New York University Press, 2002).
[70] See Glover, *Humanity*.

The horrors induced by combat are, in some sad way, almost understandable, but the torture, mutilation, and deliberate killing of prisoners and noncombatants makes the world hard to live in. Jean Améry, an Austrian philosopher, was tortured by the Gestapo. He said:

> Anyone who has been tortured remains tortured. . . . Anyone who has suffered torture never again will be able to be at ease in the world, the abomination of the annihilation is never extinguished. Faith in humanity, already cracked by the first slap in the face, then demolished by torture, is never acquired again.[71]

Those who torture commit a double crime. Not only do they harm fellow human beings physically but they reduce them as moral beings. The tortured will do almost anything to escape further torture; they, too, even though innocent, lose their moral identity. Primo Levi comments on the diminishment felt by concentration camp prisoners:

> We endured filth, promiscuity, and destitution, suffering much less than we would have suffered from such things in normal life, because our moral yardstick had changed.[72]

Despite his suffering, Levi never denied the humanness of his torturers. He attributed their moral decline to all the factors we have discussed in this chapter. Refusing even to call them *torturers*, he said of those who made him suffer:

> They were made of the same cloth as we, they were average human beings, averagely intelligent, averagely wicked: save the exceptions, they were not monsters, they had our faces, but they had been reared badly. . . . All of them had been subjected to the terrifying miseducation provided for and imposed by the schools created in accordance with the wishes of Hitler and his collaborators.[73]

In contrast to Levi's humane, if despairing, assessment, others have found it difficult to accord even legitimate enemies any respect. During World War I, W. A. Spooner, the warden of New College, Oxford, allowed the names of German graduates who were killed fighting for Germany to be listed under "Pro Patria." Although he was criticized

---

[71] Quoted in Primo Levi, *The Drowned and the Saved*, trans. Raymond Rosenthal (New York: Vintage, 1988), p. 25.
[72] Ibid., p. 75.
[73] Ibid., p. 202.

for this stand, he insisted that these graduates had done nothing wrong in fighting for their own country.[74] Glover notes that such generosity was rare.

Here we might note that Warden Spooner, who should be remembered for his moral courage, is more often thought of in connection with a mental-linguistic quirk of the sort we discussed in chapter 1. In speaking of Queen Victoria, Spooner referred to "the queer old dean" instead of "the dear old queen." This odd transposition of letters and sounds seems to be proof that our minds generate language from underlying thoughts, and sometimes our tongues run ahead of our thoughts. When students discuss mental processes and their own ways of thinking, they should be aware of Spoonerisms. For present purposes, it is sad that *Spoonerism* refers to a linguistic anomaly and not to a courageous moral stand.

Basically good people who have collaborated with or have been tribally associated with evil acts or movements understandably suffer guilt. The recognition of such guilt prompts a variety of reactions. Some defend their group by pointing out that "others did it too." Some – probably the majority – fall silent. Few have the courage to discuss both their own guilt and the suffering they have endured. Indeed, guilt may make it seem that the suffering is deserved.

Martin Heidegger, a German philosopher who supported the Nazis, remained mostly silent on the Holocaust – but not entirely. When he spoke, he seemed to take the first position. In a response to Herbert Marcuse's request that he make a statement on the Holocaust, Heidegger replied:

> I can only add that instead of the word "Jews" [in your letter] there should be the word "East Germans," and then exactly the same [terror] holds true of one of the Allies, with the difference that everything that has happened since 1945 is public knowledge world-wide, whereas the bloody terror of the Nazis was in fact kept a secret from the German people.[75]

Heidegger's response is a classic case of "they did it too," but it isn't even true. East Germans suffered terribly, but there was no

---

[74] See Glover, *Humanity*, p. 175.

[75] Quoted in Richard J. Bernstein, *The New Constellation* (Cambridge, MA: MIT Press, 1992), p. 129.

cold-blooded, systematic program to annihilate them.[76] Further, if Heidegger was unaware of the "bloody terror," he was certainly not unaware of the confiscation of property and the dismissal of Jewish professors from the universities; he actively cooperated in those immoral acts.

The guilt-induced silence of many Germans included silence on their own suffering. How, in all decency, could a people implicated in the Holocaust protest that they, too, suffered? Not many were as thick-skinned as Heidegger. The boy, Konny, in Grass's *Crabwalk* was confused and embittered by this collective silence. Why did his country-men and even his school ignore the disaster of the *Wilhelm Gustloff*? Nine thousand lives lost – thousands of them little children! Konny's confusion deserved an extended discussion. How can we talk about our own suffering when we are guilty of – or at least tainted by – a monstrous suffering inflicted on others by our people? But Germans *did* suffer, and there is no reason to suppose that the thousands of old people, women, children, dogs, cats, and canaries incinerated in the Dresden bombings somehow deserved it. Suffering, whenever and wherever it occurs, deserves compassion and relief. But silence on all this – on the guilt, the suffering, the shame, the innocence – breeds confusion. And other innocents are likely to suffer as a result.

It is only in the last few years that German writers have felt com-pelled to write about the suffering of German civilians during and after World War II.[77] How should we respond to the fact that some 600,000 German civilians died in Allied bombings and many more were left homeless? Why have Germans been unable to talk about this devastation? Is it better that we (all of us) do not discuss it, or are we breeding whole new generations of Konnys who will direct their anger at other people? It is at least conceivable that, when we refuse to discuss these things critically, we contribute by that very refusal to the permanent loss of our moral identity.

In this chapter, we discussed the attractions of war and the social con-struction of masculinity that supports its attractiveness. We looked at

---

[76] See Naimark, *Fires of Hatred*, on the important difference between ethnic cleans-ing and genocide.

[77] See, in addition to Grass, W. G. Sebald, *On the Natural History of Destruction*, trans. Anthea Bell (New York: Random House, 2003).

pacifism and women's leadership in rejecting war, and we raised the question of why peace and pacifism so rarely appear as major topics in the school curriculum. We considered the public psyche and its fickle attitude toward young people in the military. We raised questions about propaganda and the ease with which hatred is aroused. Finally, we discussed the loss of moral identity that occurs in war and its related violence. The fundamental question for educators is this: can we claim to educate young people if we do not prepare them for the psychological upheavals that accompany war and violence?

The emphasis throughout this book is on individual and group self-understanding. What powerful individuals or groups will try to influence me? How should I respond? How can I maintain my moral identity and that of the people to whom I belong? Moral identity has its origin in home and community life. Home is our next topic.

3

House and Home

For our house is our corner of the world . . . it is our first universe. . . .

Gaston Bachelard

In the *Cardinal Principles of Secondary Education* (1918), one of the seven great aims of education listed was "worthy home membership."[1] American schools, however, have done little to promote that aim, despite the obvious fact that all human beings must make some sort of home for themselves. Homemaking has for too long been considered the domain of women – one requiring no education beyond that handed down from mother to daughter. The bold suggestion of this chapter is that schools should educate secondary school students for homemaking and provide critical lessons on everyday life. The topics are both intellectually rich and relevant to all human lives.

Home as a Shelter

A home is more than a shelter from the elements, but it is at least that, and I'll start the discussion by thinking of shelters. Most of us take shelter for granted, and we rarely think about the built-places in which we live and work. What would we do if we had to build our own shelter? Where would we begin?

Once in a while, an adult human being – prompted by necessity or romantic daydreaming – takes these questions seriously and undertakes to answer them. Michael Pollan, a writer who had never engaged

[1] See National Education Association, *Cardinal Principles of Secondary Education* (Washington, DC: U.S. Government Printing Office, 1918).

64

in construction of any kind, decided to build (with some help) a place of his own – a "hut" that would function as his study.[2] Over a period of some months, he learned about footings, framing, roof, windows, and finishing. These are all essential parts of actual physical buildings, but the words are rich in metaphorical meaning as well. We hope to build our plans on a sound footing, and we refer to the sky as a roof over the earth. We speak of windows on the world and on our minds. In Gaston Bachelard's beautiful *Poetics of Space*, cellars, windows, attics, corners, doors, chests, and drawers are all described both physically and metaphorically.[3] The richness of metaphorical use points to the primal quality of houses and their parts.

Pollan's building is tiny (about 8 by 13 feet), but it hardly qualifies as a hut; its construction is too well informed by modern architecture to strike us as a hut. However, the motivation, if not the structure, is primitive. Huts – primitive shelters – appear all over the world, constructed from whatever natural materials are available. Before we even ask a question critical to today's everyday experience of home-making, we might note some of the intellectual possibilities in studying something about small buildings.

The dimensions of Pollan's rectangular building conform to the Golden Ratio – width 8 feet multiplied by 1.618 (Φ) to give a length of 12.9 feet. That fascinating number – phi (Φ) – appears in an amazing number of natural phenomena, and it has long been considered to represent the rectangular proportion most pleasing to the eye.[4] However, phi is not the only number to appear repeatedly in architectural aesthetics. The proportions of an ideal human body are used often, and the history of such use and ideas about the ideal human body are fascinating.[5] Here is a critical question for educators: How

---

[2] See Michael Pollan, *A Place of My Own: The Education of an Amateur Builder* (New York: Delta, 1997).

[3] See Gaston Bachelard, *The Poetics of Space*, trans. Maria Jolas (New York: Orion Press, 1964).

[4] See Mario Livio, *The Golden Ratio: The Story of Phi, The World's Most Astonishing Number* (New York: Broadway Books, 2002). See also, for example, its appearance in literature: Dan Brown, *The Da Vinci Code* (New York: Doubleday, 2003).

[5] See Norman Crowe, *Nature and the Idea of a Man-Made World* (Cambridge, MA: MIT Press, 1999); also John Brinckerhoff Jackson, *A Sense of Place, a Sense of Time* (New Haven, CT: Yale University Press, 1994).

is it that, despite today's insistence that all students study algebra and geometry, few learn anything about the Golden Ratio or the human proportions used to harmonize nature and the built-world?

There is, of course, a connection between buildings and the natural materials available in a given locale. John Dewey described geography as "an account of the earth as the home of man,"[6] and this suggests a careful study of the relation between the physical characteristics of a region and human-made environments. Yet schools often neglect the study of homes in their efforts to get children to memorize the names of countries, mountains, rivers, and other geographical features. Social studies text books do discuss how people use available resources to construct buildings, but the best builders care for and appreciate materials in addition to using them. Edward Casey recognizes that building is a "Promethean activity of brawny aggression and forceful imposition," but he points out that it is more than that:

> Building is also ... *Epimethean*: a matter of attentive "after-thought" (the literal meaning of "Epi-metheus," brother of Prometheus and husband of Pandora). In this latter capacity building is most effectively cultivational in character, for it seeks not to exploit materials but to care for them.[7]

In addition to matters of cultural literacy that might be discussed here (who can tell us the story of Prometheus and Epimetheus?), this passage introduces a genuine critical question. What does it mean to care for building materials? How does one care for different kinds of wood, for example? What skills are needed to prevent waste? Casey remarks that the attitude of cultivation or caring-for extends to

> matching precise grains of wood, finding that a certain column goes well with a given balustrade, realizing that one building design suits the location better than another, discovering that the same design also opens up a dialogue among those who are going to reside in the building it projects ... and others who will be affected by this eventual building in some significant way.[8]

---

[6] John Dewey, *Democracy and Education* (New York: Macmillan, 1916), p. 211.
[7] Edward S. Casey, *Getting Back into Place* (Bloomington: Indiana University Press, 1993), p. 173.
[8] Ibid., p. 174.

Perhaps few adults think critically about the shelters within which we make homes. However, most children show an almost instinctive interest in primitive shelters. Many (perhaps most) adults can remember constructing, as children, an indoor shelter from blankets, towels, and old sheets stretched across overturned chairs and anchored by piles of books. Whatever game we were playing – cavemen, Indians, burrowing animals – we snuggled into these shelters safe from the wider world. Often we used these shelters for daydreaming.[9] Indeed, the house itself may be construed as such a shelter. Bachelard comments, "If I were asked to name the chief benefit of the house, I should say: the house shelters daydreaming, the house protects the dreamer...."[10] How can we provide for this essential function in building and caring for our homes?

Building a primitive childhood shelter also satisfies the desire to construct – one of the fourfold interests of children identified by Dewey.[11] Outside, children use branches, twigs, cardboard boxes, old boards, or whatever materials they can find. Sometimes the shelter is found rather than constructed – a spot between rocks on the beach, a clear spot in a bramble patch, a cavelike niche in a riverbank, a deserted backyard. Even then, it is likely that the found place will somehow be marked as the occupant's own place. In later childhood, the special place is often a tree house.[12]

Closely related to the interest in primitive shelters and secret places is one in nests. Bachelard devotes a whole chapter to nests and the wonder they inspired in us as children. "This wonder," he writes, "is lasting and today when we discover a nest it takes us back to our childhood or, rather, to a childhood; to the childhoods we should have

---

[9] Constructing the shelter, playing a game within it, and daydreaming are all exercises of the imagination. Dewey discusses the centrality of imagination in the lives of children in *The School and Society* (Chicago: University of Chicago Press, 1900), p. 55. Kieran Egan emphasizes narrative imagination (a facet not treated in depth by Dewey) in *Children's Minds, Talking Rabbits & Clockwork Oranges* (New York: Teachers College Press, 1999) and also in *Imagination in Teaching and Learning: The Middle School Years* (Chicago: University of Chicago Press, 1992).

[10] Bachelard, *Poetics of Space*, p. 6.

[11] Dewey, *School and Society*, p. 45.

[12] For a delightful account of child-built tree houses and huts, see Robert Paul Smith, *"Where did you go?" "Out" "What did you do?" "Nothing"* (New York: W. W. Norton, 1957).

had."[13] Again, in a discussion of nests, we see almost limitless literary possibilities, but we also encounter critical questions: Why are we so fascinated with nests? What human interest is served? How shall we arrange our own shelters so that the nests of other living things can be preserved?

Schools today give some attention to environmental issues, but often the topics are treated on a global level and in an abstract fashion. Natural history and the ecology of our own backyards may be entirely ignored. For students who have a yard or hope to have one in the future, critical questions abound: What creatures live there? How does my life affect theirs? The entomologist Frank Lutz found almost 1,500 species of insects in his 75-by-200-foot suburban yard, and they were not harmful to his garden.[14] Where do all these creatures find shelter? How can we achieve balance in our gardens? Should we reduce the size of our lawns and add shrubs and flowering plants that provide food and shelter for wildlife?[15] The lawn is a feature of home landscaping that we rarely call into question, and yet there are many sound ecological reasons for reducing the size of lawns. I will return to this issue when we discuss advertising and consumerism in a later chapter.

Given that building, dwelling, and cultivating are so central to human life, it is surprising that schools give so little attention to the house or domicile.[16] The spaces in which we live shape us and are, in turn, shaped by us. In chapter 1, I suggested that students be encouraged to think about the conditions under which they work best. Now we might ask them to study their dwelling places. Casey writes:

> Built places . . . are extensions of our bodies. . . . Places built for residing are an enlargement of an already existing embodiment into an

---

[13] Bachelard, *Poetics of Space*, p. 93.

[14] See Eric Grissell, *Insects and Gardens: In Pursuit of a Garden Ecology* (Portland, OR: Timber Press, 2001).

[15] See Michael Pollan, *Second Nature* (New York: Delta, 1991); also Sara Stein, *Noah's Garden: Restoring the Ecology of Our Own Back Yards* (Boston: Houghton Mifflin, 1993).

[16] For a lovely architectural description of the development of housing forms, see Crowe, *Nature and the Idea of a Man-Made World*. For a philosophical account of dwelling, see Martin Heidegger, "Building Dwelling Thinking," in *Basic Writings*, ed. David Farrell Krell (New York: Harper & Row, 1977); for a history of the home, see Witold Rybczynski, *Home: A Short History of an Idea* (New York: Viking, 1986).

entire life-world of dwelling. . . . As we feel more "at home" in dwelling places, they become places created in our own bodily image.[17]

The dwelling places of children are chosen for them by adults, but wise adults encourage children to arrange and decorate their own rooms or corners. What does a house, apartment, or room say about the person who lives there? What are the person's interests? How are they represented? Is the space an authentic extension of a real person or that of a human impersonator – a mere copy of something considered fashionable? By whom was it planned and for what purpose? This is another topic to which we will return in the chapter on consumerism and advertising.

Like so many of the other topics for critical lessons – topics usually neglected in schools – the study of houses and shelters is intellectually rich, providing lessons in art history (the cruciform, vertical and horizontal axes), geography (materials and climate), mathematics (geometry, Pythagorean proportions, designs), literature (nostalgia, the desire to return or to escape), science (connection to nature, human biology, biophilia), religion (symbol, ritual), sociology (living patterns and homelessness), politics (the meaning of homeland), anthropology (villages, customs), and many more.

Our concentration, however, is again on self-understanding. Dare we ask students to reflect on their own living spaces? Might this not invite invidious comparisons, embarrassment, and even depression? It need not. Students can be invited to explore and reflect without making public disclosure of their living conditions. Indeed, students – like subjects of research – should always be protected from invasions of privacy that make them the instruments of their own denigration. There are ways to discuss these matters, encourage reflection, and return to the discussion at a more general, impersonal level.

Stories about people living in all sorts of shelters and conditions can be presented for student discussion and critique. What is it like to live in a trailer in Florida or a tiny adobe house in New Mexico or a log house with no indoor plumbing in the hills of North Carolina?[18] What is it like to live in a city apartment on, say, the sixteenth floor

---

[17] Casey, *Getting Back into Place*, p. 120.

[18] On trailers and adobe houses, see Jackson, *A Sense of Place*; for a wonderful story of life on a hill farm in North Carolina, see *Aunt Arie: A Foxfire Portrait*, ed. Linda Garland Page and Eliot Wigginton (New York: E. P. Dutton, 1983).

or in a row house close to a busy highway or on a lonely ranch in Wyoming? How do people create beauty, unity, and authenticity in each of these settings? Does it matter whether they do?

Historical, sociological, and anthropological accounts can also be used to moderate the effects of assessing present conditions as somehow lacking. How did earlier inhabitants cope with overcrowding, lack of adequate heat and lighting, insect infestations, faulty (or absent) plumbing, lack of privacy, and other deprivations? High school students are young and can visualize themselves as persons only temporarily caught in conditions less than desirable. The alternative – not to discuss these things at all – smacks of hypocrisy. It implicitly deprives students of an opportunity to improve both their present and future lives. Moreover, honest and open study may induce sympathy and critical appreciation for the living conditions of others.

What does it mean, for example, to be homeless? In the United States today, people who are homeless usually find some form of shelter provided by public or private charity. But no part of this temporary shelter can be made into an extension of one's own body. On the contrary, the very impossibility of doing this – of making the place one's own – devalues the homeless body and self. How would we function without an address, a telephone, a place to store our belongings, a place where others may find us?

The philosopher Heidegger tried to convince us that physical homelessness is not "our" real problem:

> However hard and bitter, however hampering and threatening the lack of houses remains, the *real plight of dwelling* does not lie merely in a lack of houses. . . . The real dwelling plight lies in this, that mortals ever search anew for the essence of dwelling. . . . What if man's homelessness consisted in this, that man still does not even think of the *real* plight of dwelling as *the* plight? Yet as soon as man *gives thought* to his homelessness, it is a misery no longer.[19]

Heidegger fails to understand the abject misery of physical homelessness. He also fails to see the evolutionary quality of building that many architectural theorists have described so beautifully. Physical forms of building evolve with customs, religion, language, and technology. Everything that develops depends on those first primitive

---

[19] Heidegger, "Building Dwelling Thinking," p. 339.

forms, and it is unlikely that the kind of thinking extolled by Heidegger could have developed in the absence of adequate physical shelter. Thinking depends on shelter (shelter for the dreamer, as Bachelard put it), and it cannot by itself relieve the real misery of physical homelessness. It is both blind and heartless to suppose that it can.[20] However, students – adequately sheltered – should be encouraged to explore Heidegger's question about the "real plight of dwelling." What might this mean? How should we respond?

I should emphasize here that a home need not be a house or permanent shelter. A home can be a trailer, tiny apartment, or series of temporary dwellings so long as the inhabitants have sufficient control to mark the place as their own. Some people move often, yet make each new place into a home. Some have even found a "home" in a school, church, or library. City children may have an advantage over isolated rural children in having so many such homes accessible to them. A home involves continuity of persons and customs; it may even be identified with a physical region or set of natural features. Many people relate more closely to a region than to a house as they think of home. Although we require a shelter, we need to think beyond shelters to places.

Before turning to the topic of place, I should put a question to educators (one that will become familiar as we move along): Where in the established school curriculum should these topics be presented? An ideal answer would be to scrap the present curriculum, which has effectively been obsolete for at least two centuries, and create a new one organized around central human problems and interests. But this is unlikely to happen. A practical alternative is to stretch each and every school subject so that it makes room for these essential topics. Then the question becomes not where but how – how can mathematics, English, science, a foreign language, social studies, and the arts include critical lessons on these topics?

Place and Time

We are often drawn to a place that we regard as home because of its natural features. Some people feel at home on the seaside, some in

---

[20] See Nel Noddings, *Starting at Home: Caring and Social Policy* (Berkeley: University of California Press, 2002).

the mountains, some in the country, some in the city. And for some, home is a particular spot on the seaside or a special neighborhood in a particular city. The house in which they live is not as important to these people as its natural location. A dwelling place close to a specific natural feature and oriented to it in just the right way is crucial to the very lives of, for example, the Navajo, and moving away is unthinkable. To be forcibly moved, even if compensated fairly, may induce deep depression, sometimes death.[21]

Just as some people feel a strong attachment to the natural attributes of a place, others become attached to features of the human-made world – particular streets, bridges, churches, markets. Or one may be attached symbolically to a place – the home of one's ancestors, the seat of one's religion, or a place made famous by one's favorite writer, composer, or painter. Consider Elie Wiesel's answer to the question of where he felt most at home: "In Jerusalem ... when I am not in Jerusalem."[22] Wiesel expresses a symbolic longing for one place, a nostalgic longing for another associated with childhood, and a practical attachment to places that satisfy his need to work.

We may also feel connected to a place because of events that occurred there. We do not wish to live on the site of the great battle of Gettysburg or that of the 9/11 disaster, but we may feel a deep connection when we visit these places. In some cultures, places are named for events. Consider the Apache names "Widows Pause for Breath," "They Piled on Top of Each Other," and "Lizards Dart Away in Front."[23] Each name tells the essence of a story. And sometimes a place that already has a name becomes a metaphor for something that happened there: a terrible defeat after great success is "a Waterloo"; giving superfluous gifts may be regarded as "carrying coals to Newcastle"; someone to be shunned is "sent to Coventry."

In talking with college and university students in the past few years, I have been surprised at how many respond, when asked about places to which they are attached, by naming vacation places. Not one in a recent class named her or his home-place! This response may

---

[21] See the account of Navajo suffering induced by a forcible move in Casey, *Getting Back into Place*.
[22] Elie Wiesel, "Longing for Home," in Leroy S. Rouner, ed., *The Longing for Home* (Notre Dame, IN: University of Notre Dame Press, 1996), pp. 17–29.
[23] The stories are told in Keith Basso, *Wisdom Sits in Places* (Albuquerque: University of New Mexico Press, 1996), pp. 28–29.

represent a need to get away from the tightly structured life associated with today's homes. As several writers have observed, people today are more governed by time than place.[24] We travel easily and quickly all over the world, move our places of residence often, and find familiar landmarks everywhere. But in almost all places, work hours are prescribed, mealtimes are set, and the evening news marks the close of a workday. Even children live by the clock. It may be understandable, then, that people seek relief from the tyranny of human-made time.

However, some occupations, some places, and some vacations tend to restore our sense of cyclic (natural) time. We allow ourselves to be guided by (or at least pay attention to) the seasons, sunrise and sunset, the growing period of various plants, the tides, the rains. Then, if we are thoughtful, the changes of cyclic time can be connected to religious rituals and place-bound customs. Church bells herald noon and twilight. Birdsong precedes and announces sunrise. The dying wind welcomes sunset. Many human beings feel the need for such connections and become closely attached to places that satisfy this need.[25] Even for those who do not seem to need a connection to nature, it is instructive to learn how the human-made world has evolved from the natural world and, of course, people may feel great love for a place, say, a city, that is mostly human-made.[26]

Such knowledge should invite thinking. Do I have a need to be near mountains or an ocean? Does it lift my spirit to see the sunrise, or is waking at such an hour unthinkable? Why and in what way is a vacation place memorable? Or is mentioning a well-known vacation place just one more characteristic of a human impersonator?

As students reflect on the importance of place in their own lives, they should be urged to consider how others feel about their native places. The topic is rich in possibilities for multicultural education. Might we be more thoughtful in recommending large dams, schemes of urban renewal, and large-scale settlements if we were

---

[24] See the discussion in Casey, *Getting Back into Place*, and Crowe, *Nature and the Idea of a Man-Made World*.

[25] The idea of a genetic need for a connection to nature is described in Edward O. Wilson, *Biophilia* (Cambridge, MA: Harvard University Press, 1984); see also Eugene V. Walter, *Placeways: A Theory of the Human Environment* (Chapel Hill: University of North Carolina Press, 1988); and Jackson, *A Sense of Place*.

[26] See Joseph Rykwert, *On Adam's House in Paradise* (Cambridge, MA: MIT Press, 1997); also Crowe, *Nature and the Idea of a Man-Made World*.

fully informed about the attachment of people to their places of residence?

It may be especially important for urban students in the United States to understand the central role of cities in our culture. Cities have been the center of knowledge and enterprise for centuries. They are clearly different from the countryside, and yet their architectural forms can be traced to natural beginnings. The mathematics of the human body, and especially that of our senses and powers of perception, appears, transformed, in our built-places. It should awaken a certain pride and sense of belonging in city students to know that, as they wander the streets of their city, they are part of what Cicero called a "second nature" – a human-made world built into the world of nature.[27] What do they love and admire in their city? Where do they feel most at home in it? A critical discussion on the vitality of cities, on finding a favorite spot in a library or museum, may be important for today's urban students. Are they using their city's educational resources as fully as did earlier city dwellers? If not, why not?

In the discussion of human-made time, we should return to the themes of chapter 1. There it was suggested that students give critical attention to their own work habits. Now we might ask them to consider how they manage human-made time in general. Do they feel in control of it? Do they use to-do lists and self-imposed deadlines to ensure free time, or do they feel driven by such devices? They should know that many happy, creative people live highly structured lives, but the structures they create serve the needs of the individual. Such structuring also reduces double-mindedness and helps to restore mental integrity. When we know that time has been allotted for a particular task or for a preferred recreation, thoughts about it are less likely to intrude on the present occupation.

A study of time can be fascinating in itself. At what point in history did time become more important to human life than place? Why? How did the first clocks imitate the movement of the sun? And how did clocks displace the observation of natural phenomena in navigation? How does the perception of time influence language and the customs governing human interactions? At bottom there remain critical questions for individuals: How do I manage human-made time? How do I

---

[27] See especially the discussion in Crowe, *Nature and the Idea of a Man-Made World*.

achieve harmony with cyclic time? Can I use the harmony with cyclic time to better manage human-made time?

Another critical question students should discuss is this: Do we live in a terrible time? Barbara Kingsolver wrote recently, "It's hard to imagine a more frightening time than this."[28] But she went on to say that almost every generation of human beings has felt this way. "It isn't new, this feeling of despair over a world gone mad with heartless and punitive desires."[29] What is new, she notes, is that we now hear immediately about horrors and miseries from all over the world. How can we manage all this with a minimum of despair and without hardening our hearts? This might be a good time to return to Swofford's confession of despair (chapter 2) and ask again about its roots. Must cycles of violence continue? Are young males inherently attracted to violence?

Was there ever a better time to live? I remember remarks made by Archibald Cox on this topic at a Stanford University commencement some thirty years ago. He was attracted to the late eighteenth century, as many thoughtful people are. He acknowledged that he might have enjoyed living then if he could have been, say, Thomas Jefferson, but not if he had been a woman bearing her child alone in the frontier wilderness. Even the best of times are terrible for some. Time, place, and social position all matter. We, as individuals, are shaped by – and help to shape – all three.

Organic Habits

Bachelard says that "the house we were born into is physically inscribed in us. It is a group of organic habits."[30] This seems to be true for people who have lived an entire childhood in one house. As Bachelard observes, we remember an uneven step, a creaking door, the exact position of a tiny latch. But his remark about organic habits may be largely true even for those who do not stay in one childhood place, for a home is not just a house, and those who make a home are likely to repeat certain arrangements wherever they move. Thus it is at least possible that our early dwelling places do induce organic habits in us.

---

[28] Barbara Kingsolver, "Small Wonder," *Peace and Freedom* 64(1), Winter 2004: 5.
[29] Ibid.
[30] Bachelard, *Poetics of Space*, p. 14.

It is surely true that our national homeland and its language are inscribed in us. General patterns of interaction – how close we stand to others in conversation, the way we open our conversations, social hierarchies – are all largely determined by national/regional cultural socialization. Many biographical accounts attest to the difficulty of adjusting to life in a culture different from that into which one was born. The difficulty is not one-sided. Groups trying to understand strangers in their midst also have a hard time, and the difficulty is aggravated when strangers insist on the religious or political superiority of their own views.[31]

Within our own native land, we may differ substantially from others by race or religion. These two categories into which we are born influence some of us enormously. They are obviously important, and I'll say more about them in the chapter on religion. Here I am more concerned with the self-understanding of personal habits.

Our habits are developed in the settings where we are born and raised. Besides the large cultural patterns that influence us for a lifetime, there are those produced by the interaction of our living conditions and personalities. Young people need to think about these. Consider a few examples. Do you prefer bright indoor light or the permanent twilight of drawn shades or draperies? Do you like open doors and windows or everything locked up safely? Are you a night person or a morning person? Do you like bright or muted colors? To be comfortable, do you require room temperatures above 72°F or below 70°F? Do you like plants around you, or do you find them messy? How about pets? If you like pets, which ones do you prefer? Do you like a quiet environment or do you feel ill at ease without sound? If a family member likes to watch sporting events on television, do you join him, retire to another part of the house, or leave with mumbled comments about couch potatoes?

Sharing a home with someone whose answers to these questions are the direct opposite of one's own can be very difficult. Most of us have enjoyed stories of dramatically different partners such as

---

[31] Many fine novels illustrate this point. See, for example, Barbara Kingsolver, *The Poisonwood Bible*; A. J. Cronin, *The Keys of the Kingdom*; Louise Erdrich, *Tracks*; E. M. Forster, *A Passage to India*; Peter Matthiesen, *At Play in the Fields of the Lord*; Jill Paton Walsh, *Knowledge of Angels*; and Eugene Burdick, *The Ugly American*.

Felix and Oscar in *The Odd Couple,* but in real life we would find living with someone so different from us a great hardship. Part of making a home is the construction of a shared aesthetic, and the more interests and habits we share at the outset, the greater our chance of success.[32]

Our intellectual interests and education may also separate us. Primo Levi describes an event in his own life that illustrates the possibilities. He was attracted to a girl, Rita, in a chemistry class they were both taking. She was obviously bright and got good grades, but she was "without the appetite" Levi had for the subject. Then one day he noticed that she was carrying Thomas Mann's *The Magic Mountain* in her bag. Because the book had been his "sustenance during those months," he asked her about it:

> And soon enough I had to realize that she was reading the novel in an entirely different way. As a novel, in fact: she was very interested in finding out exactly how far Hans would go with Madame Chauchat, and mercilessly skipped the fascinating (for me) political, theological, and metaphysical discussions between the humanist Settembrini and the Jewish Jesuit Naphta.[33]

Readers of this volume – even if they have not read *The Magic Mountain* – might discuss their own reactions to Levi's remarks. Some will, with Rita, be intrigued by the possibility of an affair between Hans and Madame Chauchat. Others (like me) – especially those who have read *The Magic Mountain* – will want to return to the wonderful discussions between Settembrini and Naphta. Never mind Hans and Madame Chauchat! And we sit for a while remembering not only the discussions but that last awful event in the mountain meadow.

How much should such differences matter? No one can really answer that question. What we need to investigate for ourselves is the question of which differences *do* matter to us and perhaps why they matter. I say "perhaps" because we cannot always answer the question why, but it is part of what we must try to do in examining our lives.

[32] See Noddings, "The Couple at Home," in *Inside the American Couple*, ed. Marilyn Yalom and Laura L. Carstensen (Berkeley: University of California Press, 2002), pp. 108–124.

[33] Primo Levi, *The Periodic Table,* trans. Raymond Rosenthal (New York: Schocken Books, 1984), p. 35.

High school students are young and inexperienced. In most cases, their store of experiences is limited, and reflection may not have much to work on. Biographical accounts, essays, fiction, and poetry can be powerful in expanding their field of experience. The events in stories provide vicarious experience, but the encounter with a story is a real experience, and imagination can make vital connections to one's actual life. Further, as educators, we want our students to grow intellectually. The experience gained through reading can increase cultural knowledge, activate the imagination, and provide rich material for personal reflection.

If we want students to find critical issues in the domain of homemaking, we have to expand their knowledge about the topic. In addition to the material discussed in the section on shelters (and we barely scratched the surface), there is much to learn about the history of homes and homemaking. It may interest students to learn, for example, that the word *comfort* was not used in connection with daily life in homes until the eighteenth century.[34] Were people not interested in comfort before that time? If not, why not? And how about privacy? This, too, is a relatively new concept applied to homes. Witold Rybczynski tells us:

> The medieval home was a public, not a private place. The hall was in constant use, for cooking, for eating, for entertaining guests, for transacting business, as well as nightly for sleeping. . . . At night, the tables were put away and the beds were brought out.[35]

And many people slept in one bed, with others scattered about the room on piles of straw. How far teachers will want to pursue this arrangement is a matter of individual taste, humor, and confidence in managing delicate questions.

Study of this sort may encourage students to ask why they cherish privacy or care nothing for it and why they might be unwilling to spend money on decoration if it means giving up comfort. Discussion of privacy and comfort can also contribute to the study of other cultures. Rybczynski notes that the concept of privacy (as Westerners think of it) is absent in Japan. "Lacking an indigenous word to describe this quality, the Japanese have adopted an English

---

[34] See the account in Rybczynski, *Home.*
[35] Ibid., p. 27.

one – *praibashii*."[36] He also suggests, citing an Australian marketing consultant, that people of some cultures give appliances a higher "psychological positioning" than Americans do. Hence, a refrigerator may appear in a Japanese living room.[37] Why would we find this unsettling and unappealing in an American home?

Self-understanding is a good enough reason to examine the origin and development of our organic habits. But another reason is that broader knowledge and reflection may help us to change those habits or to initiate the search for new ones. Why, for example, would Michael Pollan – a writer who had never been good with his hands – decide to build his own study-hut? Why do many of us grow our own vegetables and fruits when there is no economic necessity for us to do so? Why do some become deeply interested in the simple life and reject city living? Why, in contrast, do others flee from small towns to experiment with life in a great city? In most cases, our imaginations have been set afire by stories or pictures. Something touches us, and we think, "I'd like to try that."

Patterns of communication also become organic habits. Many people retain ungrammatical forms of speech despite the best efforts of teachers all through their school days. Such people may even be able to identify correct and incorrect forms on written tests, but they cling to the familiar incorrect ones. This is a matter of considerable educational and social importance, and it is also controversial. It is controversial because people associate their speech habits with their social, ethnic, and class origins. Why should any of these habits be judged wrong? Why should white majority educators insist on changing them? We need to talk about these things and invite critical reflection. When educational researchers point out – even document richly and generously – the difficulties experienced by those whose communication habits differ significantly from those of academically successful families, they are sometimes accused of advocating a deficit model or even of racism.[38] Should we insist that there are no cultural

---

[36] Ibid., p. 28.

[37] Ibid., p. 218.

[38] For two important studies that document the linguistic difficulties of poor or minority communities, see Shirley Brice Heath, *Ways with Words* (New York: Cambridge University Press, 1983); also B. Hart and T. R. Risley, *Meaningful Differences in the Everyday Experience of Young American Children* (Baltimore: Brooks, 1995).

deficits? Or should we talk about language communities and why certain forms are appropriate in some settings but not in others? To neglect this topic out of a misconceived notion of political correctness seems irresponsible.

It might actually be easier to talk about these matters with high school students than with professional colleagues. If we were to take homemaking seriously and give some time to studies of parenting, we might find that students who have never experienced genuine dialogue would be quite fascinated by the possibility. Simply disregarding – even mocking – studies that show marked differences in communication patterns between low- and middle-income parents and their children is unwise and unproductive.[39] It is an understandable reaction, one that properly resists blaming the victim, but victims are often unwittingly complicit in their own victimization.[40] To share with students the real possibility that some patterns of communication are more closely associated with academic success than others seems the right thing to do.

The differences that should concern us do not fall only along class or racial lines, and if we were to concentrate only on these, we would deserve accusations of arrogance and discrimination. There are also linguistic habits across all races and classes that denigrate women and children. There are habits that make children fear humiliation in verbal interaction with their parents. And there are widespread misunderstandings about what it means to have a dialogue. Two people are not in dialogue simply because they are talking to each other. Dialogue requires listening, a genuine respect for the partner in dialogue, and a mutual commitment to inform, learn, and make decisions.[41] All of these things could be, and should be, discussed in schools.

When we share a home, as most of us do, our organic habits affect others, and they are transmitted to children. In trying to com-

---

[39] See, for example, the treatment of this problem in Lisa Delpit, "Educators as 'Seed People' Growing a New Future," *Educational Researcher* 7(32), 2003: 14–21.

[40] See my argument in *Starting at Home*.

[41] One of the best descriptions of dialogue (as I am using it here) can be found in Paulo Freire, *Pedagogy of the Oppressed*, trans. Myra Bergman Ramos (New York: Herder & Herder, 1970); see also Nicholas Burbules, *Dialogue in Teaching* (New York: Teachers College Press, 1993); and Nel Noddings, "Stories in Dialogue," in *Stories Lives Tell*, ed. Carol Witherell and Nel Noddings (New York: Teachers College Press, 1991), pp. 157–170.

municate, to build a shared aesthetic, to raise happy children, and to promote our own growth, we must turn critical thinking on our own ways of doing things.

Household Tasks

It is not uncommon today for two or more adults making a home together to work also outside the home. To simplify the discussion, I'll use the traditional wife–husband couple in what follows, but most of what is said can apply to other arrangements as well.

Women have always worked outside the home but, in the ideal family of the nineteenth and twentieth centuries (until almost the mid-twentieth century), a stay-at-home woman took care of the house and family. Her work did not bring a salary, but in loving, appreciative marriages, a housewife's work was recognized as a contribution not only to the well-being of the family but also to a growing net worth. "A penny saved is a penny earned" was a slogan acted upon by countless women. The work was real, valuable, and necessary. One could not run easily to the corner store to buy bread, milk, and other foods. Even earlier than this, both spouses worked at home – one mainly outside, the other mainly inside – and both forms of work were recognized and valued. This is not to say that women enjoyed equality with men during any of these years. They could not exercise full rights as citizens, nor did they control their own money or life choices.

The discontent felt by women in the eighteenth and nineteenth centuries focused almost exclusively on the deprivation of their rights as citizens.[42] Work done in the home was still necessary and valuable – sometimes even interesting.[43] But as women became better educated – a move endorsed by enlightened men to produce more

[42] See the emphasis described in the lives of Elizabeth Cady Stanton and Susan B. Anthony in Geoffrey C. Ward and Ken Burns, *Not for Ourselves Alone: The Story of Elizabeth Cady Stanton and Susan B. Anthony* (New York: Alfred A. Knopf, 1999).

[43] See Ward and Burns, *Not for Ourselves Alone*, for an account of Stanton's interest in home management; for current interest and the development of a theory of domestic life, see Patricia J. Thompson's *Hestia Trilogy: The Accidental Theorist* (New York: Peter Lang, 2002); *In Bed with Procrustes*, 2003; and *Fatal Abstractions*, 2004.

interesting wives and better mothers – another area of discontent arose. Many women were clearly as bright and intellectually capable as their brothers. Their success in school and college proved it. Why could they not enter the professions and other occupational fields as men did? Success in school led to a desire for greater equality and, indeed, women made significant gains in civic and professional life in the period from 1870 to 1920.[44]

Then things started to slip backward. By 1950 women were less well represented on college and university faculties than they had been in 1920.[45] Although women were welcomed into the workforce during World War II, they were urged to return to home and hearth after the war and to make positions available to men. For a while, an increase in home ownership and child production seemed to herald a renewed interest in homemaking as the main occupation of women.

But many women were discontented with suburban life. They were not using the education that had prepared them for public life, and their work in the home – once so vital to the economic well-being of a family – was no longer necessary. What did it matter, really, whether cookies were home-baked or purchased at a bakery? Why make clothes by hand when better-looking and more fashionable garments could be bought at a department store? Malaise was widespread, but it took the critical thinking and writing of Betty Friedan to bring it to women's consciousness.[46] A new women's liberation movement started soon thereafter.

Now, at the start of a new century, a new form of discontent has been identified. It seems that many people – both women and men – are unhappy with the hard work and confusion associated with home-making. Women complain that they have been "liberated" to do two jobs, and men seem to be distressed by the demands of homemaking – whether or not they share in household tasks. Home – once thought to be a haven from the cold world of business – has become a center of confusion and drudgery, and many young parents are glad to escape home for the relative peace and quiet of the workplace. Women are

---

[44] See Linda Kerber, *Toward an Intellectual History of Women* (Chapel Hill: University of North Carolina Press, 1997).

[45] Ibid. See also Margaret W. Rossiter, *Women Scientists in America: Struggles and Strategies to 1940.* (Baltimore: Johns Hopkins University Press, 1982).

[46] See Betty Friedan, *The Feminine Mystique* (New York: W. W. Norton, 1963).

now "able to pursue marriage, motherhood, and careers with avidity and success but with a continual rueful feeling that their plates are too full for anybody's good."[47]

Understandably, there has been a rising demand that men share in household tasks. Caitlin Flanagan describes a session she, an adolescent at the time (in the 1970s), had with a psychotherapist. Temporarily ignoring her adolescent patient's problem, the therapist spoke angrily about marriage: "I mean, who's going to do the shit work?" she asked angrily. "Who's going to make the pancakes?"[48] Flanagan was astonished to hear that making pancakes was "shit work." Joan Didion had already described cooking a meal as "dog-work" (a step up perhaps from "shit work") and children as "odious mechanisms for the spilling and digesting of food."[49] But should the work of our foremothers be described in such contemptuous terms? Are there no joys in homemaking?

Much of the writing characteristic of the women's liberation movement was scornful of homemaking. It rightly criticized the exploitation of women, but it often failed to engage in real critical thinking. Is housework really so backbreaking and disgusting, or is the greater problem twofold: a lack of recognition for the great value of housework and the fact that acceptance of the role of housewife kept women out of the public world? When one has found a place in the public world of work, perhaps some enjoyment can be found in housework, or is such an admission "evidence of craven acquiescence in one's own forced labor"?[50]

Some writers have shown appreciation for housekeeping. Bachelard goes perhaps too far in romanticizing housework. He writes that polishing furniture is an act of creation:

> Objects that are cherished in this way really are born of an intimate light, and they attain to a higher degree of reality than indifferent objects.... From one object in a room to another, housewifely care weaves the ties that unite a very ancient past to the new epoch.[51]

[47] Gail Collins, *America's Women: 400 Years of Dolls, Drudges, Helpmates, and Heroines* (New York: HarperCollins, 2003), p. 448.

[48] Quoted in Caitlin Flanagan, "How Serfdom Saved the Women's Movement," *Atlantic Monthly*, March 2004: 110.

[49] Ibid.

[50] Joan Didion, quoted in ibid., p. 110.

[51] Bachelard, *Poetics of Space*, p. 68.

He credits women with building the house from the inside and, although his analysis is overly poetic, he makes an important point. There is something quite wonderful – even primal – in increasing the beauty of household objects, and one can take pleasure in both the process and the product if one is not rushed or preoccupied with other tasks that remain undone.

There are many attitudes one can take toward housework. Some professional women enjoy many household tasks and would never describe cooking as dog-work. Cookbooks are loaded with accounts of women who have combined housework and professional life. But some women hate cooking. In a local paper recently, one woman reported converting her dining room into a modish office for herself. Since she never cooked or served dinners, what was the point in maintaining a dining room? In contrast, some women maintain almost tyrannical control over their kitchens, and still others work cooperatively with spouses, children, and visitors. The kitchen can be the heart of the home or a place entered only briefly out of necessity. One of my colleagues, for example, uses her kitchen cabinets to store old files and papers. One would be hard put to find cooking utensils – or even food – in her kitchen. There is no "right" attitude toward housework, but there are approaches more or less likely to contribute to happiness.

The key seems to be authenticity. Again, the main point is to avoid becoming a human impersonator. If a woman cooks, although she hates the task, simply because that is what a good woman does, she adds resentment to the unwanted task. These days, she would do better to find a way to reduce the time and effort once required to produce meals and, in doing so, she might contribute to her own contentment as well as to that of those around her. If, on the other hand, she loves to cook, she will not pretend to be oppressed by it out of concern for Joan Didion and Alix Kates Shulman. She will apply critical thinking to her own values and embrace those that pass the tests of logic and personal interest. Among the questions to be examined critically are these: Is it unnatural for a woman to dislike housekeeping? Is it unnatural for her not to want children or even to dislike them? Is a woman in denial of her own oppression if she enjoys homemaking? Can pleasure be found in household tasks? What tasks yield such pleasure? Do real men avoid housekeeping tasks? Or do real men help with housework? (What does the phrasing of this question imply about who is properly responsible for housework?)

And now a question for educators: Where in the curriculum do students get an opportunity to explore these questions? Where are they encouraged to explore what they want in a future home? Schooling without opportunities to think critically on matters central to everyday life results in people who are easily swayed by advertising and unconsciously bound to social norms prescribing everything from home decor and clothing to their attitudes toward home, work, leisure, and childrearing.[52]

Lest some readers think that the discussions just recommended sound too much like *life adjustment* education and, therefore, should be condemned as anti-intellectual, I want to point out that there is a rich body of recognized intellectual material on the topic of work and its various forms. Before turning to that material, however, I should emphasize again that the intellectual value of a topic should not be judged by its place in the traditional hierarchy of disciplines but rather by the nature of the thinking it calls forth. Some of the best and hardest critical thinking a person can do involves questions of everyday life.

Traditional intellectual material can, however, be useful in helping students to understand why questions about certain tasks continue to be asked. Ancient Greek thinkers held labor in contempt. Hannah Arendt notes that ancient assessments of labor "rest on the conviction that the labor of our body which is necessitated by its needs is slavish."[53] It was considered respectable to exercise one's body in games, training for war, or activities chosen for challenge or delight, but not for the production of life's necessities. Such labor was to be done by slaves. Indeed, as Arendt points out, the perceived need to eliminate labor from "man's" life provided the basic justification for slavery. It was thought that beings who were not fully human should labor so that the fully human could live without having to labor.

Students should be able to see the parallel between ancient attitudes toward life-sustaining activities and modern attitudes toward

---

[52] See my discussion of socialization in *Starting at Home*; also Diana T. Meyers, *Self, Society, and Personal Choice* (New York: Columbia University Press, 1989).

[53] Hannah Arendt, *The Human Condition* (Chicago: University of Chicago Press, 1958), p. 83.

housekeeping. Housekeeping seems to be focused on maintaining physical life, hence its evaluation as drudgery. But is this evaluation correct? Is there a difference between, say, the labor of migrant field workers and that of people working in their own yards? Or between hotel maids changing beds all day and a woman taking care of beds in her own household?

Arendt retains a useful distinction between labor and work. Labor absorbs the laborer entirely in the mere production of necessities; the "person" of the laborer is obscured, and there is no investment of the self in labor. What is produced is merely piecework, not something built, shaped, or created. In contrast, work can preserve the worker as a person. The worker invests something of himself or herself in the process as well as the product, and the product is substantial. It is not simply a meal to be consumed, an element of machinery to be incorporated into a larger product, a room temporarily cleaned, a bed made to be slept in.

If one must clean rooms or make beds all day for strangers, the activity is surely labor. But if one cleans his own room, registers the objects as members of his household,[54] and enjoys the end result – and perhaps even the process – the activity may be called work and the final product *a work*. Similarly, if suburban householders plant and harvest vegetables in their own gardens, they are not laboring. Their activity is rightly called work, and a productive, lovely garden may be called a work, even a work of art.

At least two avenues of exploration are opened by this discussion. One leads to reflection on our own personal lives. How can we live an authentic life and create a home that is a genuine extension of the self we claim? The second invites an examination of social justice. What attitude should we take toward labor and those who labor for the sustenance of all? Exploring this question may lead to a study of Marxism and the reversal of evaluation found in Marx's exaltation of the proletariat over the bourgeois. One remedy for the misery of labor is to reunite the laborer with the products of his labor – to make labor into work as Arendt describes it. In this approach, workers must share in the planning, execution, and profit

---

[54] Bachelard says of polishing furniture that the worker "creates a new object; he increases the object's dignity; he registers this object officially as a member of the human household." *Poetics of Space*, p. 67.

of their work. Process and product must become united in productive work.

Another approach is to recognize the depersonalization and inevitable alienation induced by some tasks and to pay compensatory wages to those who do them. Under such a plan, those who do the least desirable tasks in society should be paid very well. Still another approach – discussed in several well-known utopian writings – is to insist that everyone in a given society spend some time laboring so that no one is forced to spend all of his or her working hours on undesirable tasks.[55] A prominent citizen of one such utopia describes the results:

> The fact . . . that you had in the poorer classes a boundless supply of serfs on whom you could impose all sorts of painful and disagreeable tasks, made you indifferent to devices to avoid the necessity of them. But now that we all have to do in turn whatever work is done for society, every individual in the nation has the same interest, and a personal one, in devices for lightening the burden.[56]

If we apply this policy to household tasks, all members of the household would contribute fairly to whatever tasks they can manage, and everyone would be interested in reducing the labor involved in doing them. No one would be condemned to drudgery. But the question I raised earlier remains. Are all household tasks drudgery, or is that assessment a legacy of the traditional evaluation of life-sustaining work – in particular, the continuing contempt for women's work? This is a question that every student should be encouraged to reflect upon. Much drudgery can be removed by seeing tasks in a new light. When I do not see a task as drudgery, it may still be labor, but it is not quite so burdensome. Some tasks even become a sort of relief – an escape into routine – from the tasks we regard as part of our true work. And, happily, some even attain the status of play.

Sharing a Home

At the beginning of the twenty-first century, *home* and *family* are concepts in transition. Same-sex couples are making homes, building

---

[55] See, for example, Edward Bellamy, *Looking Backward* (New York: New American Library, 1960); and B. F. Skinner, *Walden Two* (New York: Macmillan, 1962).
[56] Bellamy, *Looking Backward*, p. 90.

families, and demanding recognition. Many unmarried couples are openly living together – a practice that was socially condemned fifty years ago. Divorce has increased, and some people even talk about the appropriateness of serial marriages. Many children live with a single parent. Few homes include more than two generations, and many older people live in retirement homes or villages. These are significant changes in the ways in which homes are constituted, and the changes frighten many people.

Like other controversial topics, this one must be addressed if we claim to educate. One way to start might be to study past patterns of communal living – the history and sociology of communes. There are many fascinating stories of real communes – groups of people living together as a family – and of utopias, fictional communes.[57] Sometimes these communities have advocated free love and sometimes they have demanded celibacy, but almost always they have insisted on a dissolution of the traditional bonds of married couples and families. The commune or community is to be the family. The impetus for the creation of a commune may be religious, political, or psychological,[58] but the commune operates as an economic unit much like a family. Rosabeth Moss Kanter describes two great waves of commune building in America – one in the 1840s and another in the late 1960s and 1970s.[59] Many, probably most, communes have been short-lived. It seems that the problems of living together encountered in traditional families are multiplied in communal life. Aside from historical interest in these communities and the lasting literary fascination with utopias, the important point for today's students is that deviations from the traditional family are not brand new. Whenever and however people decide to share shelter, money, social

---

[57] For a history of actual communes, see Rosabeth Moss Kanter, *Commitment and Community: Communes and Utopias in Sociological Perspective* (Cambridge, MA: Harvard University Press, 1972). In addition to the utopian fictions and accounts already mentioned, see Charlotte Perkins Gilman, *Herland* (New York: Pantheon, 1979; orig. 1915) – a feminist utopia; for a comparative study of feminist utopias, see Frances Bartkowski, *Feminist Utopias* (Lincoln: University of Nebraska Press, 1989). Some also classify the Israeli kibbutz experiment with the utopias; see Bruno Bettelheim, *The Children of the Dream* (New York: Simon & Schuster, 1997).

[58] See Kanter, *Commitment and Community*.

[59] Ibid.

relations, and life-sustaining tasks, there will be pleasures, pains, and problems.

I have suggested that starting a discussion of the variety of ways in which families have been defined with a study of communes and collective communities might be less controversial than plunging into a conversation about, say, same-sex marriage. But the topic of communal life is itself controversial, and the only feature that makes it less explosively so is its currently reduced relevance. In 1970, discussion of communes in schools was highly controversial. Even now, it would be wise to differentiate carefully among noncoercive religious communities, brainwashing cults, primarily economic collectives, Mormon polygamous groups, self-actualization groups that follow the ideas of Maslow or Skinner, and collectives like the kibbutz movement in Israel. Some groups, like some families, have been abusive. Perhaps the most infamous case of an extremist, abusive cult is that of the Peoples Temple of Jim Jones, a group that committed mass suicide in Guyana.[60] There are many other examples, however, of cults that have exercised iron-fisted control over their members' minds, finances, and associations.

In addition to showing students that today's changes in family definition are not the first to appear historically, there are at least three other good reasons for discussing communes. First, such discussion, conducted in a way that invites critical thinking, may inoculate students against the ploys of those who would recruit them to cults or other questionable groups. Second, study of some of the voluntary, highly idealistic groups may convince students that many human beings have longed for and sacrificed in the search for a perfect community. Third, although such reading need not be required (and analyzed, tested, and graded), the topic may encourage some students to read utopian fiction.

Students, after learning about communes, may realize that the current interest in same-sex marriage might actually be considered an endorsement of the traditional family form. In contrast to the rules of most communes – that all traditional family ties be broken – many homosexuals today are asking only to share in the traditional

---

[60] See the discussion of cults in Rodney R. Stark and William S. Bainbridge, *The Future of Religion* (Berkeley: University of California Press, 1985).

arrangement. Instead of destroying family values, they may in fact be supporting them.

A unit on the family and sharing a home might also return to our earlier discussion of shelters and living spaces. Family living arrangements have not always demanded separate housing for each family unit and, as mentioned earlier, there was not a sharp separation between public and what we now call private quarters.[61] Again, housing arrangements for families differ across cultures. The point throughout this exploration is to help students to understand that the fiercely defended traditional family and its living arrangements are not sacrosanct.

As discussion proceeds, attention should be given to the single-parent home. This arrangement, too, has been deplored by some policymakers and religious leaders. Why? Are a mother and children (or a father and children) not a family? Economic problems often plague such families, and students should be encouraged to study why this is so.[62] Is the single-mother family more likely to suffer economic hardship than its male counterpart? Why? Some students may become interested enough in the problems introduced here that they will want to follow up with a study of the patriarchal family.[63]

In objecting to same-sex marriages or living arrangements, students may follow their parents and religious leaders in pointing to biblical injunctions against homosexuality. This objection must be handled with great sensitivity. Possibly the best response is to admit that such passages appear in the Bible but to remind students that many customs accepted, forbidden, or prescribed in biblical times have changed. That doesn't make either the original practices or the changed ones right, but it does prompt us to seek contemporary justification for present customs.

---

[61] See Rybczynski, *Home*; also see the historical novels of Ellis Peters and Zoe Oldenbourg.

[62] See, for example, David K. Shipler, *The Working Poor: Invisible in America* (New York: Alfred A. Knopf, 2004); Cynthia M. Duncan, *Worlds Apart: Why Poverty Persists in Rural America* (New Haven, CT: Yale University Press, 1999); Sonya Michel, *Children's Interests/Mothers' Rights* (New Haven, CT: Yale University Press, 1999); and Barbara Ehrenreich, *Nickel and Dimed* (New York: Metropolitan Books, 2001).

[63] See Marilyn Yalom, "Biblical Models: From Adam and Eve to the Bride of Christ," in *Inside the American Couple*, ed. Marilyn Yalom and Laura L. Carstensen (Berkeley: University of California Press, 2002), pp. 13–31.

Some religious leaders, in opposing homosexual marriage, warn the society that the "next step" will be an acceptance of polygamy. Are polygamous groups families? Certainly the families described in the Old Testament (or Jewish Bible) were polygamous, and polygamy was not outlawed by Jews until 1030 C.E.[64] Polygamy persists today in many parts of the world, and some Mormon groups (separated from the formal church) still engage in the practice and even insist on its doctrinal rightness.[65] Indeed, Joseph Smith, the founder of Mormonism, drew on the lives of Abraham, Isaac, and Jacob to defend plural marriage.[66]

I will return to this topic in the chapter on religion, but I want to emphasize here that topics in a genuinely educational curriculum need not be narrowly categorized and segregated. Teachers should be ready to discuss at least the rudiments of each question implied by the basic theme. When we start out to explore the topic "sharing a home," questions of current concern and of historical interest will arise. Both should be addressed. Sometimes, the most effective pedagogical strategy is to start, as I did here, with an exploration of a practice somewhat removed from us by time or place and then to grapple with the highly controversial current questions. On other topics, the best move seems to be to start with a current question such as "What does home mean to you?" and then explore the historic and literary dimensions of the topic. And, of course, a teacher of great artistry will weave together current questions, historical accounts, and literature in ways that move easily from the present to the past or future, from the concrete to the abstract, from the public dimension to the personal.

I will conclude this chapter by saying a little about the pains, pleasures, and problems that every group calling itself a family may encounter. Many of us form families in order to produce and/or protect and educate children, but people also group themselves into families for other reasons. We hope to share both the ordinary and the extreme situations of life. We want someone who will be with us and care for us until "death do us part," but we also want someone with

---

[64] Ibid., n. 3, p. 29.

[65] See Jon Krakauer, *Under the Banner of Heaven* (New York: Doubleday, 2003).

[66] Ibid. See also Harold Bloom, *The American Religion: The Emergence of the Post-Christian Nation* (New York: Simon & Schuster, 1992).

whom to share the day's events and to plan with us for the future. We hope to live with people who will help us to create a real haven from hectic public life and a shelter for dreaming. All hope of establishing a home in this sense depends on our capacity to communicate with understanding. How should we meet and treat the others we encounter?

4

Other People

Hell is other people. – *No Exit*

Jean-Paul Sartre

All actual life is encounter.

Martin Buber

We must love one another or die.

W. H. Auden

One of the great mysteries of human life is the contradictory and paradoxical attitudes we take toward others. On the one hand, we need one another; our happiness and well-being depend on establishing good relations with at least some human beings. On the other hand, we often fear others; we feel jealousy, envy, distrust, and even hate. In families and schools, we socialize children to conform to certain rules of behavior concerning the treatment of others and how to behave in social settings, but we rarely encourage a critical examination of the events and feelings that underlie the need for such rules. What is it about human nature and human social conditions that make these rules necessary? Should we question or even reject some of these rules?

In recent years, philosophical interest in relations and related-ness has increased,[1] and social scientists, too, have studied human

---

[1] See, for example, Jacques Derrida, *Writing and Difference*, trans. Alan Bass (Chicago: University of Chicago Press, 1978); Ruth E. Groenhout, *Connected Lives: Human Nature and an Ethics of Care* (Lanham, MD: Rowman & Littlefield, 2004); Emmanuel Levinas, *The Levinas Reader*, ed. Sean Hand

relations and confirmed their importance to personal well-being.[2] Philosophical liberalism's emphasis on individualism and autonomy has been questioned, but so has the unreflective reliance on community.[3] Clearly, human beings do not spring into the world as fully rational, mature choice-makers. We are born entirely dependent on the care of adult others. This suggests that our initial sense of the other is that this other is a "being-for-me." The fear of coming under the gaze, of being defined by the other, as described by Sartre – this "being-for-another" – comes later and is perhaps conditioned by the quality of that first relation.

The First Other

The newborn infant is perhaps just conscious – or almost conscious – of his mother as separate from himself. Still, this other of whom he was so recently a biological part is somehow known as his source of food and comfort. He (I'll use *he* simply to differentiate infant from mother) will accept a surrogate, of course, and it seems unlikely that he can sense the substitution. But the source of comfort, usually the biological mother, is – to the child – a being-for-me. What else might she be? She comes when the child summons her, comforts, feeds, responds. The well-loved child is the center of his own universe surrounded by beings – at least one being – there for him.

This start in life is a good place to begin philosophical thinking. We do not start life as fully rational beings somehow "thrown into the world." We do not start as individuals who, in full command

(Oxford: Blackwell, 1989); the earlier work of Martin Buber, *I and Thou*, trans. Walter Kaufman (New York: Charles Scribner's Sons, 1970); also Nel Noddings, *Caring: A Feminine Approach to Ethics and Moral Education*, 2nd ed. (Berkeley: University of California Press, 2003); Alexander M. Sidorkin, *Learning Relations* (New York: Peter Lang, 2002); Barbara Thayer-Bacon, *Transforming Critical Thinking* (New York: Teachers College Press, 2000).

[2] See, for example, Mary M. Brabeck, ed., *Practicing Feminist Ethics in Psychology* (Washington, DC: American Psychological Association, 2000); Daniel Kahneman, Ed Diener, and Norbert Schwartz, eds., *Well-Being* (New York: Russell Sage, 1999); Robert E. Lane, *The Loss of Happiness in Market Democracies* (New Haven, CT: Yale University Press, 2000).

[3] See Shlomo Avineri and Avner de-Shalit, eds., *Communitarianism and Individualism* (Oxford: Oxford University Press, 1992); for a critique of autonomy, see Martha Albertson Fineman, *The Autonomy Myth: A Theory of Dependency* (New York: New Press, 2004).

of our agency, then form contracts with other individuals to begin life in communities. Nor do we start out conscious of coming under the gaze of others, fearful of what these others see and think of us. We start out totally dependent, yet confident (if we are fortunate) that the attached, related other is there for us – that our summons will bring a response. We start life in relation, not as individuals.

By the third month of life (often earlier), the first form of reciprocity emerges. The baby smiles in response to his caregiver's appearance. This response – one that delights parents – is a genuine contribution to the caring relation. It sustains and encourages caregivers in their efforts. No one knows this better than those – parents or nurses – who must care for unresponsive infants or patients. The cared-for contributes to the caring relation by simply acknowledging our efforts to care. Later, as he develops, the child will be able to enter reciprocal caring relations and take his turn at caring. We tend to forget the value of cheerful, genuine, nonjudgmental responses as we mature and come to depend more on rationality and language. David Hume was one of a few philosophers who reminded us of the continuing importance of congeniality and a sympathetic response.[4]

All of this may seem unproblematic, although we will return to it in the next chapter to uncover critical questions on parenting. Here, critical questions arise in connection with the relation between caregiver and care receiver. Dependence and responsive care promote in the child both a sense of control over his own environment and an increasing vulnerability to the attitudes and judgments of the caregiver. Totally dependent on his mother (let's say), the child wants her approval and continued love. Any threat to this love, any sign of withdrawal, is frightening, and this vulnerability paves the way for years of successful socialization. The caregiver, in her limited sphere, has enormous power over the child.[5]

But the child learns early on that this power is exercised in a very limited domain. Who is this person who responds to my every summons? I love her, but do I want to be like her? Nancy Chodorow has argued that girls identify with the mother-caregiver, while boys

[4] See David Hume, *An Enquiry Concerning the Principles of Morals* (Indianapolis: Hackett, 1983/1751).

[5] See Sara Ruddick, *Maternal Thinking: Towards a Politics of Peace* (Boston: Beacon Press, 1989).

must separate themselves to establish a male identity.[6] This observation returns us to the critical questions of the previous chapter. Given a choice, who would choose a female identity? Why? Why has the work of women been so devalued, and what can be done about this devaluation?

The question reaches even deeper. Why are females themselves – and not just their work – devalued in some societies? Adrienne Rich comments:

> The fathers have of course demanded sons; as heirs, field-hands, cannon-fodder, feeders of machinery, images and extensions of themselves; their immortality. In societies systematically practicing female infanticide, women might understandably wish for boys rather than face the prospect of nine months of pregnancy whose outcome would be treated as a waste product.[7]

What a terrible start in life – to be a surviving "waste product." Today the elimination of females is still common, but mainly through abortion rather than infanticide, and some countries are actually experiencing a shortage of females. If the fetus could philosophize, she might well ask: Why is this mother-caregiver there-for-him but not for-me?

In our own society, even in the absence of killing female fetuses, disparaging attitudes still prevail. Why is a successful working woman called a *career woman* when we would not dream of referring to an ordinary working man as a *career man*? Why is it acceptable for a woman to dress like a man but not for a man to dress like a woman? In the third Harry Potter film, young wizards are taught to face the thing they fear most by making it ridiculous. One student, afraid of Professor Snape, overcomes his fear by imagining the feared teacher dressed as a woman and shouting at the image, "Ridiculous!" The study of gender – its history, psychology, and sociology – should be central to education. Material for critical lessons on this topic is plentiful.

But let's return for a bit to the development of reciprocity in the child. The initial cries of the infant and his early smiles are

---

[6] See Nancy Chodorow, *The Reproduction of Mothering* (Berkeley: University of California Press, 1978).
[7] Adrienne Rich, *Of Woman Born* (New York: W. W. Norton, 1976), p. 195.

rudimentary (and highly effective) forms of communication. Dialogue begins, and a relation of care and trust is developed. Martin Buber refers to "the child, lying with half-closed eyes waiting for his mother to speak to him" but then notes that some lucky children "do not need to wait" – "they are unceasingly addressed in a dialogue. . . ."[8] The result, writes Buber is this:

> Trust, trust in the world, because this human being exists – because this human being exists, meaninglessness, however hard pressed you are by it, cannot be the real truth. Because this human being exists, in the darkness the light lies hidden, in fear salvation, and in the callousness of one's fellow-men the great Love.[9]

The dialogue described by Buber may or may not employ words. That between caregiver and infant is certainly wordless on the part of the infant, and the words used by the caregiver are not nearly so important as her facial expression and touch. Still, language will gradually enter the picture. To communicate better with this loved other, the child will learn to talk. He will meet both approval and disapproval in encounters that grow more and more complex. He will "come under the gaze" and learn what it means to be-for-another. Yet he will strive to be-for-himself. How will he handle this? Buber tells us that no one can become a full human being without entering relation: "I require a You to become; becoming I, I say You. All actual life is encounter."[10]

Being-for-Another: Socialization

The early encounters characterized by the unconditional response of the caregiver gradually include episodes of explicit socialization. The toddler comes under a gentle gaze; a period of training occurs, and the child experiences praise and correction. Well before he can demand *why* to every suggestion, he is aware that some behaviors are approved and some disapproved.

But eventually, "why" questions will be asked. Some will be silly, and the exasperation of parents trying to respond to endless

---

[8] Martin Buber, *Between Man and Man* (New York: Macmillan, 1965), p. 98.
[9] Ibid.
[10] Buber, *I and Thou*, p. 62.

whys is well known. However, from the perspective taken here, the danger is not overindulgence in responding to questions; on the contrary, the danger is that the growing child will stop asking them. In young adolescence – when the questions should be most vital – many children simply and thoughtlessly accept or resist adult attempts at socialization. This is the time when youngsters should be encouraged to ask critical questions and develop new methods of analysis.

It is the time to start a serious discussion of socialization and how it works on all of us. What presses us to do our best in school – to complete homework, study for tests, and strive for high grades? What presses against such effort? Youngsters should come to understand that peer pressure, too, is a form of socialization. Diana Meyers has argued that reflection is our most dependable bulwark against socialization.[11] We have to *think* about how people, customs, and institutions are trying to shape us.

Teachers might start with easy, if shocking, examples to consider. Suppose that you are at a family dinner and one of the people at the table puts his head down and starts to gobble food doglike. Most students will react to this by suggesting that the diner has gone mad. (There will undoubtedly also be jokes about "my brother" who always eats this way.) Well, suppose that he eats with his hands instead of using a fork? Kids might rightly note that, in some cultures, this would be acceptable. But "we" don't eat that way. Suppose that a person holds his fork like a shovel, piles in the food, and talks with his mouth full. Bad manners! But where do manners come from, and why do we accept and use them?

Students might spend some time discussing facilitative practices to which they have been socialized. Some practices are indeed useful, facilitative, because they make our daily activities run smoothly and render our lives more predictable. What family practices are of this sort? What school rules can be accepted as useful in this way? If laws controlling traffic, health, noise, and nudity are added to the discussion, students may agree that much of socialization is both powerful and necessary. Indeed, they may begin to feel that they are being asked to preach to themselves.

[11] Diana Meyers, *Self, Society, and Personal Choice* (New York: Columbia University Press, 1989).

Now is the time to introduce some questionable cases. Why do we all stand for the playing of the national anthem? Well, to show respect. But how should we treat people who refuse to stand because they think their country is behaving badly in the world? Many of us refused to stand up for the flag or the national anthem during the Vietnam War, for example. We agreed that standing is a sign of respect, and we wanted to withhold our respect publicly. Why do *you* stand? Are you showing genuine respect or are you afraid of what others will think of you? If you were surrounded by protestors and you – you as an individual – wanted to stand up, would you dare to do so? This is an opportunity to imagine oneself first on one side of the issue, then on the other.

Today many African American students face the scorn of their peers when they accept school rules, study, and work for their teachers' approval. How do these pressures arise, and how are they best handled? We adults preach, instruct, coerce, and try to inspire youngsters to accept *our* efforts at socialization and reject the pressures of peers. "Just say no!" is a popular slogan, but it is rarely effective.

Students need to believe that they should reflect, evaluate, and make authentic decisions. That means perhaps rejecting some of what the adult community advises them to do. It means questioning some practices that seem unhelpful or even damaging. Must there be homework every night? Why? What are students learning from this practice? Is the assigned homework necessary for meaningful understanding of the subject matter? Or is the object to teach docility and obedience to authority? If it is the latter, is this bad?

The point of this important question is not to make rebels of our adolescents but to encourage their thinking. We do that best by inviting them to talk about their concerns and by responding to what they say honestly. If we educators are thoughtful, many of us will admit that much homework is meaningless, even absurd. Educational critics in the 1960s pointed this out at a time when the school curriculum was not nearly as sterile and test-driven as it is now.[12] It wouldn't

---

[12] See, for example, Paul Goodman, *Growing Up Absurd* (New York: Random House, 1960); Goodman, *Compulsory Mis-education* (New York: Horizon, 1964); Neil Postman and Charles Weingartner, *Teaching as a Subversive Activity* (New York: Delta, 1969); Charles Silberman, *Crisis in the Classroom: The Remaking of American Education* (New York: Random House, 1970).

hurt to have students read some work of Paul Goodman (*Growing up Absurd*) and discuss whether they regard their own schooling as absurd. Teachers today should certainly reflect on the words of Postman and Weingartner:

> What one needs to ask of a standard is not, "Is it high or low?", but, "Is it appropriate to your goals?" If your goals are to make people more alike, to prepare them to be docile functionaries in some bureaucracy, and to prevent them from being vigorous, self-directed learners, then the standards of most schools are neither high nor low. They are simply apt.[13]

Discussing such views will not necessarily turn kids off from school learning; most are already turned off. They may indeed experience tremendous relief to learn that some teachers share their sense of frustration and meaninglessness. Their new problem may become one explored in chapter 1 – to find efficient methods of dealing with required material that is irrelevant to their interests. What is gained by doing conscientious work and gaining the approval of teachers? Credentials and opportunities for further schooling are not negligible rewards. But they should not be confused with real learning or the creation of meaning. Is there a way to have both the rewards and real learning?

There are risks in conducting these discussions with teenagers. We want them to understand that some socialization is not only unavoidable but both necessary and desirable, that some is questionable (why not eat with our hands?) but easily shrugged off as not worth protesting, and that some should be rejected vigorously. By treating widely accepted everyday behaviors, most students will see that *to socialize* means to make people fit for life in a particular group. There are all sorts of rules that we accept tacitly. It doesn't even occur to us to question them, much less violate them. Gobbling food doglike is a violation that verges on madness. How about singing loudly in a public place where other people are working, listening to a lecture, or just quietly minding their own business? Why shouldn't we sing when the muse moves us? Raising this question without thorough discussion

---

[13] Neil Postman and Charles Weingartner, "What's Worth Knowing?" in *Radical School Reform*, ed. Ronald and Beatrice Gross (New York: Simon & Schuster, 1969), p. 167.

may induce bursts of song in algebra class. The risk may be worth taking.

If we want to encourage critical thinking with respect to socialization, we must periodically return to an examination of everyday behavior – behavior that is not governed by written laws or even explicit rules. Exploration of these behaviors should induce a sense of awe at just how dramatically we are influenced by socialization. There are no laws against singing, and I doubt that many (if any) schools have explicit rules against it. There are, of course, school rules forbidding disruption, and particularly loud singers might be charged, in almost any neighborhood, with disturbing the peace. But generally, to sing or not to sing is decided on the basis of perceived appropriateness. A young woman singing loudly as she walks down a city street is likely to occasion no more than a turn of heads. The same person singing the same song in a crowded subway car may be thought deranged. We should notice also that, since so many options are foreclosed in various social situations, the only one open – mental escape – is often chosen.

A teacher conducting such a discussion would make it clear that she is not encouraging spontaneous song in algebra class. The purpose is to explore, to reflect upon, our common socialization. She might discuss cultural differences in what is found acceptable by way of ordinary behavior. Rebecca West quotes a teacher who explains an important cultural difference:

> "You don't understand that here in Split we are very much on parade. We're not a bit like the Serbs, who don't care what they do, who laugh and cry when they feel like it, and turn cartwheels in the street if they want exercise...."[14]

Students might, understandably, think the Serbs would make fine company. But let's return to the issue of singing. Why, the teacher might ask her students, would *you* not burst into song in algebra class? Possible answers:

1. Because it's crazy! (But consider how powerful our socialization is. What's crazy about singing?)

---

[14] Rebecca West, *Black Lamb and Grey Falcon* (New York: Penguin Books, 1994/1941), p. 141.

2. I'd get kicked out and might flunk algebra. (Ah, here we have a concern about consequences. But are the consequences natural?)
3. I'm afraid my voice would crack and people would laugh at me. (Another whole world of consequences. How does this one differ from the earlier one?)
4. The teacher would have to stop teaching, and that's not fair to everyone else. (This student has already been successfully socialized to the classroom.)
5. People would think I'm nuts. (It matters what other people think.)
6. I'd do it if some other kids would, too. (And what other things might you do if you had company?)

All of these responses are worth further discussion, but the last two may be especially important. (Unfortunately, teachers influenced by some current character education programs would be so delighted with answer 4 that the discussion would end with a commendation of the student who made it.) "People would think I'm nuts" invites serious analysis. How concerned should we be about what others think?

Reflecting on that first caregiver – that being-for-me – we are able to answer confidently that we should be very concerned about what others think of us. Our earliest response to attempts to socialize us is a desire to please this much-loved other who so clearly loves us. We do not want her or any significant other to think ill of us. Indeed, our very selves are built at least in part on the images reflected back to us by others.[15] Thus it would be disingenuous to deny all interest in what others think of us.

Teachers are themselves sometimes guilty of this questionable claim. Some, insisting that they do not care what their students think of them – "I'm not in a popularity contest" – justify their attitude in terms of "what is right." They overlook the power of mutual relations to instill "trust, trust in the world because this person exists." This suggests that teachers should care deeply if their students do not like

---

[15] For an account of what is sometimes called the *looking-glass self*, see George Herbert Mead, *Mind, Self, and Society from the Standpoint of a Social Behaviorist* (Chicago: University of Chicago Press, 1934); see also Nel Noddings, *Starting at Home: Caring and Social Policy* (Berkeley: University of California Press, 2002).

them. But, of course, to be worthy of trust and to encourage trust in the world, teachers must not buy their students' affection. Rather, they must show through their care and concern that there are good reasons for students to like and trust them.

Building relations of care and trust in the classroom is part of an ongoing critical lesson in human relations.[16] Whom should we like? What does it mean to like someone? If we acknowledge that the opinion of those we like matters to us, does that give them too much power over us? Suppose we like the wrong people?

A discussion of friendship is central to this set of critical lessons. According to Aristotle, friendship is important in moral life.[17] Friends wish the best to their friends *for the friends' sake*. A friend does not seek something for himself in wishing the best for his friend. He regularly receives the special benefits of friendship and is grateful for these, but his words and acts are not designed to curry favor. He likes (even loves) the friend and wants the best for him. Even a transient friendship based on mutual, but temporary, interests is marked by such genuine concern.[18]

Friends point each other upward, and that is why friendship is so important to moral life. They do not stand by silently while their friends do things they believe are wrong. The opinions of friends matter greatly because we know they have our best interests in mind. It is in this sense, perhaps, that Aristotle once said that whatever teaching does, it does *as to a friend*; that is, the teacher wants the best for her student for the student's own sake.

This discussion reminds us again that Western culture – especially American culture – has put too much emphasis on autonomy. It is not only that we often deny economic dependence and interdependence, but we also tend to prize autonomous thinking. "Think for yourself!" parents advise their children. They don't really mean this, of course. They really mean that children should not be too easily influenced by their peers; they rarely mean that the children should think for themselves and ignore parental advice. We have all heard adults say

---

[16] See Marilyn Watson, *Learning to Trust* (San Francisco: Jossey-Bass, 2003).

[17] See Aristotle, *Nicomachean Ethics*, trans. Terence Irwin (Indianapolis: Hackett, 1985).

[18] See my discussion of lessons on friendship in *The Challenge to Care in Schools* (New York: Teachers College Press, 1992).

to the young, "If everyone else jumps off the cliff, will you do it, too?" in frustrated attempts to get kids to think – think before leaping or following. What parents and teachers should want is not autonomy in thinking (there may be no such thing) but intelligent heteronomy. Listen, think, heed the right people.

But who are the right people? To whom should we listen? Perhaps a better question to ask is, "To whom *do* we listen and why?" We listen to people we like, but we should not always have to agree with those we like, and a tolerance for disagreement is something we expect to find in true friends. We listen to teachers we trust. Those who care enough to develop relations of care gain our trust, and we listen to them. But we are subject to strong socialization, and so most of us also listen to those in whom authority is officially invested. At times we even mistake this authority for caring.

Sometimes people listen so uncritically to those in authority that their moral identity becomes bound up with authority. Disobeying that authority is then equated with behaving immorally, and this moral dependence is often encouraged by stern parents, teachers, and religious authorities. When trust in that authority is betrayed, moral identity is threatened. After all, the reaction seems to be, if the moral authority on which I've built my moral identity has failed to do what's right, how can I do what's right? How can I even know what is right?

Jonathan Shay has described the perceived failure of authorities to do "what's right" as a significant source of lasting psychological trauma in Vietnam War veterans. He writes:

> Is betrayal of "what's right" essential to combat trauma, or is betrayal simply one of many terrible things that happen in war? . . . No one can conclusively answer these questions today. However, I shall argue what I've come to strongly believe through my work with Vietnam veterans: that moral injury is an essential part of any combat trauma that leads to lifelong psychological injury.[19]

When military authorities fail to provide adequate resources, send men into unnecessarily dangerous situations, show contempt for the opposing civilian population, and reward soldiers for doing

---

[19] Jonathan Shay, *Achilles in Vietnam: Combat Trauma and the Undoing of Character* (New York: Scribner, 1994), p. 20.

things no decent person would do, the loss of moral identity may be acute, as we saw in chapter 2. I'll return to this theme in the next section.

Children may be traumatized by the moral failure of their parents, citizens by that of their government, and students by the failure of their teachers. In Erich Maria Remarque's *All Quiet on the Western Front*, it is a teacher who convinces his entire class of teenage boys to sign up for the German army in World War I. The advice was bad, and the students hate the teacher in retrospect. The story's protagonist, Paul, says: "These teachers always carry their feelings ready in their waistcoat pockets, and trot them out by the hour. But we didn't think of that then."[20] Of course they "didn't think of that then." They trusted their teacher. As they fought, suffered, and died, however, these boys expressed increasing contempt for that teacher. Moral betrayal (intended or not) by those in authority causes moral injury.

Let's return briefly to an examination of behaviors that are not controlled by law but are nevertheless tightly constrained by the customs to which we are socialized. Why would it seem odd for a businessman or an elderly woman to skip along the sidewalk? If either of them had a small child by the hand, would their skipping be more acceptable? Suppose the businessman and the elderly woman were instead engaged in a game of hopscotch? Suppose the businessman were dressed in a skirt or dress? And why is it acceptable for a woman to wear trousers but an occasion of amusement or scorn for a man to dress like a woman? A recent ad promising protection against credit card fraud shows how implicitly we depend on people to behave "in character." It pictures a conservative-looking middle-aged woman getting a tattoo in a seamy tattoo parlor. Why, the ad asks, would anyone believe that she had actually visited such a place? (A reputable credit card business, the ad implies, would not believe this.) How might such constraints affect the lives of people who are aging? And finally (for now), why do we sit silently when a preacher (in church) says things we believe are outrageous – things that would trigger fiery debate in another setting? As they are encouraged to think on these matters, students may contribute many more examples.

[20] Erich Maria Remarque, *All Quiet on the Western Front* (New York: Fawcett Books, 1982), p. 11.

The school has a heavy twofold responsibility: to socialize students and to provide them with the intellectual tools to understand, accept, shrug off, or reject parts of that socialization. It sometimes fails in the first task because teachers are not encouraged to form the relations of care and trust in which defensible forms of socialization can take place. It *usually* fails in the second task because the critical lessons we are discussing are absent from the classroom.

Interacting with Others

So far, we have mainly considered the effects *others* have on *us*, but we also influence others. Encounters are interactions, and the way we treat others has an effect on how they treat us. We learn this not only by direct experience but also as a part of the implicit socialization process. Parents, teachers, and preachers constantly remind us to "do unto others as you would have them do unto you." But when others violate that rule, we often feel justified in doing so ourselves. Moreover, schools do comparatively little to help young people learn and practice sympathetic modes of communication.

Examples of unhelpful and hurtful talk are easy to find. Such talk abounds in everyday conversation, and samples can be found in novels, on television, in movies, and in columns by Ann Landers and Dear Abby. Predicaments that require sensitive communication spring up endlessly. Recently, in an advice column, this problem was posed: A young woman was to be married at an afternoon ceremony to be followed by a reception. An acquaintance, who would have her own wedding that morning, announced that because the time between the weddings was too short to change clothes, she would attend the afternoon ceremony in her bridal gown. (The variety of human insensitivities is amazing.) The afternoon bride was, of course, opposed to this. What should she do or say?

In a mystery novel by Ruth Rendell, a young man describes the misery he suffered in a failed marriage. His wife had lost romantic interest in him:

> "I will say for Joanna she didn't pretend. She never did. She came straight out with it. 'I don't fancy you any more,' she said. 'You're going bald.' I said she must be mad...."[21]

---

[21] Ruth Rendell, *The Babes in the Wood* (London: Arrow Books, 2003), p. 130.

What sort of person would fall out of love with her husband because he was going bald? And what sort of person would come "straight out" with such a comment? Why in the world would a man marry a woman with so little human sympathy?

People crave human companionship and often don't know how to judge the worth of potential friends and intimates, and sometimes it doesn't even matter – company is all that matters. In Tom Perotta's *Little Children*, the mother, May, of a convicted child molester suffers from social isolation – particularly after her son is freed and returns home. She welcomes and appreciates the company of Bertha:

> Not because she liked Bertha exactly – Bertha was hard to like in any simple way – but because a person needed company.... So what if Bertha dyed her hair a brassy red and drank too much – or made mean jokes, and rarely had a good word to say about anyone?[22]

May was driven to Bertha because other people – once considered friends – had deserted her.

Novels are filled with examples of failed attempts to communicate, thoughtlessly hurtful comments, remarks designed to wound, and important comments left unsaid. Instead of concentrating on literary technique, mood, setting, and the like in literature studies, teachers might ask students to discuss the patterns of conversation. How might things have gone better if the characters had expressed themselves differently? How often are there failures in listening, and what does it mean to listen? Everyone knows what it is like to speak to someone who is not listening. It is as though one does not exist. Indeed, when this happens, we even say, "I might as well talk to myself." Better to talk to oneself if there is a point to what is said. The annihilation of existence that results from not being heard is a terrible thing. Understanding that, we know that, as moral beings, we must listen to one who addresses us.

The worry, of course, is that if we listen, we may hear a request and feel obligated to respond. As listeners, we are soaked in obligation.[23] But some requests are easily met: Just laugh with me! Join me for a bit of idle chatter. Imagine how I felt.... Even when we cannot satisfy

[22] Tom Perotta, *Little Children* (New York: St. Martin's Press, 2004), p. 70.

[23] As Caputo puts it, obligation continually tugs at our sleeve. See John D. Caputo, *Against Ethics* (Bloomington: Indiana University Press, 1993).

the request of a speaker (and such occasions are numerous), we can respond in a way that acknowledges the speaker's personhood. We can assure her that she has been heard. The capacity to respond in this way probably has its origin in the first days of relation with that adult who was always there for us. When the infant's cry produces a response, his or her existence is confirmed.

When we speak, we want to produce in the listener an affect consonant with our mood. If we tell a joke, we do not want our listener to respond with a dull literal comment. If we are unhappy, we do not want to be told simply to cheer up. If we are puzzled, we want clarification, not a simplistic denial of complexity. An appropriate, mood-sensitive response is a sign that the listener has really heard us.

Adults often make the mistake of responding to children in the wrong mode. Instead of treating children's comments seriously and furthering the conversation with age-appropriate comments and questions, too many adults respond with an attitude that says, in effect, "Isn't that cute!" This patronizing attitude does little to increase a child's capacity to engage in real dialogue and may even impede it. Children raised this way may exhibit frivolous habits of mind and conversation well into adulthood. They may be friendly and expect congenial responses, but they contribute nothing of substance to conversations. It seems that they expect to be liked but not taken seriously.

Another sort of mistake was mentioned in chapter 3. Sometimes loving parents adopt authoritarian methods, thinking that such methods will ensure that their children will be safe and successful. Some authoritarian parents simply do not engage in conversation with their children at all. They give orders, praise, and reprimands, but they do not enter a dialogue. Some even adhere to the notion that dialogue with children is inappropriate.[24]

---

[24] See again Shirley Brice Heath, *Ways with Words* (New York: Cambridge University Press, 1983). Heath does not charge all minority parents with this lack and she certainly recognizes the great love many such parents have for their children, but she carefully documents one regional case in which a group of parents do not engage their children in dialogue. Argument in educational circles has recently become heated over conversational patterns. See B. Hart and T. R. Risley, *Meaningful Differences in the Everyday Experience of Young American Children* (Baltimore: Brooks, 1995). For a rebuttal that, I think, misses the point, see Lisa Delpit, "Educators as 'Seed People' Growing a Future," *Educational Researcher* 7(32), 2003: 14–21.

Students may get the mistaken idea that intellectually substantial conversation must take the form of debate. Certainly many panel discussions aired on television are of this adversarial form. Panelists shout at one another, and each makes a connection only with members of the audience who are already in agreement with him. No one learns anything. The contrast with Socratic dialogue or the healthy dialogue described by Paulo Freire is dramatic.[25] True dialogue is motivated by a genuine, open question. Both parties are exploring and learning from their partner. The dialogue is marked by comments such as: "I wonder; have you read X? I hadn't thought of that; yes, but, in contrast, A says . . . ; oh, that's like Y; is there evidence for that?" We learn from such dialogues – not only from our partner but also by probing our own memory and marshalling evidence for the positions we take. And we reflect; we are persuadable. Students might be asked to judge the conversations they hear over a day's time in and out of school. How many are examples of genuine dialogue? If there are few, what explains their scarcity?

This discussion might return us briefly to topics we considered in chapter 1. If believing (temporarily) in what we read is a good learning technique, perhaps the same can be said of following the arguments of a conversational partner. We do not learn much if our minds are concentrated on our own position and how we will present it when the other stops talking.

Teachers might also suggest a small experiment in note-taking. Thoroughly attentive listeners should not need to take copious notes; merely jotting down an occasional name, title, or date should be quite enough. Slavish note-taking can get in the way of understanding and condemn the note-taker to go over the whole thing again to get the sense of what was said. Worse, the original tone and motive are lost, and what remains is inert. I think that one of my own great advantages as a student was that I became absorbed in ongoing lectures and rarely took notes. Almost always, I remembered more than classmates and found the material easier to use in my own work.

But the main reason for listening is to maintain or to establish a relation of care and trust with the other. Our partner in conversation is more important than the point we are trying to win. I don't mean by

[25] See Paulo Freire, *Pedagogy of the Oppressed*, trans. Myra Bergman Ramos (New York: Herder and Herder, 1970).

this that there are no great principles or ultimate commitments that should override personal relationships. There are times, of course, when we must disagree with our conversational partners and even oppose them. But the living other – the one present to us in conversation – is more important than the point of our argument in the sense that we owe to her or him our full attention and a thoughtful response that gives assurance of continued care even in the face of disagreement.

The main feature of caring is receptive attention on the part of the one who would care. When we receive what-is-there in the other, we are moved to respond. Usually, this response is triggered by motivational displacement; that is, our motive energy flows toward the needs of the cared-for. We are all familiar with this sequence of events. Indeed, we sometimes resist giving our full attention precisely because we fear the likely motivational shift. Not wanting to lay aside our own interests and projects, we take refuge in not listening or in listening superficially and responding politely but uselessly. Gabriel Marcel described not-listening or half-listening as "indisposability." He wrote, "When I am with someone who is indisposable, I am conscious of being with someone for whom I do not exist; I am thrown back on myself."[26] Students should think about how often this happens to them and how often they respond this way to others.

But aren't there people who are just wrong – even evil – to whom we should not listen? If, by *listen*, we mean *join* or *go along with*, of course we should not listen. However, we need to listen in order to make a justifiable decision that the other is wrong. Too often a decision is made on the basis of reputation or affiliation. If we are Democrats, for example, we decide before listening that a Republican speaker is probably wrong. Similarly, some adolescents reject out of hand advice coming from parents and teachers – even though they might accept the very same advice if it were given by a peer. Listening receptively need not lead to contamination or involvement in questionable projects.

It is understandable that parents should prefer that their children not fall into bad company. Conscientious parents do not want their

---

[26] The quotation appears in the chapter on Marcel in H. J. Blackham, *Six Existential Thinkers* (New York: Harper & Row, 1959), p. 80.

children running with kids who use drugs, skip school, and commit acts of vandalism. Young people rarely have the emotional and intellectual sophistication required to reform their companions, and they should not be expected to do so. It is a hard enough task to point their respectable friends consistently upward – as friendship requires.

Teachers can help, however. Teachers concerned about the moral development of their students can use small-group work to improve listening, resistance, recognition, and inclusion. Good kids are not likely to be corrupted by conversations with bad ones if the conversations are limited and guided, and the bad kids may be favorably influenced. In many cases, youngsters who are outsiders will change their behavior and attitudes as a result of being recognized and included. There is some evidence that lack of acceptance is a cause of antisocial behavior and violence in adolescents.[27]

Learning to listen should be a major commitment in any truly moral life. Teachers can assist their students in making this commitment by listening themselves. What a gift it is to be heard! Rowan Williams, archbishop of Canterbury, said of a revered Catholic priest, Father Joe, that he "was a listener of genius – someone who would be well on the way to meet you before you got there."[28] Here, then, is a set of critical-reflective lessons that prompts each of us to put the other first – at least long enough to listen. Listening to others does not entail being corrupted by them. Rather, it suggests the lasting gift of friendship – pointing the other toward his or her own better self.

A critical question rarely engaged anywhere in our highly individualistic society concerns shared responsibility. How much responsibility do we have for the crimes and cruelties of our fellows? This sort of talk – the very mention of shared responsibility – is rarely well received. Frequently, it is condemned as suggesting an attitude that is "soft on crime." Actually, it is a profound question that should introduce a set of important critical lessons.

---

[27] Exclusion may be especially hard for boys who feel that their masculinity has been challenged. See Jessie Klein and Lynn S. Chancer, "Masculinity Matters: The Omission of Gender from High-Profile School Violence Cases," in *Smoke and Mirrors*, ed. Stephanie Urso Spina (Lanham, MD: Rowman & Littlefield, 2000), pp. 129–162. See also Nel Noddings, "Coping with Violence," *Educational Theory* 52(2), 2002: 241–253.

[28] Quoted in Tony Hendra, *Father Joe* (New York: Random House, 2004), p. 270.

Shared Responsibility

Before launching into a discussion that should motivate some deeply significant critical lessons, I should make clear what I mean by *shared responsibility*. I will not refer to a legal definition, to collective responsibility of the sort incurred by, say, a corporation, or to attempts to fix blame. Philosophers have produced a substantial body of work on these topics, but much of it is technical and beyond the scope of this book.[29] Moreover, despite its technical and legal contributions, much of this philosophical work does not address the problem that concerns me here. I want to focus attention on the ways in which we might be said to share responsibility with wrongdoers for their wrongdoings. A few examples will get us started.

Consider a fifth-grade boy, Bob, who has become a bully. Do his classmates share any responsibility for his behavior? Do his parents? His teachers? By asking this set of questions, I am not suggesting that Bob bears no responsibility for his acts. If we were looking at the situation from a legal framework and we could provide convincing evidence that Bob has committed the acts of which he is accused, we would be right to say that he is *guilty* of bullying. And we would not say that his classmates, parents, and teachers are also guilty of these acts.[30] However, responsibility reaches deeper than guilt. Bob's classmates may have excluded or mocked him; his parents may have abused him; and his teachers may have made him feel inferior. None of these acts, if they occurred, excuse Bob's bullying. But they help to explain it, and that is important if our concern is with the prevention of acts of this sort.

At every level of human society, we seek to fix blame for acts and events that members of the society – at the given level – deplore and want to prevent. The prevailing response is to pursue prevention through rules, procedures for detecting and fixing blame, and the infliction of penalties. This approach to the prevention of unwanted acts has never been very effective, and often it makes things worse. The persons, groups, or nations that perpetrate or support unwanted

[29] See the essays in Larry May and Stacey Hofman, eds., *Collective Responsibility* (Savage, MD: Rowman & Littlefield, 1991); also Margaret Gilbert, *Sociality and Responsibility* (Lanham, MD: Rowman & Littlefield, 2000).

[30] Kurt Baier is helpful on this. See Baier, "Guilt and Responsibility," in May and Hoffman, *Collective Responsibility*, pp. 197–218.

acts and events continue to violate the rules and sometimes do so more violently. Moreover, having suffered penalty or retribution, they now feel justified in their behavior.

In a convincing description of the lives of violent offenders, the psychiatrist James Gilligan writes:

> The first lesson that tragedy teaches (and that morality misses) is that *all violence is an attempt to achieve justice,* or what the violent person perceives as justice . . . so as to receive whatever retribution or compensation the violent person feels is "due" him or "owed" to him. . . .[31]

Gilligan goes so far as to say, *"the attempt to achieve justice and maintain justice, or to undo or prevent injustice, is the one and only universal cause of violence."*[32] We don't have to agree completely with this (and, in presenting critical lessons, we should not demand agreement) to see that there is at least a germ of truth here. Is it true in the case of the young bully, Bob? It may well be that the establishment of a healthy friendship, better parenting, or the attention of a caring teacher would put an end to Bob's bullying. A teacher who understands that Bob is trying to achieve some recognition grants a positive motive for his unacceptable acts. By letting him know – explicitly or implicitly – that she sees in him a person who is better than his acts, she confirms that better person.

Confirmation is, I have suggested, one of four major components of moral education: modeling, dialogue, practice, and confirmation. The first three have been widely, and approvingly, discussed, but the last is rarely mentioned. The idea of confirmation – which I take from Martin Buber[33] – is one of the loveliest ideas in moral life. But it seems to go against a long-standing attitude that identifies moral agents with their acts and holds them solely responsible for infractions they commit. Further, confirmation can only be performed when a relation has been established. The one doing the confirming has to know the one who is confirmed well enough to make a reasonable, honest judgment of what the other was trying to do. When we confirm someone, we attribute to a questionable act the best possible motive consonant

---

[31] James Gilligan, *Violence* (New York: G. P. Putnam's Sons, 1996), p. 11.
[32] Ibid., p. 12.
[33] See Buber, *Between Man and Man.*

with reality. To do this, we must have sufficient knowledge of the other to make it plausible that this better motive was actually operating. Miscreants of all ages – but especially children and teenagers – often react with relief and gratitude: Here is someone who sees my better self![34] The better self, perceived through receptive listening, is thus encouraged.

The practical difficulties of engaging in confirmation are obvious. Without time spent in establishing relations of care and trust, attempts to confirm may sound like scripted responses; they are worthless. But an even deeper difficulty may be the traditional unwillingness to recognize moral interdependence. Philosophers have too often insisted on the autonomy of moral agents. Immanuel Kant held that "it is contradictory . . . to make another person's *perfection* my end and consider myself obliged to promote this."[35] This seems to deny that how good I can be is least partly dependent on how you treat me. Of course, we should not define another's perfection and insist that he or she live up to that ideal. Kant is right that, strictly speaking, the other's moral perfection cannot be my project. But we must always be aware of the other's moral ideal and his or her struggle in attaining it. I am arguing that the way we treat others affects – and affects deeply – their own moral behavior and growth. We are morally interdependent.

The notions of autonomy and moral independence have been much overemphasized. The revered American thinker Ralph Waldo Emerson – called by John Dewey "the philosopher of democracy" – pushed the extreme on this. "What is God?" he asked, and responded, "the most elevated conception of character that can be formed in the mind. It is the individual's own soul carried out to perfection."[36] He then went on to say:

> Know then, that the world exists for you. . . . What we are, that only can we see. All that Adam had, all that Caesar could, you have and can do – build, therefore, your own world.[37]

---

[34] See also my comments on confirmation in *Caring* and in *The Challenge to Care in Schools*.

[35] The quotation and comments on it appear in Noddings, *Caring*, p. 102.

[36] Ralph Waldo Emerson, quoted in Robert D. Richardson, Jr., *Emerson: The Mind on Fire* (Berkeley: University of California Press, 1995), p. 97.

[37] Ibid., p. 234.

Such talk is romantic and, to some, inspiring. It is also dangerously lacking in understanding. Emerson too often overlooked the hardship and lack of opportunity many people experience. Despite his strong endorsement of democracy and his clear respect for the personhood of all people, Emerson still spoke too often as though each person could fashion her own life and was responsible for doing so.

Jean-Paul Sartre, the great existentialist philosopher, also described human beings as "radically free." But he realized that radical freedom is useless if people are neither aware of it nor have opportunities to act on it. His sympathy and anger over the oppression experienced by masses of humanity led him to embrace Marxism.[38]

Often the emphasis on basic freedom or autonomy asks too much of human beings. Viktor Frankl, the eminent existentialist psychiatrist, having studied the variety of ways in which Holocaust victims responded to their suffering, concluded that although people are not free to control their own suffering, they are free to choose their attitude to that suffering.[39] This suggests that everyone, if he or she really tries, could behave as the most heroic do. It entirely overlooks the possibility that the heroic among us might not have been faced with their own worst nightmares. Noting this is not meant to denigrate anyone's heroism but to face the reality that each of us has a breaking point, and it seems either blind or hard-hearted not to recognize this.[40] A hero in one situation may collapse in another or, as we saw in the discussion of war, may become a physical hero but a moral monster.

If students read Orwell's *Nineteen Eighty-Four*, they will have an excellent opportunity to explore the issue of freedom and responsibility. Was Winston Smith entirely responsible for his betrayal of Julia? Or is the blame more properly placed on the evil O'Brien?[41] One could plausibly argue that O'Brien's most evil act was to tear from Smith the moral capacity to choose an authentic act. Smith lost his moral identity. (Bright students may well ask who shares responsibility with

---

[38] See Sartre, *Being and Nothingness*, trans. Hazel E. Barnes (New York: Washington Square Press, 1956); also Sartre, *Search for a Method*, trans. Hazel E. Barnes (New York: Vintage Books, 1968).

[39] See Viktor E. Frankl, *The Doctor and the Soul* (New York: Vintage Books, 1973).

[40] See my comments on Frankl's position in *Happiness and Education* (Cambridge: Cambridge University Press, 2003), pp. 40–45.

[41] See George Orwell, *Nineteen Eighty-Four* (New York: Harcourt, Brace and World, 1949).

O'Brien – a good question about political life.) Examples abound in real life, too. Should concentration camp prisoners have been able to resist stealing from one another? Were the soldiers who slaughtered civilians in Vietnam completely responsible for their acts? How about the guards in Abu Ghraib? Or the violent criminals whose lives were described by Gilligan?

I want to return to the concept of confirmation and how it applies to shared responsibility, but first we should consider views diametrically opposed to radical freedom. The behaviorist psychologist B. F. Skinner argued that a technology of behavior must be designed and implemented if the human condition is to be improved. The myth of autonomy stands in the way. He wrote:

> Freedom and dignity illustrate the difficulty. They are the possessions of the autonomous man of traditional theory, and they are essential to practices in which a person is held responsible for his conduct and given credit for his achievements. A scientific analysis shifts both the responsibility and the achievement to the environment.[42]

Is no one to be held responsible, then, for his or her own conduct? The prominent trial lawyer Clarence Darrow often argued this way. He even managed to save two young murderers from hanging by arguing that their elite education at the University of Chicago had warped their moral judgment.[43] They had been introduced to Nietzsche! Who can be sure what effects such reading will have on young, impressionable minds? Notice that this sort of argument could be used to promote critical thinking (read, but think, think!) or, as in Plato, to censor students' reading.

If we take the first course of action – wide, controversial reading in the service of critical thinking – we might want to include Skinner's *Walden Two*, a behaviorist utopia, and the fascinating *Erewhon*, a utopian novel by Samuel Butler. In Erewhon, those who commit crimes are considered ill and are treated, not punished.[44] This enlightened attitude is spoiled, however, by the way in which the medically ill

---

[42] B. F. Skinner, *Beyond Freedom and Dignity* (New York: Vintage Books, 1972), pp. 22–23.

[43] See the account of the "trial of the century" in Kevin Tierney, *Darrow: A Biography* (New York: Thomas Y. Crowell, 1979).

[44] See B. F. Skinner, *Walden Two* (New York: Macmillan, 1962); also Samuel Butler, *Erewhon* (London: Penguin Books, 1985/1872).

are treated. As if to remind us that human beings – even in utopias – are inevitably morally schizophrenic, the citizens of Erewhon treat the ill like criminals. It is simply immoral, in Erewhon, to be ill, and illness deserves punishment.

The idea of confirmation offers a position that rejects both radical freedom and environmental determinism. It emerges from a firm belief in moral interdependence. It requires listening that is more than a form of politeness. It means recognizing the other as *other* and entering into her frame of reference as nearly as possible. Tony Hendra says of the priest, Father Joe:

> Joe was a holy chameleon. To me he was irreverent and secular. To others he was an intensely spiritual guide; to yet others a mild but unyielding disciplinarian. To some he was a father, to some a mother. He always did what was appropriate and practical for the person he was with. There weren't two kinds of people in the world for Joe, nor three, nor ten. Just people.[45]

The idea of moral interdependence and the practice of confirmation are important not only to the lives of individuals but also to world peace and the interaction of various religious, ethnic, and national groups. I have concentrated on these topics, as with all others in this book, with respect to self-understanding, but the connection to larger social and political issues should be made.[46] The central idea, moral interdependence, is so important that we will return to it in the following chapters.

I have expressed a strong preference for the idea of moral interdependence. Teachers should express themselves and defend their beliefs. However, they should also encourage students to read and discuss the most powerful competing views available and continue to explore the questions: To what degree am I responsible for my own acts? To what degree am I responsible for things others do as a possible result of how I've treated them? How can I best contribute to the moral/ethical development of others? How should my thinking on this influence the social policies I support?

[45] Hendra, *Father Joe*, p. 270.

[46] For a discussion along these lines with respect to international affairs, see Harold H. Saunders, *The Other Walls* (Princeton, NJ: Princeton University Press, 1991).

We have concentrated in this chapter on our relations with other human beings. When we start philosophical thinking with that first relation – one in which, ideally, the other presents herself as a being-for-me – we are forced to recognize our moral interdependence. So much depends on how children are treated by the first adults in their lives.

Then we looked at the processes of socialization. We are all subjected to continuous socialization. If we are interested in critical thinking, we cannot be satisfied with the mere acceptance of our efforts to socialize. Students growing from childhood to adolescence toward adulthood must be helped to understand the processes of socialization. Which norms should I accept and endorse? Which should I question or study more carefully? Which should I reject? And why, why, why?

Finally, moral interdependence was discussed explicitly in connection with shared responsibility. An acceptance of moral interdependence implies the need for human beings to listen attentively to one another. It suggests also a commitment to confirmation as a central component of moral life. It reminds us constantly that how good I can be depends at least in part on how you treat me. Possibly no critical lesson is more crucial to moral life and happiness than this one.

5

Parenting

You know more than you think you do.

Benjamin Spock

Thou shalt be on the child's side.

A. S. Neill

N o task is more challenging and potentially more rewarding than parenting. Few of us use academic mathematics as adults, but most of us become parents. Yet, our schools require all students to study algebra and geometry, but they rarely offer serious courses – or even units of study – on parenting. The assumption has long been that young people will learn how to be parents at home – from their own parents.

There is a troubling question built into this assumption. We know that academic success is highly correlated with socioeconomic status, and it may be that certain parenting practices are also related to, or affected by, that status. This is not to say that rich parents love their children more than poor parents do; that is obviously untrue. It is not to say, either, that there is something wrong with poor parents or with those from cultural minorities. It is not a matter of blame. Further, bad parenting occurs in all socioeconomic groups, ethnicities, races, religions, and communities. But some parenting practices seem to be more readily available to the economically and educationally well off and also seem to be more effective for life in a liberal democracy; these practices could be taught and critiqued. The upward mobility so touted by policymakers in America might be better encouraged by the teaching of effective parenting than by requiring all students to study academic subjects. But we are not faced with an either-or choice. We could teach parenting *and* encourage students to study important academic subjects.

Finally, I do not mean to suggest that only the economically poor and some cultural minorities need to learn parenting skills. We could all learn a great deal from such studies, but they must be presented nondogmatically. One of the critical lessons on parenting should focus on how often experts have been wrong in the past and how they might be wrong today. As in the discussion of socialization, students need to acquire information, but they also need opportunities to reflect on and challenge that information.

Infants and Childcare

Educators have for years asked, "What knowledge is of most worth?" Usually, the question triggers a heated debate over the merits of disciplinary knowledge and arguments over content versus process knowledge. But if we were to start, as Alfred North Whitehead suggested, with life itself as the material of education,[1] we would surely name knowledge of parenting as central to human interests. Almost everyone might agree on this, but serious disagreement arises when we ask where this knowledge should be acquired.

I have long thought it indefensible to insist that parenting skills must be taught only at home or in some social institution attended voluntarily by adults seeking such knowledge. An obvious complaint against this system is that, under it, those who have been poorly parented will themselves become poor parents. I still believe this, but there is an objection to my suggestion that parenting be taught in schools, where the instruction will be available to all. The objection is that there are many demands on our schools and that our society has been awash in readily available parenting advice for about 100 years.[2] If people can read, they can find the instruction and advice they need. So! The schools should concentrate on teaching everyone

---

[1] See Alfred North Whitehead, *The Aims of Education* (New York: Free Press, 1967/1929).

[2] For a review of this literature, see Ann Hulbert, *Raising America* (New York: Alfred A. Knopf, 2003).

to read. I certainly agree that reading should be taught to everyone, but this answer will not do. One must feel a need before she seeks information through reading, and many young people simply copy whatever their parents or caregivers did by way of parenting. Further, there is a disconcerting body of evidence that few people ever read a book after high school; the percentage may be as low as 50 percent. It seems likely also that people who do not read books do not read the kinds of periodicals that would inform them about parenting. Thus, simply teaching people to read will not ensure that they will read material that will make them well informed. Moreover, many students have an unpleasant experience with reading all through their school days. They are much relieved to finish school and be done with reading. This sad state of affairs suggests a set of critical lessons for teachers: Can we motivate people to continue reading? If we reject this question – as I suggested in chapter 1 that many of us do – what natural motivation might we build upon to encourage reading? These questions are important not only for the topic at hand – parenting – but also for the more general issue of promoting a well-informed citizenry.

Another objection might be offered against providing information and teaching parenting skills to high school students: This is material that (we hope) will not be used for some years. It will be forgotten before it is needed. I cannot lightly brush aside this objection because I have myself raised it against much of what is taught in high school. However, the material to which I object is *never* used by most students. If we teach parenting in schools, students may conclude that the topic has some importance, and they may recall parts of it when the practical need arises. At least, the memory of having engaged this material may trigger a felt need to reactivate its study. We cannot easily make the same claim for teaching the French Revolution, the grammar of complete and simple subjects, and quadratic equations. Then, too, the material on parenting, wisely chosen, will have direct relevance to teenagers who are themselves still being parented. Indeed, students might take the whole of schooling more seriously if we were to introduce topics of current interest that will surely arise again in adult life.

What should we teach about parenting? It would be useful to teach the basics of infant care, using material from Spock or some other widely accepted authority.[3] It is not adequate, certainly, to have students walk around school all day with an egg in their pockets – a practice designed to convince students that one must always be attentive to the fragility and constant presence of a baby. That practice is just silly. But all older students, both boys and girls, should learn the rudiments of physical care for babies.

More important, however, students should have an opportunity to learn about and discuss the psychology of childrearing. This is more important for late teenagers than the physical care of infants because it can encourage reflection on their own experience. These teenagers are, in a sense, still being raised, and reflection on this process should induce critical thinking. In chapter 3, I suggested that students might profit from reading about and discussing patterns of homemaking, building, and the organic habits that develop in one's early home environment. There I warned against intruding on students' privacy, and here I will repeat that warning. There is a significant difference between an attitude that says "Think about it" and one that says "Tell me about it." No student should be required, or even strongly encouraged, to share publicly her personal experience of being parented. Some such experiences will come out, but they should be voluntary, and teachers should make it clear that good examples are preferred over bad ones, although the latter should not be forbidden. Again, it is part of self-understanding to recognize that most of us regret the disclosure of events that reflect badly on our families and friends.

The most basic topic to consider is how adults should interact with children. How should children be socialized? What sort of discipline is recommended? Students should learn that patterns of childrearing have changed over generations. Rigid, authoritarian methods give way to more permissive approaches, and permissive approaches are often replaced by tougher ones.[4] With enough reading and discussion, most students may be convinced that neither rigid nor permissive methods of parenting are to be recommended.[5] There is considerable evidence that children who are allowed to do as they please often

---

[3] See especially Benjamin Spock, *Dr. Spock's Baby and Child Care* (New York: Pocket Books, 1998/1946); also Spock, *On Parenting* (New York: Pocket Books, 2001). For a multitude of additional references, see Hulbert, *Raising America*.

[4] See Hulbert, *Raising America*.

[5] The work of Diana Baumrind is especially helpful on this. See Baumrind, "Parent Styles and Adolescent Development," in *The Encyclopedia of Adolescence*, ed.

become anxious and indecisive; they are simply not mature enough to handle the decisions thrust upon them. At the other extreme, children of authoritarian parents sometimes fail to develop habits of reflection and critical thinking. If they rebel, and they sometimes do, they may adopt contrary ways as unreflectively as they initially accepted their parents' orders. Diana Baumrind calls the best methods "authoritative," but just what is entailed by that label needs considerable thought.

Authoritative parents seem to know when to use authoritarian strategies – "No, you cannot play in the street, sneak into X-rated movies, drink vodka" – and when to relax and let kids have fun. Because they establish relations of care and trust, they rarely have to use authoritarian methods, and their kids rarely take advantage of permissive episodes. But there are no recipes for establishing such relations and no guarantees that the "right" method will always produce the desired result.

Many parents find it unnecessary to inflict penalties or punishment. They establish household rules cooperatively and expect everyone to live by them, but occasional infractions are treated as matters for discussion. Coming home late, forgetting chores, or being nasty to a sibling require apologies and explanations. Chronic behavior of this sort requires serious intervention, but punishment is not usually an effective response because it further weakens the relation.[6]

Communication seems to be fundamental. When parents are genuinely happy to see their kids at the end of the school/work day and engage them as equals in conversation, relations are strengthened. Conversations of this sort form the foundation not only of family life but also of democratic life more generally. John Dewey said, "A democracy is more than a form of government; it is primarily a mode of associated living, of conjoint communicated experience."[7] It is hard to exaggerate the importance of genuine conversation in a liberal democratic society. Children have to believe that

R. Lerner, A. C. Petersen, and J. Brooks-Gunn (New York: Garland Press, 1991), vol. 2, pp. 746–758; also Baumrind, *Child Maltreatment and Optimal Caregiving in Social Contexts* (New York: Garland, 1995).

[6] See my *Starting at Home: Caring and Social Policy* (Berkeley: University of California Press, 2002); also Stephen R. Covey, *The 7 Habits of Highly Effective Families* (New York: Golden Books, 1997).

[7] John Dewey, *Democracy and Education* (New York: Macmillan, 1916), p. 87.

their views are respected but that opinions must be supported, that their interests are worthy of discussion, and that their contributions to the well-being of others in the household are both expected and appreciated.

Cultural differences in styles of parenting and communicating should be discussed generously, and they should not be made into stereotypes. Individual differences occur in all racial and ethnic groups. However, differences that appear with a degree of regularity should probably be discussed. For example, is the typical Asian American family authoritarian?[8] If so, does this style help or hinder children in their school years? How? Are some styles products of hardships that parents cannot escape? Dr. Spock came to understand and appreciate poor mothers – often African American – who ignored his advice and went on weaning and toilet training their children early so that they could get back to work while their children were very young.[9] What else could poor working mothers do? And what should be said about the white upper-middle-class parents who push their toddlers into prestigious preschools and press relentlessly for academic achievement from the cradle to college?

While some parents ignore expert advice, others become almost obsessively dependent on it. The function of critical lessons in this area should be to encourage the acquisition of information and the exercise of critical thinking. By all means, learn what the experts are saying, but use your head and recognize that expert opinion often changes. A historical look at expert opinion should convince students of its variability.

Before looking at some historical material, I want to revisit an example that should be interesting to teenagers. What role should parents play in their child's homework? Many elementary schools today require parents to sign their children's homework as an indication that they have seen it completed. The idea, supposedly, is to involve parents in their children's schoolwork. The result, more often than not, is confusion and a disruption of family life. Instead of facilitating communication and harmony, this practice often produces dissension. Parents protest that they do not understand what the teacher

[8] Students may enjoy reading and discussing the novels of Amy Tan. How can we check to see if her stories ring true?

[9] See the account in Hulbert, *Raising America*.

wants and that the student – if he or she had been listening – should be able to explain what is wanted. The question I am raising for discussion is whether parents should be involved in children's homework and, if so, in what way.

Some parents take an active, even authoritarian, role in their children's homework. They specify when it will be done and insist on reviewing the results. If a child's marks are not as high as the parents would like, many parents will supervise homework more closely and even hire a tutor. This is done for the child's good, of course, but some of us have serious doubts about the effects of such efforts to control children and their futures. If homework is the student's responsibility, why not insist that it be *his* and not that of his parents?

Other parents, as suggested previously, do not supervise homework. They may ask how it's going, whether help is required, whether anything interesting is being learned, whether the load is too heavy, and so on, but the responsibility belongs to the student. These parents provide help if it is requested, but they actually resent the school's insistence on their participation. Are the children of such parents likely to shrug off homework and do poorly in school? Some students will be surprised to learn that many excellent students have parents who treat homework this way. It is the child's responsibility, and parents will help only if asked to do so.

There are also parents who are either too tired or just uninterested. Some are so poorly educated that they cannot help. Some are intimidated by teachers and schools. They are embarrassed when they don't understand the assignment. Better-educated parents may react to an unclear assignment with irritation, but parents who have a history of failure in school may interpret their lack of understanding as proof of their own incompetence.[10] Their discomfort may be turned on the child with an impatient "If you paid attention, you'd know what to do." How can these parents and children be helped?

I raised questions earlier about homework, and certainly high school students should be encouraged to continue the discussion of these questions. What function does homework serve? Is it necessary?

[10] For a poignant account of this problem, see David K. Shipler, *The Working Poor: Invisible in America* (New York: Alfred A. Knopf, 2004).

When? Should it be graded? How? Must it be a lonely task or can it be a cooperative one? When you become a parent, how will you interact with your child over homework? Why?

Whenever it is suggested that topics central to human life be treated seriously in school, there are those who will respond with accusations of anti-intellectualism, so we must point out again that the topic of parenting can include material that is recognized by disciplinary experts. It is a matter of some irony that the experts on infant care were for so many years almost exclusively male, while the ordinary caregivers were, of course, female. It is also instructive to learn how often the experts have disagreed and the lack of confidence they have induced in young mothers.

But in addition to the accounts of experts in childcare, there is a fascinating history of childhood itself. Philippe Ariès, in his prestigious study of childhood, writes:

> Medieval art until about the twelfth century did not know childhood or did not attempt to portray it. It is hard to believe that this neglect was due to incompetence or incapacity; it seems more probable that there was no place for childhood in the medieval world.[11]

Ariès's contention was widely accepted for years, and it seemed to be supported by examinations of medieval art in which infants and young children were depicted as having the same proportions as adults.[12] Students interested in art may enjoy studying some of the paintings that show strange-looking infants whose heads are unnaturally small. When this oddity is pointed out, students may think that Ariès was indeed right. Medieval thinkers and artists did not acknowledge childhood but simply saw smaller, less competent human beings.

Recently, however, scholars have challenged Ariès's view. Nicholas Orme, for example, has convincingly documented the existence of childhood in medieval times.[13] Noting that childhood was recognized

---

[11] Philippe Ariès, *Centuries of Childhood*, trans. Robert Baldick (New York: Vintage Books, 1962), p. 33.

[12] See John Cleverly and D. C. Phillips, *Visions of Childhood* (New York: Teachers College Press, 1986).

[13] See Nicholas Orme, *Medieval Children* (New Haven, CT: Yale University Press, 2001).

in medieval England for religious and legal purposes, he notes that ages and stages were also widely recognized in the Early Middle Ages and were well established by the Late Middle Ages. Referring to the depiction of stages in a famous encyclopedia, he notes that these stages appeared in a speech by the character Jacques in *As You Like It*. Orme notes:

> In these analyses, infancy became an age of its own, lasting from growth in the womb or birth until the age of seven. Childhood (typified for Jacques by a schoolboy) followed from seven to fourteen, and adolescence (by a lover) from fourteen to twenty-eight.[14]

Clearly, the concept of adolescence has changed considerably. Students may be attracted to its representation by a lover but astonished to think of it as lasting to age twenty-eight. Notice that this passage from Orme presents an opportunity to ask who the character Jacques is. The teacher doesn't have to be "teaching English" to invite students to find Jacques's speech in *As You Like It* and to draw attention to its famous opening lines: "All the world's a stage, and all the men and women merely players." The lines and their source may be remembered longer if the teacher who leads the discussion is focusing on something other than Shakespeare. It would be quite wonderful for students to discover that their teacher is an educated person, not a mere summarizer of didactic texts.

There is much to be gained in a sequence of critical lessons devoted to childhood. Not the least is the point that historians study customs and events other than war and political leadership. It is important, too, for critical thinkers to see that experts can disagree, and to learn something about the sort of evidence that makes one case better than another. When reference can be made not only to history and psychology but also to art and literature, discussion contributes to intellectual integrity. Perhaps most significant of all, however, is the potential to bring intellectual and practical life together.

In Orme's account of learning to read in medieval England, we see a precursor of current debates on the teaching of reading. Some children were taught the alphabet first, then syllables, then words and sentences. Others were taught words first and the alphabet as it

[14] Ibid., pp. 6–7.

appeared in words learned. It was also clear to teachers of reading (official teachers, parents, or relatives) that some children learned the basics of reading swiftly (sometimes in just a few weeks), while others took a very long time (several years).[15] Today, ignoring the valuable lessons of this history, policymakers demand that all children demonstrate specified reading skills at specified ages. We'll revisit this topic in the section on the literature of childhood.

Motherhood and Its Cares

Lessons on infant and childcare would be incomplete without discussion of the trials and satisfactions of motherhood. I will not include here information on conception, pregnancy, and childbirth. These are obviously important topics and are usually addressed somewhere in today's school curriculum. The present concern is with the joys, conflicts, hard work, and potential exhaustion that accompany childrearing.

Many of the attitudes toward motherhood in the West today can be traced to our Victorian heritage. Mothers – pure, unselfish, forever giving and suffering – were extolled in literature written by men. Coventry Patmore's poetic tribute, *The Angel in the House*,[16] so disgusted Virginia Woolf that she rebelled, writing:

> It was she [the angel] who used to come between me and my paper when I was writing reviews. It was she who bothered me and wasted my time and so tormented me that at last I killed her. You who come of a younger and happier generation may not have heard of her. . . . She was intensely sympathetic. She was immensely charming. She was utterly unselfish. She excelled in the difficult arts of family life. . . . Above all . . . she was pure.[17]

In short, the Angel sounds like a character in a Mother's Day card. Woolf was right to kill her. We are well rid of her. Still, free of the oppressive Angel, women can find satisfaction in household management and deep joy in motherhood. Women do not need to reject

---

[15] Ibid., pp. 246–251.

[16] Coventry Patmore, *The Angel in the House* (New York: E. P. Dutton, 1876).

[17] Virginia Woolf, "Professions for Women," in *Collected Essays*, vol. 2 (London: Hogarth Press, 1966), p. 285.

everything associated with home and children in order to construct a satisfying personal life. They should, however, be informed about the history of motherhood and have opportunities to reflect on their own values and hopes.[18] Sara Ruddick presents a balanced view of maternal experience, and I too have written about the joys of motherhood.[19]

There is something seriously amiss in an education that fails to treat the history of motherhood. Childbirth was for centuries excruciatingly painful and dangerous, and it became even more perilous when male doctors – dripping with the germs of other patients and cadavers – began to deliver babies. Every young woman should know something of this history and of Ignaz Semmelweiss, the Viennese physician who campaigned so fiercely against the puerperal fever induced by the dirty hands of physicians. Semmelweiss was not the first to implicate physicians in the contamination causing childbed fever, but he was certainly the most passionate.[20]

Physicians were not alone in aggravating the suffering of women in childbirth. Theologians and preachers were in some ways worse. They pointed to scripture to justify the suffering of women in childbirth. Women, many of these men insisted, were *supposed* to suffer in childbirth as a penalty for Eve's disobedience.[21] Theologians opposed anesthesia for the pain of childbirth on the grounds that the suffering was ordained by God. Adrienne Rich notes that Queen Victoria committed a radical act when she accepted anesthesia for the birth of her seventh child.[22]

All of this may seem so alien to contemporary life that it need not appear in the school curriculum. But also alien are the interminable wars of history (that *do* still appear in the curriculum), accounts of medical discoveries less significant than that of Semmelweiss, and

---

[18] See Adrienne Rich's classic, *Of Woman Born* (New York: W. W. Norton, 1976); also Ann Ferguson, "On Conceiving Motherhood and Sexuality: A Feminist Materialist Approach," in *Feminist Social Thought: A Reader*, ed. Diana Tietjens Meyers (New York: Routledge, 1997), pp. 38–63.

[19] Sara Ruddick, *Maternal Thinking: Towards a Politics of Peace* (Boston: Beacon Press, 1989).

[20] See Rich, *Of Woman Born*. Rich notes that Oliver Wendell Holmes made similar claims about the causes of childbed fever.

[21] For a comprehensive and lively history of Eve, see John Anthony Phillips, *Eve: The History of an Idea* (San Francisco: Harper & Row, 1984).

[22] See Rich, *Of Woman Born*, p. 169.

acts of lesser importance by Queen Victoria. Further, the point is to get young people thinking about change and the strong resistance that arises against it when tradition and its powerful advocates feel threatened.

How many people know that the Catholic Church has not always held that human life (complete with soul) begins at conception? Indeed, this notion was not officially asserted until the late nineteenth century.[23] The story of what was believed before that is interesting in itself but, more important, it illustrates again that having adequate information may change one's whole way of thinking. Experts in every field have supplied information and advice to the public, but they have also induced fear and anxiety. And then they have changed their minds!

Mothers have always had ambivalent feelings about their children. Possibly nothing about motherhood is more important than this for young people to understand. Even the best mothers are sometimes exasperated with their children.[24] When this happens, mothers need time off, time for themselves. When there is no time off and no one supports or understands the weary mother, unpleasant episodes occur, and sometimes the results are catastrophic. For a young woman whose mental health is already fragile, caring for young children can be very difficult. If, in addition, she is told, as sometimes happens, by a husband, elder, or preacher how happy she should be for the gift of children, her health may break entirely. Teenagers should be aware of the case of Joanne Michulski, a mother of eight, who one summer day chopped up her two youngest children and displayed their parts on her front lawn[25] and, more recently, the case of Andrea Yates, who drowned her five children in the bathtub. Poor woman. Whenever she begins to emerge from her mental illness, the horror of what she did overcomes her and sends her back to the relative safety of illness.[26] It may not be possible to prevent all such disasters – just as it is probably not possible to prevent entirely the loss of moral identity in combat – but we can move in the right

---

[23] See Orme, *Medieval Children*, p. 14. Rich, *Of Woman Born*, also discusses this.
[24] See Ruddick, *Maternal Thinking*.
[25] The story is told with great sensitivity by Rich, *Of Woman Born*, pp. 263–269.
[26] I discuss this case in *Happiness and Education* (Cambridge: Cambridge University Press, 2003).

direction by informing young people and helping them to understand that childrearing can be trying and exhausting, that motherhood is not adequately captured in the romantic literature, that it is forgivable to lose one's temper (so long as no real harm is done), and that it is acceptable to seek help when one's emotional health becomes shaky.

It is important, too, for students to know that men – politicians, theologians, experts – have long exercised control over reproduction. The Nazis glorified Aryan motherhood, and after World War II the Russian government awarded medals to women who had ten or more children. Both countries needed more people. In contrast, when a nation (China, for example) suffers from overpopulation, it is likely to penalize parents who have a second child or even force the mother to have an abortion. These high-level policy decisions are not based on eternal, unquestionable moral values. They are merely expedient and change with national and cultural conditions. Unreflective women are often trapped by them.

Understanding something of the history of motherhood and related political issues may assure young women that they are permitted, even encouraged, to reflect on their own deepest desires, strengths, and weaknesses. The object, again, is not to promote automatic, thoughtless rebellion against authorities and experts. Any sensible person with a sore throat will consult a physician, not a shoe salesman. And similarly, sensible people will listen to the voices of authority, but they will inform themselves sufficiently so that they can raise questions, and they will gain confidence in their right to dissent.

Students who have a religious affiliation will hear arguments against various practices that many women have deemed necessary for their health and full personhood. They may not hear, however, stories of the brave women who have sacrificed their religious affiliation to fight for the right of women to choose contraception and abortion. Without advocating a position, schools should be sure that students are at least aware of these stories. Some of them, such as that of the former nuns Barbara Ferraro and Patricia Hussey, are quite wonderful.[27] Whether students agree or disagree with the positions taken by these dissenting women, they will learn that committed

---

[27] See the story in Debra Campbell, *Graceful Exits: Catholic Women and the Art of Departure* (Bloomington: Indiana University Press, 2003), pp. 132–152.

people can, in good conscience, take very different positions on vital issues.

Whatever is learned in critical lessons on motherhood, many – probably most – students will eventually become parents. What else might our schools teach on the all-important task of parenting?

The Literature of Childhood

One of the most delightful tasks of parenthood is reading to and with children. Not only do the children love it, but the practice gives parents opportunities to revisit the literature they loved as children. Notice, again, that adults who had satisfying experiences sharing literature with their own parents have an obvious advantage over those who did not have such experience. But schools can make it more likely that future parents will read with their children.

Schools could redesign the English curriculum so that one or two semesters in high school would be devoted to the literature of childhood. For some students, this would be an opportunity to revisit childhood literature from a more advanced standpoint. For others, the experience would fill an important gap, introducing them to stories they might otherwise miss entirely.

What should be given up in order to make room for fairy tales, fables, children's poetry, classic stories, and contemporary children's books of high quality? When we face the fact that much of what we do now in high school literature classes seems to have the negative effect of destroying interest in reading, the whole curriculum should be subject to analysis and reevaluation. Why teach Shakespeare if the end result is a huge population of graduates who will avoid Shakespeare in adulthood? If some knowledge of Shakespeare is deemed essential for cultural literacy, then we should find multiple opportunities to refer to Shakespeare's work all through the curriculum. I mentioned one such possibility in citing Orme's reference to Shakespeare's character Jacques in *As You Like It*. Surely such opportunities arise frequently in history, geography, psychology, and art. Can similar opportunities be found in mathematics and science? I am not suggesting that Shakespeare be dropped entirely from the English curriculum. Rather, I am suggesting that his work be made more relevant by *showing*, not just telling, that it is part of our general culture. One work, well treated, with lots of support from the other disciplines, might increase interest considerably.

The reading of fairy tales should be accompanied by the study of psychology addressed to the topic. Why, for example, does Bruno Bettelheim recommend fairy tales and fantasy for children? Why, however, does he warn against using stories that cast mothers as witches or fathers as ogres?[28] Which fairy tales and what metaphors appearing in those tales arise frequently in adult literature?

Students might also enjoy reading *Aesop's Fables* and perhaps exchanging notes on the sayings that come from these stories: Sing all summer, go supperless to bed in winter; birds of a feather flock together; don't make much ado about nothing (another opportunity to refer to Shakespeare); might makes right; honesty is the best policy... And then there is the story of the fox and the "sour" grapes and one of the goose (or hen) that laid golden eggs. In addition to the obvious contributions to cultural literacy, students should consider the power of the morals that accompany these stories. Should literature deliver a moral message or should it provide entertainment and enjoyment? Need it do one or the other? Can a story of evil or meanness deliver a moral message?

Plato was not the only philosopher to warn against the corrupting influence of literature. Much more recently, Rousseau advised against the use of literature with young students. His advice to teachers was to abandon books and encourage students to learn from direct experience. Indeed, most educators over many centuries seem to have believed that the literature used in formal education should teach morals; any other literature should be forbidden or strongly discouraged. Today, there are those who urge us to consider whether books such as the Harry Potter series should be banned or ignored. Do these books advocate or encourage witchcraft? If they do, should they be banned? The history of attitudes toward children's literature is another bit of history well worth exploring in itself.

After studying some fairy tales and fables, teachers might invite students to form small book clubs of a sort. Suppose the teacher listed

---

[28] See Bruno Bettelheim, *The Uses of Enchantment: The Meaning and Importance of Fairy Tales* (New York: Alfred A. Knopf, 1976).

the following books: Kenneth Grahame, *The Wind in the Willows*; Louisa Mae Alcott, *Little Women*; Charles Kingsley, *The Water Babies*; A. A. Milne, *Winnie-the-Pooh*; and Beatrix Potter, *The Tale of Peter Rabbit*. Students could choose which book group to join, engage in discussion, and plan an oral review for their classmates. I wouldn't require written book reports, because they have a way of becoming the whole point of doing the reading, and the idea is to enjoy and share the books as adults do in book clubs.

One could argue that high school students need practice in writing, and that is why they should do book reports. But practice in writing should not come at the expense of sacrificing the pleasure of reading and sharing. Teachers could ask students to read the short reviews of children's books in, say, the *New York Times* and use these reviews as models for occasional reports on contemporary children's literature. Individual assignments of this sort could culminate in a collection of reviews to be compiled and shared with the entire class. Writing a review would thus serve a purpose, and it would be a fine way to become acquainted with current children's literature.

While they are reading reviews of children's books, students should learn about the Newbery and Caldecott awards and search out books that have received these awards or honorable mention. Learning that illustrators, as well as writers, are recognized in the world of children's literature, students might want to team up and write some children's stories – one writer and one artist to each story.

Time should be spent on illustrated books – particularly those for young children. As we read to children, we can point out colors, shapes, and sizes. We can also encourage tiny tots to count. Looking at a picture, we might ask a child whether she sees "birdies" on the page. Where? What color are the birdies? How many birdies? Here students can get an important lesson on learning to count. A young child may have learned to recite "One, two, three, four" without being able to use these words to count. Pointing at three birdies, she may say, "One, two-three, four," revealing that she has not yet grasped one-to-one correspondence or that she needs more practice in hand–eye coordination. Sometimes it helps (but we shouldn't push it too hard – this is supposed to be fun) to hold the child's finger and point it slowly at each bird, saying, "one" (lift finger), "two" (lift finger), "three!" Without distracting ourselves from the story, we can also point to page numbers now and then, and ask, "What will be the next page number?"

Reading together should be a pleasure, and it should strengthen the adult–child bond, but it is also an unsurpassed way to learn all sorts of things. Some books are richer in possibilities than others. *Alice's Adventures in Wonderland*, for example, provides potential lessons in logic, philosophy, mathematics, science, history, and art. *The Annotated Alice*, with notes provided by Martin Gardner, is a source of all sorts of information.[29] Gardner even addresses the question raised earlier by Bettelheim about the effects of violence in children's literature. In one of his marginal notes, he wonders about how children will react to the wicked Queen of Hearts's "constant orders for beheadings." Then he writes:

> As far as I know, there have been no empirical studies of how children react to such scenes and what harm if any is done to their psyche. My guess is that the normal child finds it all very amusing... but that books like *Alice's Adventures in Wonderland* and *The Wizard of Oz* should not be allowed to circulate indiscriminately among adults who are undergoing analysis.[30]

In today's terrorist climate, the reaction of children might be different. However, students might want to check for current empirical studies that support or cast doubt on Gardner's (and Bettelheim's) conclusions. Intrigued by Gardner's erudition and sense of humor, they might also want to read some of his columns on mathematical puzzles or the way he answers his own personal questions on religion.[31]

Before leaving *Alice in Wonderland*, we should say more about the logic (and illogic) illustrated there. In chapter 1, I shared doubts about the usefulness of teaching symbolic logic as an aid to critical thinking. I admitted that, despite doubts, I would still teach logic in both mathematics and philosophy. There are many arguments in *Alice* that would

---

[29] Martin Gardner, *The Annotated Alice: Lewis Carroll* (New York: World Publishing, 1963).

[30] Ibid., p. 109.

[31] Many of Gardner's columns from *Scientific American* are collected in *Mathematical Carnival* (New York: Alfred A. Knopf, 1975). For his perspectives on religion, see Gardner, *The Whys of a Philosophical Scrivener* (New York: Quill, 1983).

serve as starting points for instruction in logic. In one exchange, Alice is exhorted to say what she means:

> "I do," Alice hastily replied; "at least – at least I mean what I say – that's the same thing, you know."
>
> "Not the same thing a bit!" said the Hatter. "Why, you might just as well say that 'I see what I eat' is the same thing as 'I eat what I see'!"
>
> "You might just as well say," added the March Hare, "that 'I like what I get' is the same thing as 'I get what I like'!"
>
> "You might just as well say," added the Dormouse, which seemed to be talking in its sleep, "that 'I breathe when I sleep' is the same thing as 'I sleep when I breathe'!"[32]

What is the logical error here, and who makes it? All students should be familiar with the often-committed error of affirming the consequent or, as we say in mathematics, reasoning from the converse. Conversations from *Alice* might be used to introduce the rules of logic by starting with logical fallacies. If there is interest (and my experience suggests that there will be), teachers could move from the fallacies in stories and advertising to some practice with symbolic logic and truth tables, and then back to stories and everyday situations. Instruction in formal logic is certainly not sufficient for the acquisition of critical thinking, although it may help, but students must see a reason for bothering with it.

Parents and children can also enjoy word play. Besides expanding their vocabulary through stories and poetry, most children love the rhymes and rhythms of poetry. Often they will dance or sway to the rhythm of a poem, and their early fascination with sounds may grow into a lifelong love of language. High school students should consider how it is that we can make sense out of a poem like "Jabberwocky." What is it about language that enables us to derive sense from a collection of words that are, in themselves, nonsense?[33]

---

[32] *Annotated Alice*, p. 95.

[33] See "Jabberwocky" in *Through the Looking-Glass*, also in *The Annotated Alice*, pp. 191–197. Students may also become interested in mirror writing. (The first verse of "Jabberwocky" appears in mirror writing.) Mirror writing also figures among the codes in Dan Brown, *The Da Vinci Code* (New York: Doubleday, 2003), p. 298. Both high school and younger students might enjoy another word game suggested in *The Da Vinci Code*, p. 99. How many English words (no plurals!) can you make from the letters of the word *planets*?

I'll add a personal note here. I've enjoyed reading Thurber's *The 13 Clocks* to my grandchildren.[34] In this wonderful story, the wicked duke continually threatens to slit his enemies from "the guggle to the zatch." After hearing this, children are likely to run about yelling, "I'll slit you from the guggle to the zatch!" and then collapse in laughter. I've never seen any violence follow this bit of verbal mayhem, so I'm inclined to agree with Gardner on this. However, visual violence may be an entirely different phenomenon, and its effects may be pernicious.[35] Even on this, the evidence is mixed, but wise parents may want to control the amount of such violence to which their children are exposed.

Guidance and Respect

Reading together is a fine way to start conversations that provide both guidance and respect. Parents have an obligation to guide the moral growth of their children, and much can be done along these lines through vicarious experience. Sometimes it is easier to launch sensitive moral discussions about the dilemmas and decisions of fictional characters than it is to address one's own problems directly. Reading and talking about the situations faced in literature also opens the door to mutuality in dialogue. Invited to speculate on what a character will do next or why he did what he did in the latest episode, children will often reveal much of their own thinking. While encouraging and respecting that thinking, parents can also suggest alternatives that might be ethically or practically more sound.

Mealtime is another promising setting for conversation. Everyone should have an opportunity to say something about his or her day. If parents set the stage by saying a bit about the ups and downs of their day, children may also speak up. We know from long experience that if we pin a child down and ask, "What did you do in school today?" we're likely to get the well-caricatured answer, "Nothing!" In a safe setting, however, with suitable stimulation, children may enjoy contributing to the conversation, and they may learn listening as well as speaking skills.

---

[34] James Thurber, *The 13 Clocks* (New York: Donald I. Fine, 1990/1957).
[35] See Donald F. Roberts and Ulla G. Foehr, *Kids and Media in America* (Cambridge: Cambridge University Pres, 2004).

What prevents families from engaging in conversation at mealtimes? Students may respond that their families simply do not eat together or do so only rarely. This response should lead to a discussion of how family habits have changed. With both parents working outside the home and children experiencing irregular hours for schooling and other activities, it is understandable that fewer families eat together. Does the habit of "grabbing a bite" when one can lead to overloading on junk food? Do family members watch TV while eating? Have people forgotten how to set a table for dinner? Have table manners deteriorated? All of these questions are worth asking and exploring, but the one that concerns us here is this one: When *do* parents and children engage in conversation?

In recent years, some experts in childrearing have suggested scheduling time for group conversations or family meetings and also for one-to-one sessions between a parent and each child.[36] Some of these suggestions turn family life into a corporate enterprise of sorts, and many people dislike the idea of making appointments with their own family members. However, rejection of a full business model need not imply total rejection of everything suggested in such a model. Students might enjoy, for example, reading and reporting on Stephen Covey's *The 7 Habits of Highly Effective Families*.[37] And they might read the earlier account of family life governed by industrial engineering methods – *Cheaper by the Dozen*.[38] Can a family enjoy spontaneity and still establish measures of efficiency?

We are trying to figure out how to maintain a loving informality for regular conversation and how, at the same time, to ensure that such conversations actually take place in overscheduled households. One promising technique is to schedule weekly family meetings. At these meetings (attendance compulsory!), family members can decide cooperatively on mealtimes, job lists, and general household rules. Upcoming appointments and scheduled events can be announced, and complaints can be registered. Having raised a very large family, my husband and I heartily endorse the practice of holding family

---

[36] See the accounts in Hulbert, *Raising America*.

[37] Covey, *The 7 Habits of Highly Effective Families*.

[38] Frank B. Gilbreth and Ernestine Gilbreth Carey, *Cheaper by the Dozen* (New York: Bantam, 1966/1948).

meetings. The efficiencies gained by meeting regularly, agreeing on rules, and getting commitment to take on various jobs actually permit more free time for informal conversation and reduce the need for constant nagging about responsibilities. This topic may invite a return to a discussion of the efficiencies promoted by to-do lists. In today's world, it is hard to exaggerate the need to discuss and analyze time management techniques.

Students should be encouraged to think about how families teach responsibility. For more than 100 years, experts on childrearing have been divided roughly into two camps: parent-centered and child-centered.[39] Parent-centered advice focuses on the rights and responsibilities of parents in maintaining order, securing obedience, and raising moral children. Child-centered advice pays more attention to children's self-esteem, interests, and felt needs. Both groups of experts want to raise healthy, happy, moral children. Indeed, as Hulbert rightly points out, the differences between the two groups have grown smaller over the years since Benjamin Spock led the way to a middle road. Responsible experts on both sides reject or minimize the use of corporal punishment, warn against permissiveness, and recognize the needs of both parents and children. However, the matter of teaching responsibility is a good one to illustrate differences of emphasis.

Responsibility may be taught forcefully, with explicit rules and penalties assessed for infractions. Oddly, we often see this approach used by college teachers who are teaching (or preaching) child-centered methods of teaching and childrearing. Late papers are penalized in the name of teaching responsibility, and all student responsibilities, together with penalties for their neglect, are laid out precisely. I have never found such methods attractive, and they are certainly not consistent with student-centered methods. My own syllabi contain dates when assignments are due, but these dates are just guidelines. I accept papers whenever they come in, and I do not assess penalties for lateness. It is better to submit a good paper a bit late than a mediocre one on time. The greater responsibility is to do an adequate job, not merely to be on time.

[39] See the discussion in Hulbert, *Raising America*.

More consistently, many parent-centered advocates today recommend forms of moral education (character education, usually) that attempt to teach virtues, including responsibility, directly. The virtues are explicitly defined, taught, and monitored. Rewards and punishments are used to induce conformity.[40] To child-centered thinkers, these methods are questionable.

Child-centered adults also want to produce responsible children, but they are more likely to concentrate on the environment than on the child. In a happy, safe environment, children will want to cooperate in the smooth operation of the home or classroom. They will understand why responsible behavior is desirable, and they will want to please the adults who sometimes remind them of their obligations. Because they are granted respect, these children will return it. Punishment is not required because children in optimal environments will be appropriately moved by the disapproval or disappointment of beloved adults.

If cruelty is ruled out and instruction (including reprimands and expressions of disapproval) is conducted kindly, probably either approach will have a positive effect. My own sense is that the child-centered approach may be more powerful in encouraging critical thinking, because it involves active choice and participation rather than obedience. The parent-centered approach may guide parents in socializing their children gently, but its emphasis is still on inculcating desired beliefs and behaviors through the process. In contrast, the child-centered approach is more likely to help children understand the processes of socialization – believing that such understanding is necessary for critical thinking. But students should hear stories of people who became critical thinkers despite rigid (and even cruel) childhoods. Sometimes we learn to think in reaction to methods we evaluate as wrong.

---

[40] For a discussion of the pros and cons of character education, see my *Educating Moral People* (New York: Teachers College Press, 2002). For a strong argument in favor of character education, see Thomas Lickona, *Educating for Character: How Our Schools Can Teach Respect and Responsibility* (New York: Bantam Books, 1991). For a strong argument against character education, see Alfie Kohn, "The Trouble with Character Education," in *The Construction of Children's Character*, ed. Alex Molnar (Chicago: National Society for the Study of Education, 1997), pp. 154–162; also Kohn, *Punished by Rewards: The Trouble with Gold Stars, Incentive Plans, A's, Praise, and Other Bribes* (Boston: Houghton Mifflin, 1993).

Where does religious training fit into teaching responsibility? I will say much more on the role of religion in moral training and moral life generally in the chapter on religion, but here it must be noted that many parents and teachers believe that religion is necessary in moral training. This is clearly untrue; many atheists and agnostics are highly moral people. However, some students will want to acknowledge the influence that religion has had in their lives, and they may argue for the role they hope it will have in the lives of their children. Surely, religion provides one solid framework from which to design moral education. If the religion espoused rejects cruelty and emphasizes loving kindness, it may provide lifelong guidance for moral life. However, hell and damnation have *no* place in moral education, and I will argue that schools should actively protect children from belief in such horrors and their pernicious effects.

We see again a contrast that falls roughly along the parent-centered/child-centered lines. Some religious perspectives insist that adults, drawing on religious instruction, must define what is good and steer their children firmly toward that good. Child-centered approaches – with or without religion – are more likely to engage in a cooperative construction of the good based on universal and concrete needs. This does not imply relativism. The universal needs for sustenance, protection, acceptance, affiliation, and opportunity to grow are sufficient to trigger reflection and sensitivity to the plight of others.

The contrast is sometimes revealed vividly through interpretations of *confirmation*. In traditional religious perspectives, confirmation is the culminating ceremony of initiation into adult beliefs and practices. In Christianity it includes acceptance of rituals of accusation, confession, penance, and forgiveness. From the non-religious perspective of care ethics, confirmation involves receptivity by the adult, discovery, and affirmation of the better qualities of the child. From her knowledge of the child – gained through daily life in a relation of care and trust – the adult attributes to the child's acts the best possible motive consonant with reality. Confirmation, described in this fashion, need not be the product of a secular ethic; in Buber, it is part of a religious framework and life.[41]

---

[41] See Martin Buber, *I and Thou*, trans. Walter Kaufman (New York: Charles Scribner's Sons, 1970).

Further, confirmation can be practiced among adults and friends of any age. It is not a technique or strategy for use by adults on children. One can see that the first notion of confirmation fits well with parent-centered views, while the second is clearly child-centered in its orientation.

Critical lessons on parenting must address current problems. What should a good parent do to control television watching, overeating, and failure to exercise? Why were these not major problems two or three generations ago? These questions should lead to a review of earlier explorations. Living conditions and organic habits have changed, and children spend less time in free activity outdoors. Are communities really so unsafe that children should not be allowed outside unsupervised? Do children spend too much time in front of the television (and eating) because their parents are guiltily afraid for their safety outdoors? And are parents feeling guilty because they have become busy with their own lives? Has food become a substitute for affection and conversation? How much TV is too much? Should parents control what is watched? Should kids have TVs in their bedrooms?[42] All of these questions have the potential to get students to think not only about what they will do as parents but also about what they are themselves doing now. Students should be encouraged to use the distinction between parent- and child-centered patterns to explore remedies. Is it best to exercise firm, direct control over these habits or to build on the interests of the children to steer them in the desired direction?

No exploration of parental guidance would be adequate without discussion of drugs. However, most schools include drug education as part of the regular curriculum, and we are concentrating on matters the schools might teach but usually do not. We should, then, ask how parents may inadvertently contribute to the drug problem by trying to solve so many childhood problems with medication. For example, is Ritalin too often prescribed for "itchy" kids who just need time to run and let off steam? Students cannot be expected to answer this question, and they should not be led to believe that it has been answered definitively by anyone, but they should be aware of controversy on the matter.

---

[42] For a summary of kids' media habits, see Roberts and Foehr, *Kids and Media in America.*

In general, broad questions of drug use should be raised. If parents turn to medication for weight control, enhanced sex life, more energy, and a good night's sleep, are kids likely to adopt similar habits? Why are there so many drug ads on television? (We'll look at this question more closely in the chapter on advertising.) How can American society at one and the same time be soaked in medications and wage a war on drugs?[43]

There are, of course, many social/political problems that arise in connection with the war on drugs, and schools should treat these also.[44] But our main concern in this book is self-knowledge and how learners may be affected by knowledge or ignorance of questions we are addressing. Accordingly, I believe we should spend more time on the history of drug use, the widespread use of (legal) drugs, the harm caused by such use, and the things that cause people to turn to drugs. Half of the battle in education is getting the students to trust us. As Emerson once said, the key to education lies in respecting the student. If we respect our students, we will share with them the long-running tragic-comedy of human drug use.

There is both humor and grief in this story. From tales of Dionysus to present wine tastings and alcoholic revelries, the story of humankind is flavored by alcohol. Adolescents should learn that Johnny Appleseed was loved for bringing the apple – and thus apple cider – to the alcohol-deprived early frontier.[45] Present educational efforts to preach abstinence only from drugs, sex, and alcohol to kids living in a society immersed in all three teach more about our hypocrisy than anything else. Of course, abstinence should be presented as a desirable alternative, but good sense and moderation should also be recognized. Humans have always sought greater powers, increased beauty, consolation, fun, and escape from hardship through various substances. How successful has the quest been? Why would you join in this experiment?

---

[43] For an introduction to the problem, see Jeffrey A. Schaler, ed., *Drugs: Should We Legalize, Decriminalize or Deregulate?* (Amherst, NY: Prometheus Books, 1998); also Steven Wisotsky, *Beyond the War on Drugs* (Buffalo: Prometheus Books, 1990). An interesting account of marijuana appears in Michael Pollan, *The Botany of Desire* (New York: Random House, 2001).

[44] See 43. Also see Donaldo Macedo, *Literacies of Power: What Americans Are Not Allowed to Know* (Boulder, CO: Westview Press, 1994).

[45] See Pollan, *Botany of Desire*.

Among the many problems facing today's parents is how to promote the education of their children. I have already said a little about differences of opinion on how parents should be involved in their children's homework. We can see that the prevailing attitude now is parent-centered; that is, there is widespread acceptance of the idea that parents should make sure that children do an adequate and timely job on their homework. A more child-centered perspective would consider educational activities that parents and children might share. Homework is rarely an educational activity. Reading together and engaging in conversation have been discussed. Attending musical or dramatic performances, visiting museums or historical sites, traveling, and dining out occasionally together are all potentially rich educational activities.

Often, well-intentioned, generous educators say, "Poor children can learn as well as rich children." What they mean, of course, is that intelligence and learning capacity are not dependent on economic status. But their well-intended slogan is highly misleading. It suggests that schools can make up for deficiencies – sometimes enormous deficiencies – in homes. It is unfair and short-sighted to suggest this, and students should think ahead to how they will use their economic resources to promote their children's education. It is not simply a matter of finding the best school, although living in a good neighborhood is certainly important. More important, parents must share their resources in ways that contribute to their children's learning, and a wise society would concentrate on eliminating poverty – not on insisting that teachers and students succeed in spite of poverty.

Perhaps the most troubling educational problem for parents today is the tremendous and misguided pressure on children to succeed academically. This pressure is not an invitation *to learn*, to wade joyously into the waters of intellectual life. Indeed, the dominant effect of this pressure is to produce students who are interested only in marks, not in learning. One quite good student interviewed by Denise Clark Pope confessed frankly that he sought a 3.7 or higher average to satisfy his father and get "50 bucks":

"I mean look, grades are the focus. I tell you, people don't go to school to learn. They go to get good grades which brings them to college, which brings them the high-paying job, which brings them to happiness, so they think...grades is where it's at."[46]

How many students would affirm this assessment? Although I worry about the loss of genuine intellectual interest, I would remind students that there is nothing basically wrong in trying to get good grades. Grades are the currency for mobility in academic and thus professional life. The problem – a surprisingly difficult one – is to achieve a balance that does not destroy real interest and passion for learning. So, too, accepting the necessity to complete tasks one would prefer to avoid is part of responsible life. We make the problem more difficult than it needs to be by insisting that "good" students should be motivated to do – should even like – everything we set out to teach. In discussing the responsibilities of parents, students should be reminded of the lessons of chapter 1. To avoid the trap of double-mindedness, we need to admit that we sometimes do not want to do a particular bit of homework but that we will do an adequate job as quickly as possible and then get on with something we really want to do.

Students should be allowed, even encouraged, to criticize the current emphasis schools put on competition, standardization, and the accumulation of trivial knowledge. Teachers, too, need to learn the fundamental lesson of how to do an adequate job of teaching the required curriculum and then move on to critical lessons on things that matter.

In this chapter, we've looked at what the schools might teach on the universally important topic of parenting. We've talked about the basic knowledge of childcare, the contribution of experts, the history of motherhood and its romanticization, children's literature, the debate between parent-centered and child-centered orientations to child-rearing, the need for both respect and guidance in raising children, and the role of parents in promoting their children's academic success. At the end of the chapter, we considered some of today's most pressing problems in childrearing – too much TV, too much junk

---

[46] Denise Clark Pope, *"Doing School": How We Are Creating a Generation of Stressed Out, Materialistic, and Miseducated Students* (New Haven: Yale University Press, 2001), p. 11.

food, too little exercise, too little meaningful free time, and too much pressure for academic success.

Our discussion of parenting is far from complete, and readers may already have thought of topics that should be introduced or extended. Children are usually fascinated by animals, for example; that interest shows up early in children's literature. Moreover, many young people today, appalled by our society's treatment of animals, have become vegetarians. To lead a satisfying and morally sensitive life, what should be our attitude toward animals – and, for that matter, toward plants and nature in general? That will be our next big topic.

6

Animals and Nature

> When necessity leads us, we arrogate to ourselves the right to wreak massive destruction, and we can do no other. But precisely because we do stand so clearly under the terrible law of nature, which permits living beings to kill other living beings, we must watch with anxiety that we do not destroy out of thoughtlessness.
>
> Albert Schweitzer

I have treated the topic of human relations with animals and nature in other places.[1] Here, in keeping with our major theme, I want to invite critical thinking and self-reflection on the topic.

It is obvious that animals play a significant role in human life. We eat them and use their products in clothing and shelter. At some times, and in some places even today, we fear them; we, not they, become prey. Some animals work for us, and some are regarded as much-loved companions. Do we have moral obligations to nonhuman animals? If so, what are they?

There is increasing interest also in the human connection to nature. Do we properly (as the Bible suggests) have dominion over the whole natural world? What does this mean? And what might a connection to nature mean in each of our individual lives?

Themes we have already addressed will emerge again in connection with animals and nature: children's literature, teaching responsibility, traditions and socialization, organic habits, being moved by feeling,

---

[1] See, for example, Noddings, *Caring*, 2nd ed. (Berkeley: University of California Press, 2003); *The Challenge to Care in Schools* (New York: Teachers College Press, 1992); and *Happiness and Education* (Cambridge: Cambridge University Press, 2003).

listening and persuading, and coming to understand our own habits of thought.

Animal Companions

In Western societies today, many families have pets. Children who do not have a pet animal often long for one, and "a dog" (or cat or horse) is possibly the most frequent response to the question of what a child would like to receive as a gift. Pets give us much pleasure. There is increasing evidence, too, that pets contribute to our health as well as our happiness. A pet often eliminates or reduces depression in the elderly, and there is now some reason to believe that growing up in a house that contains pet animals actually reduces the likelihood of developing allergies.

Some parents purchase a pet for their children in order to teach them responsibility. It becomes Joey's job to feed and walk Rover or Alice's job to feed Kitty and change her litter box. This is fine if the animal is not treated as a mere means to teach responsibility. If parents really dislike the animal and continually threaten to get rid of it unless Joey and Alice shape up, the experience can be harmful for everyone. Joey may begin to think of Rover as a burden and even a troublemaker. Alice may want to trade the cat for a turtle or a bowl of fish. To reap the benefits of pets, we have to want and enjoy them. A father who says to Joey, "I fed Rover because I knew you'd be getting home late" shows his consideration for both Joey and Rover. At the same time, such expressions remind children that the responsibility they have accepted is serious.

Life with pets, handled considerately, teaches us not only about responsibility in the sense of duty or obligation but also about response-ability. Dogs clearly have the ability to respond with gladness, excitement, fear, affection, curiosity, and pain. Some scientists might want to modify this list by placing *what seems to be* in front of *affection, curiosity,* or *gladness.* There was a day when many scientists even insisted that nonhuman animals do not really feel pain. The screams, howls, and whimpers of creatures in painful situations were thought to be mere machine-like responses.[2]

---

[2] See accounts critical of such thinking in Marc Bekoff, *Minding Animals* (Oxford: Oxford University Press, 2002); David DeGrazia, *Taking Animals Seriously*

The first critical lessons on the human relationship to nonhuman animals center on the responsibility to provide pets with food, affection, and play. Even the smallest children can respond positively to such lessons. Older children, especially those in senior high school, should be asked to think about and discuss the fate of abandoned animals. If a family is moving, is it all right to discard Kitty? If students agree that it is wrong to simply abandon Kitty, is it acceptable to leave her at an animal shelter? What is likely to happen to her there? How many erstwhile pets are euthanized every year in the United States?

This discussion can quickly get emotional and, in a way, that is good. We want students to feel something when they encounter pain, loss, and abandonment. But feeling should not displace rationality entirely. (Another good question: Can feeling and rationality be so separated?) Surely, there are situations in which an animal must be given up. Suppose a family is moving overseas to a country that does not welcome immigrant pets? Suppose Rover is persistently resistant to house training or likes to nip the mailman? Or suppose Kitty refuses to use the litter box? What solutions can students offer to these problems? Which are ethically defensible? Which ask too much and trigger comments such as "It's only a cat, for Pete's sake!"?

What are we to say about people who are irresistibly attracted to baby animals – puppies at Christmas, bunnies at Easter – but lose interest in the adult animals? Do we make a contract of sorts when we take an animal into our home? A deeper question underlies this one. What accounts for the paradoxical behavior of a society that is at once highly sentimental about animals and almost cavalierly negligent in its treatment of them? As we will see, some of this strange behavior may be traced to an unwillingness to examine our relationships rationally. The use of *contract* in relation to animals will also arise again and demand some analysis.

Discussing these questions – exploring all sides, raising new questions, giving examples, seeking evidence, respecting legitimate differences – could make a huge difference in the lives of companion

(Cambridge: Cambridge University Press, 1996); and Jeffrey Moussaieff Masson and Susan McCarthy, *When Elephants Weep: The Emotional Lives of Animals* (New York: Delacorte Press, 1995).

animals and the people who care for them. Such discussions also set the stage for an exploration of still more difficult issues. When, for example, are we guilty of anthropomorphism – that is, of attributing human qualities to nonhuman animals? Jane Goodall describes the reaction of other scientists when she first wrote of chimpanzees having personalities: "I was ascribing human characteristics to nonhuman animals and was thus guilty of that worst of ecological sins – anthropomorphism."[3] Goodall did not back down on her claims, however. On the contrary, she has presented evidence to convince many of us that the so-called higher animals do indeed have feelings and personalities.

It is fair to point out, however, that we are surrounded by examples of anthropomorphism in our stories and films – animals that talk, wear clothes, make detailed plans, and the like. Such stories delight us – especially our children – but they may add to our confusion. Little children served a fish dinner may ask, Could this be Nemo? Most of us reassure our children that Nemo is just a character in a wonderful story, not a real fish. However, I recently heard of a small girl who answered this response with "But still – it was *somebody*!" Conversations about our relations with nonhuman animals begin early. They should be extended and deepened into adolescence. Was the little girl right to think of the fish on her plate as "somebody"? How about the mouse in the pantry? Or a spider in the bedroom? Or a roof rat in the attic? In her foreword to Marc Bekoff's lovely *Minding Animals*, Goodall writes:

> Children learn quickly from those around them.... They are fascinated by animals, but just as they can learn to be kind to them, to accept them as wonderful beings...so too can they learn to treat them as objects, put in the world for the benefit of humans. And they can learn to be cruel.[4]

Goodall is clearly right that children can learn to be either kind or cruel. But what does kindness require of us? And what must we do to avoid cruelty?

---

[3] Quoted in Masson and McCarthy, *When Elephants Weep*, xviii.
[4] Jane Goodall, Foreword, in Bekoff, *Minding Animals*, xii–xiii.

Magic, Sacrifice, and Cruelty

Today we believe that a child who is cruel to animals is in some form of psychological distress, and it is true in our culture that cruelty to animals is often a precursor of antisocial behavior. We properly worry about it. Not so many years ago, however, wanton cruelty was widely accepted and even celebrated. As recently as three centuries ago, animals were sacrificed in horrible ways. James Fraser describes the early modern French practice of burning snakes, cats, or foxes alive at midsummer celebrations. Imagine burning a basket or sack full of live cats! Fraser notes:

> At Metz, midsummer fires were lighted with great pomp on the esplanade, and a dozen cats, enclosed in wicker cages, were burned alive in them, to the amusement of the people.[5]

Amusement? Such a reaction is hard to imagine in today's France (or anywhere else in the Western world). Perhaps, after all, human beings have made some moral progress.

What were earlier people trying to do when they burned animals alive? The most frequent victims were cats, and the cats were thought to be witches who had taken on the feline form. A community got rid of its witches by burning cats. We should remember, of course, that many communities in the period from 1400 to 1700 also burned human beings – usually women – as witches.[6]

Fraser describes the movement of human thinking from magic to religion to science. It is, however, hard to see a sharp, practical difference between magic and religion. Scattering blood on a field in the belief that this will magically produce a better crop is little different from spilling blood to satisfy some supernatural deity who will, in turn, bless the field with fertility. And Fraser himself observes that magical practices and beliefs are often incorporated in religion and persist to the present day. After giving an account of the "savage" practice of eating the body of a deity (perhaps the corn-god) or drinking the god's blood (the vine-god), he writes:

---

[5] James Fraser, *The Golden Bough* (New York: Macmillan, 1951/1922), p. 760.
[6] There are many accounts of the witch craze. See, for example, Joseph Klaits, *Servants of Satan* (Bloomington: Indiana University Press, 1985).

151

Thus the drinking of wine in the rites of a vine-god like Dionysus is not an act of revelry, it is a solemn sacrament. Yet a time comes when reasonable men find it hard to understand how any one in his senses can suppose that by eating bread or drinking wine he consumes the body or blood of a deity. "When we call corn Ceres and wine Bacchus," says Cicero, "we use a common figure of speech; but do you imagine anybody is so insane as to believe that the thing he feeds upon is a god?"[7]

If we have made some moral progress in refusing to be amused by the suffering of cats being burned alive, we may yet have a long way to go in living up to Cicero's expectations. We'll return to related topics in the chapter on religion.

It would be too much to expect high school students to read Fraser's *The Golden Bough*. The lovely old secondhand volume in my possession is inscribed by a previous owner with "started 4/30/75; finished on p. 36, 5/2/75/ too much!" But teachers could certainly share parts of it and invite critical discussion on the topics of magic, religion, and the human relationship to nonhuman animals. They should also raise questions about Fraser's work. What is his reputation today? What objections have been raised about his treatment of "savages" and "primitives"? Are his reports entirely dependable? Are there people today who enjoy the suffering of animals? In what context? Should such practices be unlawful?

People have fed upon gods, but they have also long believed it necessary to feed the gods – to make sacrifices to them. All sorts of creatures have been sacrificed to meat-loving gods: sheep, birds, llamas, oxen, goats, deer – rarely lizards or insects. Barbara Ehrenreich notes that sacrificial animals had to be thought edible.[8] However, although insects, spiders, snakes, and lizards were rarely thought to be sufficiently appetizing as offerings to the gods, they played a significant role in other magical rites. Fraser recounts many stories of practices designed to propitiate insects, rats, and mice so that fields of corn and other grains would be spared.[9] Farmers sometimes even posted written messages warning rats and mice to stay out of their fields.

---

[7] Fraser, *Golden Bough*, p. 578.
[8] See Barbara Ehrenreich, *Blood Rites: Origins and History of the Passions of War* (New York: Henry Holt, 1997).
[9] See the account in Fraser, *Golden Bough*.

The identification of killing with religious duty and celebration has a long, blood-soaked history, but there is another side to the story. Rene Girard writes:

> In many rituals the sacrificial act assumes two opposing aspects, appearing at times as a sacred obligation to be neglected at grave peril, at other times as a sort of criminal activity entailing perils of equal gravity.[10]

Thus, the people sacrificing an animal might ask its forgiveness, pray to its spirit form, or seek some kind of purification after committing the act. It seems likely that this ambivalence toward the ritual killing of animals arose out of a suspicion that animals value their lives and feel pain. It thus seems wrong to inflict needless suffering and death on them. If one believes, as Descartes did, that animals are mere mechanisms devoid of the capacity for pain, he or she would have no reason to feel guilty about carving up or burning a live animal. Thus facts and beliefs are important in fixing or unseating our attitudes. Will increased knowledge about the lives and emotions of animals make people more hesitant to abuse them?

We must consider another possibility in the ambivalent feelings described by Girard. For primitive people, there existed a constant fear that large animals might attack and eat them. People were not only hunters; they were also prey.[11] Oddly, a fear of large animals persists in many young children even today, and parents are often awakened at night by children crying that there is a bear or tiger in their bedroom. This fear may be a genetic legacy of sorts. Do stories have an effect on these fears? What kinds of stories aggravate the fear? Are there stories that reduce or eliminate the fear?

Still another possible reason for human ambivalence about the killing of animals arises from the belief (or suspicion) that a given animal might have been human in a previous life or might be destined for human status in a future life. Then killing the animal comes perilously close to killing a human being.

As students explore the historical connection between humans and nonhuman animals, they will certainly raise the issue of using animals

[10] Quoted in Ehrenreich, *Blood Rites*, p. 33. She cites Rene Girard, *Violence and the Sacred* (Baltimore: Johns Hopkins University Press, 1979), p. 1.
[11] See again Ehrenreich, *Blood Rites*.

for food. Is it cruel to kill animals for food? Views range from the traditional biblical view that gives "man" dominion over all other life on earth to one that rejects all exploitation of animals for food or clothing. Sorting through these views with careful, critical intelligence is a major job. I'll say more about this in the next section on ethical obligations.

There was a time when human beings in climates with cold winters had little choice but to eat animal products. Students may learn much from reading literature that includes the description of meals in medieval and early modern times.[12] With no source of fresh vegetables and great difficulty in preserving such foods, people ate meat – often several varieties at one meal. It was no more cruel for humans to eat deer, rabbits, and quail than it was for nonhuman predators to do so. Unfortunately, the world was created in such a way that its creatures have to eat one another to survive. This fact alone, as we will see in the chapter on religion, has driven some people away from religion.

Today, however, it is possible to sustain human life without eating meat. Should we all become vegetarians? Are we obliged to do so? The discussion here should be reasonable and comprehensive. Could we allow large animals (cattle, pigs, sheep) to live at all if we did not use their bodies for food and other purposes? Are those farmers who raise nonhuman animals automatically guilty of cruelty? Do certain religious laws and rituals aim at keeping the suffering of animals to a minimum even though the animals are killed for food? What are these laws, and are they effective?

It may be instructive at this stage for students to hear the views of the philosopher Arthur Schopenhauer, who saw life as inevitably a chain of suffering. The only escape, Schopenhauer believed, lies in giving up earthly life entirely. This solution could be interpreted as embracing suicide, refusing to reproduce, or simply detaching oneself from any worldly interest whatsoever. The end result under any of these interpretations fully activated would be the end of human life in this world. Most of us refuse this solution. However fraught with suffering our lives might be, we seek to preserve them and find what joy we can. A question arises, then, for those who recommend an end to all animal farming. True, such a decision would put an end to

[12] The novels of Ellis Peters and Zoe Oldenbourg are especially useful on this.

animal suffering. But if the animals themselves had the choice, would they accept life that ends in quick, violent slaughter in preference to no life at all? Are the few months grazing in sunlit pastures, perhaps the joy of mating and giving birth, attractive enough to bear the bitter end? It is clear that human beings, knowing full well that their end will come – perhaps after great suffering – still choose life. What would the animals choose? One can't imagine a greater dilemma.

This set of critical lessons cannot be left at the level of a simple either/or – to use animals for human purposes or not to do so. There are other considerations. Might we consume meat, for example, if the animals whose bodies we use are allowed to live free, healthy lives before slaughter? Students should know that many people who are not vegetarians nevertheless deplore the practices of factory farming. Many of us have given up eating veal, most pork, and lamb, and many seek out free-range poultry and eggs. Are such people simply squeamish? Are they unable to make a clear decision? Or are they as nearly right as we can get in this imperfect world?

Ethics and Animals

When we think about ethics, we usually refer to human conduct in a moral community – that is, in a community of moral agents. Within this community or society – it could be worldwide – all rational people, people capable of accepting moral responsibility, are included. This way of looking at a moral community has raised problems for our treatment of those who are not capable of moral reasoning – infants, the severely retarded, the senile and, of course, nonhuman animals. Philosophers manage to include infants in the moral community by acknowledging their potential to be future members or by granting them protection because they are loved by full members of the community. Similarly, the retarded and senile are often included marginally because of their relationship to moral agents. From some religious perspectives, all human beings are part of the moral community because human life – at any stage, in any condition – is deemed sacred. Religious perspectives seem to give us the clearest, most unequivocal answer to the question of who belongs to the moral community, but the beliefs that underlie the answer are fraught with contradictions and even magical thinking. (More on this in the chapter on religion.)

Where does this leave nonhuman animals? Clearly, they are not able to reason in the way we expect of moral agents, and they cannot behave as moral agents in their interactions with us. But, as mentioned previously, neither can infants, the severely retarded, or the senile. Shall we say, then, that some animals must be included in the moral community because they are loved by some people in that community?

Can we find help for animals in religious perspectives? Historically, the answer to this – at least with respect to Western religion – is no. Peter Singer castigates both Judaism and Christianity for their "thoroughly religious idea that humans are at the center of the moral universe."[13] Although he is correct in much of what he says about religion's insensitive attitude in the past, he entirely overlooks changes that represent a much more compassionate approach. On this, E. O. Wilson is more generous, noting that religious leaders now often interpret the Genesis passage that gives humans dominion over all other life as a call to stewardship. He cites impressive statements on this stewardship from Pope John Paul II, Patriarch Bartholomew I, and Reverend Stan L. LeQuire, director of the Evangelical Environmental Network to support his claim that contemporary religion is no longer supporting cruelty to animals or exploitation of the natural world.[14]

Still, the more powerful approaches did not originate with religious thinkers. The early utilitarian philosopher Jeremy Bentham argued strongly that, in deciding how people or animals should be treated, we should take account only of relevant differences. The color of one's skin, for example, cannot provide a reason for treating human beings as other than fully human. With respect to nonhuman animals, Bentham wrote, "The question is not, Can they reason? nor Can they *talk*? But, Can they *suffer*?"[15] The implication is clear: Creatures that can suffer should not be made to do so unnecessarily.[16]

---

[13] Peter Singer, "Taking Humanism Beyond Speciesism," *Free Inquiry*, October–November 2004, 20.

[14] Edward O. Wilson, *The Future of Life* (New York: Alfred A. Knopf, 2002), pp. 157–160.

[15] Jeremy Bentham, *Introduction to the Principles of Morals and Legislation* (Oxford: Clarendon Press, 1996/1789), ch. 17.

[16] John Rawls, too, makes this claim, albeit briefly. Justice as fairness, for Rawls, applies only to the community of those who can understand the concept of

Notice that if one believes, as Descartes did, that animals cannot suffer, there would be no reason, under Bentham's view – to abstain from those acts that we now know do cause pain. No responsible person would make Descartes's claim today but, as we will see, some – even scientists – stubbornly refuse to recognize pain when it occurs.

Adopting Bentham's perspective does not remove all problems. Which animals experience pain? We know that the so-called higher animals do, but what about reptiles and fish? Does the fish whose mouth is torn by a hook feel pain?[17] What about insects? Does a fly feel pain when its wings are ripped off? Students may decide that it is safest to avoid acts that might cause pain if it is possible to do so.

What should we think, then, about hunting and fishing? It is no longer necessary for most people in Western societies to engage in these activities in order to supply their families with food. However, some people want to keep old skills and traditions alive. Just as some women continue to make quilts, can tomatoes, and make their own blackberry jam, some men want to engage in the activities of their forefathers. One can argue, of course, that quilt-making and canning tomatoes do not cause pain to any creature. But hunters respond that limited, responsible hunting actually improves the health of deer herds by eliminating the surplus population and preventing starvation. Before brushing aside this argument, students should consider the range of options open to humans in our relationship to large animals. If we do not raise or hunt them for food, it will surely be necessary to control their numbers. How is this to be done?

As we explore the issue of hunting, we might return to the earlier discussion of the ambivalence and contradictory emotions that arise in sensitive people when they kill a healthy animal. Speaking strongly against hunting and fishing for sport, Bekoff quotes Richard Nelson on the mixed feelings he experiences on killing a deer:

> I raise the rifle back to my shoulder. . . . I carefully align the sights and let go the sudden power. . . . The gift of the deer falls like a feather in the snow. . . . I whisper thanks to the animal, hoping I might be

justice and enter reciprocal relations, but this does not mean that we have no obligations to those outside the moral community of justice. See Rawls, *A Theory of Justice* (Cambridge, MA: Harvard University Press, 1971).

[17] The answer to this appears to be yes. See Bekoff, *Minding Animals*, p. 143. According to Bekoff, we don't yet know about insects.

worthy of it. . . . Incompatible emotions clash inside me – elation and remorse, excitement and sorrow, gratitude and shame.[18]

What might it mean to be "worthy" of an animal's death? Does it make a difference that the hunter uses the animal for food? Suppose the deer is killed merely for its antlers?

As students consider these difficult questions, they should be reminded that the natural world is "red in tooth and claw." Humans are not the only predators. Our decision not to eat meat would not make the lion, wolf, or coyote vegetarians. Fish would continue to eat one another, and lizards and birds would still gobble insects. The natural world is aesthetically beautiful, but it is ethically deplorable. Indeed, the problem of animal pain is one of the most difficult problems in theodicy – that branch of religious thought that tries to reconcile God's goodness with the existence of pain and evil in the natural world. Many theologians simply avoid the issue, but we will return to it in the chapter on religion.

It seems heartless to ignore the widespread suffering from natural evil, not only that of animals in the wild but also that of humans from storm, accident, and illness. Yet some religious writers continue to do so. They are so determined to defend God's goodness that they deny the evil in the natural world – sometimes even all evil. By way of preview, consider an astonishing suggestion from Huston Smith, who seems to admire the view that there really is no evil:

> If a two-year-old drops her ice-cream cone, that tragedy is the end of the world for her. Her mother knows that this is not the case. Can there be an understanding of life so staggering in its immensity that, in comparison to it, even gulags and the Holocaust seem like dropped ice-cream cones?[19]

My own answer to this is a definite "No," and I turn from such notions in disgust. We do not live in that "immensity." We live finite lives in which our misery is real. Still, instead of cutting the discussion short, I would have students read at least part of Elie Wiesel's *Night*.[20]

---

[18] Quoted in Bekoff, *Minding Animals*, p. 134. From Richard Nelson, *The Island Within* (New York: Vintage Books, 1991).

[19] Houston Smith, *Why Religion Matters* (San Francisco: HarperCollins, 2001), p. 254.

[20] Elie Wiesel, *Night*, trans. Stella Rodway (New York: Hill and Wang, 1960).

After reading this account of human suffering in the Holocaust, they will never be able to think of it as an event comparable to a dropped ice-cream cone. Besides, a good mother replaces the dropped cone for her child.

Acceptance of our place in the natural world can lead us either toward or away from flesh-eating. Many thinkers have argued that since the world was created with prey and predators, there is nothing wrong with our taking part in it as predators. We have already seen that people living in northern climates in earlier times really had no choice but to eat meat. Is the fact that meat-eating is natural sufficient justification for doing so today? Peter Singer argues that animals' eating one another does not justify our doing so, since we have alternatives that they do not, and we are able to think about and seek out those alternatives.[21] It is indisputable that we have alternatives, but our capacity to think in ways unavailable to other animals actually weakens another of Singer's arguments – his argument against "speciesism" – as we will see in a bit.

Before turning to that argument, however, we should revisit a comment made earlier. Observing that law-abiding people no longer burn cats alive in ritual celebrations, I suggested that we have perhaps made some moral progress. Students might add that we have also given up burning humans at the stake and executing them by other horrible methods. Is this moral progress or a mere aesthetic aversion? We know, for example, that humans still burn others alive and scatter their parts in terrible explosions and bombings. Still, it could be argued that good people do not do these things deliberately. These horrors happen unfortunately while we are trying to accomplish morally acceptable aims. Is this convincing? Can suicide bombers make a similar argument?

Fraser argued that humans have progressed in their thinking from the magical to the religious to the scientific. If this progress in thinking implies moral progress, we should be able to claim a reduction in cruelty. But, although we no longer condone the deliberate torture of animals, we allow physical and emotional pain to be inflicted on them by factory farming and by scientists. In the name of science, pain-sensitive animals have been poisoned, shocked, exposed

---

[21] See Peter Singer, *Animal Liberation* (New York: New York Review of Books, 1990), ch. 5.

to extreme temperatures, infected with diseases, cut up, poisoned by radiation, kept immobile, deprived of companionship, blinded, deafened, and deliberately depressed.[22] It is hard to read the accounts of such research without experiencing revulsion. Is this research necessary? Singer claims, "Among the tens of millions of experiments performed, only a few can possibly be regarded as contributing to important medical research."[23] Today, with the availability of computer simulations, cutting up animals to learn anatomy is even less essential. Still, students should think carefully and collect information on the use of animals in medical research. Few of us, after such study, can reject all such research.

Young people are often intensely sympathetic, and critical lessons on our treatment of animals may lead some to extreme positions. Nurtured from infancy on anthropomorphic tales, they may find it hard to see both sides of the issues discussed here. Indeed, one could argue convincingly that, with respect to some practices in research, there is no "other side" to entertain. Unnecessary cruelty should be stopped, and that's that. However, just as they should listen to the arguments in favor of animal farming, hunting, and fishing, students should also listen to the powerful arguments scientists use to defend research on animals. They should be encouraged to exercise critical intelligence in analyzing arguments that have great emotional appeal.

"Speciesism" and Rights

Singer argues against an attitude he calls "speciesism" – "a prejudice or bias in favor of the interests of members of one's own species and against those of members of other species."[24] He writes:

> It should be obvious that the fundamental objections to racism and sexism ... apply equally to speciesism. If possessing a higher degree of intelligence does not entitle one human to use another for his or her own ends, how can it entitle humans to exploit nonhumans for the same purpose?[25]

[22] See the powerful account in Singer, *Animal Liberation*.
[23] Ibid., p. 40.
[24] Ibid., p. 6.
[25] Ibid., p. 6.

Can students, properly aroused against cruelty to animals, find major difficulties in the concept of speciesism? An examination of practical situations may be sufficient to raise doubts about it. If you were driving a car and had to choose between hitting a human child or a deer, what would you do? Is your choice justified or is it a product of unjustified cultural conditioning?

There is an opportunity here to do some real philosophical thinking. Although humans and nonhumans have much in common, it is unlikely that nonhuman animals can produce theories, literature, history, or any of the great bodies of thought that require both well-developed language and logic. As John Rawls points out in a paragraph of great sensitivity:

> A conception of justice is but one part of a moral view. While I have not maintained that the capacity for a sense of justice is necessary in order to be owed the duties of justice, it does seem that we are not required to give strict justice anyway to creatures lacking this capacity. But it does not follow that there are no requirements at all in regard to them, nor in our relations to the natural order.[26]

Rawls goes on to speak against cruelty but notes that we must go beyond a theory of justice to argue the case. Certainly we must go beyond a contract theory, because animals are unable to make contracts as humans do. I asked earlier in this chapter whether, in taking pets into our homes, we enter into a sort of contract with them. If students are attracted to this idea, we must now point out that such a contract is only a way of speaking – albeit a powerful one that, taken seriously, binds us to provide care and affection.

To compare speciesism with racism and sexism is almost certainly a logical mistake. In *Happiness and Education*, I wrote:

> To associate speciesism with racism, sexism, and classism is a powerful emotional move, but it may involve a category mistake. At least in principle, each of the big "isms" applies to all the entities involved – all human beings. We usually think of racism in connection with the oppression of blacks by whites, but clearly, if power relations were reversed, the oppression of whites by blacks would still be racism.[27]

---

[26] Rawls, *Theory of Justice*, p. 512.
[27] Noddings, *Happiness and Education*, pp. 134–135.

Nonhuman animals simply do not have the capacity to participate in justice or in the arguments that support it. They could not be guilty of speciesism by preferring their own species to another. As Bentham pointed out, this is not even the right question to ask. Instead, we should govern our relations according to the capacities of the entities with which we are dealing. Nonhuman animals can suffer pain, love (or something like it), fear, and loneliness, and therefore we should not inflict unnecessary pain, deprive them of companionship, or cause them anguish. The concept of speciesism does not really further this cause. It may, in fact, injure the cause of those who would alleviate animal suffering by suggesting that too much is demanded of us. What reasonable person would *not* put her own species first in moral thought? As in our earlier example of the deer and the child in the road, we naturally and rightly put a higher value on human than nonhuman life. Wilson notes that, in life-or-death conflicts, the priority should be "first humanity, next intelligent animals, then other forms of life."[28] We are bound together in the long run, however, and "a sense of genetic unity, kinship, and deep history are among the values that bond us to the living environment."[29] Even Albert Schweitzer, advocate of reverence for life, whose quotation appears at the beginning of this chapter, admitted sadly that we must destroy some forms of life in order to preserve our own and some others.

Should animals have rights? A similar difficulty arises with this idea. When people claim that animals should have the same rights as people, what do they mean? Surely, they cannot mean that animals should have a college education, be allowed to vote, and choose their own occupation. What then? The only reasonable interpretation of rights with respect to nonhuman animals is that their needs should be considered carefully within the framework of their capacities. We should acknowledge, as we are considering, that we could be wrong about animal capacities, and we *were* wrong on this issue for many years. With new, more dependable knowledge, our responsibilities change. A basic question for critical discussion remains: Does the concept of rights advance the cause of animals or is there a better way to approach the problem?

[28] Wilson, *Future of Life*, p. 133.
[29] Ibid., p. 133.

Some advocates for the well-being of animals do use the language of rights.[30] Others hold that this is a mistake,[31] and Singer argues simply that it is unnecessary.[32] On this, as I argued earlier, Singer seems to be correct; we need only respond compassionately to suffering and refrain from inflicting it. But students should give some critical attention to the concept of rights.

The U.S. Declaration of Independence states that "all men are created equal, that they are endowed by their Creator with certain unalienable Rights, that among these are Life, Liberty and the pursuit of Happiness." These are powerful words, and they have been used to further the cause of equality and freedom in the Western world. But what do they mean, and how many of the founding fathers actually believed them? It is, first, doubtful that the founders – many of them deists – really believed that rights were initially conferred by God; after all, the language of rights rarely appeared in philosophical or legal language until the seventeenth century. Can they have believed that all human beings ("men") are created equal? How, then, could they justify slavery? How could they justify restrictions on voting and land ownership? How could they justify the denial of many rights to women?

The purpose of critical discussion on rights is not to disillusion students about the founders or their statements. It is to encourage thinking on the close connection between rights and needs. When a group expresses a need and has the power to demand that it be met, it may well succeed in establishing a right.[33] Sometimes, too, a powerless group is defended by another that can press for its rights. The powerless group is said to "have a right" even though it is unable to exercise it. The idea here is that the powerless group has a *moral* right of some kind, but to actually have the right in any real sense, the right must be acknowledged by those who have the power to confer it.

---

[30] See, for example, Tom Regan, *The Case for Animal Rights* (Berkeley: University of California Press, 1983).

[31] See, for example, M. Levin, "Animal Rights Evaluated," *Humanist* 37, July–August 1977: 14–15; also C. Perry and G. E. Jones, "On Animal Rights," *International Journal of Applied Philosophy* 1, 1982: 39–57.

[32] See Singer, *Animal Liberation*, ch. 1.

[33] I've argued this at some length in *Starting at Home: Caring and Social Policy* (Berkeley: University of California Press, 2002).

As Singer points out, the language of rights is often used as a short way of acknowledging interests and needs. Indeed, such language has proliferated to the point of occasional nonsense. What can it mean to say that one has a right to walk on the grass, to dress in a slovenly way, to raise one's children in a fundamentalist religion, or to talk back to authorities? Some such claims are established, with considerable disagreement, by law. Others become just a way of speaking – "I have my rights" – when someone wants to have his or her own way.

Despite the ambiguous nature of many claims to rights, most of us would not want to give up the language of rights. The language of the Declaration was pointed to again and again as various groups sought equal protection under the law and the privileges once held by only a few. It was used to condemn slavery and to further the liberty and full participation of women. In 1948, the United Nations adopted the Universal Declaration of Human Rights, which includes civil, political, economic, and cultural rights. This document is continually under interpretation, and so far, its recommendations have been difficult to enforce. Still, as many writers have emphasized, the language is powerful and provides a starting point for vigorous debate.

Throughout the history of debate on rights, much has depended on definitions, beliefs, and knowledge. Slavery was defended on the grounds that black people were not really men as the Declaration and Constitution intended. White women were men in the sense that they were considered to be fully human, but it was thought that, because of their limited and specialized functions, they did not have the capacity to govern. Even today, there are those who insist that women are too emotional to hold political office. (Those who make this silly claim should look more closely at the antics of male athletic teams, road rage, violent crime, and berserk behavior in combat.)

Definitions central to the granting or withholding of rights usually involve a set of beliefs about cognitive, emotional, and moral capacity. Fraser tells us that the people of Darfur once believed that "the liver is the seat of the soul, and that a man may enlarge his soul by eating the liver of an animal."[34] "Women," he writes, "are not allowed to eat

---

[34] Fraser, *Golden Bough*, p. 576.

liver, because they have no soul."[35] Or perhaps the men feared that women might acquire a soul by indulging in liver. Are there people in Darfur or other parts of the world who still believe this? When certain beliefs are shown to be untrue – that black people are not fully human, that women are intellectually (or morally) inferior to men, that animals are not capable of suffering – we are led to rethink our stand on rights. Even if we put aside the question of rights – recognizing rights language as a convenience of sorts – we have to revise our patterns of response.

Careful critical thinkers will probably not reach full closure on the issue of our moral obligations to animals. We may agree that the infliction of unnecessary pain is wrong and thus refrain from eating veal because of the physical and emotional suffering induced by life in a small cage. We may condemn whaling because we now appreciate the great beauty and intelligence of these creatures and because we no longer need the products their bodies provide. We may object to painful experiments on animals for frivolous human interests such as cosmetics. We may reject wearing fur; we no longer need to kill animals for their skins and hides. We may speak out against factory farming and insist that animals raised for food be treated humanely. But it is hard to make final statements on our complicated relationship with animals, and we have to consider the impact of our decisions on fellow humans who depend on farming or ranching as a way of life. At bottom, as we will see in the chapter on religion, this world was not created as a kind, nonviolent place. The horrors of nature have led many thoughtful people – Darwin, for example – to question the Christian description of an omniscient, omnipotent, and all-good God.

So far in this chapter, we have noticed once again how critical issues have a tendency to overlap – to run into one another and force us to extend our thinking. Humans and animals have been connected throughout our common existence. We treasure some animal companions, and most of us – especially as children – enjoy animal stories. We have related to animals through magic, religion, and science. We now see that it is time to subject that relationship to the kind of critical thinking suggested here. It is also time to let the conversations on this topic lead us to a host of related questions, equally critical.

[35] Ibid., p. 576.

The Natural World

It is obvious that human beings are part of the natural world and utterly dependent on it for our survival. If Wilson is right, we also have a genetic attraction to it:

> The phenomenon has been called biophilia, defined as the innate tendency to focus upon life and lifelike forms, and in some instances to affiliate with them emotionally.[36]

Children show this interest early and, Wilson suggests, even go through critical stages in the development of biophilia.[37] In chapter 3, we noted the attraction of children to huts, caves, and tree houses. They also tend to seek out cavelike spots in the natural environment. Gary Nabhan tells us what he learned about children's interest in the great outdoors:

> Over time, I've come to realize that a few intimate places mean more to my children, and to others, than all the glorious panoramas I could ever show them.[38]

Children enjoy hiding in thickets and under shrubs. They like to poke around for worms and bugs. It has been my experience that they also like to learn the names of plants and insects – so long as the fun of learning isn't ruined by some form of test. A central lesson for parents is that much childhood learning takes place informally in the daily give-and-take of conversation in the home, yard, and neighborhood. The learning goes both ways. Like Nabhan, I have learned much by walking around gardens with small children. Closer to the ground and less preoccupied with daily tasks, they see all sorts of things, and then we have the fun of tracking some of them down both by direct observation and in books. We sometimes gather caterpillars and put them in jars with plenty of the vegetation on which we found them, and then watch their progress to chrysalis and eventually to butterfly or moth.

[36] Wilson, *Future of Life*, p. 134.

[37] Ibid., pp. 137–138; see also Peter Kahn, *The Human Relationship with Nature* (Cambridge, MA: MIT Press, 1999).

[38] Gary Paul Nabhan and Stephen Trimble, *The Geography of Childhood: Why Children Need Wild Places* (Boston: Beacon Press, 1994), p. 7.

Attitudes of curiosity and preservation start early, but often they fail to develop. Many adults have an aversion to insects, worms, and caterpillars. I have had to stop adults who wanted to help me in the garden by squashing or drowning the caterpillars that will eventually become black swallowtail butterflies. Children should learn early that appreciative gardeners can share what they plant with other forms of life. Always? Of course not, and another of life's lessons is that sometimes we must use methods that we would prefer to reject. The basic lesson, however, is to strive for a balance and to welcome those creatures that help to preserve it so that extreme measures will rarely have to be invoked.[39]

Striving for balance – in both gardening and thinking – is a major critical task. Wilson provides illustrative stereotypes of environmentalists and "people-first" advocates, and he advises strongly that we drop these adversarial forms; they are not helpful. He writes:

> The first step is to turn away from claims of inherent moral superiority based on political ideology and religious dogma. The problems of the environment have become too complicated to be solved by piety and an unyielding clash of good intentions.[40]

This means that both tree huggers and tree slashers must think more deeply. Our discussions on listening and persuading (chapter 4) become important here. Other people, whose views we may strongly oppose, are nevertheless members of the moral community and must be treated with care and justice. Finding and using language that confers respect while it argues for a point is challenging work. It helps to believe that we may learn from those with whom we differ.

There are also personal preferences and interests to be examined critically. Do you believe that people have an innate tendency to affiliate with nature? What draws you to the natural world? What do you fear in it? Recent studies have shown convincingly that people prefer to live in parklike environments. They want to be near water, and they would like to have an open view. In cities, people try to create

[39] See Eric Grissell, *Insects and Gardens: In Pursuit of a Garden Ecology* (Portland, OR: Timber Press, 2001).
[40] Wilson, *Future of Life*, p. 152.

natural settings with house plants; if they can afford to do so, they live near parks or close to a river.[41]

How do you enjoy the natural world? Some of us like to run or walk in a park; some backpack in the wilderness; some prefer boating and fishing; and some of us get close to nature by gardening. For all of these preferences, there are books to be read, stories to be told, art that attracts us, and serious study if we are so inclined. Children should have wide experience with the natural world so that their thinking has content; that is, they should know what they are talking about and not simply adopt an ideological position. Too often in schools, we either ignore critical issues entirely or fail to provide the experience necessary to apply critical thinking usefully.

It is widely recognized that there is a spiritual aspect to our relation with the natural world. Celia Thaxter, a gardener and writer whose personal life was not a happy one, wrote:

> When in these fresh mornings I go into my garden before anyone is awake, I go for the time being into perfect happiness. In this hour divinely fresh and still, the fair face of every flower salutes me with a silent joy that fills me with infinite content.... All the cares, complexities, and griefs of existence, all the burdens of life slip from my shoulders....[42]

Others report similar experiences walking by the ocean, standing on a mountaintop, looking at the star-studded desert sky, or just breathing in the fragrance of newly mown grass. Belief in the connection between spirit and place is as old as humanity. Socrates, in *Phaedrus*, states that he prefers the city over the countryside because he cherishes the conversations and debates he holds with other city dwellers However, he seems to fall under the spell of the nymphs and other spirits of the lovely place where he and Phaedrus stop to rest. Places, E. V. Walter tells us, have the power to lead our souls, a power Plato called "psychagogy."[43] In extreme conditions, one might experience *topolepsy* – a condition of being seized by a place or its resident demons. Every culture has its tales of sacred places and places

---

[41] See Wilson, *Future of Life*, on this.

[42] Celia Thaxter, *An Island Garden* (Boston: Houghton Mifflin, 1988/1894), pp. 112–113.

[43] E. V. Walter, *Placeways: A Theory of the Human Environment* (Chapel Hill: University of North Carolina Press, 1988), especially pp. 146–150.

haunted by good and evil spirits. American Indian cultures are especially rich in such stories.[44] But we do not need to believe in place spirits to feel the spiritual lift that some places bring to us. It is just a matter of finding such places and cherishing them.

Returning to a topic introduced in chapter 3 – that of organic habits acquired in our first homes – what childhood experiences have influenced our attitude toward the natural world? Returning to our discussion of parenting, what attitudes do we hope our children will develop, and what experiences will we provide to encourage them?

We have identified many critical issues in discussing the human relationship to animals and nature. We live so completely in the midst of these matters that possible issues often escape our attention. Yet, surely, our ethical obligations toward nonhuman animals – if we have any such obligations – should be of deep moral concern. Similarly, to think adequately about the place of humans in the natural world requires us to think about our own personal behavior in and attachment to that world.

I have tried to emphasize connections in this chapter. Topics discussed in earlier chapters on making a home, relating to other people, and parenting arose again here, and some of our discussion points ahead to topics that will emerge in the next chapters. In thinking about where and how we want to live, for example, we may need to ask ourselves what we are willing to give up in order to secure the natural environment we want for ourselves and our children. We will examine that and similar issues in the next chapter on advertising and propaganda. How should we conduct our economic lives so as to preserve the health and beauty of the natural world?

[44] See Keith Basso, *Wisdom Sits in Places* (Albuquerque: University of New Mexico Press, 1996); see also the Navajo detective stories of Tony Hillerman.

7

Advertising and Propaganda

Thrift is now un-American

William H. Whyte, 1957

Billions of dollars are spent every year on advertising by those who want to promote their products, and advertising itself has become very big business. The appeals to consumers through advertising are obviously successful; the business keeps growing. How is it that people are persuaded to buy products they do not need in addition to those that are needed? And how is it that they are persuaded by advertising tactics that consist mainly of messages that no one really believes?

In this chapter, we will discuss the rise of a consumers' republic – one that defines citizenship more in terms of consumption than of civic action.[1] We will see that the topic is loaded with complexities: Should we buy only what we really need, or is it our duty as citizens to maintain the economy by buying as much as we can? Has mass consumption furthered or hurt the American work ethic? Does advertising serve an educational purpose? How do advertising and propaganda overlap? What should be the school's role in educating consumers? Why has pharmaceutical advertising grown so rapidly, and should we believe what is advertised? Should we regard ourselves as a free society because there are no legal constraints against our speaking out, or should we worry that we are enslaved by a huge system that manipulates our opinions?

---

[1] See Lizabeth Cohen, *A Consumers' Republic* (New York: Vintage Books, 2003).

Becoming Consumers

Schools today usually provide some form of consumer education, although – with the current concentration on college preparatory academics – the trend may be toward less of it. The emphasis in such courses is usually on comparative shopping, learning how to evaluate the safety of products, how to manage credit, and the application of some basic mathematics. In addition, social studies text books often include small sections on changes in how people shop (from general stores to malls and mail order catalogs), consumer protection movements, amounts spent on advertising, and changes in consumer spending. These are all worthwhile topics.

However, when we consider the enormous changes that consumerism has made in our conception of citizenship, we might well renew our worries about what the schools do *not* teach. At least implicitly, there is some consideration of changes in the role of citizen embedded in discussion of the Industrial Revolution. The wide availability of manufactured and mass-produced goods had mixed effects. On the one hand, people no longer had to make their own clothing or raise their own animals or hunt for food. On the other, they had to take on unfamiliar jobs to pay for the new products. History is filled with stories that describe the hope, excitement, disappointment, and alienation that these changes caused. Moving from an agrarian to an industrial society brought enormous changes to ordinary lives.

Becoming a consumer, then, can be interpreted in several ways. In today's schooling, it usually refers to students' gradual transition from childhood to adult, responsible forms of buying. In a historical sense, it may refer to a whole society – what is sometimes called the *consumers' republic*. I am using it to launch deeper questions about the individual's role as consumer: How is it that I am defined primarily as a consumer from infancy on? How far should I resist advertising campaigns? How far is it possible to engage in such resistance?

As we saw with other critical topics – childhood, the psychology of war, parenting, socialization, homemaking, our relationship to animals and nature – there is a substantial history that is barely touched in schools. Students should learn, at least, about the deliberate attempts of business and advertising to influence the daily lives of citizens.[2] They should hear about planned obsolescence and the role of dissatisfaction in enticing buyers. They should hear Simon Patten's words written in the early twentieth century:

> It is not the increase of goods for consumption that raises the standard of life ... [but] the rapidity with which [the consumer] tires of any one pleasure. To have a high standard of life means to enjoy a pleasure intensely and to tire of it quickly.[3]

There is also a scholarly sort of critical lesson to be learned from my use of this passage. In Joel Spring's book, where I found this quotation, Patten is referred to as an "ideologue of consumerism,"[4] but what exactly does this mean? Patten was also deeply worried about the alienation induced by the move from rural life to city life. The question arises of whether he was advocating, explaining, or trying to make the best of the new consumerism. One gets an entirely different view of Patten in reading Scott Nearing's almost worshipful account. Nearing took an advanced course in economics with Patten in 1903 and found him to be a responsive and caring teacher, one who followed students "out into the world, gave them advice, got them positions."[5] He was apparently a brilliant teacher. None of this would prevent him from also being an ideologue. But he was interested in social work as well as economics. Nearing remarks, "He was concerned with the underdog: the poor, the ignorant, the untrained, the misfits, the delinquents."[6] Perhaps it was this concern that led Patten to find something good about the new consumerism. In her brief mention of Patten's work, Lisbeth Cohen refers to Patten's argument that "the realm of consumption and leisure offered workers ... more satisfaction and pleasure than degrading industrial work and provided the nation with the chance to build a more cohesive society free of class and ethnic divisions."[7] The critical lesson for students is that we should be slow to judge a writer, work, or position on the basis

---

[2] Ibid.; see also Joel Spring, *Educating the Consumer-Citizen* (Mahwah, NJ: Lawrence Erlbaum, 2003).

[3] Quoted in Spring, *Educating the Consumer-Citizen*, p. 55.

[4] Ibid., p. 55.

[5] Scott Nearing, *The Making of a Radical: A Political Autobiography* (White River Junction, VT: Chelsea Green, 2000), p. 23.

[6] Ibid.

[7] Cohen, *Consumers' Republic*, p. 10.

of one short quotation. Another lesson that follows right on its heels is that social/economic life is so enormously complex that we rarely find the pursuit of a pure or perfect position fruitful. Compromises are required. We must ask what motivates a compromise and what is accomplished by it.

Closely related to the continual search for pleasure – whether we approve of it or not – is the tendency to accept manipulation by advertising. By and large, people do not *believe* advertising messages, but they are nevertheless *moved* by them. They are moved by pictures, catchy phrases ("I'd walk a mile for a camel"), and associations. A product endorsed by a celebrity usually does well on the market. Do people really believe that the celebrity has tried and enjoyed the product? A product advertised during big sporting events is likely to appeal to watchers who identify with the players as well as the fans. Cars advertised in pictures with beautiful women appeal to some men. Images of speed and control appeal to others.

Learning something about the history of advertising, students may ask themselves how we have allowed ourselves to be so easily led. Can't we just say no? Here we should return to our earlier critical lessons on socialization. An individual might well say no to a particular product, but advertisers do not aim their messages at individuals. They aim to manipulate – or, some would say, educate – whole classes or groups. They study children, teenagers, young mothers, sports-loving men, the elderly, and so on. Thus, although I might well resist ads for a particular style of clothing, my resistance weakens when everyone around me – everyone, that is, like me – adopts the style. Teenagers should find this easy to understand. How do they treat the kid who is courageous or indifferent enough to resist current styles?

In *The Sunday Philosophy Club*, the main character, Isabel, listens to a young man defending his spiked facial piercings. When he says that the piercings show he "doesn't care," Isabel responds:

> "Don't care about what?" "About what people think. It shows that I have my own style. This is me. I'm not in anybody's uniform." Isabel approves, "Uniforms are not a good idea" but then adds, "Unless, of course, you have donned another uniform in your eagerness to avoid uniforms."[8]

---

[8] Alexander McCall Smith, *The Sunday Philosophy Club* (New York: Pantheon Books, 2004), p. 195.

The young man acknowledges this possibility but makes clear that he has *chosen* this "uniform." Is that how most of us justify our choices – teenagers in their own special way? This discussion may extend the analysis of socialization processes and also reopen the door to serious study of how we treat one another.

Students may ask whether people have ever intervened in this vast program of manipulation. The answer is "yes," but with mixed results. In the 1930s, for example, women's organizations were prominent in demanding safer food, fairer prices, and more dependable household goods. Men, too, were involved in consumer protection and product testing organizations.[9] They had considerable success – so much, in fact, that business struck back, accusing many of these groups of anti-American, subversive, and even Communist leanings.[10] At the same time, business launched powerful new advertising campaigns designed to convince workers that the surest way out of the Depression was to spend as much as possible, thereby fueling the economy. Since then, periodically, political leaders in the United States have made similar arguments.

From the start of the consumer age, some people worried about the moral effects of consumerism on the citizenry. In particular, what would happen to the Protestant work ethic? When people no longer had to raise their own food, make their own clothing, and hack out their own livelihoods, would they become soft and succumb to hedonism? Simon Patten argued that there was nothing to worry about on this score. With so many new goods continually emerging, people would work harder than ever to secure them.[11] The Protestant work ethic was safe. Still, to assuage such fears, early advertisers emphasized the usefulness of products, not the pleasures they might bring. It might be worthwhile to have students compare early ads with today's highly hedonistic "because you deserve it" ads.[12]

Moral concerns continued to arise. Would people begin to define their citizenship almost entirely in terms of their consumership?

---

[9] See the comprehensive account in Cohen, *Consumers' Republic*.
[10] Ibid.
[11] See Spring, *Educating the Consumer-Citizen*, pp. 2, 96.
[12] Ibid.

Would that lead to a decline in civic participation? Has it, in fact, done so?[13]

Another moral concern was created by new technologies. When movies became popular, there was widespread concern about their effect on the morals of viewers. Educational and religious leaders counseled control; they even recommended censoring both movies and radio programs. On radio, educators wanted more educational programming but, on this, commercial interests carried the day, arguing more or less accurately that people wanted entertainment, not lessons. Both film and radio, however, complied with the expressed desire to keep programming clean in language, unshakably against crime, and thoroughly American.[14]

Self-censorship codes did not, however, dampen advertising. Children's programs advertised cereals in which various prizes were hidden or could be obtained by submitting a certain number of box tops. Further, by establishing hero worship as a legitimate goal of their programming for children, advertisers ensured themselves of large audiences and the support of powerful organizations that promoted Americanism. Such programming could also be easily adapted to teens and adults and would play an important role in national propaganda.

Some of the concerns expressed in the 1930s and 1940s strike us as amusing today. Criminals were not to be portrayed as attractive; the good must always win in the end; there must be no swearing, no sexually titillating scenes, and Americanism should always be promoted. The Catholic Legion of Decency, the American Legion, and the Hays Office all watched over these concerns diligently.

Because some of these concerns seem prudish and parochial to us today, does that mean that we should have no concerns about the effects of consumerism, media, and advertising on our moral life? Do many young people spend too many hours watching TV and playing

---

[13] Many such critiques have appeared in the past two decades. See, for example, Mary Ann Glendon, *Rights Talk* (New York: Free Press, 1991); Robert Putnam, "Bowling Alone: America's Declining Social Capital," *Journal of Democracy* 6, 1995: 65–78; Michael Sandel, *Liberalism and the Limits of Justice* (Cambridge: Cambridge University Press, 1982).

[14] See the lively and informative account in Spring, *Educating the Consumer-Citizen*.

video and computer games?[15] How does this expenditure of time pose a moral threat? Does the pervasive violence in the media have an undesirable effect? What about the explicit sex in movies and the widespread availability of pornography on the Internet? All of these questions are important to address, but so is the basic question of the overall effects of consumerism and advertising on our personhood. Are we becoming, en masse, human impersonators, as Maslow feared?

Person, Citizen, Consumer

We should surely be concerned with the possible loss of personhood and individuality. But, equally, we should think about the changed concept of citizenship. Lizabeth Cohen expresses concerns about this and notes that many writers – especially "communitarians" – have warned against the dangers of sacrificing community and public goods to consumer goods.[16] Regretfully, she writes:

> As much as I might prefer a public sphere inhabited by voting citizens rather than demanding consumers, by public-spirited taxpayers rather than self-interested tax cutters, and by communities committed to cooperation with neighbors rather than wrapped in isolated localism or destructive competition, I fear that such an alternative hopelessly resides in an unregainable past – if it ever existed at all.[17]

To avoid hopelessness, the solution may be to increase the standards for both roles – for both citizen and consumer. If this is possible, it is a good example of the kind of compromise thoughtful critics must consider. Cohen suggests:

> Taking nothing for granted, we can hold our mandate to be both citizens and consumers to the highest standards of democracy, freedom, and equality, dwelling not so much on whether we should

---

[15] For the numbers on this, see Donald F. Roberts and Ulla G. Foehr, *Kids and the Media in America* (Cambridge: Cambridge University Press, 2004).

[16] Cohen mentions Michael Sandel and Christopher Lasch. I would add Glendon, *Rights Talk*, Alasdair MacIntyre, *After Virtue* (Notre Dame, IN: University of Notre Dame Press, 1981), and Charles Taylor, *Sources of the Self* (Cambridge, MA: Harvard University Press, 1989).

[17] Cohen, *Consumers' Republic*, p. 409.

simultaneously be citizens and consumers but rather accepting that, like it or not, we are.[18]

The question for Cohen, then, is what sort of republic will this citizen-consumer build?

But can't we just reject the consumer role? As they study and think critically about the machinations of advertising, students may become angry. Feeling duped, they may swing from being avid buyers – "wanting things" – to critics who would like to turn back the clock and start over. Why not retreat to Walden Pond, as Thoreau did? But even Thoreau did not stay permanently at Walden. As Cohen has pointed out, we are consumers, like it or not. Still, students might like to read the story of Scott and Helen Nearing, who, in recent times, came close to the ideal of a minimal consumer/active citizen.[19] Committed to a sustainable way of life, they built their own home, grew most of their own food, and continued an active political life promoting equality, frugality, and deep concern for the environment. Could everyone live as the Nearings did? Students might at first react by demanding, "Why not?" But remember that the Nearings did have to purchase some things and, when they were invited to lecture, they were dependent on modern modes of travel. When they wrote books, they needed editors and publishers. We all live in an interdependent world, and there is no escaping that.

We could try a form of religious escape. Isaiah Berlin describes this choice as a "retreat to the inner citadel."[20] Under this choice, I reject all worldly desire and give up anything by which a tyrant or evil agent might force me to comply with his will. Berlin writes:

> This is the traditional self-emancipation of ascetics and quietists, of stoics or Buddhist sages, men of various religions or none, who have fled the world, and escaped the yoke of society or public opinion, by some process of deliberate self-transformation that enables them to care no longer for any of its values, to remain, isolated and independent, on its edges, no longer vulnerable to its weapons.[21]

---

[18] Ibid., p. 410.

[19] See Scott Nearing and Helen K. Nearing, *Living the Good Life* (New York: Schocken Books, 1970). See also the extensive list of other readings in Nearing, *Making of a Radical*.

[20] Isaiah Berlin, *Four Essays on Liberty* (Oxford: Oxford University Press, 1969), pp. 135–141.

[21] Ibid., pp. 135–136.

Students attracted to the ascetic possibility (there might be a few) should read more extensively on it. How often and in what ways are those who have retreated still dependent on others? And what should we feel about those left behind? Finally, we might ask whether it is really possible, by total self-abnegation, to be safe against tyrants and evil agents. It may be that truly evil people can *always* find a way to get us to betray those we love and the beliefs we hold.[22] And what sort of life have we achieved if we succeed in coming to a point where nothing in this world matters to us?

Deciding, as virtually all of us must, to live as fully as possible in this world, how do we achieve a desirable balance between our roles as citizen and consumer? It is reasonable to look at ads critically and ask which products we can eliminate from our list of needs or wants. Of those that remain, why do we need or want them? If we buy and use them, will any harm be done to us, to other people, or to the environment? Making and comparing lists of items that would be rejected might be interesting. Would you buy, even if you could afford it, a recently advertised dog bed for $6,000? What else might an animal lover do with $6,000?

Smart consumers want to be sure that their purchases are worth the money and that they are adding something useful or beautiful to their acquisitions. They ask not only whether an item is useful but how it fits into their set of possessions and, more generally, into their lives. They do not want to buy with enthusiasm and "tire of it quickly." They ask whether certain expenditures may prohibit future plans – a new car today, less for education tomorrow. They learn that well-advertised brands may not represent the best buys. And they learn to plan and to budget. For smart consumers, frugality is not un-American; it is just smart.

Citizen-consumers are interested in more than their own welfare. They are interested in the well-being of both the natural environment and their social communities. Are there good arguments, for example, against buying sport utility vehicles (SUVs) and other large vehicles that use too much gasoline and perhaps further pollute the atmosphere? How have advertising campaigns encouraged consumers to damage the environment and weaken their own prospects

---

[22] Consider the evil O'Brien in George Orwell's *Nineteen Eighty-Four* (New York: Harcourt, Brace and World, 1949).

for affordable fuel in the future? It is fairly easy to find arguments against off-road vehicles (why not hike?), leaf blowers (what happened to nice, quiet rakes?), speed boats on tranquil lakes (try a canoe!), and a host of other products to which people are attracted through advertising for convenience or thrill.

But sometimes a source of environmental damage is so familiar, so fully accepted in a community, that we don't even think about it. Consider the large green lawns that are so popular in the United States. When trees are cut down to make room for housing developments, the quickest and easiest replacement is lawn, but lawns require upkeep. Tons of water, pesticides, and fertilizers are poured onto lawns, and lawns must be cut regularly to preserve their appearance. If the lawn is large, it will probably be mowed by a power mower – a gas guzzler that spews pollution into the atmosphere. Ted Steinberg points out, "One hour spent mowing grass is the equivalent in terms of emissions produced to driving a car 350 miles."[23] Sara Stein tells us that because a lawn "is cut off from the life support systems on which the natural survival of grass depends, ... it must therefore remain permanently in intensive care."[24] Ads then urge us to buy herbicides "to kill the clover and, having thus purged the patient of this source of nitrogen," they tell us to pour on lime to "enhance the uptake of petrochemicals [to keep] the grass growing fast...."[25] This fast growth, in turn,

> forces it to sprout still more blades, more rhizomes, more roots, to become an ever more impenetrable mat until it is what its owner has worked so hard or paid so much to have: the perfect lawn, the perfect sealant, through which nothing else can grow – and the perfect antithesis of an ecological system ... an acre of grass where not even a honeybee could find a flower to sip.[26]

Advertisers played a large role in urging American homeowners to install and maintain large lawns. Steinberg refers to Frederick Taylor (the efficiency and standardization expert well known to educators) and his experimentation with lawn grasses. The hope was to produce a grass "made in [the] way that an article is manufactured in a machine

---

[23] Ted Steinberg, *Down to Earth* (Oxford: Oxford University Press, 2002), p. 222.
[24] Sara Stein, *Noah's Garden: Restoring the Ecology of Our Own Back Yards* (Boston: Houghton Mifflin, 1993), p. 136.
[25] Ibid., p. 137.
[26] Ibid., pp. 138–139.

shop or factory."[27] One of the Scott company's ads told homeowners, "Your lawn is the symbol of peace at home and its proper maintenance a vital factor in keeping up morale."[28] The producers of lawn seed, fertilizers, pesticides, and equipment made it virtually a patriotic duty to maintain a beautiful lawn.

A well-kept lawn is beautiful, however, and students would be right to point this out. Some people do nurture lawns because of their beauty, but many more maintain them because of social pressure. If everyone else in the neighborhood has a green, well-clipped lawn, you had better have one, too. Michael Pollan tells the story of his father's refusal to maintain a proper lawn and the outrage this induced in his neighbors. He also writes of a Thoreau scholar who tried persistently to defend his right (is there such a right?) to nurture a wildflower garden instead of a lawn in his front yard. He was ordered to mow it or face a fine. "When last heard from," Pollan writes, "his act of suburban civil disobedience had cost him more than $25,000 in fines."[29]

Open, continuous, and well-manicured lawns were even promoted as Christian and democratic, in contrast to the English and European custom of building walled gardens. It may strike students as odd that *democratic* should mean in this case – and in many others, it turns out – the "same." It was thought simply undemocratic to take an individualized approach to one's relationship with nature – at least insofar as that relationship extends to front yards. Pollan remarks:

> And just as the Puritans would not tolerate any individual who sought to establish his or her own back-channel relationship with the divinity, the members of the suburban utopia do not tolerate the homeowner who establishes a relationship with the land that is not mediated by the group's conventions.[30]

Like Steinberg and Stein, Pollan refers to the enormous influence of advertising in producing a nation of lawn lovers. All three remind us, too, that most of the turf grasses advertised and sold in the United States are not native to this climate and require, therefore, considerable maintenance. "America now has some 50,000 square miles of

[27] Quoted in Steinberg, *Down to Earth*, p. 222.
[28] Ibid., p. 222.
[29] Michael Pollan, *Second Nature* (New York: Delta, 1991), p. 68.
[30] Ibid., p. 72.

lawn under cultivation, on which we spend an estimated $30 billion a year...."[31] We have incurred enormous costs and sacrificed ecological health, and we have done this more or less mindlessly at the urging of advertisers.

Are there no aesthetically pleasing alternatives to lawns? There are, and students should learn enough natural history to enable them to do some planning along these lines. Sara Stein gives detailed plans for converting suburbia into a lovely landscape of woods, thickets, shrubs, and meadows. She also provides instructions for bird houses, shelters for toads, and watering places for butterflies.[32] We can't all live on properties large enough to include a pond, but – if we have a yard at all – we can learn how to include shelter for native plants and animals. Students can also learn how to introduce nonnative plants responsibly to their gardens. Eric Grissell, in teaching us about insects and their ways, notes that balance – creating "an ecological community" – should be our objective.[33] Responsible experimentation and faithful stewardship are required.

Another alternative is to live in a densely populated city. Oddly, although cities generate more pollution and use more energy per square foot than residential alternatives, their per capita damage is far lower. David Owen points out that spreading people out increases the ecological damage that can be done by each household – more cars, swimming pools, lawns and their enormous cost, septic tanks, huge rooms and houses to heat. He notes:

> [I]f you made all eight million New Yorkers live at the density of my town, they would require a space equivalent to the land area of the six New England states plus Delaware and New Jersey.[34]

Is Owen right on this? Check the arithmetic. But, in any case, there are drawbacks to living in cities. Childhood asthma is often rampant in large cities, space is at a premium, and contact with nature may be limited to public parks and the few house plants one can sustain. Are there alternatives besides the city or suburb? Students may want

---

[31] Ibid., p. 66. Presumably, the figure is even higher now.

[32] See Stein, *Noah's Garden*; also Pollan, *Second Nature*.

[33] See Eric Grissell, *Insects and Gardens: In Pursuit of a Garden Ecology* (Portland, OR: Timber Press, 2001).

[34] David Owen, "Bright Green Mega-City," *New Yorker*, Oct. 18, 2004: 112.

to study the village concept and consider its feasibility for a growing population.

Wherever they decide to live, they should be prepared to think hard about the influence of advertising. There should be a liberating effect of learning to think critically about advertising and, more generally, the patterns and effects of socialization. When we decide that a certain convention – such as a large lawn – is not only unnecessary but possibly even harmful to the ecological community, we may become free to try alternatives. Similarly, when students learn how they are manipulated by big-name brands and pressed further by their peers who have accepted their own manipulation, they might feel suddenly, wonderfully free to seek out attractive, less expensive, little-known brands. The odds are against this happening, however, because our schools – the very institutions that should be promoting critical thinking – actually sustain and even invite advertising.[35] To those of us who believe that critical thinking is central to education, this way of operating is a dereliction of duty.

Students should also be asked to consider whether people who think the way I've been writing here are un-American and anticapitalist. What would happen if we all ignored most advertising, watched only those TV channels (public television) that show little advertising, boycotted popular brands, rejected social pressures to buy products or adopt customs we regard as ecologically or personally unsound? Would our economy collapse? It might. But what does that tell us about the road we are on? Is it possible to develop a sustainable way of life? These questions should find a permanent and central place in the school curriculum.

Another aspect of the problem is that of becoming a genuine, whole person, and this has been the main focus of the present book. Must we all resign ourselves to being human impersonators, or can we develop ourselves as semi-independent thinkers? Notice that I say *semi-independent* because I have already argued that we are necessarily interdependent and that an appreciation of interdependence at every level is essential to our human future. But a recognition of interdependence does not reduce the importance of critical – semi-independent – thinking. Precisely *because* we are physically, socially,

[35] See Alex Molnar, *Giving Kids the Business: The Commercialization of America's Schools* (Boulder, CO: Westview Press, 1996).

182

and emotionally interdependent, we must think critically and develop a network of intelligent heteronomy. We are necessarily consumers, but we want also to be good citizens and fully developed persons.

Health and Advertising

In the week before I started writing this section, the drug giant Merck withdrew its best-selling painkiller, Vioxx – used in treating arthritis – because of its association with increased heart attacks and strokes. There is some doubt now about other brand-name drugs in the same molecular family, although their makers have been quick to assure the public that their products are safe. Critical consumers should be skeptical of these assurances.

Since 1997, when drug companies were allowed to market their wares directly to consumers, the number of ads for drugs has increased dramatically. Merrill Goozner notes, "Ad spending tripled from $788 million in 1996 to $2.5 billion in 2000."[36] Spending on advertising and the demand for more and pricier drugs are synergistic; each encourages the other. Goozner writes, "Retail spending on prescription drugs doubled in just five years, reaching $154.5 billion in 2001.... Utilization [the primary source of the increase] soared."[37] If we ask why so many more people are demanding brand-name drugs, the answer is almost certainly "advertising." Critical thinkers would not be so easily swayed. But government plays a role here, too. Perhaps the U.S. government should forbid the advertising of pharmaceuticals directly to consumers. Many other nations, including Canada, already forbid such advertising.

The American public seems to be convinced that there is a drug for every ailment and complaint. Kids who were once described as itchy or restless are now given drugs to make them sit still in school. People who are too lazy to exercise look for weight reduction drugs, and the alarming increase in childhood obesity has not so far induced a clear call for more effective physical education in schools. To make matters

---

[36] Merrill Goozner, *The $800 Million Pill* (Berkeley: University of California Press, 2004), p. 233; for other critiques of the pharmaceutical industry, see Marcia Angell, *The Truth About Drug Companies* (New York: Random House, 2004); also Jerry Avorn, *Powerful Medicines* (New York: Alfred A. Knopf, 2004).

[37] Goozner, *The $800 Million Pill*, p. 232.

worse, the people who should be exercising are more often watching television, where they see more ads for junk foods and miracle drugs to control the effects of indulging in them. An oddity in all this is that when people turn to illicit drugs for similar purposes – to feel better, to escape depression and boredom, to get smarter, stronger, or sexier – they become criminals.[38] Yet, far more people are killed by mistakes (by both doctors and patients) in the use of prescribed drugs than by illicit drugs.

Advertising for drugs is somewhat different from other advertising, because consumers are more likely to believe these ads. In this sense, pharmaceutical ads are more like national propaganda than the innocuous (if bothersome) ads for vacuum cleaners, detergents, cosmetics, and romantic vacations. It is often belief born of desperation and/or hope. But the immediate belief rests on a deeper one – that the marvels of drugs have contributed enormously to well-being and longevity. The truth is almost certainly that improved sanitation and living conditions have been the primary causes of increased longevity. The single most important move we could make globally to increase health would be to ensure a safe water supply for all of the world's people. An even deeper belief underlies the one in miracle drugs; many Americans believe that they have the best health care system in the world. Easily verified facts show that, on the contrary, the United States lags behind several nations in longevity, infant mortality, access to health care, and other indicators.

Critical thinking is relatively scarce in the general population, but many people suppose that it is regularly exercised by those in science and medicine. This belief also influences the vulnerability of consumers to advertised drugs and advice on health care. In addition to feeling unwell, consumers are made to feel guilty if they do not use the latest medicines.

It would seem the duty of educators to reduce this vulnerability. One way to do this is to acquaint students with historical accounts of stubborn resistance to evidence in the scientific world. Students need to know that the world of science and medicine is not populated entirely by wise, critical thinkers. We have already mentioned

---

[38] See my discussion in *Starting at Home: Caring and Social Policy* (Berkeley: University of California Press, 2002).

the story of Ignaz Semmelweiss and puerperal fever. In J. G. Farrell's
The Siege of Krishnapur (set in 1857), two doctors argue heatedly
over the causes of cholera. The story, although fiction, is historically
accurate on this debate and includes a summary of the evidence that
showed conclusively that cholera is spread through contaminated
water. Yet, as in real life, listeners decide to believe the doctor they
like best – never mind who has the best evidence and argument.[39]
Students might enjoy reading of other cases in which passion and
likeability have overridden logic and evidence, at least for a time.[40]

Scientific organizations try to hold their members to the highest
standards of truth and objectivity, but violations occur. Under pressure to succeed and to acquire prestige, some scientists have engaged
in questionable practices, and a few have even fabricated research.[41]
Moreover, scientific research is sometimes misreported or even sup-
pressed by political interests.[42] It might be argued that students –
especially those not preparing to major in a science – would be better
served by courses that look carefully at the sociology and philosophy
of science than at the basic structure intended to prepare them for
the next science course.

Besides learning to use critical thinking in questioning the thinking of others, there is another point to be made here. There is much
to be learned from literature. Not everything must be taught specifically and learned in preparation for appropriate responses on tests.
The Siege of Krishnapur, for example, also includes discussion of
England's involvement in the opium trade, its disastrous experience
in the Crimea, and its imperious treatment of India's intellectuals
and its religions. Students who read this book with pleasure might
also want to read E. M. Forster's *A Passage to India*, and younger students might still enjoy the much earlier works of G. A. Henty such

---

[39] See J. G. Farrell, *The Siege of Krishnapur* (New York: New York Review Books, 2004/1973).

[40] Mathematically inclined students may enjoy the account of the feud between Wallis and Hobbes in Hal Hellman, *Great Feuds in Science* (New York: John Wiley & Sons, 1998).

[41] See Horace Freeland Judson, *The Great Betrayal: Fraud in Science* (Orlando, FL: Harcourt, 2004).

[42] See the account in Richard Lewontin, "Dishonesty in Science," *New York Review of Books*, Nov. 18, 2004: 38–40.

as *With Clive in India*. Then there are the poems of Kipling, biographies of Gandhi, and essays by Orwell. We often make the mistake of supposing that critical thinking is learned systematically and by being exposed only to the side that turned out to be right historically. Thus objections might be raised to Henty's books and to some of Kipling's work. But it is often salutary to read stories of likeable people whose beliefs and attitudes we now question, even despise. Such experience should lead us to consider our own beliefs and attitudes and subject them to careful scrutiny.

When we are teaching material related to health, we should try to avoid preaching (which doesn't seem to help) and instead provide a wide range of vicarious experience through literature and historical accounts. Students may be astonished to learn, through fiction such as Caleb Carr's *The Alienist*, that drug use (especially opium derivatives) was rampant in New York City in the early twentieth century. As they study the long, and often violent, history of humankind's experience with drugs and mind-altering substances, students should be led to think critically not only about their own lives but also about major social issues.

One important related social issue is society's treatment of drug use and abuse. Surely, reasonable people will agree that it is undesirable for people to harm themselves through the use of drugs. Should society, then, make a list of illicit and/or controlled drugs and make it a criminal offense to buy, sell, or use them? Reasonable people may well differ on this question, but anyone advancing an opinion should be prepared to answer a further question: Has the criminalization of drugs made things better or worse?[43] This is a hard question to answer because we do not have a clear way to decide how much worse things might be if the drug laws were amended. One of the few related efforts that might shed some light on the problem is the experience the United States had with Prohibition. It seems clear that Prohibition made the situation worse, not better, but there are those who would argue even against this judgment. There are some questions, however, that should be considered as we attempt to decide the issue. What proportion of the prison population is serving time for

---

[43] See the essays in Jeffrey A. Schaler, ed., *Drugs: Should We Legalize, Decriminalize or Deregulate?* (Amherst, NY: Prometheus Books, 1998); also Steven Wisotsky, *Beyond the War on Drugs* (Buffalo, NY: Prometheus Books, 1990).

drug offenses? How much does this cost the society in terms of lost productivity and expenditure for the support of prisons? What effect has the war on drugs had on police officers and, more generally, on the whole system of law enforcement? If money were diverted from the legal control of drugs to drug education, would matters improve? What evidence can we find for this? As in all critical lessons, all sides should be heard and encouraged to improve their arguments.

If we review what has been said so far in this section, we might well ask, What are we teaching here? Is it history? Geography? Science? Literature? The best answer is offered by Whitehead in his argument for what should constitute the school curriculum, "and that is Life in all its manifestations."[44] Taking Whitehead seriously, we are forced to the conclusion that the present school curriculum is obsolete – dangerously so.

As we encourage students to think critically about advertisements for legal drugs and about the medical profession itself, we must again strive for balance. Well-informed people have a justified respect for modern medicine, even as they question its representation in popular ads. High school students are only gradually acquiring the cognitive tools to handle ambiguities and extreme positions.[45] We do not want them to reject the medical establishment, but neither do we want them to be manipulated by greedy people who have invaded that field. It is not easy to be well informed in a land awash in advertising and propaganda.

One health-related issue does not even require critical thinking, just common sense. It should be a straightforward matter of integrity that schools should not allow commercial companies to force television ads on the captive audiences of students in schools.[46] Similarly, schools should not permit the sale of sodas and other junk foods on their premises. Schools have to set an example. They should not preach one story and act out one contrary to it.

---

[44] Alfred North Whitehead, *The Aims of Education* (New York: Free Press, 1967/1929), pp. 6–7.

[45] See Kieran Egan, *An Imaginative Approach to Teaching* (San Francisco: Jossey-Bass, 2005).

[46] For an account of this widespread and shameful practice, see Molnar, *Giving Kids the Business: The Commercialization of America's Schools.* See also Juliet B. Schor, *Born to Buy: The Commercialized Child and the New Consumer Culture* (New York: Scribner, 2004).

In attending to questions of health in schools, more attention should be given to the study and critical appraisal of lifestyles. Both individual and social issues should be addressed. What constitutes a healthy lifestyle? What forms of recreation benefit individuals, the larger society, and the ecological community? Should we, for example, reject individual sport vehicles on land or sea that pollute the air and water? Should there be a law against such use, or would such a law be an infringement of personal rights? Are there recreational activities that are just as much fun but cause less harm to the environment? How is it that people became so interested in these sports?

It might be worthwhile for students to keep a health log for several weeks – entering what they eat and when, how long they sleep, how much time they spend on television and computer games, and how much and what sort of exercise they get. In addition, they might be asked to watch CNN for an hour and record how many ads for medications appear. Then they should watch MTV and note the content of ads there. Who is being targeted and for what? As part of a unit on health practices, students might also interview their parents and grandparents (or people of similar ages) and ask whether present popular medical ads mention ailments that were not discussed twenty, thirty, or forty years ago. Is it possible that drug advertisements have invented diseases? Are people led to believe that they need medication when actually they do not? Perhaps elders need a new form of health education, too.

Along the same lines, an analysis of health-related items and ads in the local newspaper could be undertaken. In my own local paper on the morning I was writing this, many such items appeared. On the front page, a well-dressed man was being arrested for blocking traffic near the site of President Bush's scheduled campaign talk. The purpose of his protest, and presumably of his blocking traffic, was to advocate the legalization of marijuana for medical use. On a later page, a large ad placed by the New Jersey State Police offered "up to $1,000" for information on the growing of marijuana. Students should consider the ethical implications of such an offer. What sort of person would report his or her neighbor in order to "earn" $1,000? One can predict a lively argument on this. On one side is the clear fact that growing quantities of marijuana is illegal; those who do it commit a crime.[47] On the other side is worry about a law that makes good people bad and bad people even worse. If real harm is being done, should not good citizens report the harm without expectation of monetary reward? Is it time to rethink a practice that so demeans citizens?

In the same edition of the paper, there were ads for alternative medicine, getting thin through hypnosis, the relief of menopausal symptoms, breast care, cholesterol control, and dental implants. There were two ads from law firms offering to help victims of Vioxx to sue Merck. And there was a very interesting story about a group bringing suit against AstraZeneca for exaggerating the benefits of Nexium. The complaint sounds like one well documented by Goozner. It is alleged that AstraZeneca knew it would lose money when patent protection for its best-selling drug, Prilosec, expired. It is alleged that it therefore produced and marketed a substitute, Nexium (a slightly changed version of Prilosec), to maintain its dominance in the treatment of heartburn. Whether or not this claim is shown to be true, it is only one of a multitude of such stories.[48] It is enough to drive one to antidepressants. But this would not be a wise move because some of those drugs are now being blamed for an increase in suicides among teens. Well, perhaps, we elderly folks can still get a lift from them. Until...?

What makes us so gullible, and why do we exercise so little control over the many efforts to socialize us? In *Tuesdays With Morrie*, an old professor tells his former student:

> "Here's what I mean by building your own little subculture.... I don't mean you disregard every rule of your community. I don't go around naked, for example. I don't run through red lights. The little things, I can obey. But the big things – how we think, what we value – those you must choose for yourself. You can't let anyone – or any society – determine those for you."[49]

---

[47] See Michael Pollan's account of the vigor of new strains of marijuana and the harsh penalties for growing it. His description of the universal desire for changes in consciousness is also both interesting and useful: Pollan, *The Botany of Desire* (New York: Random House, 2001).

[48] See the account in Goozner, *The $800 Million Pill*; also Angell, *The Truth About Drug Companies*, and Avorn, *Powerful Medicines*.

[49] Mitch Albom, *Tuesdays with Morrie* (New York: Broadway Books, 2002), p. 155.

Propaganda

There is a clear connection, induced by advertising techniques, among "Americanism, free enterprise, and consumerism."[50] Those who have launched groups for consumer protection and sometimes even organized boycotts have been accused of un-American behavior. Similarly, those who advocate a fairer distribution of wealth are often branded as Communists – even when they reject that association and clearly favor modified forms of socialism or liberalism. The use of epithets such as *un-American*, *Communist*, or *pinko*, cut short the need to provide a cogent argument. Today, even *liberal* is hurled as an epithet. One wonders how the people who so easily condemn liberalism feel about child labor laws, social security, the forty-hour work week, unemployment benefits, voting rights, bank insurance, and school desegregation. Critical thinkers insist that complaints and epithets be backed by arguments and evidence.

The most dangerous advertising is that which demands belief, not simply a rush to buy. As pointed out earlier, much advertising has little to do with belief; it just attracts customers. But medical advertising urges belief. It suggests that well-informed consumers will buy the advertised products *because* they are knowledgeable and believe in the efficacy of what is advertised. Similarly, propaganda aims to strengthen a belief system or sometimes to install a new one. With hindsight, we can easily identify propaganda. When we are in its presence, we are too often inclined to believe what it says.

In our earlier discussion of the psychology of war, we made a start at discussing propaganda. Here, that discussion will be extended. The basic idea is to engender doubt and reject unfounded certainties. One can reject an ordinary advertisement with little risk. At worst, one who does so may be considered "out of it." Among teenagers, this risk is sometimes considerable. Rejecting medical advertisements carries the further risk that, if illness occurs or worsens, one will be chastised for failing to be well informed. Not only does the person who ignores such ads risk illness (it is suggested), but she may be accused of bringing the problem on herself. Doubting or challenging propaganda is even more risky, for now a doubter may be labeled unpatriotic, even treasonous.

---

[50] Spring, *Educating the Consumer-Citizen*, p. 126.

World War I saw a huge propaganda campaign launched in the United States. "The campaign had two aspects. On one hand, it promoted patriotism. On the other hand, it manufactured hate."[51] Before the war, President Wilson warned:

> Once lead this people into war and they'll forget there ever was such a thing as tolerance. To fight you must be brutal and ruthless, and the spirit of the ruthless brutality will enter into the very fiber of our national life, infecting Congress, the courts, the policeman on the beat, the man in the street. Conformity would be the only virtue, and every man who refused to conform would have to pay the penalty.[52]

Wilson was right on this. When the United States entered the war, however, he did little to reduce the tensions and ruthlessness he had predicted. I have already discussed some of the home-front atrocities that came with full mobilization and the horrors experienced by young men on the battlefield. Except in rare cases (World War II was one), the majority of citizens must be convinced by propaganda that they should support a war. In World War I, this involved painting Germans as brutal, almost monstrous, Huns. German soldiers were not portrayed as scared kids conscripted for war – very like their counterparts in Britain, France, and the United States – but as helmeted monsters. Every German atrocity, and of course there were some, was grossly exaggerated, and those committed by the Allies were covered up or excused. As we have already seen, citizens at home – in England, the United States, or Germany – were more rabidly attracted to the war than were the soldiers who knew its full horror.[53] Propaganda was employed to whip up enthusiasm, and manipulation of news from the front was used to maintain interest and faith in the war.

It is not only future soldiers, then, who must be prepared for the psychological changes that come in wartime. All citizens are affected, and propaganda is used on both sides. It is widely recognized that Saddam Hussein used propaganda ranging from the crude and obvious to more sophisticated forms. People were forced to praise

---

[51] Gerald A. Danzer, J. Jorge Klor de Alva, Larry S. Krieger, Louis E. Wilson, and Nancy Woloch, *The Americans* (Evanston, IL: Houghton Mifflin, 2000), p. 571.

[52] Quoted in ibid., p. 572.

[53] See again some of the literature cited in chapter 2, especially Robert Graves, *Goodbye to All That* (London: Folio Society, 1981/1929), and Erich Maria Remarque, *All Quiet on the Western Front* (New York: Fawcett Books, 1982/1929).

him, and stories of that praise appeared as part of the propaganda in daily newspapers.

But the United States also conducted a campaign of propaganda and control during the first Gulf War. Iraqi atrocities in Kuwait were exaggerated, and it seems now that some stories were simply fabricated (the one about Iraqi soldiers removing babies from incubators, for example). On the other hand, the massacre of retreating Iraqi soldiers at Mutla Ridge was kept as quiet as possible. Only a few broke the silence and revealed what had happened there. Jonathan Glover notes, "The television pictures of the massacre are said to have influenced President Bush's decision to stop the war before the public pleasure in victory turned into revulsion."[54]

Those in government have to be concerned with public opinion – with public pleasure and revulsion. In 1922, Walter Lippmann published *Public Opinion*.[55] It presented a devastating critique of contemporary American democracy. Lippmann noted that the American people, for the most part, had neither the time nor the inclination to study social problems and draw rational conclusions. Further, they had no direct access to the events requiring analysis. A democracy of the whole people required what Lippmann called "omni-competent" individuals, and such people do not exist. Certainly it is a myth that they exist in large numbers.

John Dewey had to agree with large parts of Lippmann's argument, even though he rejected Lippmann's elitist solution. He saw that the public on which true democracy depends had not yet taken form. Open and rational dialogue had not yet been developed. Dewey wrote, "The belief that thought and its communication are now free simply because legal restrictions . . . have been done away with is absurd."[56] Public opinion, uninformed by inquiry and dialogue, is actually harmful to democracy:

> [A] belief in intellectual freedom where it does not exist contributes only to complacency in virtual enslavement, to sloppiness,

---

[54] Jonathan Glover, *Humanity: A Moral History of the 20th Century* (New Haven, CT: Yale University Press, 2000), p. 172.

[55] Walter Lippmann, *Public Opinion* (New York: Free Press, 1965/1922). For a solid summary of Lippmann's analysis, see Robert Westbrook, *John Dewey and American Democracy* (Ithaca, NY: Cornell University Press, 1991).

[56] John Dewey, *The Public and Its Problems* (New York: Henry Holt, 1927), p. 168.

superficiality and recourse to sensations as a substitute for ideas: marked traits of our present estate with respect to social knowledge.[57]

Much the same can be said about the public today. Thinking ourselves free – continually bragging about our freedom – we are manipulated, as Lippmann and Dewey said, by unreflective habits, slogans, pictures, symbols, and stereotypes. Dewey expressed the hope that art (both literature and the visual arts) might function to encourage intelligent thought, a hope expressed again by Maxine Greene.[58] As we saw in chapter 2, that idea had been explored by Virginia Woolf and more recently (and with less hope) by Susan Sontag. But the art that has actually worked to "manufacture consent" has not been the sort envisioned by Dewey, Greene, Woolf, and Sontag. On the contrary, it has been bound up inextricably with advertising and propaganda – appealing to myths, national pride, and questionable visions of the heroic. Even newspapers, Lippmann pointed out, depend on advertising for their survival, and thus they are influenced by the opinions of those who want to advertise their products. The advertisements, in turn, influence consumers who exert even more pressure on the papers to conform to public opinion.

The scientific approach to inquiry on political/social issues that Dewey saw as a requirement for the establishment of true democracy has been employed instead in developing methods for the control of public opinion. The success of these methods is demonstrated in the enormous success of advertising as an industry. It is reflected, too, in political advertising, in strategies designed to induce belief and allegiance without inquiry and critical thinking.

Election year 2004 was filled with such attempts. Some were frighteningly similar to the methods Orwell warned us about in *Nineteen Eighty-Four*.[59] Legislation that allowed increased logging was referred to as the "Healthy Forests Re-forestation Act"; an act that permitted industry to spew more pollution into the atmosphere was called the "Clean Air Initiative"; and a law that encouraged schools to retain children in a grade or prevent their graduation if they failed

---

[57] Ibid., p. 168.

[58] Maxine Greene, *The Dialectic of Freedom* (New York: Teachers College Press, 1988).

[59] See Orwell, *Nineteen Eighty-Four*.

a statewide test was named the "No Child Left Behind Act." To argue against such legislation requires one to analyze and show persuasively that the names or labels do not describe the intended results. This is difficult to do in a political climate in which people are persuaded (or charmed) by the words themselves. How can you be against healthy forests, clean air, or no child left behind? But advocates of these acts should also want true dialogue. Perhaps they can advance arguments that will show the labels to be correct or, if not literally correct, in the best interests of the environment, the society, or children in the long run. Such crucial dialogue is cut short by the use of attractive labels and slogans. We seem to have entered the linguistic world of newspeak and doublespeak.

The fault does not lie with one political party; this dangerous shift in the use of language has been bipartisan. Citizens seem delighted to hear that their country is number one, their health system the best in the world, their soldiers the bravest and best equipped, their teams the strongest, their living conditions the most advanced, and so on. Many seem to believe even that all our children can be above average. If a political candidate makes the mistake of saying something unappealing, the simplest remedy is to deny having said it. Even when proof to the contrary is readily available, repetition of the denial seems to win the day. (We will see in a bit how the denial can be technically true if one omits or adds a word.)

One of the most troubling events of that political year was the scenario generated by the so-called Swift Boat ads against John Kerry. Critical thinkers need not have been Democrats or Kerry supporters to find the ads and their results worrisome. Instead of analyzing and explaining, the Kerry campaign simply emphasized Kerry's wartime heroism. It did not offer a logical defense of Kerry's anti-war activities. Among the unfortunate results of this exchange is an important one for educators: it will now be even harder for conscientious high school teachers to discuss the Vietnam War honestly with their students. Surely, it would be wrong to label all Vietnam veterans as war criminals; Kerry certainly did not do that. However, the acts described by Kerry in 1972 have been well documented by historians, journalists, psychologists, military people, and poets. Atrocities were widespread. That shameful war should have been revisited with careful analysis in the current debate. Why did otherwise good young men do such terrible things? What effects could be traced to the use of language such as *free fire zones* and *body counts*? Why were soldiers rewarded for committing acts they themselves found despicable? Why did so many common soldiers feel that their leaders had betrayed them? And perhaps most important of all: How will we learn to solve our problems without war if we are unwilling to face the truth about the wars already waged? Kerry could have defended his antiwar record as vigorously and honestly as he did his war record, but doing so effectively would have required an audience capable of critical thinking. We seem no closer to having such an audience now than we were in the days of Lippmann and Dewey.

In examining the language used in propaganda and in politics more generally, students should be invited to study the status of the word *liberal*. The word is now often used as an epithet, and few politicians are willing to stand up and say, "I'm a liberal and proud of it!" Certainly, there is a legacy to be proud of. As noted earlier, many social reforms are properly credited to liberals. The object of the discussion is not to produce a whole new generation of liberals but rather to see why the label was once a proud one. Students should also explore the possibility that liberals have somehow gone wrong. They should examine the charges that liberals are guilty of loose spending, big government, weakness on crime, and high taxes. Is there evidence to support these charges? Does this explain why the label has fallen into disrepute? The message to students is again: listen, analyze, think.

Students might profitably spend some time analyzing techniques that obfuscate by omitting, adding, or concentrating on single words. A case in point is President Clinton's notorious "It depends on what the meaning of 'is' is." Denials – "I never said that" – are technically correct if a single (even unimportant) word differs from the original statement. It is also worth mentioning that this exasperating technique is frequently used by children and teenagers in response to parents' questioning. For example: "Did you eat all the cookies this afternoon?" "No!" ("I ate some this morning. Or I hid some away for later"). Such statements are honest to the letter but, in spirit, maddeningly dishonest. Responses of this kind are close to the *mental reservation* that was both widely used and widely castigated by the Catholic Church. The idea was to escape whatever ill fate threatened by saying something not entirely true but adding (silently, of course) the strict truth as a mental reservation. Thus, God at least "heard" the truth.[60]

More closely related to propaganda is the so-called noble lie used by rulers and others in government. A noble lie is told in a good cause – sometimes to protect a government's strategic plans but often because it is believed that those governed cannot cope with the truth.[61] It is probably impossible to avoid entirely the noble lie in political life, but it is a dangerous ploy in real democracies or in societies that see themselves as democracies. Imagine, for example, what might happen if it were learned that a president of the United States had actually betrayed the country. It might well be better for the country if that president were removed from power but his perfidy covered up. The necessity to avoid social upheavals, loss of faith in government, and even civil war explains why the noble lie is still employed. However, its use and the widespread knowledge that it is used also helps to explain why conspiracy theories develop and linger for years after questionable events. Citizens know that their leaders lie to them, but they find it difficult to know exactly which statements are lies, and they are reluctant to charge a prominent figure who should merit trust with lying. In the case of assassinations or major disasters, it is predictable that suspicions of lying will be aroused. Indeed, most thoughtful citizens would prefer a lie that preserves the fabric of their society to the truth that might tear it apart.

Critical thinkers must learn to analyze and assess arguments, to resist slogans, and to probe their own psyches when they find themselves irrationally moved. But they must also learn to think carefully about possible effects both on themselves as individuals and on the groups to which they have given allegiance. They should be able to resist manipulation, but they should also be able to make commitments.[62] When we come to believe that our society and its leaders are mired in dishonesty and corruption, we may become cynical, even paralyzed. It is perhaps the hardest job of education to produce

---

[60] The practice has a long and fascinating history. See Sissela Bok, *Lying: Moral Choice in Public and Private Life* (New York: Vintage Books, 1979).

[61] See ibid. Also Plato, *Republic*, trans. B. Jowett (Roslyn, NY: Walter Black, 1942).

[62] The worry is that critical thinkers may become bystanders, unwilling or unable to make commitments. See Jane Roland Martin, "Critical Thinking for a Humane World," in *The Generalizability of Critical Thinking*, ed. Stephen P. Norris (New York: Teachers College Press, 1992), pp. 163–180.

people who will think but not give up working rationally and passionately for a better life, a better world.

In this chapter, we have discussed matters central to critical thinking – becoming rational consumers, advertising, the effects of advertising on health, and a range of topics associated with propaganda. Throughout the discussion, we have been concerned with the effects of manipulation on both individuals and the larger society. What should I believe? Whom should I believe? What will be the effects of my accepting or rejecting certain claims? These are among the difficult questions that critical thinkers must ask.

We are not just consumer-citizens, however. We also contribute to our society as workers. Indeed, it is our gainful work that makes it possible for us to be consumers. How should we make our living?

8

Making a Living

> To find out what one is fitted to do and to secure an opportunity to do it is the key to happiness.
>
> John Dewey

M any of the things we've discussed so far come together in this chapter. Everyone wants to make enough money to live comfortably, but what does this mean? Should one aim to make millions? Or is this a questionable aim for a moral life? Should one aim at a profession in order to achieve high status? Should one aim at a profession even if one would prefer to run a fishing boat, do carpentry, dance, or play the trumpet? Are there (legal) jobs that a socially conscious person should decide to avoid? The big questions: What kind of work will contribute to my becoming a whole person and also contribute to my community, and what are my chances of finding this kind of work?

Realistic Expectations

When inner-city fifth or sixth graders are asked what they want to be when they grow up, a surprising number say that they will be doctors or lawyers. Sometimes that answer persists into secondary school but, more often, it disappears and is replaced by an awful nothingness. Teachers, who have been strongly warned not to have low expectations for poor children, generally praise the initial response. Why shouldn't poor kids expect to enter the professions?

This is a difficult question – one filled with pitfalls for critical thinkers. On the one hand, no considerate person should want to destroy the idealistic hopes of children, and the easy way out is to be politically correct and praise the high expectations. On the other, it seems dishonest to encourage highly unrealistic expectations. If children are doing poorly in school and have no knowledge of what it takes to become, say, a physician, it seems almost irresponsible to encourage the expectation. Indeed, a suspicion arises that teachers accept such statements to prove that *they* don't have low expectations for their poor students. Critical thinkers must find a sympathetic way to talk about realistic expectations – a way that is supportive and constructive but not delusional.

Very like the discussion of linguistic patterns in poor families, frank discussion of occupational expectations can arouse anger in those who are strong and generous advocates of the poor. Certainly the advocacy is admirable, but some forms of advocacy verge on the romantic. Critical thinkers must be willing to look critically at even those positions they admire.

What is wrong with having high expectations even if those expectations are unrealistic? The danger is that, when it becomes clear that an expectation is unrealistic, there will be no reasonable aspiration to replace it. Boys whose hopes are built totally on a career in basketball (such as those in *Hoop Dreams*) sometimes drift into unemployment, an unstable succession of low-wage jobs, or crime when those hopes are shattered. The critical task is to guide kids in a way that doesn't ridicule high expectations but provides strong backup for secondary aspirations.

The story of upward mobility in America includes Horatio Alger rags-to-riches tales, but the main narrative has been one of generational steps. Children with working-class origins go to college and become teachers, nurses, social workers, police officers, and technicians. Their children may become doctors, lawyers, ministers, and professors. There is nothing sacred or obligatory about this stepwise mobility, and there are inspiring accounts of exceptions. There are also many stories of downward mobility. However, gradual, generational mobility has much to recommend it. It tends to preserve family and community ties and to provide role models that ease the transitions.

How might we use this historical account to advise students? Surely, we should not tell a student that she isn't "good enough" to be a doctor – that instead she should plan to be teacher. That is wrong on all counts. Only the most serious, dedicated students should be encouraged to teach, and educators should not support the pernicious hierarchy of occupations that denigrates teaching. Perhaps the first critical task is to challenge the hierarchy that supposedly describes upward mobility. But, given its wide acceptance, a sensitive teacher might well point out to a fine student from working-class origins that the road to teaching is somewhat easier to follow than that to medicine. For example, one can enter a state college or spend one's first two years at a community college, get a fine education, and not put a tremendous strain on the family budget. Further, the social transition will be easier; it usually does not cause a feeling of stark difference in social background.[1] We need not discourage really fine students from applying to top-ranked private institutions, but we should help them to understand the dramatic differences they will encounter. Not only will they be faced with demanding academic requirements, but they will also meet a whole new world of social expectations. Even their most admirable organic habits may be challenged and shaken.

There are several general social lessons to be considered in this discussion. Why, for example, do we hold a hierarchical view of occupations? Why, for example, do we think of it as better to be a lawyer than a teacher? Why is it better to be a teacher than, say, a construction worker? The quick answer from most students will be "money," but teachers can show that salaries do not always conform to hierarchical status. "Prestige" is another likely answer and, again, teachers should be ready to press the "why" question. Why should teachers have higher prestige than construction workers? Why, in fact, is the status of teachers relatively low in the United States? These and related questions should be explored critically, but the existence of the hierarchy should not be denied. We don't want to jump from unrealistic expectations on one level to a denial of reality on another.

One aim of exploring occupational hierarchies is to encourage genuine appreciation of economic and social interdependence. All students should become generously aware of how dependent we are on the work of others. In chapter 3, we discussed some utopian schemes

---

[1] The true story told by Ron Suskind illustrates the great difficulties experienced by poor minority students at Ivy League schools, but it also provides evidence that "skipped generation" mobility sometimes works. See Ron Suskind, *A Hope in the Unseen* (New York: Broadway Books, 1998).

designed to equalize occupational standing and to remove the burden of unattractive labor from the shoulders of the unfortunate few. These ideas should be revisited with a practical question in mind: Which, if any, of these ideas could actually be employed in today's society?

Again, all students – and not just those living in city or rural poverty – should be aware of the complex condition we call *poverty*. Can it be cured by education? This is a question that has been investigated in some depth by critical theorists in education. Michael Apple, for example, warns us that "the assumption that we will find long-term answers to the drop-out dilemma and to the realities of poverty and unemployment by keeping our attention within the school, is dangerously naïve."[2] If everyone completes high school, who will work at the low-wage jobs so many now perform? Will the market respond by raising these wages in order to get workers or will the wages of those at the next higher level go down? If our society could, under pressure from the market, pay the lowest wage earners at a higher rate, why not do it now and help people to achieve some economic stability and respect?

Students, especially economically poor students, should be helped to understand that the messages they receive in school about the value of education are only half true. It is true that an individual's economic life chances, on average, will be improved by more years of schooling. It is not true that poverty in general can be eliminated by education. The structure of the larger society either supports or discourages poverty.[3] When we advise students that they can "escape" poverty by diligent study, we should remind ourselves that a moral society should do its best to eliminate poverty so that there would be no need to escape it. Then more fully human reasons to continue one's education might arise.

Students should also understand that it is not easy for individuals to escape from poverty. Many people living in poverty work very hard – sometimes holding two or even three low-wage jobs. All sorts of difficulties keep them on the edge of destitution or even homelessness.

---

[2] Michael W. Apple, *Cultural Politics and Education* (New York: Teachers College Press, 1996), p. 70.

[3] See Apples's persuasive argument and figures comparing the numbers who live in poverty in the United States with several European nations in Apple, *Cultural Politics and Education*.

Lack of an address, for example, can make getting any job difficult; a low-wage job can make it hard to find decent housing or any housing at all.[4] Lack of benefits causes minor illnesses to become major financial emergencies. And the poor are regularly exploited by check-cashing fees, a lack of public transportation that necessitates the use of taxicabs, exorbitant rents, and higher prices in local stores.

The children we call *at risk* – those we urge to escape poverty through schooling – also suffer from lack of role models. In listening to inner-city teachers, I've heard repeatedly that many young people have no one in their lives who works at a regular job. These kids have no idea what it takes to get and hold a job or what it would be like to have one. Although we often hear about the poor parents who are working two jobs and the teenagers who put in long hours at part-time jobs and come to school exhausted, we rarely hear this other part of the story. In situations such as these, it is important for students to hear from people who work at decent jobs. The few heroic stories of inner-city kids who have made it into Ivy League schools may not be so important in inspiring hope as the everyday accomplishments of people who have made a first working-class step toward upward mobility. Teachers, especially those from working-class backgrounds, can serve as daily models of what can be done with a good education. Instead of preaching, exhorting, and threatening, teachers should spend time explaining how they got their education and what it means to them. The task of career advising cannot be left entirely to guidance counselors. Students need to know that people with backgrounds roughly similar to theirs can succeed in school.

Promoting school success is crucial. Good teachers help students to succeed by providing a variety of ways in which requirements can be satisfied. The present standardization movement, requiring all students to meet the same standards in academic subjects, will almost certainly work against the very students it purports to help.[5] The

---

[4] See Barbara Ehrenreich, *Nickel and Dimed* (New York: Metropolitan Books, 2001).

[5] There is considerable evidence to support this contention. See, for example, Linda Darling-Hammond, "From 'Separate but Equal' to 'No Child Left Behind': The Collision of New Standards and Old Inequalities," in *Many Children Left Behind*, ed. Deborah Meier and George Woods (Boston: Beacon Press, 2004), pp. 3–32.

best teachers build on students' interests and talents; they do not try to force everyone into the same mold. If students repeatedly fail at school subjects, they not only turn away from school but may also develop an aversion to anything resembling training or retraining, and they may fear authorities of all sorts. David Shipler has described in convincing detail how adults who failed in school are afraid to sign up for retraining programs of any kind.[6] After ten or twelve years of failure, why should they suppose that training of any kind will yield success? I'm not arguing here that students should simply be *given* some symbol of success; the success has to be earned. This is what critical thinking educators must figure out: How can I help this student to *earn* success? What might that success look like? Surely, it does not have to be success on a standardized test. Just as success in adult life takes many forms, it should be possible to succeed in school in more than one way.

Discussion of realistic expectations should be factual, open, and respectful. Kids should know that much of what they hear in schools is economic propaganda. It is not true, for example, that most jobs in the next two decades will require higher education. To the contrary, most job openings will be in occupations that do not require a college education. Why do educators persist in passing along this false message? Students should be prepared, however, to think about continued learning. Instead of forcing everyone into traditional academic courses, we would do better to give some eleventh and twelfth graders strong vocational preparation and opportunities for post-secondary education other than college. What we encourage students to do should have a basis in facts and real possibilities. Our respect should be real, and the methods we use to help students succeed should be matched to their needs. Mike Rose comments:

> It is interesting that virtually all of our current discussions of academic standards are framed either in the quasi-technical language of assessment and accountability or as a lament for diminished performance. There could be a whole other discussion of standards in a language of expectation, respect, and democratic theory.[7]

---

[6] See David K. Shipler, *The Working Poor: Invisible in America* (New York: Alfred A. Knopf, 2004).
[7] Mike Rose, *Possible Lives: The Promise of Public Education in America* (Boston: Houghton Mifflin, 1995), p. 414.

Expectation, respect, and democracy, yes. Help each student to find out what he or she is fitted to do and to assess the realistic chances of getting such an opportunity. This means not only granting respect to the choices of individual students but also teaching for a wider appreciation of interdependence. But, although respect for all honest work should be encouraged, romantic views of labor should be avoided. It is easy to speak of the "dignity" of all labor but, as we saw in chapter 3, not all labor can rightly be called dignified. Some labor is backbreaking, smelly, and unhealthy. It is this sort of labor that utopians would like either to eliminate or to distribute equitably over the entire population.

Work also lacks dignity if the one performing it is compelled by circumstances to do this work instead of that for which he or she is – by nature or training – really fitted to do.[8] Many new immigrants have found themselves in this unhappy situation – trained physicians and teachers, for example, forced to work at menial jobs, sometimes temporarily, sometimes permanently. These are individual tragedies of which students should be at least aware, and they should be reminded that it is not the menial work itself that lacks dignity but the loss of what one is fitted to do.

I want to emphasize once more that the development of expectations should be a cooperative task. Students have ideas, interests, and longings, but they need facts, encouragement, and some assurance that the choices they are considering are real possibilities. The cooperative construction of expectations requires sensitive and continuous interaction. Teachers who know their students well must contribute to this task. It can't be done by specialists working with test scores and brief statements.[9]

Thinking about An Occupation

There's nothing wrong with high expectations so long as they are balanced by realistic ones that are also satisfying. There's nothing inherently wrong with daydreaming either. Remember that Gaston

---

[8] See Herbert Kliebard, *Schooled to Work: Vocationalism and the American Curriculum 1876–1946* (New York: Teachers College Press, 1999).
[9] See again Suskind, *A Hope in the Unseen.*

Bachelard wrote that the house is a shelter for daydreaming – that "the values that belong to daydreaming mark humanity in its depths.... It [daydreaming] derives direct pleasure from its own being."[10] Daydreaming gives us pleasure, and it can also be used to escape boredom but, at its best, it leads to productive thinking. There is evidence that some workers even prefer routine, boring jobs because such jobs free them to daydream. E. V. Walter writes, "The major unacknowledged activity in classrooms and factories, then, is daydreaming."[11]

How can daydreaming lead to productive thinking? I'll give a personal example that might be useful. I rarely read science fiction, but one night – having run out of my recreational mystery novels and too tired to tackle professional reading – I started a novel about interplanetary colonization. One colony was so far from Earth that it took about twenty-five years to reach it. People making the round trip would find their friends on Earth fifty years older, although they themselves would have aged only about two years, thanks to the astonishing relationship between time and speed. Putting the book down, I began to think about how many spaceships, each carrying 50 to 100 frozen passengers, would be required to establish a colony of about 5,000 over a year. Assuming that the new planet has fine air, good soil, pure water, and attractive weather, the colonists will not have to live in an artificial environment. I thought about the kinds of workers the colony would need. (There are, by the way, many exercises that ask questions of this sort – what to take on a wilderness expedition, whom to include on an interplanetary mission, etc.) But the question that turned me from daydreaming to productive thinking was this: How would we educate children in such a colony? I won't go into the details of my thinking here, but my musings led to the confirmation of a suspicion that has nagged me for some time: The contemporary school curriculum in America is obsolete – very nearly useless for current life. In a colony many light years away, we would not dare to squander our educational efforts on such material.

---

[10] Gaston Bachelard, *The Poetics of Space*, trans. Maria Jolas (New York: Orion Press, 1964), p. 6.

[11] Eugene V. Walter, *Placeways: A Theory of the Human Environment* (Chapel Hill: University of North Carolina Press, 1988), p. 13.

My musings also led directly to reflection on Jane Martin's interesting *Cultural Miseducation*.[12] Martin is rare among educational theorists in worrying about cultural conservation; that is, she is concerned with ways in which we can preserve the cultural knowledge that has grown enormously. Clearly, no one person could master all of it or even a significant part. The only way to preserve it is to be sure that some segment of the youth population learns something substantial about each component we want to save. That means teaching different things to different people, not persisting in the outdated practice of forcing the same curriculum on everyone. But are there not some things – of the sort I've been discussing in this book – to which all students should be exposed? Can we do this and, at the same time, provide a variety of curricula? A whole world of reflective and productive thought has been generated by what started out as daydreaming.

The purpose of my example is to trigger discussion and reflection on our habit of daydreaming. I made assumptions about the nature of the planet, the number of colonists, and the availability of spaceships. How often do we make assumptions to give the next phase of daydreaming a foundation in pseudo-reality? Do some people daydream without regard for such foundations? Do some of us regularly put the daydream "on pause" in order to check facts and keep things as reasonable as possible? Do others of us fear that such fact checking would reduce or destroy the pleasure sought in daydreaming?

At what point does daydreaming turn into productive thinking? My daydreaming about a space colony was converted into productive thinking when I started to wonder how children would be educated in a technologically sophisticated but entirely isolated community. Teachers should share experiences in which daydreaming led them to productive thinking, and students should be encouraged to reflect on their own daydreams. It is foolish to resolve to put an end to daydreaming; people will continue to engage in it. But how much of our daydreaming is mere escapism? From what are we trying to escape?

Daydreaming can be explored in a review of organic habits. Students should consider questions such as: Do I make a sharp separation between work and play? Does my daydreaming contribute to

12 See Jane Roland Martin, *Cultural Miseducation* (New York: Teachers College Press, 2002).

both – perhaps even unite them? Do I want a job that dependably ends each day at 5 P.M.? Am I willing to live with job-related thoughts all day, every day? What are my priorities: location, money, autonomy, low stress, working with people, working with things? Am I a morning or evening person? Is order important for me? Do I need to feel that what I am doing contributes to the public good?

It is also worth reviewing the discussion of double-mindedness. In what tasks do I find myself most distracted? What tasks make me wish I were doing something else? When am I completely, happily occupied? Are there paid occupations that might provide this sort of satisfaction? Which of these do I find appealing, and which of these offer real possibilities? Obviously, students who will go directly to work after high school need to attend to these questions earlier than those who plan to go to college, and they deserve help in exploring them. The topics considered here should not be organized into a sequential curriculum. They should be suggested, followed up as interest is expressed, returned to, deepened.

As daydreaming is explored, we should deepen our discussion of double-mindedness. How free is daydreaming? It is lovely to be free, at peace, daydreaming to our favorite music or just awaiting sleep. It is another thing to use daydreaming as an escape. One who does this often is in danger of leading a Walter Mitty life – one in which the only interesting, wonderful things happen in daydreams. Why do we use daydreaming as an escape? It would be worthwhile – perhaps very enlightening – to ask students to keep track of when they daydream. (They need not disclose the content of their daydreams and, as we'll see in a bit, we may want to discourage such disclosure.) Do certain classes induce more daydreaming than others? Why? Do I drift into daydreams during homework? Is the drift caused by double-mindedness? That is, do I long to be doing something else, chastise myself to get back on task, and float off again into daydreams that I will later count as study time? Are there topics and/or problems that rarely trigger this chain of events? What occupations are suggested by these keen interests?

The content of daydreams can profitably be discussed in general, but teachers must protect the privacy of students, and they must remember the great worry expressed earlier by critics of a curriculum of self-understanding. Our function is not individual therapy. Teachers are not usually licensed therapists, and the classroom is not in any case the place for such therapy. We should help our students to understand, for example, that many people (perhaps most) sometimes enjoy in fantasy what they would abhor in reality. Just knowing that others go through this will relieve some students of guilt and the fear that they are psychologically sick. But if a student offers an example and asks, "Is that sick?" a teacher would have to respond that, if the question worries the student, he or she should take it up with a therapist. It would be better to establish guidelines that would make such disclosures out of bounds. Examples to be invited are those that have led to productive thinking.

The matter of protecting privacy while discussing critical issues is a crucial one for teachers. Setting boundaries for conversations about daydreams is necessary. Teachers are already familiar with the need to set boundaries in other valuable learning tasks. For example, English teachers often have students keep logs of their activities and thoughts. Wise teachers counsel students not to share events or memories that might cause embarrassment or harm. Teachers are compelled by law to report certain situations – abuse or illegal immigration, for example – and they protect their students by advising caution in what they reveal. Advisory lessons of this sort are valuable for both teachers and students.

To help with fearful daydreams, we can use a technique discussed in an earlier chapter. Instead of talking directly about present teenagers' problems, we can ask them to think as parents. We might again put the conversation into historical context. In the 1950s, for example, many children had fearful daydreams (and nightmares) about nuclear war. Schools made things worse by having emergency drills during which children had to take shelter under their desks and use their hands to protect the backs of their necks. Some terribly frightened children believed that they were holding their heads on. (I don't know what the purpose of that posture was.) Now if you had been a parent at that time, how might you have reassured your children?

More recently, schools have responded to frightful world events by forbidding their discussion. Secondary school teachers have sometimes been forbidden to discuss the war in Iraq and, to protect small children, the events of 9/11 are not mentioned in primary school classrooms. But, of course, high school students need to talk about war in general and, in particular, any current war. And young children have heard about the destruction of the World Trade Center; their daydreams – acted out in classrooms where such activity is permitted – show just how afraid they are. Vivian Paley has documented the fears and has also suggested ways to relieve them through fantasy play.[13]

For those who fear that explorations of this sort will lead to a neglect of subject matter knowledge, I should point out that a lengthy discussion of nuclear fears in the 1950s might instill more historical knowledge than the usual chronological recitations. Readings in fine literature and poetry – including the spy thrillers of John le Carré – might be suggested. Biographical accounts of scientists involved in the development of the atomic bomb and the uneasiness, grief, and fear they experienced afterward should be discussed. Discussion might include the political policy called *mutually assured destruction* (MAD), which – after the advent of the hydrogen bomb – was opposed by many people, including Bertrand Russell, who believed that MAD really was mad and sought a reduction, if not elimination, of nuclear arms.[14] Opportunities arise, too, to study the statistical likelihood of being caught in disasters such as 9/11. As students are comforted by the probability that they will remain safe, they should be encouraged to think of ways to promote the safety of others.

As they discuss the fears of young children, teenagers may admit that they, too, have fearful daydreams. Even more troubling, they may confess that daydreams that start out in dread sometimes become confusingly enjoyable. If we were attacked again, there might be no regular classes – no tests! – for at least a while. I might be a hero. Some of the people I hate might die. No, I don't wish that! Do I? Here is that attraction to violence that we saw in the discussion of war. Students need reassurance that their guilty, confused daydreams do not make them sick or evil people. But if the daydream of violence really is attractive, then reflection on their lives is strongly recommended. Why am I so unhappy, bored, or discouraged that disaster seems an attractive escape? And, remember, bad daydreams as well as good ones can lead to productive thinking.

A direct connection can be made from reflection on daydreams to thinking about occupations. Answers to the questions "Who am I?"

---

[13] See Vivian Gussin Paley, *A Child's Work* (Chicago: University of Chicago Press, 2004).

[14] See Alan Ryan, *Bertrand Russell: A Political Life* (New York: Hill and Wang, 1988).

and "What sort of person am I?" help to suggest directions to pursue in seeking an occupation. What do you see yourself doing in fantasy emergencies? How do you handle the fears of others? How do you handle your own? What occupations might suit your character and personality?

Many successful high school students do not worry much about how they will make a living. They may be accepted by fine institutions of higher education without even declaring a major. Indeed, some of these lucky students will amble through their undergraduate years, perhaps taking off a year or more to "find themselves." When they are ready, they may enter graduate school ready to specialize in some field but still not forced to choose an occupation. Preparation and planning are as important for this group – if not quite so urgent – as for the students who will move directly from high school into the job market.

In thinking about an occupation, self-analysis is essential for all groups. The question "Who am I?" is as important as "What should I do?" Indeed, it may be more important, because answering it provides a direction rather than an explicit answer. A careful exploration may suggest study of a mechanical nature, but it will not say "Be a plumber or an electrician." Similarly, it may direct an academically proficient student interested in medicine to consider pathology rather than general medicine. Aptitude, interest, personality, background, and potential resources are all factors to be considered. Early on, it is as important to eliminate certain occupations as it is to think more deeply about others.

I do not mean to suggest that high school students should be obsessed with questions concerning their future occupation. Rather, the explorations I suggest here address the larger issue of becoming a real person and not a human impersonator. It is perhaps as great a mistake to focus obsessively on making the grade and getting ahead as it is to allow unrealistic expectations to foreclose one's future opportunities. Denise Clark Pope has documented the distortion of young lives that occurs when teenagers become overly concerned with test scores, GPAs, and college admission.[15] Many such youngsters sacrifice not only present happiness but real learning as

---

[15] See Denise Clark Pope, *"Doing School": How We Are Creating a Generation of Stressed Out, Materialistic, and Miseducated Students* (New Haven, CT: Yale University Press, 2001).

well. The joy of intellectual life is lost and one wonders, in reading these accounts, whether the grade-grubbing teenager will become a status-and-money-obsessed professional. The habits of stress and pernicious competition documented by Pope may well carry over into job searches and work itself. There is already some troubling evidence that young people afflicted by stress in the workplace may sacrifice their integrity to get ahead.[16] Teacher-guided discussions should direct attention to the larger issues of personhood, including character and happiness.

To understand oneself is surely important in finding out what one is fitted to do, but one must also learn what the possibilities for employment are in order to establish realistic expectations. Frank examination of help-wanted ads should occur regularly, and students should be aware that probably fewer than half of America's families today can survive on one salary.[17] Without shattering high expectations, the task of educators is to remind students that there is more to life than money and more to an occupation than the salary it provides. Among the vital issues to be discussed is whether there are some occupations to be shunned for ethical reasons.

Ethical Considerations in Occupations

High school is an ideal time to talk with students about ethics and occupational life. Once they enter the job market, economic anxiety may overcome ethical considerations. It is hard to refuse a job when one is desperate to obtain gainful employment. It might be helpful to start with stories of people who have made sacrifices to avoid jobs they considered ethically questionable.

Dan is a young man who completed high school with some difficulty; he was not much interested in academic studies. After

[16] See Wendy Fischman, Becca Solomon, Deborah Greenspan, and Howard Gardner, *Making Good: How Young People Cope with Moral Dilemmas at Work* (Cambridge, MA: Harvard University Press, 2004).

[17] See Andrew Hacker, "The Underworld of Work," *New York Review of Books*, Feb. 12, 2004: 38–40; also Simon Head, *The New Ruthless Economy: Work and Power in the Digital Age* (Oxford: Oxford University Press, with the Century Foundation, 2004); and Eileen Appelbaum, Annette Bernhardt, and Richard J. Murnane, eds., *Low-Wage America: How Employers Are Reshaping Opportunity in the Workplace* (New York: Russell Sage Foundation, 2004).

graduation, he was accepted into a community college program preparing police officers. He completed the program, received a certificate, and got a job as a police intern near his hometown. At first, this seemed perfect. He could live at home, and the city that employed him was large enough to offer both a variety of activities and the promise of advancement. After a few months, however, Dan came home and announced that this work was not for him. He said that he couldn't stand the way his fellow officers treated the people they questioned or arrested. His parents were proud of him, and they began to explore other possibilities for Dan's future.

We certainly do not want to condemn law enforcement as unethical. Indeed, we usually regard our police officers as people who enforce the moral/legal standards of the community. What problems can students identify in this story? Should Dan have tried a police job in another community? Do officers of the law sometimes use questionable methods? Some young people enter the profession with ethical ideals and manage to maintain a high level of integrity. Others become as bad as or worse than the people they arrest. And some, like Dan, just object to treating people as the job sometimes requires. There is no one defensible conclusion to be drawn from this story, but students should see how important it is to understand themselves before they enter an occupation that may contribute to either their growth or their moral deterioration. We have already discussed similar concerns with respect to joining the military.

Another story: Professor Smith, a philosophy professor at a major university, describes a conversation with a law student. Jack, the law student, had not taken a course with Professor Smith, but he had read some of her work, and so he stopped in to talk during her office hours. Jack was distressed by the very power of the education he was getting in law school. He said that the proudest thing his colleagues could say when faced with a case was, "I could win either side of that case, any case!" Jack wondered and worried about what happens to the search for truth in such a system. Professor Smith sympathized and recommended some readings that endorse Jack's way of thinking, but she had to admit that this way of thinking – one that would replace the adversarial system with one in which everyone pursues the truth – has little chance of becoming the norm. It amounts to utopian thinking. Can students envision a system that might satisfy Jack? What character and personality traits might make it difficult for

Jack to succeed as a lawyer? Is law, then, an ethically questionable occupation?

It is hoped that no student will defend drug dealing as an ethically acceptable occupation, but complicated questions may arise even on this issue. Should we condemn the farmers in Afghanistan for their growing of opium poppies or those in Colombia and Bolivia for growing coca? It is hard to maintain standards of ethical judgment and, at the same time, to recognize that blame and credit must be considered in context. We must ask what choices were available to a person whose conduct we question. The poor coca farmer in Bolivia has far fewer choices than the teenager in New York City who decides to deal in drugs.

Every occupation can be examined from an ethical perspective. Should one work at growing tobacco? At logging in old forests? At advertising harmful products such as cigarettes? It is easy for young people far removed from the possibility of such employment to condemn it. But just as we make allowances for the poppy growers of Afghanistan, we might see that people brought up on a tobacco farm or in a logging community might have relatively few opportunities. Further, their work might even be ethically defended.[18] How? Can students find biographical or fictional accounts that portray these communities sympathetically?

Open discussion of this sort might lead students to suppose that moral principles and conclusions are relative – that is, totally dependent on context and the beliefs of individual moral agents. When we ask questions about the morality of police work, law, logging, tobacco farming, and drug farming, the answers seem to start with "It depends...." And indeed, many ethical judgments (I am using *ethics* and *morality* synonymously[19]) are largely dependent on context and individual belief. But some are not. For example, it is always wrong to commit murder, to inflict unnecessary pain on another human being, or to torture innocent animals. The words *absolute* and *relative* – offered as discrete categories to describe the status of moral

---

[18] See, for example, Wendell Berry, *Another Turn of the Crank* (Washington, DC: Counterpoint, 1995).

[19] Many (perhaps most) philosophers today use the terms synonymously, but some see morality as the larger category and ethics as a subtheme treating rules of interaction. Others use ethics as the larger category and morality to refer to matters of personal conduct such as sexual behaviors.

principles – have never served us well. One who accepts one or more absolute rules is certainly not a relativist, but she may not be accurately described as an absolutist either, because she may accept the relative nature of many judgments. Further, even in her absolute principles, she may agree that much depends on the definitions of *murder*, *pain*, *unnecessary*, and *torture*. We should not allow students to conclude a discussion of the ethics of occupations with the faulty notion that "it all depends" on what the individual feels or believes. If it is clear that an act will cause unnecessary pain, we are absolutely enjoined to refrain from doing it. Difficulties arise when we are unsure whether the expected pain is unnecessary. Then a lot does depend on the background and personality of the one making a judgment. Dan did not say that police work requires one to inflict unnecessary pain but, for him, it was too close a call for comfort.

Students should explore the question of whether an occupation requires the infliction of unnecessary pain or whether that pain can be avoided by conscientious conduct, whether the employing agency produces harmful products (but perhaps also produces helpful ones), and whether employment in this work necessitates the deliberate and regular use of deception. Am I hurting people directly by my actions or indirectly through the products my company produces? Must I be willing to lie and deceive in order to succeed at this job? Will my work hurt or help the environment?

We might share the story of Bill, an engineer, who found himself out of work during the Vietnam War. Bill had a large family to support and could not afford to remain unemployed for long. He was offered a job at a good salary with a large chemical manufacturer. But he learned that they were making the poison Agent Orange and, deeply opposed to both the war and environmental destruction, he turned down the job. He was supported with pride by his wife and children.

But should the person who accepted the job be judged immoral or unethical? See, students may say, it does just depend. Well, not quite. We have to ask whether Bill's replacement asked the crucial questions and how he answered them. Did he regret the harm he was doing but believe it was necessary for the good of his country? Or did he think only of his own economic well-being? Did he hope, once hired, to get a transfer to another branch of the company and thus distance himself from involvement with Agent Orange? And what sort of justification is that?

So far, we have been exploring ways in which students can ask about the effects their chosen occupation will have on others and the natural world. But they should also consider the effects of their lifestyles on what others must do as occupations. There are many dull and dirty jobs that must be done to allow others to live in relative comfort. Earlier, we discussed ways in which utopian thinkers have suggested sharing objectionable jobs. Some of their answers, however, are a bit too glib. In *Looking Backward*, when Dr. Leete's wife is asked who does the housework, she responds, "There is none to do.... We have no use for domestic servants."[20] This remark may well bring a snort of derision from female students and teachers. The writer has little understanding of what it takes to maintain a home. Both women and men should consider the domestic burden that might be increased by their working outside the home.

There was a day when few women faced the kinds of problems described by Dan, Jack, and Bill. Even today, women often avoid these problems because they enter the caring professions. The effects of their work on others is mostly, sometimes overwhelmingly, positive.[21] But to do any work outside the home often requires another woman to provide childcare. Even if that woman works at a day-care center or preschool, her life and workday are affected by the first woman's choice to work outside the home. The effect could be positive; paid work is now available. But young women, in demanding affordable childcare, should study the effects of their demand on other women. Should committed feminists forge their own success through the exploitation of other women?

High school students cannot solve these difficult social problems, but they should be aware of them. If they are able to avoid a life of hardworking poverty, they should continue to think how best to bring about a better life for others.

Thinking about others should lead back to a further, deeply reflective examination of self. The questions we have been exploring throughout this book are broadly moral questions. Classical philosophy gave much attention to these questions: What sort of person am

---

[20] Edward Bellamy, *Looking Backward* (New York: New American Library, 1960), p. 90.
[21] See the essays in Suzanne Gordon, Patricia Benner, and Nel Noddings, eds., *Caregiving* (Philadelphia: University of Pennsylvania Press, 1996).

I? What sort of person should I become? What does it mean to be good? To be happy? Today, too often, these questions are ignored in both technical philosophy and education. They have been exiled to the domain of religion, but one does not have to embrace religion in order to answer them thoughtfully and well.[22]

John Dewey's statement at the beginning of this chapter invites exploration of these questions. To find out what one is fitted to do requires more than an assessment of talent. It also requires consideration of the sort of person one wishes to be and the kind of life one wants to live. Careful thought on these matters may help students decide that they do not want to pursue money and fame but, rather, a life of deep satisfaction – one rich in relationships, social commitment, satisfying leisure, and continuing wonder at both the natural and intellectual worlds. The guiding question should be: What sort of occupation will permit me to become the person I want to be and live the life I envision?

The Hypocrisy of Schooling

We have so far discussed the task of preparing for work in a way very different from the typical approach in schools. Instead of recommending training for a specific occupation or opposing that recommendation with an insistence that all students must study the traditional academic curriculum before thinking about an occupation, we have talked about realistic expectations, daydreams, self-understanding, appreciation of economic interdependence, and the ethics of occupations. This approach should, I will argue, make us more open-minded and appreciative of vocational education.

For more than 100 years, American educators and policymakers have argued over the value of vocational education.[23] It was clear as early as 1895 that the high school curriculum had to change if more young people were to attend and perhaps graduate. Because there

---

[22] In the late 1800s, many people gave up religious affiliation and even religious belief for ethical, not epistemological, reasons. See, for example, Susan Jacoby, *Freethinkers* (New York: Metropolitan Books, 2004); also James Turner, *Without God, Without Creed* (Baltimore: Johns Hopkins University Press, 1985).

[23] See Kliebard, *Schooled to Work*; also David L. Angus and Jeffrey E. Mirel, *The Failed Promise of the American High School: 1890–1999* (New York: Teachers College Press, 1999).

was an increasing demand for industrial workers and a decrease in the use of apprenticeships, the logical solution was to introduce vocational education into public high schools. The National Association of Manufacturers expressed support for this solution; it suited their purposes.

Why did many educators object to vocational education? Two reasons stand out. First, some educators simply rejected practical studies as a form of *education*. Schools, they argued, should educate, and vocational training should take place after an adequate education. There are still many people who argue this way, entirely ignoring the fact that large numbers of young people reject what is so proudly called education. The second reason, closely related to the first, was the expressed fear that children would be shunted into vocational preparation too early. It was undemocratic, these people believed, to steer youngsters away from the academic learning that promised a brighter future. Both reasons ignore the possibility that genuine education might take place in a vocational program.

The debate was far too shallow. Few questioned the superiority of the highly abstract academic curriculum. Worse, few addressed the issues we have been exploring here and the basic question of how vocational programs might be designed so that they would merit the label education. Jane Addams did so, but her ideas – focused on the growth and well-being of the industrial worker rather than the success of the industry – were not adopted, indeed were hardly heard.[24] It is time to revive some of Addams's ideas and subject vocational education to conscientious study.

Educators like John Dewey were right to object to a form of schooling that branded children early on as incapable of academic work and consigned them to plumbing, cosmetics, or auto mechanics. They recognized, and we must too, the hierarchy of occupations that establishes earning power in our society. But often they overlooked their own pronouncements on education. Education is not, or should not be, aimed only at economic outcomes. The knowledge, skills, and attitudes that contribute to real personhood can be embedded in industrial or commercial education, as Addams suggested. It is not

---

[24] Kliebard, *Schooled to Work*, p. 40; also Jane Addams, "Humanizing Tendency of Industrial Education," in *Jane Addams on Education*, ed. Ellen Condliffe Lagemann (New York: Teachers College Press, 1985), pp. 120–123.

necessary to complete a classical education in order to acquire these attributes.

Another great error made in the long conflict between vocational and academic education is to assume that schools should *assign* students to courses of study. In 1908, Charles Eliot – who had ten years earlier recommended the same curriculum for all students – now startled his colleagues by recommending the establishment of industrial tracks and, worse, suggesting how students should be placed in appropriate tracks: "The teachers of the elementary schools ought to sort pupils and sort them by their evident and probable destinies."[25]

Eliot's statement cries out for critical thinking. He was right, I believe, to note that democracy cannot make all people equal in abilities. Quite the contrary, a robust democracy should celebrate the differences that contribute to its health. It does not follow, however, that schools should deliberately sort pupils. One of the most basic and cherished ideas in the theory of liberal democracy is choice, and an important function of schooling in a democracy is to help people make well-informed choices. Teachers and guidance counselors should use aptitude tests, interest scales, school records, and interviews to guide, not to assign, students to appropriate programs. Choice should be taken seriously. It should be talked about regularly, and students should be convinced that their choices will be respected. Students should be allowed to overrule the advice they get from teachers, and no student should be denied an opportunity to try any program offered at the precollege level. Well-informed choice coupled with fine programs of study from which to choose should be the educational ideal in a liberal democracy.

Educators and policymakers should also take a more critical attitude toward the recommendations of business leaders. By a *more critical attitude* I mean one of attentive listening and critical evaluation. The suggestions of the National Association of Manufacturers and the Business Roundtable should not be rejected out of hand, but neither should their ideas be allowed to ride roughshod over the schools. A genuine partnership would require educators to listen to the needs of the business community but reserve to themselves the right to respond in educationally sound ways. Educators must never forget that our task is to contribute to the development of fully human

[25] Quoted in Kliebard, *Schooled to Work*, p. 43.

beings, not merely to provide productive workers for the national economy.

Some educators have tried to make vocational education more respectable by integrating academic and vocational studies.[26] This solution might be fine if both academic and vocational programs had been carefully designed. However, the favored program – the academic – is in sore need of revision. If all we want to do is sort students according to their academic capacity – and this capacity involves patience, persistence, and docility as well as aptitude – the present program will do nicely. But if we want to educate people capable of critical thinking, generous social attitudes, and personal happiness, we should rethink the academic curriculum. Although it has for years been reputed to accomplish these goals, there is little evidence to back the claim.

Alasdair MacIntyre has said (rightly, I think) that it would be wonderful "if fishing crews and farmers and auto mechanics and construction workers were able to think about their lives critically."[27] In response to this, I said and now repeat, "It would be equally wonderful if the same could be said of the graduates of our finest institutions of liberal education."[28] Some of our graduates are capable of such critical thinking; many are not. MacIntyre's point about workers is still well taken, but his assumption that a traditional academic education will do the trick is mistaken. Carefully and generously designed, vocational education programs may produce critical, reflective thinkers. This will not be accomplished by forcing future workers into traditional programs where they are constantly reminded that they are not really "up to it," and those courses do not produce the desired result even for many of those who succeed at them.

There is something fundamentally wrong with the traditional academic courses organized into discrete disciplines. If students are preparing for college, they must study four or five of the prescribed disciplines in high school. Why? The easy answer is that such study is required for college entrance. If we ask why, we will likely get some

---

[26] See W. Norton Grubb, *Education Through Occupations in American High Schools*, vols. 1 and 2 (New York: Teachers College Press, 1995).

[27] MacIntyre is quoted thus in Joseph Dunne and Padraig Hogan, eds., *Education and Practice* (Oxford: Blackwell, 2004), p. 14.

[28] Nel Noddings, "Is Teaching a Practice?" in *Education and Practice*, p. 164.

variant of a general response that claims disciplinary knowledge as that which characterizes an educated person. But is this true? High school students work daily with teachers who, as ostensibly educated persons, studied the disciplines in high school and college. Yet the vast majority of high school teachers know only one subject, and sometimes they do not know even that one well. The profession of teaching, more than any other profession, requires a broad interdisciplinary grasp of human knowledge – exactly the kind of preparation claimed for traditional education. But traditional education does not deliver on its own promise. College students, even those who study in institutions espousing breadth, undergo a series of courses in discrete specialties. As a result, they cannot talk easily about the historical, philosophical, religious, social, political, aesthetic, ethical, or even practical aspects of their subject.

The pressure to specialize is understandable, if mistaken. Certainly we want a high school mathematics teacher to know all of the mathematics offered at the high school level and to know it well. But, instead of pushing secondary school teachers to take more courses in higher mathematics, we would do better to encourage their study of the aspects of knowledge listed in the previous paragraph. To teach, to teach well, one must be able to connect with all sorts of interests in an authoritative and inspiring way. To do this, we must be able to cross disciplinary lines. I have talked with science teachers, for example, who say that they cannot teach some topics in their own discipline because students do not have the necessary preparation in mathematics. "Are these topics central to your discipline?" I've asked. "Absolutely!" "Well, then why don't you teach the necessary math?" The usual answers are discouraging: "I'm not a math teacher; that's not my job; I'm not trained to do that." I've even heard college teachers of sociology and economics make similar remarks about their students' preparation in statistics.

Eventual specialization is made necessary by the sheer volume of knowledge that has accumulated. It is almost certain, too, that some form of sequential study is necessary in preparation for specialization, but that does not imply that every high school and college subject should be taught as though it is preparation for specialization. Students see their teachers as living proof that this structure is weak; their teachers have forgotten most of what was forced on them in high school and college. We should either let students begin to specialize much earlier (as many nations do) or we should redesign the curriculum around human problems that draw effectively on the disciplines. Specialization at the high school level need not result in a lack of breadth. On the contrary, well taught, mathematics (or any other subject) can be presented in a way that includes history, biography, literature, religion, psychology, politics, ethics, and aesthetics.

Some time ago, Florida's governor, Jeb Bush, was asked by a student to answer a math question that appeared on the state's math examination. It was asked in a way unfair to the governor, because he was not given the choices from which an examinee must select the correct answer. But his response was illustrative of the hypocrisy that I'm talking about. He didn't know where to begin in answering the question but said that because a fifty-year-old man could not answer the question was no reason not to require fifteen-year-olds to do so. What this suggests to students is that they must learn volumes of material today that, by the time they are fifty, they may safely have forgotten. To make matters worse, with respect to this story, the honors student who had asked the question replied with confidence that she knew the answer, but in fact she had it wrong. Neither student nor governor thought to talk about the problem, try things out, ask further questions; that is, neither considered engaging in genuine problem solving.

It should be possible for students to address the great human questions prized by traditional educators (and by me, too) without sacrificing their own intellectual interests. If we found a way to do this, many students who struggle now might come alive in school. They would not be made to feel inferior for twelve important years of their young lives.

Traditional educators often argue, in the name of democracy, that all students (K–12) should have the same education. Mortimer Adler argued this way in *The Paideia Proposal*. His insistence that all children should have a high-quality education is admirable; few of us would contest this. However, does a high-quality education for all entail the *same* education for all? Adler spoke approvingly of Robert Maynard Hutchins's famous remark, "The best education for the best is the best education for all."[29] He then wrote, "The shape of the

---

[29] Hutchins is quoted in Mortimer Adler, *The Paideia Proposal* (New York: Macmillan, 1982), p. 6.

best education for the best is not unknown to us."[30] It follows, Adler advised: "The one-track system of public schooling that *The Paideia Proposal* advocates has the same objectives for all without exception."[31] Like MacIntyre, Adler failed to see the many weaknesses in the traditional curriculum.

I contend that we do *not* know what constitutes the best education for the best. Who are these *best*? Clearly, Hutchins and Adler have in mind the most privileged and the most academically talented. But many privileged children have suffered miserably in this system of schooling, and the academically talented should not be used as standard setters for all children.

If we are going to argue in the name of democracy (and I have already emphasized the role of choice in that perspective), we would do better to build on Walt Whitman's vision. He heard the songs of mechanics, carpenters, masons, boatmen, shoemakers, woodcutters, housewives, seamstresses, and ploughboys.[32] Occupations have changed, but Whitman's celebration of diversity remains a beacon of democracy. Students should read his words over and over and look forward to the day when they can contribute constructively to their community and when the whole society lives by Whitman's words, "I will be even with you, and you shall be even with me."[33] Except in specific, well-defined tasks and lines of work, there should be no best that dictates the standards for everyone.

If teachers talk the way I am talking here, students may well ask what happened to the earlier advice on realistic expectations. They would be quite right to do so. The world does not live up to the ideals expressed by Whitman. However, it is good to have ideals and work toward them. What we reject, as critical thinkers, is delusion, deceit, arrogance, and ignorance. As Henry Giroux describes the task of teachers:

> To be a teacher who can make a difference in both the lives of students and in the quality of life in general necessitates more than acquiring a language of critique and possibility. It also means having

---

[30] Adler, *The Paideia Proposal*, p. 7.
[31] Ibid., p. 15.
[32] Walt Whitman, "A Song for Occupations," in Whitman, *Poetry and Prose* (New York: Library of America, 1982), pp. 89–99.
[33] Ibid., p. 89.

the courage to take risks, to look into the future, and to imagine a world that could be as opposed to simply what is.[34]

Much of what we have discussed here requires real courage.

In this chapter, I have taken a somewhat unusual approach to preparing students for an occupation. Instead of focusing on the nation's economic needs and how individuals might best climb the economic/occupational ladder, I've concentrated on the relation between occupation and personhood, urging students to ask: "What sort of work might contribute to my full development as a person? What attitude should I cultivate toward the work of others?" With such a humanistic focus, our schools could provide strong and inspiring programs in both vocational and academic education. The details of such programs will have to wait for another book.

We briefly touched on some gender differences experienced in occupational life, noting that women have often been employed in the caring professions. In the next chapter, we take a broader look at critical issues associated with gender.

---

[34] Henry A. Giroux, *Schooling and the Struggle for Public Life* (Minneapolis: University of Minnesota Press, 1988), p. 215.

9

Gender

> A woman must have money and a room of her own if she is to write fiction; and that, you will see, leaves the great problem of the true nature of women and the true nature of fiction unsolved.
>
> Virginia Woolf

In this chapter, we'll first look at another aspect of choosing an occupation – that of discrimination against women in salaries and promotion. Although the entire occupational world is now technically open to them, women often experience great difficulty advancing in historically male-dominated occupations. However, women who choose the caring professions – the kind of work women have been allowed (even forced) to do – can expect to earn considerably less than those who dare to enter male domains. We'll look at some of the conflicts that girls face in choosing an occupation.

As in previous chapters – in discussions of motherhood, homemaking, advertising, and socialization – I'll concentrate on issues that are critical for individuals. Scholarly work in feminist studies has grown enormously in the past twenty years, and the temptation is to gather volumes of significant work, construct a curriculum, and pour the material into captive students. But I've been arguing all through this book against that way of schooling. Some students may indeed become so interested in matters related to women's studies that they will decide to pursue various topics in greater depth. Wonderful. The material in this chapter should be available to all students and should be used to launch critical investigations.

In chapter 2, we gave some attention to problems of male identity in the discussion of masculinity and the warrior model. Here, we'll extend the conversation by looking at both female and male "natures" and, with respect to the latter, at the more general problem of violence. Finally, we'll consider the problems homosexual students encounter in school. Existing programs designed to promote tolerance often concentrate on helping all students to understand the experience of gay and lesbian students who suffer abuse. I'll argue, in keeping with a consistent emphasis on critical/reflective analysis, that more attention should be given to exploring the root psychological causes of hatred and abuse. We need to understand ourselves if we are to understand others.

Women's Work

Whatever work women do, they earn on the average, considerably less than men:

> For full-time workers, the ratio of women's to men's annual earnings increased from 60.2 percent in 1980 to 71.6 percent in 1990, but between 1990 and 2000 that ratio increased only 1.6 percentage points, from 71.6 percent to 73.2.[1]

There are several reasons for this difference in earnings, but one studied carefully by Linda Babcock and Sara Laschever is that women do not speak up for themselves; they do not demand more equitable pay.[2] This observation triggers a conflict, for, on the one hand, we've been emphasizing that work is about more than money but, on the other, no one can be entirely content knowing that she is paid less than a man doing the same work and that he is more likely to be promoted than she even if his performance is not as good as hers. Thus, although there is something commendable about women's unselfish attitudes with respect to salaries, there is also something to worry about. Is it commendable to cooperate in one's own oppression?

In a review of their own and others' studies of women and the process of negotiation, Babcock and Laschever at first suggest that women just don't know how to negotiate. It often doesn't occur

---

[1] Linda Babcock and Sara Laschever, *Women Don't Ask: Negotiation and the Gender Divide* (Princeton, NJ: Princeton University Press, 2003), xii.
[2] Ibid.

to women that salaries, prices, and working conditions can be negotiated and, if negotiations do get underway, women concede too quickly. However, later in their study, the authors admit that, in fact, women are often very good negotiators – but not for themselves. It isn't, then, that women are poor negotiators. Rather, they aren't comfortable pushing themselves, and especially pressing for more money. After listening to stories that describe differences between the ways in which men and women negotiate their salaries, one middle-school girl shook her head and said, "Men are such gimme pigs!" From an early age, many girls look on self-aggrandizement with some discomfort, if not contempt.

The conflict here is genuine. Should women learn to be as self-promoting as men, or should men learn to be less self-interested? There is much to be said on both sides. Girls should learn to stand up for their occupational rights, but it would be a loss to the social world if, in doing so, women became less sensitive to social issues. As things stand now, survey after survey shows that, in general, women are far more sensitive to the needs of the poor, minorities, children, and the disabled, elderly, and imprisoned than are men.[3] Can this sensitivity to the needs of others be maintained while, at the same time, a healthier approach to self-promotion is cultivated? One purpose of engaging in critical examination of gender attitudes in schools is the hope that an optimal answer to these questions can at least be formulated, if not enacted. More cooperative, less aggressive men and stronger women – women refusing to cooperate in their own exploitation – may both contribute to a more equitable and peaceful world.[4]

I noted in chapter 8 that women in the recent past managed to avoid some questions of occupational ethics that men had to face. In the caring professions, they had the comfort of knowing that they were doing good in the world, even if they were poorly paid for doing it. However, the history of nursing provides an important exception to this comfortable feeling of doing good. Early on, female nurses

---

[3] See, for example, the statistics reported yearly in *The Chronicle of Higher Education* – for example, the *Almanac Issue*, 2004–2005, August, 27, 2004.

[4] See the essays in Emilie Buchwald, Pamela R. Fletcher, and Martha Roth, eds., *Transforming a Rape Culture* (Minneapolis: Milkweed Editions, 1993).

were not always regarded as doing good or even, as moral persons. Susan Reverby notes:

> Before the 1870s, no nurses had any formal training or schooling for the work. Hospital nurses were considered the dregs of female society – mainly women who drank themselves into oblivion to endure their seemingly thankless and wretched labors of cleaning, feeding, and watching over the hospital's inmates.[5]

The first women to enter training for nursing had to withstand the thinly veiled scorn of society in addition to bringing order to their occupation. It isn't necessary for all students to know something of the history of nursing as a profession, but interested students should be advised on sources that will tell them more about a hard-won profession.

Today, when all of the caring professions are respectable yet relatively ill paid, students should know that women still fill most of these positions:

> As recently as 2001, 98 percent of child-care workers, 82 percent of elementary school teachers, 91 percent of nurses, 99 percent of secretaries, and 70 percent of social workers in the United States were women.[6]

Another conflict arises. Should today's girls refuse to enter traditionally female occupations? By joining one of these occupations, one is assured of doing something that helps others. That matters to many women. But one may also be reinforcing society's tendency to exploit women. To make matters more complicated, academically successful girls are now frequently advised against preparing for the caring professions: "You're too smart for that!" As I noted before, this is a socially insensitive message. It suggests that we do not need or want the very best teachers, nurses, and social workers, and it discourages girls from doing what they may really want to do. It encourages the idea that traditionally male work is worth far more than traditionally female work. Again, we have to face reality. In terms of money and prestige, that unfortunate statement of value is true. But in terms of how things should be, how we want them to be, it should be a call

---

[5] Susan Reverby, *Ordered to Care* (Cambridge: Cambridge University Press, 1987), p. 22.

[6] Babcock and Laschever, *Women Don't Ask*, p. 65.

for transformation. Both individual girls and the community at large suffer from the reinforcement of faulty values.

It is worth spending more time on the predicament faced by today's young women. The world of occupations is certainly more open to them now than ever before, although there are still many horror stories about how women are treated when they dare to enter male domains.[7] But the new freedom has, paradoxically, brought new constraints. Instead of asking girls what they would like to do – what they see themselves as fitted to do – school advisors too often tell them what they *should* do. The old norms for female aspirations have rightly been rejected, but the new ones can be almost as coercive. To tell a bright young woman that she *should* study math, for example, may weaken the self-confidence she has built up through an entirely different area of study. I have talked with several bright female undergraduates who are confused over their own unhappiness with the majors into which they were lured by well-intentioned advisors. We risk repeating old errors in our hard-won new world. Indeed, I wonder (this is speculative) whether this new coercion may account for the fact that, while women still do not score as well on the math SAT as men, they have lost their former advantage on the verbal SAT. Perhaps young women are once again afraid to design and build their own futures.

There is yet another major conflict that emerges for women in the caring professions. Caring is associated with subservience. It is thought, mistakenly, to be synonymous with caregiving. The concept of caring in an ethics of care is applicable to every aspect of human interaction, not just to caregiving.[8] It addresses, at the most basic level, how we should meet and treat others and ourselves. But the word *caring* is part of everyday language, and it is easy to slide from the technical concept involving attention and response to one that emphasizes tender, hands-on, sympathetic caregiving. The difficulty is aggravated by the obvious fact that caring in the technical sense is ethically necessary in the practical activities of caregiving. Thus, because caregiving has long been the domain of women, and because

[7] Ibid.

[8] See Nel Noddings, *Caring: A Feminine Approach to Ethics and Moral Education*, 2nd ed. (Berkeley: University of California Press, 2003); also Noddings, *Starting at Home: Caring and Social Policy* (Berkeley: University of California Press, 2002).

the ethics of care seems to have its origin in female experience,[9] some astute critics fear that an emphasis on caring in ethics will contribute to the continued exploitation of women.[10]

Fear of continued exploitation is not to be brushed aside lightly. The history of the caring professions is rife with examples of how their caring has been used against women. Women in general have been expected to care (that is, to provide tender, hands-on caregiving) and, as essential to that care, to put the needs of others above their own. Reverby titles her history of nursing *Ordered to Care*, and the implication is clear:[11] It is the hands-on nurse, the underling, who is ordered to care. Hospital administrators and head nurses are exempt from the order. Even today, nurses who want to get ahead are advised to spend less time with patients and more time writing reports, conferring, and organizing.

In education, too, there has been an expectation that caring is something one does with young children. As children grow, they need less care, and caring is almost eliminated at the level of school administration. In the so-called golden age for female school superintendents (roughly 1910–1940, peaking in 1930), a major complaint against prominent female superintendents was that they were too democratic, too soft on teachers, in a word – too caring.[12] These women were implicitly using an ethic of care – relating to teachers with attention and a positive response. There was nothing soft or wishy-washy about their style, and they seem to have been highly effective. But they were *women* and they *cared*. The faulty perception was that such behavior was appropriate for subordinates, not for leaders.[13] If women insisted on maintaining this caring style, then they should not expect to be leaders.

---

[9] See Noddings, ibid.; also see Carol J. Gilligan, *In a Different Voice* (Cambridge, MA: Harvard University Press, 1982).

[10] See, for example, Jean Grimshaw, *Philosophy and Feminist Thinking* (Minneapolis: University of Minneapolis Press, 1986); Barbara Houston, "Caring and Exploitation," *Hypatia* 5(1), 1990: 115–119; and Helga Kuhse, *Caring, Nurses, Women, and Ethics* (Oxford: Blackwell, 1997).

[11] Reverby, *Ordered to Care*.

[12] See Jackie M. Blount, *Destined to Rule the Schools* (Albany: State University of New York Press, 1998).

[13] See Lynn Beck, *Reclaiming Educational Administration as a Caring Profession* (New York: Teachers College Press, 1994).

Students should be aware of the multiple paradoxes in the situations just described. Because women's work has long been economically devalued, girls are now advised to aim for occupations traditionally held by men. But, a girl may well ask, what if I *want* to be a nurse or preschool teacher? Turning her critical eye beyond her own interests to those of society, she may ask: Wouldn't it be better to work toward a reevaluation of women's work? Her critical thinking may lead her to question the hypocrisy in a society that ostensibly cherishes its young but denigrates those who work with them.

Another paradox is revealed in a pervasive attitude toward women who care at managerial levels. It is not only female school superintendents who have suffered from an attitude that misconstrues caring as touchy-feely. Although there is considerable evidence that caring (as an ethical way of being) is effective in negotiating and leading, the very fact of its association with women still arouses suspicion. Leaders are supposed to be tough, single-minded, and aggressive. Again, students must consider whether it is women or the society that must change. And we should probably avoid a simplistic this-or-that answer. Women should probably learn how to promote themselves and protect their own interests, but society should become more appreciative of the values long associated with women. This is tough, loving, critical work.

Female and Male Natures

We should consider the possibility that women are drawn to the caring professions because the propensity to care is biologically inherent in the female. This doctrine, *essentialism*, is rejected by most feminists because it has been used with devastating effect against women.[14] For centuries it was believed that women were created to be wives and mothers, and this idea was often supported by reference to biblical passages. Feminists have raised the question of why so many writers, preachers, and everyday followers promote the Adam and Eve story

---

[14] See the discussions in Mary M. Brabeck, ed., *Practicing Feminist Ethics in Psychology* (Washington, DC: American Psychological Association); also Deborah L. Rhode, ed., *Theoretical Perspectives on Sexual Difference* (New Haven, CT: Yale University Press, 1990).

(in Genesis 2) over the more simple and egalitarian story in Genesis 1: "So God created man in his own image, in the image of God created he him; male and female created he them." Elizabeth Cady Stanton, in *The Woman's Bible*, wrote:

> If language has any meaning, we have in these texts [Genesis 1] a plain declaration of the existence of the feminine element in the Godhead, equal in power and glory with the masculine – the Heavenly Mother and Father.... [15]

But we would be getting ahead of ourselves to pursue Stanton's line of thinking here. More will be said on religion in the next section and in the chapter on religion.

The notion that woman (the singular was often used – as though women were an interchangeable commodity) was created as an indispensable aide to man, especially in procreation, was promoted as scientific truth in the early twentieth century. The influential psychologist G. Stanley Hall insisted that women should be educated for their biologically determined role as wives and mothers, and he expressed the fear that women educated in the male-oriented liberal arts would lose interest in sex – perhaps even become barren.[16] It was thought to be tantamount to race suicide to educate girls as we educate boys, because the brightest females – those who represented the best biological stock – might refuse to reproduce.[17]

The view that women were intellectually inferior to men and would be harmed by serious intellectual effort was further complicated by attempts to glorify the role of mother and homemaker. The basic conflict between seeking equality in the public world and defending the importance of making a home and raising children created a dilemma for thoughtful educators. Women like M. Carey Thomas, president of Bryn Mawr, insisted on the standard (traditionally male)

---

[15] Quoted in Geoffrey C. Ward and Ken Burns, *Not for Ourselves Alone: The Story of Elizabeth Cady Stanton and Susan B. Anthony* (New York: Alfred A. Knopf, 1999), p. 200; see also Stanton and the Revising Committee, *The Woman's Bible* (Seattle: Ayer Press, 1974).

[16] See G. Stanley Hall, *Adolescence: Its Psychology and Its Relation to Physiology, Anthropology, Sociology, Sex, Crime, Religion, and Education*, 2 vols. (New York: D. Appleton, 1904).

[17] Edward L. Thorndike took this position (on white women, of course). See Thorndike, *Education: A First Book* (New York: Macmillan, 1912).

liberal arts curriculum for women, but opportunities for women so educated were few in comparison with those available to men.[18] As noted earlier, despite the increased participation of women in education, the percentage of women in prestigious academic positions and in educational leadership actually declined after 1930. It was not only the opposition of men that stood in the way of women's progress in the public domain. At the root of the conflict was a belief, held by many women, that the proper (and tremendously important) work of women was to be done on the domestic scene.[19]

Today the conflict is seldom cast in terms of women's intellectual inferiority or the competing glories of motherhood.[20] Women and men share the conflict between professional and domestic success, but many features of the contemporary conflict are a legacy from an earlier struggle, and girls should be aware of that history.

Although essentialism has been used to keep women in their place (out of public activity), it has sometimes glorified the feminine. Carl Jung and his followers described female and male psyches as essentially different but complementary.[21] Much of this literature is fascinating and has the merit of drawing on myth and religion. The great danger, of course, is that it suggests (and sometimes accepts outright) the notion of a "true" woman and a "true" man. Most of us today reject this idea. Can students think of people who still accept the idea that women and men have different, biologically inherent natures? If it doesn't emerge spontaneously, teachers should point

---

[18] See Margaret W. Rossiter, *Women Scientists in America: Struggles and Strategies to 1940* (Baltimore: Johns Hopkins University Press, 1982); also Barbara M. Cross, ed., *The Educated Woman in America* (New York: Teachers College Press, 1965).

[19] For an account of this conflict, see Patricia J. Thompson, *The Accidental Theorist* (New York: Peter Lang, 2002).

[20] However, even today a prominent man questions whether women have the genetic capacity for science. The story appears in Piper Fogg, "Harvard's President Wonders Aloud About Women in Science and Math," *The Chronicle of Higher Education*, Jan. 28, 2005: A12.

[21] Some good sources: Irene Claremont de Castillejo, *Knowing Woman* (New York: Harper Colophon, 1974); Marie-Louise von Franz, *Shadow and Evil in Fairy Tales* (Dallas: Spring, 1983); M. Esther Harding, *Woman's Mysteries* (New York: Harper & Row, 1971); and Estella Lauter and Carol Schrier Rupprecht, eds., *Feminist Archetypal Theory* (Knoxville: University of Tennessee Press, 1985); but see my critique in Noddings, *Women and Evil* (Berkeley: University of California Press, 1989).

out that essentialism is accepted doctrine in many religious groups; it is not restricted to Islam but appears in some Christian and Jewish sects as well.[22]

Some nineteenth-century feminists, accepting essentialism, even argued for the moral superiority of women.[23] One argument in favor of granting women the right to vote was that the moral climate of society would be improved when women were allowed greater participation in public life. While this prediction has not been fully realized, there is a significant gender gap (as noted earlier) on matters of social welfare.

The question of essentialism remains open to investigation. Although most feminists (I include myself here) have rejected it, some of us do so for pragmatic reasons and remain agnostic on its basic claims. Its consequences have been bad for women; therefore, we avoid it. But, scientifically, it seems right to say that we do not yet know what aspects of femaleness and maleness are biologically inherent. There do seem to be inclinations or fairly regular tendencies that are gender related, but it is not unreasonable to attribute these to centuries of experience and social expectations.

A voluminous literature on gender similarities and differences has accumulated over the past thirty years. Many, perhaps most, feminists describe gender as a social construction; that is, the attributes and habits observed in the genders are not the result of biology but, rather, of socialization. But within the group who believe this, there are differences. Cynthia Epstein, for example, takes the position

> that most gender differences are not as deeply rooted or immutable as has been believed, that they are relatively superficial, and that they are socially constructed ... kept in place by the way each sex is positioned in the social structure.[24]

[22] For a description of contemporary sex roles in a fundamentalist school, Bethany Baptist Academy, see Alan Peshkin, *God's Choice: The Total World of a Fundamentalist Christian School* (Chicago: University of Chicago Press, 1986); see also Paula Kane, James Kenneally, and Karen Kenneally, eds., *Gender Identities in American Catholicism* (Maryknoll: Orbis Books, 2001).

[23] See the discussion in Noddings, *Women and Evil.*

[24] Cynthia Fuchs Epstein, *Deceptive Distinctions: Sex, Gender, and the Social Order* (New Haven, CT: Yale University Press and New York: Russell Sage Foundation, 1988), p. 25. For further theoretical discussions of gender differences, see Rhode, ed., *Theoretical Perspectives on Sexual Difference.*

Others, while agreeing that gender is socially constructed, do not believe that the observed differences are superficial. I agree with those who believe that the differences are very deeply rooted and very nearly universal in human experience. Moreover, the differences are supported not only by minor cultural customs but by enormous bodies of religious belief and the ages'-long dependence on war to solve political problems. Thus femininity has been defined in terms of subservience and masculinity in terms of the manliness of warriors. Differences so deeply rooted will be hard to eradicate. Perhaps the most important practical question for students to explore is this: Which of these differences (whatever their source) should we try to eliminate and in which direction?

Are males, for example, inherently competitive and aggressive? There certainly is a long history of association between manliness and the traits of warriors. Even William James, strongly opposed to war, found military life "congruous with human nature" and feared that many saw war as a "bulwark against effeminacy."[25] His search for a moral equivalent of war recognized the importance of hardihood:

> Militarism is the great preserver of our ideals of hardihood, and human life with no use for hardihood would be contemptible. Without risks or prizes for the darer, history would be insipid indeed; and there is a type of military character which every one feels that the race should never cease to breed, for every one is sensitive to its superiority.[26]

The quotation from James illustrates the problem young people need to consider. What are the traits associated with hardihood? Are they necessarily manly? Which such traits should be encouraged in everyone? Which should be discouraged?

Michael Kimmel has discussed the social construction of masculinity. Citing Robert Brannon, he lists four rules of American manhood:

> (1) No Sissy Stuff: Men can never do anything that even remotely suggests femininity. Manhood is a relentless repudiation and devaluation of the feminine. (2) Be a Big Wheel: Manhood is

---

[25] William James, *The Varieties of Religious Experience* (New York: Modern Library, 1929/1902), p. 284.
[26] William James, "The Moral Equivalent of War," in John J. McDermott, ed., *The Writings of William James* (New York: Random House, 1967), pp. 660–671.

measured by power, wealth, and success. Whoever has the most toys when he dies, wins. (3) Be a Sturdy Oak: Manhood depends on emotional reserve. Dependability in a crisis requires that men not reveal their feelings. (4) Give 'em Hell: Exude an aura of manly daring and aggression. Go for it. Take risks.[27]

Remember Virginia Woolf's comment on *manliness* and *womanliness* – "both so horrid."[28] Which of the preceding rules should be rejected? Which should be modified? Can we encourage dependability, some daring, some aggressiveness in both males and females? Are some of the manly traits named in the rules simply false?

Consider the emotional factor. Men have often claimed that women should not be placed in positions that require impartiality and decision making. Women, it has been said, are too emotional. Some years ago, a student in one of my classes made an impressive presentation on this topic. She assembled a set of pictures, anecdotes, and historical accounts showing the emotional behavior of men: athletes leaping into one another's arms after a victory, crowds (all men) shouting against political rivals, warrior-berserkers on a rampage, male drivers in the throes of road rage, saloon fights in western films, heat-of-the-moment murders, impassioned ravings from the pulpit. At the end of her presentation, she said simply: "Tell me again. Who's too emotional?" An exercise such as this might be worthwhile for high school students.

At least one more critical issue on gender differences should be considered before we move on. What happens to boys who do not, or seem not to, fit the socially constructed model of masculinity? Sometimes they adjust and proudly become "new men," but sometimes they suffer greatly. In some cases, their suffering becomes so intolerable that they turn to violence – perhaps, in the most terrible way, to prove their masculinity. Jessie Klein and Lynn Chancer remind us that almost all of the mass killings in schools a few years ago were committed by boys who believed that their masculinity had

---

[27] Michael S. Kimmel, "Clarence, William, Iron Mike, Tailhook, Senator Packwood, Spur Posse, Magic... and Us," in Buchwald et al., *Transforming a Rape Culture*, p. 123.

[28] The Woolf comment appeared in chapter 2. It was quoted in Sara Ruddick, *Maternal Thinking: Towards a Politics of Peace* (Boston: Beacon Press, 1989), p. 154.

been challenged.[29] "However," they note, "the social construction of masculinity was not among the problems the media cited to explain the killings."[30] We will return to this important problem later in a brief discussion of homosexuality.

It is clear that both women and men have suffered from expectations arising out of society's construction of masculinity and femininity. But women have borne a particularly heavy burden, and we turn to that next.

The Second Sex

Simone de Beauvoir opened her well-known book this way: "Woman? Very simple, say the fanciers of simple formulas: she is a womb, an ovary; she is a female – this word is sufficient to define her."[31] Hearing this, high school girls may rightly protest that no one talks or thinks like this today. But the attitude, covered over with language required by political correctness, lies deep in the masculine psyche and is supported by accepted practices in religion, politics, art, and employment. We can't engage here in a full historical account of societies' treatment of women, but students should be aware of crucial points that still affect the lives of women.

In all of the world's great religions – especially the three great monotheistic traditions – women have been an afterthought. Considering Aristotle's description of the female as a "misbegotten male," Aquinas asks whether "woman" should even have been created and then expends space, energy, and questionable logic in explaining that she is necessary as a helper to man – not in great worldly tasks where another man would be a better helper but in generation. Many women in my graduate classes have reacted to this remark – and others to be mentioned shortly – with outrage. One fortyish woman slammed a book on her desk and demanded, "Where does he get off at with such a remark? And why haven't I heard this stuff before?" Hers

[29] See Jessie Klein and Lynn S. Chancer, "Masculinity Matters: The Omission of Gender from High-Profile School Violence Cases," in Stephanie Urso Spina, ed., *Smoke and Mirrors* (Lanham, MD: Rowman & Littlefield, 2000), pp. 129–162.
[30] Ibid., p. 130.
[31] Simone de Beauvoir, *The Second Sex*, trans. H. M. Parshley (New York: Bantam Books, 1952), p. 3.

was a double indictment – one of male thinkers who have regularly insulted women and one of an educational system that refuses to discuss such matters.

If students begin to read religious literature with critical eyes, they will see that the male bias is pervasive. "God" is *he*, although (rarely) he reveals feminine attributes. Wisdom, in what Jack Miles calls the "marriage of Torah and Wisdom," appears as a woman in Proverbs but, as Miles remarks, her message "scarcely goes beyond 'If you make a fool of yourself, don't say I didn't warn you.'"[32] I mention this episode because many of today's religious thinkers strive mightily to show that the female does appear with some dignity in sacred literature. It would be worthwhile for students to seek out and report on such passages. What are some of these passages, and does their occurrence refute my claim that male bias is pervasive?

Material of this sort must be handled with sensitivity. I'm not sure it can be handled at all in public schools, although it is material well known to many members of the college-educated population. As advised earlier, it should not be presented in the spirit of laying out the final and absolute truth. Rather, it should be introduced as significant cultural knowledge: Here is what some scholars have claimed; here is what others have concluded from the evidence available. I admit that we may not be able to do this but, with a heavy heart, I ask readers to consider why not. What does it say about our view of education that we cannot even raise these issues in public high schools?

Let's set religion aside for the moment. Philosophers, psychologists, artists, and sociologists have also contributed to the status of women as a "second caste."[33] Virginia Woolf (less than a century ago) asked young women, "Have you any notion how many books are written about women in the course of one year? Have you any notion how many are written by men?"[34] Women and their activities were

---

[32] Jack Miles, *God: A Biography* (New York: Alfred A. Knopf, 1995), p. 293.

[33] Beauvoir writes of "two castes" in *The Second Sex*.

[34] Virginia Woolf, *A Room of One's Own* (New York: Harcourt Brace, 1929), p. 26. Also, the film, with Eileen Atkins as Woolf, is wonderful and worth viewing by high school students.

directed by men. Even childbirth and mothering were directed by men. The subject of *woman*, said Woolf,

> attracts agreeable essayists, light-fingered novelists, young men who have taken the M.A degree; men who have taken no degree; men who have no apparent qualification save that they are not women.[35]

The pages from which these comments are drawn are funny, informative, enormously sad, and ultimately enraging. If I were not basically opposed to coerced reading, I would suggest that these pages be made required reading. Woolf writes of "Professor von X" (he is legion) and "his monumental work entitled *The Mental, Moral, and Physical Inferiority of the Female Sex.*" Her musings about Professor X (the personification of male attitudes toward women) are hilarious – his heavy build, great jowl, small eyes, red face. She draws unattractive doodles of X. She speculates on what has made him so irritable and unhappy. She admits to being upset by the accusation of inferiority: "My heart had leapt. My cheeks burnt. I had flushed with anger."[36] Of course. Most thinking women react the same way. And writings similar to those that upset Woolf continued to appear long after 1929.

Psychologists had been discussing the *variability hypothesis* since 1894, with interest falling off after 1936 and picking up again in the 1960s and 1970s. The hypothesis states that males vary more than females in intellectual capacities; that is, more males are found among the highest and lowest scorers. Females are more nearly alike, and not so many extremes are found.[37] Although research on the hypothesis was often done with objectivity, the hypothesis itself echoes a long-held and contemptuous view of women. In 1885, for example, Max Nordau wrote:

> Woman is as a rule, typical; man, individual. The former has average, the latter exceptional features ... there is incomparably less variation

---

[35] Ibid., p. 27.
[36] Ibid., p. 32.
[37] The hypothesis is still around. See Alan Feingold, "Sex Differences in Variability in Intellectual Abilities: A New Look at an Old Controversy," *Review of Educational Research* 62(1), 1992: 61–84.

between women than between men. If you know one, you know them all, with but few exceptions.[38]

This *sameness* of women was attributed to biology, not to the social restrictions by which women were bound. One could argue – and students should consider this possibility – that respectable scientific studies were needed to overturn the centuries'-long bias that maintained the claim of female mediocrity. However, because of the cultural constraints and expectations controlling women, one could accurately predict that the hypothesis would hold up, especially if the traits chosen for study were those already thought to favor men. An early female researcher, Helen Thompson, studied a wider range of intellectual and personality traits than her male colleagues, and she found no significant gender differences.[39] I have argued that we should add still more items to the test battery:

> listening skills, oral and written text interpretation, interpersonal reasoning, production of constructive (nonadversarial) responses, resistance to the use of verbal or physical violence as a mode of response, interruptibility (the capacity to carry on an intellectual task through a series of interruptions), and managing several tasks simultaneously.[40]

Like essentialism, the variability hypothesis works to the detriment of women. If they are told that they are mediocre or inferior intellectually, their performance may fulfill the prediction. It is hard to excel when the expectation that you will not do well is clear. An explanation like this, called *stereotype threat*, has been advanced with respect to black–white differences on various tests.[41] If test takers are told in advance that people from their group usually do less well than others, they do in fact do less well. But much more is operating here than

---

[38] Quoted in Bram Dijkstra, *Idols of Perversity: Fantasies of Feminine Evil in Fin-de-Siècle Culture* (New York and Oxford: Oxford University Press, 1986), p. 129.

[39] See Helen B. Thompson, *The Mental Traits of Sex* (Chicago: University of Chicago Press, 1903).

[40] Nel Noddings, "Variability: A Pernicious Hypothesis," *Review of Educational Research* 62(1), 1992: 85–88.

[41] See, for example, Claude M. Steele, "A Threat in the Air: How Stereotypes Shape Intellectual Identity and Performance," *American Psychologist* 52, 1997: 613–629.

threat and achievement on a particular test. When a whole culture and its traditions are soaked in negative attitudes toward a group, the effects spread into every facet of life. Both threats and effects seem to live permanently in the collective unconscious.

Many young women know that they are deeply affected by the stereotype every time they take a test in mathematics or science. But even those who feel personally unaffected – both girls and boys – should develop a sympathetic understanding for the women who preceded them. The story of Mary Somerville (1780–1872) is useful here. Self-taught, Somerville became a scientist, and her book became a "standard text for advanced students at Cambridge."[42] However, although she achieved many honors, she was never accepted into the formal societies of male science. David Noble comments:

> Her book was used as a required text in a university in which she could not teach nor have her daughters study. Her bronze likeness was placed in the Royal Society's Great Hall, from which she herself was barred. (Although her nonscientist husband early became a fellow of the Royal Society, no such honor was ever even contemplated for her.)[43]

Perhaps saddest of all was the evaluation she made toward the end of her life. Noble quotes her:

> "I have perseverance and intelligence, but no genius," she wrote. "That spark from heaven is not granted to the sex, we are of the earth, earthy, whether higher powers may be allotted to us in another existence God knows, original genius in science at least is hopeless in this." Her despair haunts us still.[44]

The effects of the stereotype have been pervasive and destructive,[45] and the basic dilemma arises again: Should members of oppressed groups, those said to be inferior, struggle to prove that they are as good as white males in male-dominated activities or should they strive to raise the valuation of activities in which they already excel? The goal should be to make this an individual decision proudly made on the

---

[42] David F. Noble, *A World without Women* (Oxford: Oxford University Press, 1992), p. 280.
[43] Ibid., p. 280.
[44] Ibid., p. 281.
[45] See also Rossiter, *Women Scientists,* for more stories of this sort.

basis of sound thinking and evaluation. Education should promote the knowledge and confidence required to make either decision, and we should teach for a world in which the despair of Mary Somerville is not repeated.

Before leaving this topic, we must address one more issue of fundamental importance. We have been concentrating on the question of women's intellectual competence. Surely, it is insulting to be regarded as intellectually inferior a priori – with no basis for the judgment in personal experience. But it is perhaps even more insulting to be considered morally inferior. Yet this assumption is deeply rooted in the world's religions.

The idea that woman brought death and evil into the world appears in classical mythology, although the story may be a distortion of earlier myths more favorable to women. In any case, Hesiod's version of the Pandora story is the one that influenced Christianity, and the church fathers found room for Pandora alongside Eve. John Chrysostom, for example, wrote:

> What else is woman but a foe to friendship, an inescapable punishment, a necessary evil, a natural temptation, a desirable calamity, a domestic danger, a delectable detriment, an evil nature, painted with fair colors?[46]

Even though it is mainly men who slaughter people in war and rebellion and who commit most of the world's violent crimes, women are portrayed as the root of evil and as morally inferior in all three of the great monotheistic systems and in much of philosophy as well. The basic story of Adam and Eve – of Eve's seduction by the serpent especially – is so well known that we need not spend time on it here. What most teenagers do not know, however, is that the story has been told and retold in both orthodox and heterodox religion, in art, literature, philosophy, and politics. The story of Eve's weakness and guilt has been enormously damaging to women.

If high school teachers attempt to teach the myth of Eve, they are likely to encounter either of two reactions. The first – one I encountered quite recently in talking with a class of seniors at a prestigious college – is "but that's not a myth!" Without expressing astonishment

---

[46] Quoted in John Anthony Phillips, *Eve: The History of an Idea* (San Francisco: Harper & Row, 1984), p. 22.

at this, teachers must patiently help students to understand that a myth is not simply a falsehood believed by primitive people in other lands or times. A myth captures some cultural interpretation of truth and gains its power from its potential to be cast and recast in endlessly fascinating ways.[47] Scholars do not insult the Adam and Eve story by calling it a myth. In part, we bring this reaction on ourselves in education by regularly teaching Greek, Roman, Egyptian, and Norse myths and carefully avoiding those that appear in Christian, Muslim, and Judaic traditions. We shouldn't be surprised, then, when affronted students object to our naming the myth of Adam and Eve with "that isn't a myth!"

The second predictable reaction is "but no one believes that anymore." Here we have to be careful. We can acknowledge that quite a few people still believe the myth in the sense just discussed; that is, they find something significant in it to guide (or disrupt) their lives. But there may be people in the class, and there are surely people in the larger society, who believe in the literal truth of the story.[48] We can only remind students that we must remain respectful of those who express views we find objectionable or we will not be able to discuss these matters at all. Respecting the speaker does not imply respecting the view expressed. Further, even if it were true that no one now believes the Adam and Eve story, the myth is so much a part of world culture that it continues to influence our lives. To those who think the story has lost its relevance, J. A. Phillips says:

> But the myth of Eve is neither unintelligible nor irrelevant. It remains deeply imbedded [sic] in both male and female ideas about the nature and destiny of women, and the attitudes it has engendered are embodied in the psychology, laws, religious life, and social structures of the Western world. . . . Eve is very much alive, and every member of Western society is affected by her story.[49]

If students still express doubt about the current impact of the story, they should be asked to watch an hour or two of world news and record the number of women they see around conference tables in political settings: How many do they count at the table with the

---

[47] Teachers might refer students to Joseph Campbell, *The Power of Myth* (New York: Anchor, 1991).

[48] See again Peshkin, *God's Choice*.

[49] Phillips, *Eve*, p. 172.

242

leaders of Israel, Europe, Palestine, or the United States? How many on the floor of the U.S. Senate? How many in the British House of Commons? How many priests? What accounts for the scarcity of women in these settings? (This is not a multiple-choice or one-answer question to which the answer is "the Eve story.")

Educators should ask themselves why the material discussed in this section almost never appears in the public school curriculum. Is it less important than the War of 1812 or the rise of the Republican Party? And why is it that women are only mentioned in connection with activities already dominated by men? The suggestion in this material is that a few women have also done interesting things.

I'll close this section with a poignant account of the harm that has been done to some women by religious insistence on their moral inferiority. There are many, many such stories. Pearl Buck tells the story of her mother's suffering under the doubts of her fundamentalist preacher husband concerning her moral status. Her mother (called "Carie" in *The Exile*) was warm-hearted, generous, and tempted toward open-mindedness. Her tolerance caused her husband to worry over the condition of her soul. Commenting on her father, whom she loved and cared for in his old age, but sympathizing with her mother, Buck wrote:

> Strange remote soul of a man that could pierce into the very heavens and discern God with such certainty and never see the proud and lonely creature at his side! To him she was only a woman. Since those days when I saw all her nature dimmed I have hated Saint Paul with all my heart and so must all true women hate him, I think, because of what he has done in the past to women like Carie, proud, free-born women, yet damned by their very womanhood. I rejoice for her sake that his power is gone in these new days.[50]

What did St. Paul say that harmed women? Can students find anything on the topic in his favor? But it will not help to hate St. Paul. He was not the first to denigrate the intellectual and moral worth of women, and he is certainly not the last. But students should consider whether his power is really gone in these times. Is it? Should it be?

However, women are not the only ones to suffer under gender bias. Those with a homosexual orientation do also.

---

[50] Pearl S. Buck, *The Exile* (New York: Triangle, 1936), p. 283.

Homosexuality

Many students get at least some information about homosexuality in sex education courses provided by their school. The main objective in this setting is to help young people avoid sexually transmitted diseases, especially acquired immune deficiency syndrome (AIDS). This is well and good, but another conversation should take place somewhere – perhaps everywhere – in schools, and that is an exploration of the hatred often expressed toward homosexuals.

Why do so many people hate gays and suppose that somehow their hatred proves their own righteousness? This is a question that should launch a set of critical lessons. First, perhaps, students should be asked to consider what it is like to be threatened, harassed, and insulted on a regular basis. Rita Kissen has documented a host of cases describing the suffering of gay students:

> One of them went to the principal and said, "This is going on and I'm being harassed and pushed around." The principal actually said to him, "Conform and that won't happen. Change your dress." ... And so with that kind of support the kid said, "Forget this. This is not safe for me to be here." ... And so he dropped out.[51]

Before discussion gets started, teachers should make it clear that these conversations will provide an opportunity to *talk* about hatred and abuse, *not* to express hatred or to engage in verbal abuse. Like so many other topics addressed in this book, the topic of homosexuality has to be handled with great sensitivity. Disclosure of one's status as homosexual should be neither encouraged nor forbidden, but it should be made clear that the need for this rule is deplored. Why must a person hide his or her full identity? One reason is, of course, that disclosure of identity may evoke verbal abuse of astonishing nastiness. Kissen recounts conversations that took place in Colorado during a campaign to eliminate special laws designed to protect gays and lesbians from discrimination. Kids felt no moral compunction in asking, "Are you a fag?" Or in saying such things as "Well, faggots should all be hanged." "I don't want to have to work with anybody that's gay." Even some teachers used hate language. "One guy was saying, 'Oh, I

---

[51] Rita Kissen, *The Last Closet: The Real Lives of Lesbian and Gay Teachers* (Portsmouth, NH: Heinemann, 1996), p. 58.

think it's right [to eliminate laws protecting gays]. I think these people should be taken out and shot. . . . '"[52]

What accounts for such brazen hatred? We've encountered hatred before in discussing the psychology of war, and we know that racial hatred was freely expressed in the United States not long ago. In some settings, it still occurs, and it may simmer just below the surface in many more. A moving passage in *The Siege of Krishnapur* explores the issue. Mr. Hopkins, the Collector of Krishnapur, is digging a grave for three more victims of the siege:

> And as he dug, he wept. He saw Hari's animated face, and numberless dead men, and the hatred on the faces of the sepoys. . . . and it suddenly seemed to him that he could see clearly the basis of all conflict and misery, something mysterious which grows in men at the same time as hair and teeth and brains and which reveals its presence by the utter and atrocious inflexibility of all human habits and beliefs, even including his own.[53]

This kind of thinking could be the beginning of wisdom. Does hatred grow in us like hair and teeth? Is the socialization about which we've talked the source of our inflexibility? Some people do not develop hate, although – because of its prevalence – they may maintain a wary distrust. If hate does not develop in everyone, is it because some have learned how to think critically about patterns of socialization? Is that sort of reflection one way to overcome the tendency to develop inflexible habits?

Hatred always has an object.[54] One individual may hate another for perceived wrongs done to her or out of envy. Such individual hatred may be deserved; that is, the one who is hated may have done real harm to the hater. In such cases, apology and restitution may reduce the hatred. But sometimes nothing can alleviate the hatred. The hater sees acts of kindness as condescension. Assurances of support are assessed as hypocrisy. Smiles become sneers. Tears are "crocodile" tears. This hatred is nourished in the heart of the hater. Therapy is required to understand and relieve it.

---

[52] These comments and many more appear in Kissen, *The Last Closet*, pp. 112–113.
[53] J. G. Farrell, *The Siege of Krishnapur* (New York: New York Review Books, 2004), p. 192.
[54] See Willard Gaylin, *Hatred: The Psychological Descent into Violence* (New York: Public Affairs, 2003).

The hatred that concerns us here is hatred for a group of people identified as somehow *other* – immorally different. That form
of hatred can also be nurtured from within, but it gets started in
the external world and is almost always supported by a like-minded
group. In war, as we saw earlier, hate flourishes, but it often disappears when the war ends. In that sense, some hatred is situational,
and a deeper understanding of how it is encouraged by propaganda
may serve to lessen it.

Hatred or moral condemnation of homosexuals is not situational,
but it is often brought to the surface by situational factors. For example, when campaigns have been launched either to give homosexuals
more legal protection or to cancel laws that already do so, animosity
seems to grow, and haters seem to feel empowered to use language
that they would otherwise curb.[55] The attitude of those who hate
homosexuals does not change when the situation changes, but manifestations of hatred may be fewer.

What supports this hatred? We know that, besides fear and anger, a
warped form of patriotism supports hate in wartime. National leaders
exploit this warped patriotism through systematic programs of propaganda. It is hard not to hate the enemy when everyone around you
expresses hate and looks upon nonhaters as somehow suspect. In the
case of homosexuality, a warped form of religious devotion is a prime
suspect, and I'll come back to this for a fuller discussion. For now,
it is enough to notice that religious beliefs are almost impossible to
discuss in public school classrooms, and it is not surprising that educators who want to make schools safer for gay and lesbian students
almost never mention religion. If this discussion is opened, those who
oppose homosexuality on religious grounds must be allowed to voice
their opinions, and that may be hard on homosexual students. But
the object is to reduce hatred and eliminate violence. Honest disagreement does not have to eventuate in abuse.

Most programs designed to promote understanding of homosexuality and acceptance of homosexuals provide information – stories
of prominent homosexuals in history or the arts, accounts of the
abuse and suffering of homosexual youths, the horrible rate of suicide
among them, criticism of the harmful language used so freely among
teenagers, and the deplorable practices in schools that, in essence,

---

[55] See the accounts in Kissen, *Last Closet*.

blame the victim.[56] These are useful programs, but they depend on the questionable assumption that greater knowledge of a group (race, nationality, religion) will reduce prejudice. The assumption is logical, but there is little evidence to support it. The apparent suspension of prejudice sometimes achieved seems to move below the surface, ready to burst forth when circumstances permit it to do so.

Hard as it is to consider, the problem is probably a form of mental/emotional illness in the haters. Can this be addressed in schools? Well, almost certainly not in the way I have just phrased it. We can't tell students that they are sick and need treatment. But we can ask them to consider why they feel as they do. If religious conviction inspires their hatred, does it not also counsel them to hate the sin but love the sinner? Are cruelty and abuse ever supported by genuine religion or are they a result of faulty interpretation? Why do so many people who profess religious belief feel free to use abusive language?

Let us suppose that some students are, at least indirectly, influenced by religion. Certainly it is true that all three great monotheistic faiths have spoken against homosexuality.[57] But all three have also made women subservient, allowed or endorsed slavery, and (at some time in their history) defended the slaughter of innocents. If all three have now rejected the killing of innocents and turned against slavery, it would seem that sacred pronouncements on homosexuality can properly be reinterpreted as people think more deeply on human problems. Some groups within each of the great religions have even renounced their former teachings on the nature and role of women. So why not on homosexuality? Why is homosexuality often associated with "pedophilia, sadism, and masochism"?[58]

When these questions have been posed and reflection advised, it might be well to retreat temporarily from the focus on religion and transfer attention to some of the curricular topics designed to reveal homosexuals as "regular" people. Jane Addams, for example, lived

---

[56] See the essays in *Theory and Research in Social Education*, Special Issue: Social Education and Sexual Identity 30(2), 2002; also Stephen J. Thornton, "Silence on Gays and Lesbians in Social Studies Curriculum," *Social Education* 67(4), 2003: 226–230.

[57] For an account of Christianity's intolerance of homosexuals, see John Boswell, *Christianity, Social Tolerance, and Homosexuality* (Chicago: University of Chicago Press, 1981).

[58] See Kissen, *Last Closet*, on the content of Oregon's failed Measure Nine (1992).

in a community of women for her entire professional life. She may or may not have had a lesbian relationship with Mary Rozet Smith. It is none of our business. But if she had, would that diminish our admiration for her accomplishments? Eleanor Roosevelt, too, may have had a same-sex relationship. So what? The purpose of programs that emphasize information is to disabuse students of their initial evaluation that something is wrong with "these people." Accounts of gay and lesbian couples should also be introduced. Here are ordinary, decent, hard-working people who live like the rest of us, except that they live with partners of the same sex. When it has been shown that gays and lesbians are usually law-abiding, pleasant people, the discussion can return to religion.

But wait. Students may object that not all gays and lesbians are ordinary, decent folks. Look at the way some dress and behave in public. Look at the disgraceful displays in the so-called gay parades. It can be admitted that many of us find these antics distasteful. We don't have to romanticize a group by creating a false, positive stereotype. There are many displays and habits in all kinds of people (even in our friends) that we find distasteful or even offensive, but we do not usually feel justified in abusing those who so offend our sensibilities.

Let's suppose that students want to return to the topic of religion. (They may not want to do this.) Can students find passages in the Bible that speak against homosexuality or do they depend on the words of current preachers and opponents of homosexuality? Do they know that many religious leaders have spoken out against the abuse of homosexuals? This is a good time to talk again about mixed messages. When religious leaders advise parishioners to hate the sin but love the sinner, they create a tension that is difficult to manage. Usually, when we follow this advice, we are committed to helping the sinner overcome the sin. We do not expect him to go on sinning. But what does it do to an individual to be told that his or her very identity is sinful? At best, the message to love the sinner might reduce some of the physical and verbal abuse that homosexuals suffer, but this is by no means guaranteed.

Students should also consider the terrible comments made by some religious leaders suggesting that AIDS is a punishment visited on homosexuals by a wrathful God. Would a good, loving God do such a thing? Was the catastrophic Indian Ocean tsunami of 2004 a manifestation of God's anger? Some religious leaders have said so.

What kind of person could believe that God would kill small children, mothers trying desperately to save their children, whole families, whole villages? What kind of God do such people believe in? Is it possible that angry, jealous people project their own anger and jealousy on the God they worship? These things have to be considered.

As I was writing this section, two interesting things happened that make this discussion even more important. The *Chronicle of Higher Education* carried a story about the dilemma facing several public institutions of higher education.[59] Should campus Christian groups be allowed to discriminate against non-Christians and homosexuals by denying them membership? One could argue that freedom of religion should allow these groups to determine their own membership. But each of these large institutions has antidiscrimination rules that apply to all campus groups that receive recognition and financial support. Perhaps the solution will be to allow the exclusionary practices but withhold all public money. It is a story worth following.

The other story is more troubling. The new secretary of education, Margaret Spellings, has ordered that an episode of a film sponsored by her department not be shown in public school classes. Why? The episode includes a lesbian family, and Spellings has expressed fear that some families will not want their young children to be exposed to that way of life. Should schools pretend that lesbian and gay parents do not exist? This event reveals just how difficult it will be to discuss matters of sexual orientation in schools. How can we combat cruelty, abuse, and violence if we are not allowed to talk about the conditions that give rise to them?

In this chapter, we have looked at problems of gender – feminine and masculine identity, occupational conflicts, the centuries'-long oppression of women, and the current intolerance and abuse of homosexuals. Some of the issues raised here involve religion, and it is very hard to talk about religious beliefs in public schools. But that is the topic to which we turn next.

---

[59] See Burton Bollag, "Choosing Their Flock," *The Chronicle of Higher Education*, Jan. 28, 2005: A33–A35.

10

Religion

Goodness is the best source of spiritual clear-sightedness.

Miguel Unamuno

There are certain questions that every thoughtful human being asks, and most of us long to hear how other reflective people have answered them. To "educate" without addressing these questions is to engage in educational malpractice. It won't do to argue that such questions should be explored in religious institutions, not in public schools. In most religious institutions, students will hear only one set of answers and, although some people find such answers deeply satisfying, single answers – accepted unreflectively – are intellectually unsatisfactory. How would a person committed to one view respond if she or he heard another well-articulated view?

Then, of course, there are many students who have no formal religious education. For most of them, the great existential questions still arise but, met with silence, they remain unexplored. Students may even be embarrassed to admit that they have such questions. Asked by others whether they believe in God, they may answer that they do, because they have never heard a respectable opinion to the contrary.

Teachers in public schools should not give specific answers to these questions. The idea is certainly not to proselytize, and any attempts to convert students to a particular religious view are clearly unconstitutional. The idea is to introduce students to a rich and fascinating literature that addresses the great existential questions from a variety of perspectives. Although these questions will be general with respect to religions and theological perspectives, the answers we explore here will be drawn mainly from Christian traditions. The reason for this is twofold. First, the topic is huge, and I am not outlining a course on comparative religion. Second, Christianity and its legacies affect every citizen of the Western world, and all students should know something about its myths and beliefs. Certainly, students should also be encouraged to explore each of the questions from their own religious perspective. The task is challenging, but let's consider how we might approach it.

Does God Exist?

The vast majority of Americans profess a belief in God, and a recent survey found that 84 percent of U.S. adolescents declare such a belief.[1] It is hard to say what this professed belief means or even whether the profession of belief is honest because, when interviewed at some length, many of those who say that they believe in God also say that their belief has little effect on their daily lives and conduct.[2]

What should teenagers know about approaches to the question of belief? First, perhaps, they should know that many believers have been afflicted by doubt and uncertainty. The epigraph at the beginning of this book warns us that we get a "dusty answer when hot for certainty in this our life." Hans Kung also asks, "Where, we wonder, is there a rocklike, unshakable certainty on which all human certainty could be built?"[3] After presenting 702 pages of religious history and debate, Kung concludes that God does indeed exist and that belief is anchored in faith but compatible with reason. Teenagers cannot be expected to wade through a volume as long and dense as Kung's, but they should know that the question has inspired such monumental investigations.

Faith or reason? Theologians and philosophers tried for many centuries to prove logically that God exists. The proofs have taken several forms and, again, rigorous examination of their logic is probably beyond the capacity (or patience) of most teenagers. However, I have

---

[1] Christian Smith, *Soul Searching: The Religious and Spiritual Lives of American Teenagers* (Oxford: Oxford University Press, 2005).
[2] Ibid.
[3] Hans Kung, *Does God Exist?* (Garden City, NY: Doubleday, 1980), p. 1.

seen a simplified version of the ontological proof discussed in a mathematics class. This version of the ontological proof was offered by Descartes – hence its applicability in a math class. It goes something like this:

1. The idea of God is that of a perfect being.
2. If God did not exist, he would lack perfection.
3. Therefore, God must exist.

Can students find a flaw in this argument? The great philosopher Immanuel Kant argued that perfection is an idea and does not imply that the perfect exists. He also destroyed the so-called cosmological proof, which argues that the universe must have had a creator – that creator we call God. But, Kant writes, that is a mistake, for we can still ask about the origin of God:

> We cannot put off the thought, nor can we support it, that a Being, which we represent to ourselves as the highest among all possible beings, should say to himself, I am from eternity to eternity, there is nothing beside me, except that which is something through my will, – *but whence am I?*[4]

And, thus, once that question is asked, we have to ask also, "Why couldn't the universe have created itself?"

The third great proof (which Kant also discredited) is important because it has reappeared in current arguments. The teleological proof argues that, where there is design, there must be a designer and a purpose. Kant argues that, at most, this proof would give us an architect, not a creator. David Hume, before Kant, had already argued that the analogy of the universe to a mechanism might be faulty.[5] Hume's reference is to the argument that infers from the existence of a watch that there must have been a watchmaker. But, Hume asked, what if the universe were not a mechanism but, say, more like a living organism?

Even if the analogy between the universe and a watch or clock is thought to hold, we still get no proof that the watchmaker is God. Why

---

[4] Immanuel Kant, *Critique of Pure Reason*, trans. F. Max Muller (Garden City, NY: Doubleday Anchor Books, 1966), p. 409. For a lucid and not too difficult discussion of the proofs, see Simon Blackburn, *Think* (Oxford: Oxford University Press, 1999).

[5] See David Hume, *Dialogues Concerning Natural Religion*, ed. Richard Popkin (Indianapolis: Hackett, 1980).

not a blind watchmaker, say evolution or the laws of physics as the engineer who, without purpose, produces the wonderful mechanism through repeated trial and error?[6]

Most philosophers today believe that attempts to prove God's existence by reason alone are hopeless. There are those, however, who are still trying to prove (by logical demonstration) that God does *not* exist.[7] These proofs are difficult, and there is no need for teenagers to struggle with them. It is enough for them to know that people are still engaged in such activities and that most of us believe that the existence or nonexistence of God will never by established by logic. However, they should also hear arguments that cast serious doubt on the ways in which the monotheistic God has been described, and some of these arguments will be explored briefly a bit later. These proofs show that God cannot be all-powerful, all-knowing, and all-good. Notice, however, that even if they are successful, they would not prove that God (under some definition) does not exist.

But let's return to the design argument as it is currently promoted. There is a set of ideas called *creation science*, and these ideas are directly contrary to evolution theory. Prominent among these ideas is the claim that all living species were created directly and completely by God; species do not evolve. Most scientists reject creation science as unscientific, and it is important for students to know this. If scientists are right in this rejection, it does not mean that a creator, design, or purpose is ruled out. Simon Conway Morris, in a long, difficult, and fascinating work on the inevitability of certain products of evolution, firmly rejects creation science but leaves open the possibility of a creator. In his preface, he writes:

> [If] you happen to be a 'creation scientist' (or something of that kind)...may I politely suggest that you put this book back on the shelf. It will do you no good. Evolution is true, it happens, it is the way the world is, and we too are one of its products.[8]

---

[6] See Richard Dawkins, *The Blind Watchmaker* (New York: Norton, 1986); see also Michael Ruse, *Darwin and Design* (Cambridge, MA: Harvard University Press, 2003).

[7] See Michael Martin and Ricki Monnier, eds., *The Impossibility of God* (Amherst, NY: Prometheus Books, 2003).

[8] Simon Conway Morris, *Life's Solution: Inevitable Humans in a Lonely Universe* (Cambridge: Cambridge University Press, 2003), xv.

But evolutionary evidence is loaded with signs of what might be described as purpose; at least, there seems to be a drive to satisfy certain natural or physical needs. Certain avenues or solutions are tried repeatedly, modified, perfected. Intelligence, Morris says, is an inevitable product, and he urges us to use that intelligence to probe existential and metaphysical questions more deeply. He concludes his examination of evolution and inevitability with lines that religious teenagers may find comforting:

> None of it presupposes, let alone proves, the existence of God, but all is congruent. For some it will remain as the pointless activity of the Blind Watchmaker, but others may prefer to remove their dark glasses. The choice, of course, is yours.[9]

The bottom line at present is that creation science and its more sophisticated offspring, intelligent design, are both rejected by most working scientists.[10] That does not mean, however, that scientists reject God. Indeed polls in the 1990s showed that about "40 percent of American scientists continued to believe in a personal God."[11] They simply refuse to consider supernatural causes when they are doing science. Is their position absurd? We'll see, as we move the discussion along, that human interest and belief in religion is riddled with contradictions.

If the most we can hope for from reason and logic is an argument for compatibility, is there something else that might induce a commitment to belief in God? The time-tested answer is faith. The mathematician/philosopher Blaise Pascal rejected all attempts to demonstrate the existence of God by logical proof.[12] Instead he offered a wager: Suppose you believe in God, and it turns out that God exists. You win immortal life! (Pascal was a Catholic and believed in heaven and hell.) If you do not believe in God, and God exists, you spend eternity in hell. On the other hand, if you believe, and God does not

[9] Ibid., p. 330.
[10] There are many works to consult here, for example, David Lindberg and Ronald L. Numbers, eds., *When Science and Christianity Meet* (Chicago: University of Chicago Press, 2003); Ruse, *Darwin and Design*; Niall Shanks, *God, the Devil, and Darwin* (Oxford: Oxford University Press, 2004).
[11] See Ronald L. Numbers, "Science without God: Natural Laws and Christian Beliefs," in *When Science and Christianity Meet*, pp. 265–285.
[12] See Blaise Pascal, *Pensées*, trans. A. J. Krailsheimer (Baltimore: Penguin Books, 1966); for the refutation, see Blackburn, *Think*.

exist, what have you lost? Some philosophers would argue that, in this case, you have lost something substantial: an opportunity to live a full, moral, happy life without coercion or guilt, a chance to assert yourself as a moral agent, the possibility of teaching others to abandon the fear of hell. But from a logical point of view, there is an even more devastating reply to Pascal. If we do not know that God exists, how do we know what he would want and reward? Perhaps he would reward those who best use their intelligence and free will, and discard those who, unreflectively, make this weasellike wager.

Søren Kierkegaard is perhaps the best-known philosophical proponent of belief by faith. He even defined faith, not virtue, as the opposite of sin.[13] The pattern of his life – a constant, continued reaffirmation of faith in the face of uncertainty – is not appealing to many. But his insistence on the inward, personal search for God does appeal to some who espouse spirituality rather than formal religion and ritual.

Many students will find the emphasis on faith compatible with their Christianity, but most will know little about the philosophical debate over reason and faith; they deserve a chance to hear at least some of it. Further, all students should master a basic vocabulary concerning belief in God. A *theist* believes in one God who can and sometimes does intervene in the lives of individuals and nations. One need not belong to a religious institution to be a theist; there are philosophical theists.[14] A *deist* believes in a creator-God who does not reveal himself or intervene in human affairs. An *atheist* believes there is no God. An *agnostic* believes the question of God's existence is undecidable. And a *polytheist* believes in the existence of many gods. There are variations and refinements of all these terms, but students should understand at least the basic definitions in order to ask intelligent questions about the various positions that might be held.

I do not mean to suggest that teachers use exactly the same examples and references that I have used here. The question of God's existence has generated an enormous literature, and there are many possibilities from which to choose. The important thing is for students to become familiar with the most significant approaches. It is

---

[13] See Søren Kierkegaard, *Fear and Trembling* and *The Sickness Unto Death*, trans. Walter Lowrie (Princeton, NJ: Princeton University Press, 1941).

[14] See Martin Gardner, *The Whys of a Philosophical Scrivener* (New York: Quill, 1983).

also important to make choices that add to the cultural knowledge of students. It is for this reason that I have mentioned Descartes, Kung, Kant, Hume, Pascal, and Kierkegaard. Other teachers might select different thinkers.

What Must I Believe?

Many students who profess a religious belief are troubled by the fact that they do not really believe everything that appears in their church's doctrine. I use *church* here because, recall, that I am speaking mainly of Christianity. The ideas, questions, and modes of approach should have wider application, but it should be noted that Jewish students may be somewhat baffled by the emphasis on belief. For them, the important questions center on conduct, not belief: What am I commanded to do? It is primarily Christians who are enjoined *to believe*. Must one give up her or his religious affiliation if one rejects some of its beliefs?

Clearly, many religious leaders have challenged the way their institutions conduct themselves. Martin Luther is a primary example here. However, it has not been unusual for believers to express doubt about particular bits of doctrine. For example, Henry Van Dusen, a Presbyterian theologian, refused at the time of his ordination exam to affirm the virgin birth of Jesus.[15] Disagreements have arisen and still arise not only between faiths but also between individuals. In general, there continues to be a fierce debate between those who see Christianity (or any of its divisions) as a growing, changing faith and those who see it as a body of fixed doctrine. The latter view has been expressed not only by preachers in fundamentalist sects but also by distinguished theologians in mainline churches. In 1872, the prominent Presbyterian theologian Charles Hodge described his seminary's mission:

> "I am not afraid to say," he asserted, "that a new idea never originated in this Seminary." ... "The Bible is the word of God.... If granted; then it follows that what the Bible says, God says. That ends the matter."[16]

[15] See the account in D. G. Hart, *The University Gets Religion* (Baltimore: Johns Hopkins University Press, 1999), p. 118.
[16] Quoted in ibid., p. 46.

Some students may welcome such confidence and absolute acceptance. Others may be deeply troubled by it. Should we, for example,
accept St. Paul's pronouncements on the status and participation of
women in the church, or should we judge his statements as reflections of the time in which he lived, and revise our beliefs along more
empirically accurate and generous lines?[17] We could, of course, join
those scholars who insist that Paul was not really the source of the
misogynist statements charged to him. Mary Daly reminds us that
this scholarly effort matters little to the concerns of women:

> The point is that for nearly two thousand years the passages [at-
> tributed to St. Paul] have been used to enforce sexual hierarchy.
> They represent an established point of view. It is rather obscene to
> be more concerned with justifying an author long dead and with
> berating women for an alleged lack of scholarship than with the
> deep injustice itself that is being perpetrated by religion.[18]

In chapter 9, we saw that Pearl Buck wrote even more angrily about
St. Paul. Growing up in a household dominated by a fundamentalist
preacher-father, watching her much-loved mother suffer, Buck said
that she "hated St. Paul with all my heart."[19]

Despite the rejection of some teachings and doubts about certain
doctrinal assertions, many people (including angry, suffering women)
remain members of their faith's congregation. Belonging is more
important than believing. Moreover, as Harold Bloom suggests, Americans tend to be highly individualistic in their religious beliefs even
though, paradoxically, they often speak a rigid party line.[20] Religious
criticism, like the attempts to prove God's existence logically, may
be too sophisticated for teenagers, but they should be aware that
there is such an enterprise. Among other purposes, it tries to explain
how people can use fantastic stories and language without pausing

---

[17] Many Christian groups still insist on the "submission" of women and, of course,
the Catholic Church does not ordain women. On the teachings in a fundamentalist Christian school with respect to the place of women, see Alan Peshkin,
God's Choice: The Total World of a Fundamentalist Christian School (Chicago:
University of Chicago Press, 1986).

[18] Mary Daly, *Beyond God the Father* (Boston: Beacon Press, 1974), p. 5.

[19] Pearl S. Buck, *The Exile* (New York: Triangle, 1936), p. 283.

[20] See Harold Bloom, *The American Religion: The Emergence of the Post-Christian
Nation* (New York: Simon & Schuster).

to reflect on what they say they believe. Are they afraid to express doubts? Of whom or what are they afraid? Christian Smith, in interviewing teenagers about religion, found that many of them believed God was always watching them, so it may be that some people believe God will "get them" if they deviate from official doctrine. Yet many of these "believers" do not let their beliefs guide their daily conduct, nor do they know very much about what they believe.[21] It might be instructive for teenagers to hear at least a little religious criticism. They may disagree vigorously with, say, Bloom and yet come away with the new notion that one can talk as Bloom does and yet not be struck by lightning.

Discussion of belief and how various thinkers have treated it should be culturally informative as well as personally helpful. There is apparently a good deal of conceptual confusion among teenagers about religion. Not only is there the odd paradox revealed by the expressed belief that God is always watching, but people do as they please anyway. There is also confusion about the meaning of terms and what certain beliefs commit us to. Smith found, for example, that many teens who said they were deists or spoke as though they were deists contradicted themselves in other responses to his questions: "22 percent of teen 'deists' in our survey reported feeling close or very close to God (the very God they believe is not involved in the world today). Go figure."[22]

Conceptual confusion is not confined to teenagers. Many American citizens refuse to believe that Benjamin Franklin, Thomas Jefferson, George Washington, and Thomas Paine were deists; yet all four are discussed as deists in *The Encyclopedia of Philosophy*, and Washington is credited with ensuring that neither *God* nor *Christianity* appeared in the U.S. Constitution.[23] People who refuse to accept even the possibility that some of the founding fathers were deists often react to the charge with fear and indignation. What causes this reaction? Would a more detailed and sensitive study of the Enlightenment relieve some of this anxiety? We see here another illustration of how the discussion of critical questions and the search for information

---

[21] See Smith, *Soul Searching*.
[22] Ibid., p. 42.
[23] See Ernest C. Mossner, "Deism," in *The Encyclopedia of Philosophy*, ed. Paul Edwards (New York: Macmillan, 1967), pp. 326–336.

interact with and support each other. In thinking about their own religious beliefs – prompted, perhaps, by a survey such as Smith's – students may want to probe more deeply into deism. If they ask, "Could I be a deist?" they may also want to know something of the history of deism and the lives and beliefs of well-known deists.

Some forms of conceptual confusion might be described as "theological incorrectness."[24] People who seem to believe firmly in the sovereignty of God go on believing also in luck, ghosts, and demons, and some consult astrological tables and fortune tellers. Drawing on studies in cognitive science, Jason Slone describes some religious concepts as maximally counterintuitive and others as minimally counterintuitive. Maximally counterintuitive concepts need reinforcement and may be supported in either a doctrinal mode or an imagistic mode.[25] In the doctrinal mode, concepts are constantly reinforced by the official repetition of words and rituals. This may help to explain why Roman Catholics accept the veneration of Mary as virgin mother, while Presbyterians are (reluctantly) willing to overlook Van Dusen's rejection of the virgin birth. But, Slone notes, "Survival of maximally counterintuitive concepts in the doctrinal mode depends on effective policing by a religious hierarchy."[26] This is yet another example of coercive socialization that students should be encouraged to reflect upon.

The survival of maximally counterintuitive concepts in the imagistic mode depends largely on the high-arousal property of various exercises – events such as revivals. Obviously, high arousal contributes to wide variation in how people interpret the concepts, and so we may find concepts upheld vigorously even though they are poorly understood.

Information can also help to dispel other tenaciously held beliefs that are related to religious history. Some people suppose that U.S. currency has always included the motto "In God We Trust." In fact, the motto was introduced during the Civil War on the recommendation of Salmon P. Chase, secretary of the treasury. Congress first authorized

---

[24] See D. Jason Slone, *Theological Incorrectness: Why Religious People Believe What They Shouldn't* (Oxford: Oxford University Press, 2004).

[25] Here Slone is drawing on the work of Harvey Whitehouse, *Modes of Religiosity: A Cognitive Theory of Religious Transmission* (Walnut Creek, CA: Alta Mira Press, 2004).

[26] Slone, *Theological Incorrectness*, p. 63.

the motto for "a new two-cent coin issued in 1864. By the end of 1865, the original permission had been extended to engrave the motto on coins of nearly all denominations."[27] Similarly, the addition of "under God" to the pledge of allegiance was accomplished during a period of national stress (1954) – the Cold War – to dramatize the difference between American democracy and "godless communism." As an aside, the pledge itself is hardly a sacred document. Written in 1892 by a Christian Socialist, Francis Bellamy (a strong advocate of the separation of church and state), it was intended to promote unity in the public schools and, not incidentally, to celebrate the opening of the Chicago World's Fair.[28]

In asking themselves what they should believe, students might appreciate discussion of the attributes of God. The great monotheistic religions describe God as all-knowing, all-powerful, and all-good. The most powerful and effective disproofs of God show incompatibilities among these attributes. But, even if we are able to show convincingly that the existence of evil in the natural world implies that God cannot be both all-powerful and all-good, that does not prove that God does not exist. It just means that at least one of the three alleged attributes must be modified.

The so-called proofs from evil are important. One can argue that an omniscient, omnipotent, and all-good God cannot prevent moral evil because he has given human beings free will. But this cannot explain natural evil. Why do innocent children suffer and die? Why are there destructive storms and earthquakes? What sort of God would create a world in which its creatures must eat one another to survive?

For centuries, the existence of natural evil was blamed on the fall of Adam and Eve. Before the fall, it was claimed, there was no natural evil. With regard to animal pain, this explanation will not do. Even C. S. Lewis, a committed Christian, has admitted that modern science has eliminated this explanation as a possibility. Since animal life predated human life by many centuries, the fall could not have initiated animal pain.[29] Still, some theologians insist that

---

[27] Susan Jacoby, *Freethinkers* (New York: Metropolitan Books, 2004), p. 107.

[28] Erik Larson, *The Devil in the White City* (New York: Vintage Books, 2004); see also Jacoby, *Freethinkers*.

[29] See C. S. Lewis, *The Problem of Pain* (New York: Macmillan, 1962).

natural evil cannot be traced to God; instead, they trace it now to the fall of angels.[30] The problem of evil in connection with God is so central to Christian faith that it has been given a special name, *theodicy*.[31]

Today, there are respectable philosophers and theologians who, because logical consistency demands it, have adopted weaker versions of the three universal godly attributes. Some say that, although God knows far more than humans ever can know, he is not omniscient. Some even say that God exists within time, not outside of it. Others weaken the attribute of omnipotence; they believe that God is constrained by the rules of logic, and some take the view that God did not create matter but rather fashioned it to form the universe. This is a variant on Kant's view of God as architect.[32] A very few explore the possibility that God, while desiring the good, has not yet achieved all-goodness. Carl Jung went so far as to suggest that God was taught a moral lesson by the goodness of a human being, Job.[33] The desired effect of these discussions, besides cultural knowledge, is for students to learn that it is morally acceptable to question and even to reject some beliefs propounded by their religious traditions.

Perhaps the best solution to these ambiguities and contradictions is to refrain from describing God. Martin Buber warns us that God cannot be made into an *It* – something to be measured and described. We can know God as spiritlike and personlike because we can encounter him, but we cannot identify and describe his infinite attributes. We can only address "him":

> By its very nature the eternal You [Thou] cannot become an It; because by its very nature it cannot be placed within measure and limit, not even within the measure of the immeasurable and the limit of the unlimited; because by its very nature it cannot be grasped as

[30] See Alvin Plantinga, *God, Freedom, and Evil* (Grand Rapids, MI: Eerdmans, 1974).

[31] For an excellent overview, see John Hick, *Evil and the God of Love* (New York: Macmillan, 1966). The word *theodicy* comes to us from the title of a book on the subject by Leibniz.

[32] For an introduction to process theology, see David Ray Griffin, *God, Power, and Evil: A Process Theodicy* (Philadelphia: Westminster Press, 1976).

[33] See Carl G. Jung, *Answer to Job*, trans. R. F. C. Hull (Princeton, NJ: Princeton University Press, 1973); see also Jack Miles, *God: A Biography* (New York: Alfred A. Knopf, 1995).

a sum of qualities...because we transgress against it...if we say: "I believe that he is" – even "he" is still a metaphor, while "you" is not.[34]

From this perspective, God is to be received, encountered, addressed, and found in relation. When we meet human others, animals, and the objects of nature in reciprocal relation, we may encounter God. The more we describe the entity we think of as God, the more we seek to establish the truth of statements that begin, "God is...," the further we move away from God.

Although this discussion could go on for volumes, I will mention just two more beliefs that might be questioned. In an earlier chapter I noted that the Catholic Church has not always believed that human life and ensoulment begin at conception; indeed, this doctrine was not officially announced until the late nineteenth century. The long debate over the time of ensoulment is another example of the historical importance of establishing and questioning beliefs.

The concept of original sin (deeply involved with the problem of evil) is another belief that might well be questioned. The concept does not appear, as often supposed, in the Bible itself. It is rather a product of Augustine's thought. Paul Ricoeur remarks on it:

> The harm that has been done to souls, during the centuries of Christianity, first by literal interpretation of the story of Adam, and then by the confusion of this myth, treated as history, with later speculations, principally Augustinian, about original sin, will never be adequately told. In asking the faithful to confess belief in this mythico-speculative mass and to accept it as a self-sufficient explanation, the theologians have unduly required a *sacrificium intellectus* where what was needed was to awaken believers to a symbolic superintelligence of their actual condition.[35]

And that is, of course, exactly what we are aiming for in educating for intelligent belief or unbelief.[36]

---

[34] Martin Buber, *I and Thou*, trans. Walter Kaufmann (New York: Charles Scribner's Sons, 1970), pp. 160–161.

[35] Paul Ricoeur, *The Symbolism of Evil* (Boston: Beacon Press, 1969), p. 239.

[36] See Nel Noddings, *Educating for Intelligent Belief or Unbelief* (New York: Teachers College Press, 1993).

Myths

Some features of myth have already been discussed, but myths and their legacies confront us repeatedly in different contexts. Schools could make a significant contribution to genuine education by helping students to understand something about the nature of myths, but this rarely happens. Students graduate from high school believing that myths belong to ancient and primitive cultures. I recalled earlier my astonishment when seniors at an elite college responded to my mention of the Adam and Eve myth with a quick "but that's not a myth!"

Referring to the Adamic myth, Paul Ricoeur says that to understand it, "In the first place, it means accepting the fact that it is a myth."[37] Acceptance of the nonhistorical character of myth leads to

> [t]he discovery of the *symbolic* function of the myth. . . . But then we should not say, "The story of the 'fall' is *only* a myth" – that is to say, something less than history – but, "The story of the fall has the greatness of myth" – that is to say, has more meaning than a true history.[38]

This is not to suggest that everyone will agree on the meaning of this or any myth. Most will agree that the story deals with the origins of evil. Adam and Eve are disobedient; they commit a sin and are punished by exile. But should the fall be considered the beginning of evil in the world? As we have already seen, it cannot explain the existence of animal suffering or, more generally, what is called *natural evil*. Ricoeur suggests that the activity of the serpent is a sign that evil was already present in the world. Adam and Eve did not introduce or cause evil. This line of interpretation shifts attention a bit from the Adamic myth to myths of the tragic God and the wicked God. We can let Adam and Eve off the hook. But why was the serpent chosen as a sign of already existing evil? In the next section, we'll return to this question and explore some feminist responses to it.

Because we can't analyze even one of the great Judeo-Christian myths in any depth here, and because it may be impossible to do an adequate job in schools, what can we expect schools to accomplish

---

[37] Ricoeur, *Symbolism of Evil*, p. 235.
[38] Ibid., p. 236.

with respect to myths? First, of course, is the understanding that many religious stories are in fact myths and that myths have tremendous power. But students should also be invited to consider what the main themes of some important myths are and how those themes have been interpreted. Are there, for example, reasons to question some interpretations? Are there political as well as religious dimensions to the myths and their interpretations?

Students might consider the following paragraph from Martin Gardner, a philosophical theist (one who believes in a personal God):

> I do not, for example, believe that God ever drowned all men, women, and children on earth (not to mention innocent animals) except Noah and his family. Even as a myth it is hard to admire the "faith" of a man capable of supposing God could be that vindictive and unforgiving. I do not believe that God asked Abraham to murder his only legitimate son as a blood offering. I know how Abraham's obedience has been justified, and I have read Kierkegaard's little book about it, *Fear and Trembling*, but unlike Kierkegaard and the author of Hebrews I am under no obligation to find anything beautiful or profound in this abominable story. To those outside the Judaic-Christian tradition, Abraham appears not as a man of faith, but as a man of insane fanaticism.[39]

What sort of God is portrayed in these stories? What might be the writer's purpose in describing God as cruel and manipulative? Are there other stories that raise questions about God's goodness? Students may point out that God stayed Abraham's hand; Isaac was spared. But then they might read about Jephthah, who killed his own daughter and gave her as a burnt offering to keep a vow he had made to God. (See Judges 11.) And this daughter is not even named. In whose interest was it to tell stories that betray human love and emphasize obedience to God and authority – to inspire fear, induce guilt, and ensure obedience? Is obedience to God more important than love and compassion for human beings – more important even than ethics, as Kierkegaard claimed? And when people answer a command of God's, how do they know that it is God speaking? These are crucial moral

---

[39] Gardner, *Whys of a Philosophical Scrivener*, p. 210. See also my discussion of the Abraham story in *Caring: A Feminine Approach to Ethics and Moral Education* 2nd ed. (Berkeley: University of California Press, 2003).

questions in today's world. Students should be encouraged to consider why they easily challenge claims to know God's will when they are made by Muslims but fail even to think about such claims made in the past by members of the Judeo-Christian tradition.

As students discuss the many myths that tell stories of evil committed and punished, they should also be invited to consider myths about evil suffered. Ricoeur reminds us that such myths return us to a tragic view and help us to realize that not all suffering is deserved. Much suffering has been inflicted on the innocent.[40] The story of Job is important to read as great literature, but it is also significant as a vivid illustration of suffering deliberately inflicted on innocent people. Although Job was ultimately spared and vindicated, what of his children and servants – all slain with God's permission? Again, these innocents go unnamed. In the end, when good fortune was restored to Job, he had "seven sons and three daughters." These three new daughters are named. What are we to think of the others who were sacrificed to test the steadfastness of Job? And if God is omniscient, why was the test necessary? Didn't he know that Job would pass the test? What are we to think of a God who would behave this way?[41]

Traditional Jewish interpretations of the *horror* myths are, in many ways, more logical than the traditional Christian ones; they recognize the dual personality of God. Christian interpretations are handicapped by the perceived necessity to preserve God from all involvement in evil. To believe that the God of the Old Testament is both all-good and capable of the cruelty and willful destruction depicted there is indeed maximally counterintuitive. Most teenagers are familiar with at least some of the great myths. How do they reconcile the

---

[40] There is widespread recognition that much suffering is undeserved. See Fyodor Dostoevsky, *The Brothers Karamazov*, trans. Constance Garnett (New York: Modern Library, n.d.); see also Miguel De Unamuno, *Tragic Sense of Life*, trans. J. E. Crawford Flitch (New York: Dover, 1954). Some of us insist that the deliberate infliction of pain or suffering is never deserved. People may bring pain upon themselves by foolish or immoral behavior, but this does not justify the deliberate infliction of pain. See my *Starting at Home: Caring and Social Policy* (Berkeley: University of California Press, 2002).

[41] Jack Miles notes that Bertrand Russell wrote of this God: "The world in which we live can be understood as a result of muddle and accident, but if it is the outcome of a deliberate purpose, the purpose must have been that of a fiend." See Miles, *God*, p. 309.

content of those myths with the requirement to believe in an all-good and loving God? Probably, they just don't allow themselves to think about it. But the ambiguities and contradictions discussed here may well help to explain the odd responses we find in Smith's survey. Again, Jewish students may be encouraged more often to think about the contradictory events and messages in sacred texts and, therefore, experience lower levels of ignorance and conflict. Public schools surely have a role in helping all students to become aware of our mythic past.

It is important for students to understand that myths can be used to maintain dominance, fear, and cruelty. But the study of stories illustrating courage, love, and justice should also be encouraged: David and Goliath, Joseph in Egypt, Ruth and Naomi. On the last, however, we can raise an important question. Ruth is traditionally admired for her devotion to her mother-in-law, Naomi. Her words have been adapted to beautiful wedding music: "For whither thou goest, I will go. Your people will be my people, and your God my God." The question is this: If a man, instead of a woman, had made such a pledge, how would it have been evaluated? Would he have been admired or shunned as a deserter?

Gender Again

In an earlier chapter, we discussed how the myth of Eve's disobedience has been used for centuries to subordinate and control women. Ricoeur recognizes this:

> No doubt it must be granted that the story gives evidence of a very masculine resentment, which serves to justify the state of dependence in which all, or almost all, societies have kept women.[42]

But he goes on to say that the real target is an "eternal feminine" in which both women and men share – its main feature being frailty. Talk about making things worse! In this move, Ricoeur misses the point of feminist criticism. Like the attempts to rescue St. Paul from charges of misogyny, the tack taken by Ricoeur ignores the devastating effects of identifying both Adam and Eve's frailty with *women,* not with a gender-neutral conception.

[42] Ricoeur, *Symbolism of Evil*, p. 254.

Women are doubly injured by the myth of Adam and Eve. The serpent, arch representative of evil in the Adamic myth, was a feminine icon. It seems unarguable that the serpent was long associated with woman. On the positive side, the serpent has been identified with self-renewal, knowledge, and healing. It also seems to have been associated with the secretive and mysterious.[43] Quite naturally, because of its capacity to shed its skin and appear newly garbed, it has been associated with the moon, which also renews itself periodically. It is not hard to understand how moon, serpent, and woman (with her monthly periods) became identified as entities that renew themselves regularly.

Feminist thought has concentrated on the link between serpent-as-healer and woman.[44] Much interesting work has been done in showing that the serpent was a very special symbol of woman's power – particularly her power to heal and renew. It is interesting, too, to note that the physician's symbol is a caduceus – a staff bearing two entwined serpents. There is little doubt about the importance of the serpent as a symbol of feminine religion and power.

It is therefore understandable that the male God would put enmity between the serpent and the woman. It was necessary to put an end to female religions and powers. Mary Daly quotes Marina Warner on this:

> In Christianity, the serpent has lost its primary character as a source of wisdom and eternity. It is above all the principal Christian symbol of evil, and when it sprawls under the Virgin's foot, it is not her direct attribute, representing her knowledge and power as it does in the snake-brandishing statue of the goddess of Minoan Crete, but illustrates her victory over evil.[45]

Does this crushing of the serpent represent repentance and a turning to the true God, or does it signify a rejection of women's elemental power and total submission? Certainly, it is significant that the writer of Genesis 3 would take such pains to separate the woman and the

---

[43] See M. Esther Harding, *Woman's Mysteries* (New York: Harper & Row, 1971), p. 53. More generally, consult other Jungian writers on this.

[44] See Merlin Stone, *When God Was a Woman* (New York: Dial Press, 1976); also Joseph Campbell, *The Power of Myth* (New York: Anchor Books, 1991).

[45] Quoted in Mary Daly, *Pure Lust* (Boston: Beacon Press, 1984), p. 390. See also my discussion in *Women and Evil* (Berkeley: University of California Press, 1989).

serpent. But the feminist interpretation of the myth is but one view. We cannot claim that everything in an earlier woman's religion was good, any more than we can claim all-goodness for the male deity of Genesis. Nor can we claim that women enjoyed more political power in the age of feminine deities. This early age is shrouded in mystery and may have been as oppressive for actual women as anything that succeeded it. Nevertheless, the separation of women from their religious symbols is an important and perhaps tragic event.

We should not suppose, however, that the serpent was the exclusive property of women. The power of the serpent appears very early and pervades Greek hero stories. As Catherine Keller has pointed out, Joseph Campbell and many feminist theorists who depend on his work may have oversimplified the world of mythology, subsuming

> all religious and cultural history under this dramatic dialectic of two world orders, that of the original mother myths and that of the conquering heroes with their supreme father.[46]

In the discussion of a myth, it would be a mistake to claim any one interpretation as true or correct. If we could decide that, the myth would become an item in the history of ideas – one more or less fixed and undebatable. There is no question but that the serpent has been thought of as the carrier of dark secrets; identified with renewal, wisdom, and healing; depicted as a phallic symbol; and considered a symbol of the sacred, of evil, and of women's power. The questions to ask of a myth's interpretation include: How much explanatory power does a particular interpretation offer? Who benefits and who is harmed by this interpretation? How is the interpretation confirmed or undermined by subsequent literature?

Nina Auerbach writes that the persistence of some images associated with women suggest an enormous, mysterious power:

> The mermaids, serpent-women, and lamias who proliferate in the Victorian imagination suggest a triumph larger than themselves, whose roots lie in the antiquity so dear to nineteenth-century classicists.[47]

---

[46] Catherine Keller, *From a Broken Web* (Boston: Beacon Press, 1986), p. 54.
[47] Nina Auerbach, *Woman and the Demon: The Life of a Victorian Myth* (Cambridge, MA: Harvard University Press, 1982), pp. 8–9.

But the continual revival of these images can hardly be regarded as a triumph for ordinary women and their condition. If it is true that Victorian art and literature "force us to look into the serpent-woman's face and to feel the mystery of power, endlessly mutilated and restored, of a woman with a demon's gift,"[48] this fact will do little to advance the cause of women's equality in the current world and may well impede it.

There is little doubt that the legacy of myth is not a positive one for women. What about current attitudes in the three great monotheistic faiths? Historical evidence shows clearly that the condition of women was more hopeful in the early days of Islam, Christianity, and perhaps Judaism. Both Islam and Christianity started as liberation movements, and both promised more nearly equal status for women.[49] But the texts of all three religions (both orthodox and heterodox) demonstrate conclusively that women are an afterthought. The texts are addressed to men; women are often blamed but rarely named.[50]

Students should be allowed, better encouraged, to read historical and current accounts of how women are treated by their religious institutions. Eventually, they will probably ask, "Why don't women simply abandon these institutions?" It is apparently hard to do. Belonging (even as second-class members) trumps believing, and the feeling expressed by many women is that the faith belongs to them as well as they to it. Why should they be forced to leave, to abandon a cherished faith? Still, one wonders. If women had the courage to walk out in large numbers, change might be dramatic.[51]

One problem involved in walking out is that all of us find it difficult to overcome the organic habits of our early life. Those habits become part of us, and change often involves obvious loss in the promise of a good only vaguely defined. Sara Maitland even suggests an analogy between faithful Catholic women and the battered

---

[48] Ibid., p. 9. See also Bram Dijkstra, *Idols of Perversity: Fantasies of Feminine Evil in Fin-de-Siècle Culture* (New York: Oxford University Press, 1986).

[49] See Karen Armstrong, *A History of God* (London: Vintage, 1999); also Rosemary Radford Ruether, *Sexism and God-Talk* (Boston: Beacon Press, 1983).

[50] For a comprehensive review of women's status in Jewish and Christian traditions, see Ruether, *Sexism and God-Talk*.

[51] See Debra Campbell, *Graceful Exits: Catholic Women and the Art of Departure* (Bloomington: Indiana University Press, 2003).

women in a shelter. Both know "that they had been hurt and would be hurt again [but this knowledge] could not totally outweigh the passionate longing to be involved again in that relationship which was the source of all emotions...."[52] Novels of religious childhood and autobiographies can be very helpful in coming to grips with one's hopes and disappointments with respect to religious affiliation.

Mary McCarthy represents an important case to consider. A devout Catholic as a young woman, McCarthy raised serious questions about the rigid and often cruel education she received in Catholic schools and at home.[53] She was aware of Pascal's wager and rejected what I have called a weasely choice. "I prefer not to play it safe," she wrote.[54] Some readers deplore McCarthy's decision to abandon the church and become an atheist. Others celebrate the decision. Students should have an opportunity to consider both opinions.

Of course, students should also read accounts that affirm life within religious faiths. I have already mentioned Dorothy Day. Students might also find the personal account of joy and serenity told by Kathleen Norris both interesting and inspiring.[55] There are lovely accounts from both Jewish and Muslim women, and these, too, should provide material for discussion.[56] Despite oppression and continued lack of recognition, many women have found deep spiritual satisfaction without leaving patriarchal institutions.

Hell and Damnation

It is a continuing source of astonishment to nonbelievers that so many professing Christians believe both in an all-good God and in hell. These logically incompatible beliefs contribute to both theological incorrectness and conceptual confusion. One teenager, Kristen,

---

[52] Sara Maitland, Introduction to *The Hound and the Falcon: The Story of a Reconversion to the Catholic Faith* by Antonia White (London: Virago Press, 1992), pp. vii–viii.

[53] See Mary McCarthy, *Memories of a Catholic Girlhood* (San Diego, CA: Harvest/Harcourt, 1985).

[54] Ibid., p. 27.

[55] See Kathleen Norris, *The Cloister Walk* (New York: Riverhead Books, 1996).

[56] See, for example, the accounts in Ruth E. Groenhout and Marya Bower, eds., *Philosophy, Feminism, and Faith* (Bloomington: Indiana University Press, 2003).

interviewed by Smith, first expresses some doubt about her faith, because there are "so many other religions and they all claim to be true," but then she says: "Those who trust in Jesus as their personal Lord and Savior will go to heaven when they die and those who don't will go to hell."[57] Hearing this, one wonders just how much Kristen knows about other religions and whether she has ever reflected on the logic of a religion that preaches both love and hell.

> Another teen (15 years old) told the interviewer that religion is good because it helps people specifically to go to heaven and not go to hell: "People should always have religion, 'cause when you die you can either go to heaven or hell, and if you don't believe that there's a God then you're gonna have a really bad life and there's no way to change that."[58]

Statements such as this one should embarrass educators far more than the much-bewailed ignorance of historical dates and mathematical processes. Hasn't this boy ever heard of good people who do not believe in God? Is unbelief the main or only reason for going to hell?

Several other teenagers in Smith's survey specifically mentioned avoiding hell as a primary reason for their religious practices. How much credence can we give to expressions of belief when so many fear that a confession of unbelief will lead straight to hell? Not only is there a distinct possibility that many express belief to be "on the safe side," but also the ignorance that accompanies such expressions of belief is appalling. Smith comments on how inarticulate many teenagers are when asked to talk about their faith:

> Indeed, it was our distinct sense that for many of the teens we interviewed, *our interview was the first time that any adult had ever asked them what they believed and how it mattered in their life.*[59] (Italics in the original)

Without telling students that there is no hell, a genuine education would expose them to views that express this idea. Surely, they should

---

[57] Quoted in Smith, *Soul Searching*, p. 20.
[58] Ibid., p. 125.
[59] Ibid., p. 133.

learn that Darwin's agnosticism was prompted not only by the cruelty he saw in nature but also by the cruelty of Christianity:

> I can indeed hardly see how anyone ought to wish Christianity to be true; for if so, the plain language of the text seems to show that the men who do not believe, and this would include my father, brother and almost all my best friends, will be everlastingly punished. And this is a damnable doctrine.[60]

One need not give up all of religion to abandon the notion of hell. As a nun, Karen Armstrong came to question the wisdom of teaching children religion-by-fear:

> What was the church asking me to do? Here I was, pumping these children with the Catholic mechanisms of guilt that would probably haunt them all their lives! Was that what the love of God was all about? I was startled by the violence of my anger.[61]

When a religion preaches love and peace, how can it also use threats of eternal punishment to keep its people in line? Why does it need to do this? There are many touching stories of thoughtful people who have left organized religions because of contradictions in their belief systems. Some of these people turn to less dogmatic faiths, some become philosophical theists, some seek spiritual life without religion, and some abandon both religion and spirituality. Many, perhaps most, do not know that prominent theologians and lay thinkers in their own institutions have given up a belief in hell.[62] They would find themselves in good company if they did also.

Bertrand Russell, after speaking admiringly of some of Jesus' teachings, criticized him specifically for his attitude toward hell:

> There is one very serious defect to my mind in Christ's moral character, and that is that He believed in hell. I do not myself feel that any person who is really profoundly humane can believe in everlasting punishment. . . . There is, of course, the familiar text about the sin against the Holy Ghost: "Whosoever speaketh against the Holy Ghost it shall not be forgiven him neither in this World nor in the world

---

[60] Quoted in Janet Browne, *Charles Darwin: The Power of Place* (New York: Alfred A. Knopf, 2002), p. 432.

[61] Armstrong, *History of God*, pp. 98–99.

[62] See, for example, Kung, *Does God Exist?*

to come." That text has caused an unspeakable amount of misery in the world. . . . I really do not think that a person with a proper degree of kindliness in his nature would have put fears and terrors of that sort into the world.[63]

It is argued by some, however, that hell is required to ensure justice. We know that evil people often escape justice in this world, so there must be a way to right things in the next world. Both Augustine and Leibniz (author of *Theodicy*) believed, however, that justice might require that most human souls suffer eternal damnation.[64] Leibniz, however, did not accept the damnation of unbaptized infants or of those who did their best by the light God had given them. That concession still leaves us with a situation many find impossible to reconcile with an all-powerful, all-knowing, and all-good God. One has to have a cruel heart or a twisted mind to believe that unbelievers, heretics, unbaptized adolescents, women who have had abortions, active homosexuals, and Adolf Hitler all belong together in hell. (Of course, we could introduce circles of deepening misery in hell, and students might consider Dante's *Inferno*.)

We educators owe our students opportunities to question the concept of hell. It is irresponsible to let them suffer the terrors that accompany the threat of hell without informing them that many good people – both religious and irreligious – reject the concept entirely.

Sources of Morality

Is God the source of morality? There are many who argue that this is true and that, without God, "everything is permitted." This pronouncement seems downright silly to others. This second group argues that human beings are social creatures; we depend on one another for pleasure, to get work done, for help in time of need, even for life itself. Our thorough interdependence is enough to generate moral thought. Self-interest, fellow feeling, practical reason, mother love, and God have all been suggested as sources of moral conduct.

[63] Bertrand Russell, *Why I Am Not a Christian,* and *Other Essays on Religion and Related Subjects* (New York: Simon & Schuster, 1957), pp. 17–18.

[64] See Hick, *Evil and the God of Love*. See also Gottfried W. Leibniz, *Theodicy*, trans. E. M. Huggard (New Haven, CT: Yale University Press, 1952).

The purpose of discussing religion and morality is not, once again, to promote a particular answer but rather to make students aware of various views. There is considerable evidence that belief in God ("God is watching") helps many teenagers to avoid the temptations of alcohol, tobacco, drugs, and sex. But clearly, belief in God has not reduced violence and cruelty in the world. I would not dwell on the violence induced by religion, but I think it should be discussed: the slaughters committed in biblical times by the Israelites, the Crusades, the Inquisition, the witch craze, the current wave of Islamic violence.[65] And how would students answer Bertrand Russell, who said that "the Christian religion, as organized in its churches, has been and still is the principal enemy of moral progress in the world"?[66]

The rejection of religion is often motivated by moral objections. In the nineteenth century, when there was no longer a threat of trial for heresy and execution for unbelief, many thinkers turned away from religion on moral grounds. James Turner writes:

> Declarations of unbelief often sounded more like acts of moral will than intellectual judgments. [Robert] Ingersoll said that "I cannot worship a being" whose "cruelty is shorelesss." Darwin was so appalled by the harshness of natural selection that he could no longer bring himself to believe in God: better that this horror should have sprung from blind chance.[67]

Students can be reminded that Darwin's agnosticism did not spring entirely from his naturalistic studies. As we've seen, there arose a question about God's goodness and the concept of hell. He was deeply troubled by the idea of hell for unbelievers – that "damnable doctrine." John Stuart Mill also expressed his disapproval of the biblical God who falls so short of the good: "I will call no being good who is not what I mean when I apply that epithet to my fellow creatures, and if such a being can sentence me to hell for not so calling him, to hell I

---

[65] This, too, is a huge topic. For recent examples, see Mark Juergensmeyer, *Terror in the Mind of God: The Global Rise of Religious Violence* (Berkeley: University of California Press, 2000); also Jon Krakauer, *Under the Banner of Heaven* (New York: Doubleday, 2003).

[66] Russell, *Why I Am Not a Christian*, p. 21.

[67] James Turner, *Without God, Without Creed* (Baltimore: Johns Hopkins University Press, 1985), p. 207.

will go."[68] In connection with God and the good, Russell invites us to look at the problem logically: If whatever God says is, by fiat, good, then we need only follow blindly what God says (if we can agree on what that is). But if we are going to say that God is good – that he chooses the good – then the concept of good is "logically anterior to God."[69] We should, then, continue to study and debate what is meant by *good*. This conclusion is attractive in many ways. In today's world, it cautions us to be very careful in doing what we suppose is the will of God.

Possibly the most important thing for students to learn is that many atheists, deists, and agnostics are good people – good defined as our conventional system of morality describes it. These are people who would not kill, steal, rape, inflict unnecessary pain, or ignore the suffering of sentient beings. They are people most of us would regard as good neighbors. Fundamentalists in all three monotheistic faiths would have people believe differently. Alan Peshkin describes the views of Mr. McGraw, head of a Christian fundamentalist school, on "humanism":

McGraw presents the "five basic tenets of humanism" as: (1) atheism; (2) immorality; (3) evolution; (4) the belief that man can do anything he wants to do; (5) ecumenism.[70]

At least, students should learn that humanists may be atheists, agnostics, or deists, but there are religious humanists as well (Erasmus was one), and humanists do not advocate immorality. Because most humanists are well educated, they do indeed accept evolution and, because they promote love and forbearance of their fellow beings, they may advocate ecumenism.[71] The statement that "man can do anything he wants to do" is meaningless without interpretation.

When we see that astonishing falsehoods of this sort are taught in religious schools, we should be led to think critically about any plan that would provide for the use of public funds in such schools. Can

---

[68] From Mill's *Examination of Hamilton*, quoted in J. B. Schneewind, "J. S. Mill," in *The Encyclopedia of Philosophy*, p. 321.

[69] Russell, *Why I Am Not a Christian*, p. 12.

[70] Peshkin, *God's Choice*, p. 77.

[71] For more on humanism and secular ethics, see my *Educating for Intelligent Belief or Unbelief*.

a society honestly promote an agenda of equality and tolerance and, at the same time, allow public funds to be used for school programs that undermine this agenda? Certainly, in a liberal democracy, citizens have a right to voice illiberal views, but they have no right to demand public monies to support those views.

Time should also be spent on a problem at the other end of the spectrum. Surely, students should learn something about the moral and democratic views of atheists and humanists, but they should also learn something about the lives and beliefs of fundamentalists. Too often, academics mock these people and insist that we can't engage in dialogue with them – "You can't talk to these people!" That's wrong if our aim is not only to understand but to maintain democratic dialogue. I have had friendly conversations with fundamentalists in train stations, at my front door, and at the garden gate. Like most atheists, fundamentalists are usually good neighbors – people who would hasten to help our children in a bicycle fall and protect our pets from injury. We can talk about gardens, the weather, our local schools, recipes, health, vacations, our grown children, and a host of other topics that concern all human beings. Now and then, we can even talk gently and tentatively about religion.[72]

Fundamentalist students should be welcomed in our public schools. That does not mean that we should abandon our social/ liberal agenda or neglect the sort of critical lessons I have been recommending. But no child should be made to feel foolish or stupid – either for her failure in mathematics or her religious beliefs. Our democracy depends on bringing our children together, not alienating them.

The work of Jane Addams stands as a model for this work. She was a builder of bridges across cultures – working to help immigrants make their transition to America without losing the cherished language and ways of the "old country." Although she believed in evolution, she nevertheless expressed admiration and sympathy for the hill farmers who laid down their work and traveled long distances to provide witness for their biblical beliefs at the Scopes trial. She admired their honesty and commitment. It is that sort of spirit we need in discussing

---

[72] For an important attempt to encourage dialogue across Christian, Jewish, and Muslim lines, see Yossi Klein Halevi, *At the Entrance to the Garden of Eden* (New York: Perennial, 2001).

religion. It is worth pointing out in concluding this section that Addams, like so many well-educated people, suffered grave doubts about the religion in which she had been brought up. Eventually,

> [by] putting to rest the question of whether she was or was not a believer, Addams freed herself to ask the questions that would eventually lead her to enduring conviction: to the belief that religion was a matter of ethics and discipline, a means of aligning individual private action with the ever changing requirements of social need.[73]

Spirituality

Can we reject formal religion and embrace something called *spirituality*? Robert Wuthnow presents evidence to support the contention that many Americans have done exactly this. In *After Heaven*, his first chapter carries the title "From Dwelling to Seeking."[74] Unhappy or unsatisfied with the answers provided by conventional religion, people still ask the questions we have been considering in this chapter. They seek the sacred but, in most cases, they seek with little guidance and negligible knowledge. A longing for the sacred coexists with the ignorance I have already noted. Wuthnow comments:

> [M]ost Americans say they pray generally to God or a supreme being rather than specifically to Jesus or Christ, most pray for themselves rather than seeking to worship through their prayers, only half of adult Americans know that Genesis is the first book of the Bible and only a third know that Jesus delivered the Sermon on the Mount, only 39 percent of teenagers believe the Bible is completely true (compared with 62 percent who held this belief in 1961), and more people perceive religion to be declining in influence than perceive its influence to be increasing.[75]

But, on the last claim, why would we take seriously the perception of people so demonstrably ignorant? Asking again in 2005, we

---

[73] Ellen Condliffe Lagemann, ed., *Jane Addams on Education* (New York: Teachers College Press, 1985), p. 19.

[74] Robert Wuthnow, *After Heaven: Spirituality in America since the 1950s* (Berkeley: University of California Press, 1998).

[75] Ibid., p. 128. On the last, Wuthnow depends on a 1994 Gallup Poll.

find many people worried that the influence of religion is increasing dangerously. The significant points for educators are that a longing for the sacred persists and that there is widespread ignorance on religious matters. The response typical of educational policymakers is that our schools should do something about the ignorance – perhaps teach the Bible as literature. But unless the longing to explore existential questions is addressed, teaching factual material on the Bible will be yet another case of "in one ear and out the other."

In addition to learning about traditional religious answers to existential questions, students should hear about answers classified as "spiritual but not religious." People who are seeking the sacred without the authority of an established religious institution ask about the sources of spirituality, the location of holiness, the meaning of life, and the possibility of response from a deity or deities.[76]

Many people who have abandoned official religion find an awakening of spirit in nature – in mountains, ocean, desert, lakes, and forests. Indeed, it is hard for some of us to separate a developed biophilia from a sense of spirituality. It is not necessarily that God is found in all living things – pantheism – but rather that natural things take on the status of the miraculous and cause the spirit to soar. Emerson saw miracles in "the blowing clover and the fallen rain"; he had no need of the biblical miracle stories that he regarded as fiction.[77] Many gardeners describe what they see in their gardens as miracles. Others feel a special serenity in quietly watching a sunrise or sunset. Paradoxically, the cruelty of nature that leads people away from institutional religions on ethical grounds is offset aesthetically by the grandeur and beauty of that same nature.

Female students especially may find contemporary discussion of women's spirituality inspiring.[78] The recognition of childbearing, homemaking, gardening, and nurturing as spiritual experiences may

---

[76] See, for example, Carol Ochs, *Women and Spirituality* (Totowa, NJ: Rowman and Allanheld, 1983).

[77] Quoted in Bloom, *American Religion*, p. 24.

[78] There are many sources. See, for example, Paula M. Cooey, Sharon A. Farmer, and Mary Ellen Ross, eds., *Embodied Love: Sensuality and Relationship as Feminist Values* (San Francisco: Harper & Row, 1987); Christine Downing, *The Goddess* (New York: Crossroad, 1984); Judith Ochshorn, *The Female Experience and the Nature of the Divine* (Bloomington: Indiana University Press, 1981); Charlene Spretnak, ed., *The Politics of Women's Spirituality* (Garden City, NY: Anchor Books, 1982).

give girls a sense of wholeness and spiritual well-being that is hard
to achieve within a religion that sees them as the devil's gateway, an
attractive evil, a second thought, a mere helpmeet to man, a creature
to be controlled. To hear one's life *as a woman* celebrated is deeply
satisfying.

Anne Morrow Lindbergh describes a "perfect" day as one involving
physical work, conversation, intellectual work, play on the beach,
sipping sherry by the fireside, lying on the beach under bright stars,
and silent communion with her companion. That whole perfect day
might be described as an exercise in spirituality.[79]

I, too, have described my own transition to a skeptical spirituality:

> From the colors of sunrise to the soft purring of my cat as we both
> fall asleep at night, the day is filled with moments of contentment
> and, sometimes, even spiritual ecstasy. Both Lindbergh and Norris
> write of the need for solitude, and, although I do not believe that
> long periods of silence and isolation are necessary, I do believe that
> moments of solitude are essential. When I am deeply affected by
> a sunrise or its spectacular pre-glow, there is always a moment of
> reflection – time to simply "be with" the beauty. It may be that others
> require longer periods of solitude for the recovery of their souls. Each
> of us has to find a way that fits her own life and, of course, what fits
> in one period of life may not fit in another.[80]

Students might welcome opportunities to write about their own
spiritual experiences, but they should not be required to do this. They
might, if they prefer, find and share such descriptions written by others. They might also share music and poetry that inspire them. This
sharing should not be rushed. Each piece of music or poetry should
be followed by a short interval of silence. Then, some day, students
might also discuss the meaning and effects of these silent periods.

Discussion of spirituality must include New Age beliefs and practices. Robert Nash describes the movement:

> New Age spirituality is a loose, all-purpose designation meant to
> describe a higher consciousness. New Age is an eclectic synthe-
> sis of such disparate beliefs as reincarnation, karma, paranormal

---

[79] Anne Morrow Lindbergh, *Gift from the Sea* (New York: Random House, 1955).
[80] Nel Noddings, "A Skeptical Spirituality," in *Philosophy, Feminism, and Faith*, ed.
Groenhout and Bower, p. 224.

power, UFOs, holistic healing, pantheism, astrology, channeling, biorhythms, shamanism, and trance induction, among others.[81]

As students sort through these ideas, separating what Nash calls the "hype" from the spiritually promising, they may want to explore Eastern religions and learn something about the richer, deeper concepts that appear superficially in much New Age literature. They may also want to reread parts of Maslow's work on spirituality.

Spirituality – seeking instead of dwelling within an established religious organization – can be a tendency found on the edges of those organizations. In most religious institutions, there are those who voice discontent and continue to search for the God that eludes them in authorized rituals. Sometimes these people are accepted as they are; in other cases, they are silenced or punished. Some have expressed concern, for example, that the Catholic Church will experience a new wave of doctrinal correctness under Benedict XVI.[82] If this happens, seekers may find it difficult to remain within the faith. Dwelling within the church may come to violate their spiritual integrity.

People who describe themselves as spiritual but not religious may be seeking a direct encounter with God, or they may be seeking a deeper meaning in everyday life. Deeply moving experiences with nature, with infants, with pets, with human beings who need help, with gardens, even with freshly cleaned houses – earthly dwelling places – may satisfy the quest for spiritual life. These possibilities should be addressed as part of a genuine education.

In this chapter, we have looked at questions that are central to human life. People tend to feel strongly about the answers they favor, and this makes it difficult to tackle the questions in public schools. Is there a God (or gods)? What is "his" nature? Must I believe everything that my religious denomination teaches? What is a myth, and what meanings are attached to those myths that have been (and still are) powerful in Western culture? Can we live moral lives without God? Should we reject the notions of hell and damnation as incompatible with the belief in God's goodness? Should we consider the

[81] Robert Nash, *Faith Hype and Clarity* (New York: Teachers College Press, 1999), p. 107.
[82] See Peter J. Boyer, "A Hard Faith," *The New Yorker*, May 16, 2005: 54–65.

possibility that God is not good in the way humans define good? Has religion done more harm than good in the world? Have women been oppressed by the major religions? How should they respond? Can we have a satisfying spiritual life without religion?

I have suggested a way in which to approach these questions. By introducing students to a wide range of well-known conflicting views, we can offer opportunities for reflection. By choosing such material carefully, we can also contribute powerfully to our students' store of cultural knowledge.

11

Preparing Our Schools

R eaders may rightly question whether the topics and issues discussed in this book can be addressed in public secondary schools. I think they can be, but the task is not an easy one. In this brief concluding chapter, I'll try to identify the obstacles to be overcome and suggest a realistic way to begin.

Preparing Teachers

How can teachers be prepared to conduct critical lessons and, in particular, to conduct such lessons on issues that do not appear in the standard curriculum? Perhaps we are asking too much. Both teacher educators and policymakers today insist that every classroom be staffed by a highly qualified teacher.[1] But what does this mean for the sorts of lessons I have suggested?

In most states in the United States, teachers are considered highly qualified if they have received the prescribed training required for a credential; thus, *highly qualified* is synonymous with *credentialed*. To evaluate the worth of a credential requires considerable analysis. Even properly credentialed teachers sometimes exhibit deplorable ignorance. In recent talks with young teachers, I heard many of them express concerns about their own deficiencies. One young man, a fifth-grade teacher, was worried about teaching science; he didn't "know much science." Another was afraid of teaching arithmetic and, watching her, I was convinced that she was very shaky on operations

---

[1] See Linda Darling-Hammond and John Bransford, eds. *Preparing Teachers for a Changing World* (San Francisco: Jossey-Bass, 2005).

with fractions. Still another revealed in his written work that he had not mastered the rudiments of spelling and punctuation. How, I asked myself, are these deficiencies to be explained? How is it that a person can study an academic curriculum in high school, go through four years of college, obtain a degree, and still have an insufficient grasp of fifth-grade subject matter?

Subject matter deficiencies are not solely, or even primarily, the fault of education departments, because education departments no longer have primary responsibility for subject matter training. Students learn (or fail to learn) mathematics, English, and science in the various departments of liberal arts, not in education courses. Professional education, striving to develop and organize its own material in disciplinary fashion, has produced mountains of material for teacher candidates to master – material on child and adolescent development, multicultural education, special needs students, students with limited English proficiency, educational technology, testing and assessment, reading in the various subject areas, learning styles, theories of learning and motivation, classroom management, and many other topics. Even if there were time in the professional course of study to treat subject matter in some depth, educators would face a turf problem. In too many institutions today, mathematics belongs to the math department and pedagogical methods to the education department. The gap between content and pedagogy is often enormous. One great strength of the old teachers' colleges was their dedication to the integration of content and pedagogy. Their graduates were not often exposed to the higher reaches of a particular discipline, but they knew the material of the K–12 curriculum and how to teach it.

Looking at the history of teacher preparation, we encounter a paradox. The teachers' colleges were disdained. For example, their female graduates, holders of bona fide BAs, were not eligible for membership in the American Association of University Women and, in general, graduates of teachers' colleges had low status. Today, beginning teachers usually (there are still exceptions) hold a degree in some disciplinary major, and so they have equal status with other college graduates. But a degree in English (lovely as that may be) is of little help to the young teacher who must teach math, science, and social studies to fifth graders. We may have traded competence for status.

Even at the secondary level, it may be shortsighted to define competence entirely in terms of the mastery of a single subject. Surely we want teachers to know the subject they teach and to know it very well, but that knowledge is not enough. Nor is it enough to know how to teach just that subject as it appears in today's textbooks. To teach well at the high school level, teachers need a breadth of knowledge that will enable them to connect the various subjects their students are required to study and also to connect that material to the issues of everyday life. If, as Whitehead advised, the content of the school curriculum should be Life itself, we are a long way from preparing teachers for this curriculum.

When we ask seriously how it is that college graduates can have difficulty with fifth-grade (or ninth-grade) subject matter, we are reminded of the massive problem of forgetting. Unless we use certain information and skills regularly, we forget them. In most occupations, it probably doesn't matter that most school-day material is forgotten. If a lawyer is not too sure about converting fractions to decimals or continues to believe that summers are warmer because the sun is closer to the earth, it may not matter. Physicians may not need to use algebra to determine appropriate dosages; carefully constructed charts do this for them. But the school curriculum *is* the fundamental subject matter of teachers, and they should know it well. This suggests a dramatic change in the curriculum of teacher education.

Not only should the curriculum be changed, but the ways of learning it should also change. The great strength of the current movement called *constructivism* is that it urges people to think, to try things out, not to depend on rote memory. However, it may be that teacher educators spend too much time preaching constructivism and teaching the specific methods associated with it and far too little encouraging student teachers to use its basic approach: try things out, reflect, hypothesize, test, play with things. Instead, too many teachers do exactly what, as constructivists, they advise their students not to do; they try to remember what they were taught and move directly to a solution or strategy.

Sometimes, in the heat of the moment, confused by stress, a teacher will tell children that $a/b + c/d = a + c/b + d$. (I've seen this happen.) But slow down and play with this a bit. If it were correct, then $\frac{1}{2} + \frac{1}{2} = \frac{1}{2}$! (2/4). Even a young child knows that this can't be right. Thus, clearly, the formula is wrong. Well, now we can look for a mathematically correct way to add fractions, but we have also demonstrated for our students that we need not be at the mercy of our limited memories. We can figure things out, and that willingness to explore is fundamental to the preparation of critical lessons. When questions of the sort discussed in this book arise, we do not want teachers to respond with prespecified, memorized answers. We want them to be prepared for exploration and critical analysis.

Transformed Curriculum

Curricula at both K–12 and college levels should be revised. To conduct critical lessons, teachers need practice in their own studies, and they need time, materials, and encouragement to engage in such lessons when they start to teach. As organized today, almost every academic course is designed to serve as preparation for the next course: algebra one for algebra two, tenth-grade English for eleventh, and so on. Indeed, the status of a course is directly proportional to its function in promoting the next higher level of a discipline. Courses designed for usefulness in everyday life or simply for their own sake rarely stand high in the academic hierarchy. The only justification for much of what is taught in secondary school is that it is needed or required at the next level of schooling. No wonder people forget so much of what is learned in high school as soon as there is no next course looming.

But the issue is complicated. These sequential courses are not useless. Some students will need them and use the material taught in a hierarchical sequence, and so the courses must be available. However, other choices should be available as well, and the sequential courses could be – should be – broadened and enriched. The usual argument against such enrichment is that there is so much material to be "covered" that there is no time for divergent discussion, no room for additional topics. In responding to this objection, we might return to Bruner's sage advice that we attend to the big ideas and central concepts of a discipline and discard the clutter. But this is not a simple task. [*Bruner*]

High school students preparing for life in a liberal democracy should be offered real choices among rich courses focused on (1) sequential study of the discipline; (2) a general humanistic approach to the discipline and its place in the culture; (3) practical applications that are clearly useful in everyday life; or (4) practical applications focused on a particular set of occupations. The first two choices are compatible with college preparation; the second two are more closely identified with vocations, and I have already urged increased attention to vocational education.

There are several advantages to this approach. When students have a choice in what they will study, they are more likely to engage the material with interest and energy. There is no compelling reason, for example, why all college-bound students should study standard sequential courses in academic mathematics. (Students in many parts of the world are offered a choice between scientific and humanistic studies in high school.) Those students planning to major in nonscientific subjects might be offered intellectually rich courses including some mathematical processes necessary to informed citizenship (what are these processes?); some history of mathematics, broadened to include political and social issues of the times; some logic and philosophy; some mathematically related literature; some units of study connecting math to other subjects; and some discussion of existential questions (e.g., proofs of God's existence/nonexistence). Some of these topics should appear, in some form, in all of the courses offered, but the time devoted to them and the particular subtopics might vary greatly.

What would such an approach suggest for, say, social studies? Chances are that the old debate over the priority of process or content would arise again with some urgency, and almost certainly educators would have to answer the question "What skills and understandings should students gain from their courses in social studies?" Making *process* a starting point for course construction does not imply that content is unimportant. We still must ask what content is most likely to produce the understandings we seek, and we should also ask what content is crucial in its own right. Ignoring content is a mistake that was made in several process curricula of the 1960s and 1970s.[2] We should have learned from that experience that content is indeed important and that sustained work with any important content that is chosen is necessary. However, we should also have learned that merely choosing content such as a chronological history of the United States is no guarantee that students will remember the material studied in such courses. Further, we should be critical of the "wars, rulers, and

---

[2] See, for example, the program called "Science – A Process Approach" that was popular in the 1970s.

laws" approach that characterizes these courses. Instead, we might offer courses in the history of the arts, of parenting and homemaking, of religion, of time and place, of the Enlightenment, of war and peace, of science, of work and industry. There are many fascinating possibilities. Again, we would ask that each of these courses include knowledge fundamental to social studies such as geography and map-reading,[3] connections to other subjects, and the great existential questions.

It would require another volume to describe this approach to curriculum in adequate detail, but it should be clear that this sort of change in the K–12 curriculum would require a substantial change in the curriculum for teachers. Teaching is perhaps the only current profession that requires "Renaissance" people – people who have a broad knowledge of many disciplines and perennial questions. A teacher in grades K–12 is not, and perhaps should not be, a mathematician, scientist, historian, literary critic, psychologist, or statistician. We encounter again a status problem. Many bright young teachers want to identify themselves with the basic discipline in which they have majored. The young math teacher may, for example, consider herself a mathematician. But mathematicians will not regard her as a mathematician. To be accepted as a mathematician, she will have to earn a Ph.D. in mathematics or produce some original mathematics. Neither achievement is likely. Why not identify proudly and whole-heartedly with the profession of teaching? "I am a teacher" should be a proud declaration.

We can agree that a mathematics teacher should know a good deal of mathematics and still recommend significant changes in the curriculum that prepares mathematics teachers. Mathematics *teachers* do not need a hierarchical sequence of courses in advanced calculus, topology, abstract algebra, and real and complex analysis. They need instead a thorough knowledge of elementary mathematics from a higher standpoint, a knowledge of other subjects sufficient to make the connections recommended here, and a grasp of how mathematics might contribute to intelligent encounters with existential and everyday questions. Teachers also need to know how to teach, of course, but it is not only pedagogical knowledge that marks their competence.

---

[3] See Stephen Thornton, *Toward Social Studies That Matters: Enacting Curriculum* (New York: Teachers College Press, 2004).

Rather, it is an incredibly rich breadth of knowledge that we do not demand of any other specialists.

High school mathematics teachers are rightly considered incompetent if they cannot perform the mathematics required in the secondary school curriculum. But, as teachers, they are also incompetent if they cannot help students to write a decent paragraph, decipher pages in a biology text, interpret a journalistic account, or suggest defensible responses to ethical problems.

The breadth required to teach well is not often acquired by simply taking an array of courses in college, because each of these courses is, as pointed out earlier, designed for the next higher course in the discipline addressed. Teacher candidates, like those in engineering, should study courses especially designed for them in all of the disciplines. Such courses would emphasize *connections* – to other disciplines, to the common problems of humanity, and to personal exploration of universal questions of meaning.

I do not mean to suggest that high school teachers should be able to teach any subject in the secondary curriculum. Expertise in a particular subject is certainly necessary. English teachers will not usually be expert in biology, but they should be able to help students read a page of biology text and ask questions to facilitate study: What definitions do we need here? Where can we find them? What fundamental concepts (if any) are involved? Are there current social problems connected to this material? Intelligent, well-educated English teachers should be prepared to discuss scientific topics and issues that matter to interested, intelligent citizens. When teachers, who should qualify as models of well-educated citizens, cannot discuss matters outside their own narrow discipline, students understandably wonder why they must study all this material that will, in a few short years, be relegated to the trash bin of memory.

What is the difference between what I am advocating here and the sort of education recommended by Adler, Hutchins, Bloom, and MacIntyre? Didn't teachers educated in the great books and standard academic subjects display the breadth I want? Some surely did, and we should acknowledge that fact. The difficulty is that these thinkers insisted that *all* students should be required to study this one great curriculum and that these studies would somehow, almost necessarily, produce intelligent citizenship and a deeply satisfying personal/intellectual life.

This, it seems to me, is mistaken on both counts. It puts the motivational cart before the horse. Many, possibly most, students are not interested in academic studies for their own sake, and they are not convinced that these studies have much actual use. That is why I recommend a variety of programs in secondary education. When we begin with topics, problems, and issues of interest to students, we may be able to expand those interests. There is no reason to suppose that, by cramming their heads with material of little interest, a magic moment will occur when "all this makes sense," and highly accomplished students will be ready to make important decisions as individuals and citizens. It does happen sometimes, and the appearance of wonderful exemplars causes us to think and rethink our position. We should want the traditional material to be available for those attracted to it, and teachers should be able to allude to it – to use it to make vital connections. What better way is there to show the value of traditional material than by using it effectively and appreciatively?

Well-educated teachers should help students to understand that knowledge is not adequately described as a set of easily retrievable answers to unambiguously stated questions. Much real knowledge consists of well-developed capacities to figure things out. Nor is it solely a matter of knowing where to look, although that is important. It is more a matter of being unafraid to inquire, to experiment, to face the possibility that one might not succeed.

Critical Lessons for All Programs

I have argued that educators should take the advice of Socrates seriously: we should teach for self-knowledge. This does not imply a psychoanalytic approach, although we might learn much from psychoanalytic pedagogy.[4] The approach I've suggested does not turn inward to examine the unconscious or the id. Rather, it suggests looking at the self in connection to other selves and to both the physical and social environments. How and why do we act on the world? How does it act on us?

---

[4] See Carol Ascher, "The Force of Ideas," *History of Education* 34(3), May 2005: 277–293.

Critical lessons should pervade the curriculum. Planning for every course – academic, vocational, or general – should include consideration of how the topics and skills to be taught connect to everyday life, personal growth and meaning, other school subjects, and spiritual questions. To do this effectively, much junk will have to be removed from the curriculum. The basic structure of the secondary curriculum – organization around the traditional disciplines – probably will not change in the foreseeable future.[5] However, every discipline can be stretched from the inside to provide richer, more meaningful studies.

I have argued, too, that a variety of curricula designed to meet the needs of widely different talents and interests would be more compatible with preparation for participatory life in a democratic society. All talents, interests, and honest occupations should be respected and encouraged, and critical lessons can be vigorously engaged in every curricular program. Students do not have to study traditional academic courses to become critical thinkers but, when their own interests are respected, they may listen attentively to what the great thinkers have said about those interests. They may even add productively to that thinking.

Stretching the disciplines from within suggests that, paradoxically, breadth might well be achieved by specialization. It is rarely achieved through the coerced study of unconnected specialties, however many of them are stuffed into the required curriculum. Students specializing in mathematics or science can, in the process, learn something of history, biography, philosophy, literature, aesthetics, religion, and how to live. A large part of every curriculum should be devoted to Life itself, as Whitehead suggested, and many lessons – not just an odd one here and there – should be *wonderful* – that is, designed to excite wonder, awe, and appreciation of the world and the place of human beings in it.

---

[5] I recognized this when I suggested teaching themes of care. See Noddings, *The Challenge to Care in Schools*, 2nd ed. (New York: Teachers College Press, 2005).

Bibliography

Addams, Jane. *Peace and Bread in Time of War*. New York: King's Crown Press, 1945.

Adler, Mortimer J. *The Paideia Proposal*. New York: Macmillan, 1982.

Albom, Mitch. *Tuesdays with Morrie*. New York: Broadway Books, 2002.

Angell, Marcia. *The Truth about Drug Companies*. New York: Random House, 2004.

Angus, David L. and Mirel, Jeffrey E. *The Failed Promise of the American High School: 1890–1995*. New York: Teachers College Press, 1999.

Appelbaum, Eileen, Bernhardt, Annette, and Murnane, Richard J., eds. *Low-Wage America: How Employers Are Reshaping Opportunity in the Workplace*. New York: Russell Sage Foundation, 2004.

Apple, Michael. *Cultural Politics and Education*. New York: Teachers College Press, 1996.

Ardrey, Robert. *The Territorial Imperative*. New York: Atheneum, 1966.

Arendt, Hannah. *The Human Condition*. Chicago: University of Chicago Press, 1958.

Ariès, Philippe. *Centuries of Childhood*, trans. Robert Baldick. New York: Vintage Books, 1962.

Aristotle. *Nicomachean Ethics*, trans. Terence Irwin. Indianapolis: Hackett, 1985.

Armstrong, Karen. *A History of God*. London: Vintage Books, 1999.

Ascher, Carol. "The Force of Ideas," *History of Education* 34(3), May 2005: 277–293.

Auerbach, Nina. *Women and the Demon: The Life of a Victorian Myth*. Cambridge, MA: Harvard University Press, 1982.

Avineri, Shlomo and de-Shalit, Avner, eds. *Communitarianism and Individualism*. Oxford: Oxford University Press, 1992.

Avorn, Jerry. *Powerful Medicines*. New York: Alfred A. Knopf, 2004.

Babcock, Linda and Laschever, Sara. *Women Don't Ask: Negotiation and the Gender Divide*. Princeton, NJ: Princeton University Press, 2003.

Bachelard, Gaston. *The Poetics of Space*, trans. Maria Jolas. New York: Orion Press, 1964.

Bailin, Sharon and Siegel, Harvey. "Critical Thinking," in *Philosophy of Education*, ed. Nigel Blake, Paul Smeyers, Richard Smith, and Paul Standish. Oxford: Blackwell, 2003, pp. 181–193.

Bartkowski, Frances. *Feminist Utopias*. Lincoln: University of Nebraska Press, 1989.

Bartlett, F. C. *Remembering*. Cambridge: Cambridge University Press, 1932.

Basso, Keith. *Wisdom Sits in Places*. Albuquerque: University of New Mexico Press, 1996.

Baumrind, Diana. "Parent Styles and Adolescent Development," in *The Encyclopedia of Adolescence*, ed. R. Lerner, A. C. Petersen, and J. Brooks-Gunn. New York: Garland Press, 1991, vol. 2, pp. 746–758.

Baumrind, Diana. *Child Maltreatment and Optimal Caregiving in Social Contexts*. New York: Garland, 1995.

Beauvoir, Simone de. *The Second Sex*, trans. H. M. Parshley. New York: Bantam Books, 1952.

Beck, Lynn. *Reclaiming Educational Administration as a Caring Profession*. New York: Teachers College Press, 1994.

Bekoff, Marc. *Minding Animals*. Oxford: Oxford University Press, 2002.

Bell, E. T. *Men of Mathematics*. New York: Simon & Schuster, 1965.

Bellamy, Edward. *Looking Backward*. New York: New American Library, 1960.

Bentham, Jeremy. *Introduction to the Principles of Morals and Legislation*. Oxford: Clarendon Press, 1996.

Berlin, Isaiah. *Four Essays on Liberty*. Oxford: Oxford University Press, 1969.

Bernstein, Richard J. *The New Constellation*. Cambridge, MA: MIT Press, 1992.

Berry, Wendell. *Another Turn of the Crank*. Washington, DC: Counterpoint, 1995.

Bettelheim, Bruno. *The Children of the Dream*. New York: Macmillan, 1969.

Bettelheim, Bruno. *The Uses of Enchantment: The Meaning and Importance of Fairy Tales*. New York: Alfred A. Knopf, 1976.

Blackburn, Simon. *Think*. Oxford: Oxford University Press, 1999.

Blackham, H. J. *Six Existential Thinkers*. New York: Harper & Row, 1959.

Bloom, Harold. *The American Religion: The Emergence of the Post-Christian Nation*. New York: Simon & Schuster.

Blount, Jackie M. *Destined to Rule the Schools*. Albany: State University of New York Press, 1998.

Bok, Sissela. *Lying: Moral Choice in Public and Private Life*. New York: Vintage Books, 1979.

Bollag, Burton. "Choosing Their Flock," *The Chronicle of Higher Education*, Jan. 28, 2005: A33–A35.

Boswell, John. *Christianity, Social Tolerance, and Homosexuality*. Chicago: University of Chicago Press, 1981.

Boulding, Elise. *One Small Plot of Heaven*. Wallingford, PA: Pendle Hill, 1989.

Boyer, Peter J. "A Hard Faith," *The New Yorker*, May 16, 2005: 54–65.

Bibliography

Brabeck, Mary M., ed. *Practicing Feminist Ethics in Psychology*. Washington, DC: American Psychological Association, 2000.

Brock-Utne, Birgit. *Educating for Peace: A Feminist Perspective*. New York: Pergamon Press, 1985.

Brown, Dan. *The Da Vinci Code*. New York: Doubleday, 2003.

Brown, Stephen I. and Walter, Marion I. *The art of problem posing*. Philadelphia: Franklin Institute Press, 1983.

Browne, Janet. *Charles Darwin: The Power of Place*. New York: Alfred A. Knopf, 2002.

Buber, Martin. *Pointing the Way: Collected Essays*, trans. Maurice Friedman. New York: Schocken Books, 1957.

Buber, Martin. *Between Man and Man*. New York: Macmillan, 1965.

Buber, Martin. *The Way of Response*, ed. Nahum N. Glatzer. New York: Schocken Books, 1966.

Buber, Martin. *I and Thou*, trans. Walter Kaufmann. New York: Charles Scribner's Sons, 1970.

Buchwald, Emilie, Fletcher, Pamela R., and Roth, Martha, eds. *Transforming a Rape Culture*. Minneapolis: Milkweed Editions, 1993.

Buck, Pearl S. *The Exile*. New York: Triangle, 1936.

Burbules, Nicholas. *Dialogue in Teaching*. New York: Teachers College Press, 1983.

Butler, Samuel. *Erewhon*. London: Penguin Books, 1985/1872.

Callan, Eamonn. "Liberal Legitimacy, Justice, and Civic Education," *Ethics* 111, October 2000: 141–155.

Campbell, Debra. *Graceful Exits: Catholic Women and the Art of Departure*. Bloomington: Indiana University Press, 2003.

Campbell, Joseph. *The Power of Myth*. New York: Anchor Books, 1991.

Caputo, John D. *Against Ethics*. Bloomington: Indiana University Press, 1993.

Casey, Edward S. *Getting Back into Place*. Bloomington: Indiana University Press, 1993.

Cashman, Greg. *What Causes War?* New York: Macmillan, 1993.

Castillejo, Irene Claremont de. *Knowing Woman*. New York: Harper Colophon, 1974.

Chappell, David W., ed. *Buddhist Peacework: Creating Cultures of Peace*. Boston: Wisdom Publications, 1999.

Chodorow, Nancy. *The Reproduction of Mothering*. Berkeley: University of California Press, 1978.

Cleverly, John and Phillips, D. C. *Visions of Childhood*. New York: Teachers College Press, 1986.

Cohen, Lizabeth. *A Consumers' Republic*. New York: Vintage Books, 2003.

Cole, David. *Enemy Aliens: Double Standards and Constitutional Freedoms in the War On Terrorism*. New York: New Press, 2003.

Coles, Robert. *Simone Weil: A Modern Pilgrimage*. Reading, MA: Addison-Wesley, 1987.

Collins, Gail. *America's Women: 400 Years of Dolls, Drudges, Helpmates, and Heroines*. New York: HarperCollins, 2003.

Cooey, Paula M., Farmer, Sharon A., and Ross, Mary Ellen, eds. *Embodied Love: Sensuality and Relationship as Feminist Values*. San Francisco: Harper & Row, 1987.

Covey, Stephen R. *The 7 Habits of Highly Effective Families*. New York: Golden Books, 1997.

Crocco, Margaret S. and Davis, O. L., eds. *"Bending the Future to Their Will."* Lanham, MD: Rowman & Littlefield, 1999.

Cronbach, Lee J. *Educational Psychology*. New York: Harcourt Brace Jovanovich, 1977.

Cross, Barbara M., ed. *The Educated Woman in America*. New York: Teachers College Press, 1965.

Crowe, Norman. *Nature and the Idea of a Man-Made World*. Cambridge, MA: MIT Press, 1997.

Daly, Mary. *Beyond God the Father*. Boston: Beacon Press, 1974.

Daly, Mary. *Pure Lust*. Boston: Beacon Press, 1984.

Damrosch, Leopold, Jr. *Symbol and Truth in Blake's Myth*. Princeton, NJ: Princeton University Press, 1980.

Danzer, Gerald A., Klor de Alva, J. Jorge, Krieger, Larry S., Wilson, Louis E., and Woloch, Nancy. *The Americans*. Evanston, IL: Houghton Mifflin, 2000.

Darling-Hammond, Linda. "From 'Separate but Equal' to 'No Child Left Behind': The Collision of New Standards and Old Inequalities," in *Many Children Left Behind*, ed. Deborah Meier and George Wood. Boston: Beacon Press, 2004, pp. 3–32.

Darling-Hammond, Linda and Bransford, John, eds. *Preparing Teachers for a Changing World*. San Francisco: Jossey-Bass, 2005.

Dawkins, Richard. *The Blind Watchmaker*. New York: W. W. Norton, 1986.

Day, Dorothy. *The Long Loneliness*. San Francisco: Harper & Row, 1952.

DeGrazia, David. *Taking Animals Seriously*. Cambridge: Cambridge University Press, 1996.

Delpit, Lisa. "Educators as 'Seed People' Growing a New Future," *Educational Researcher* 7(32), 2003: 14–21.

Derrida, Jacques. *Writing and Difference*, trans. Alan Bass. Chicago: University of Chicago Press, 1978.

Dewey, John. *The School and Society*. Chicago: University of Chicago Press, 1900.

Dewey, John. *Democracy and Education*. New York: Macmillan, 1916.

Dewey, John. *The Public and Its Problems*. New York: Henry Holt, 1927.

Dewey, John. *Human Nature and Conduct*. New York: Modern Library, 1930.

Dijkstra, Bram. *Idols of Perversity: Fantasies of Feminine Evil in Fin-de-Siècle Culture*. New York: Oxford University Press, 1986.

Dostoevsky, Fyodor. *The Brothers Karamazov*, trans. Constance Garnett. New York: Modern Library, n.d.

Downing, Christine. *The Goddess*. New York: Crossroad, 1984.

Duncan, Cynthia M. *Worlds Apart: Why Poverty Persists in Rural America*. New Haven, CT: Yale University Press, 1999.

Bibliography

Dunne, Joseph and Hogan, Padraig, eds. *Education and Practice*. Oxford: Blackwell, 2004.

Early, Frances, H. *A World without War*. Syracuse, NY: Syracuse University Press, 1997.

Egan, Kieran. *Imagination in Teaching and Learning: The Middle School Years*. Chicago: University of Chicago Press, 1992.

Egan, Kieran. *Children's Minds, Talking Rabbits, and Clockwork Oranges*. New York: Teachers College Press, 1999.

Egan, Kieran. *An Imaginative Approach to Teaching*. San Francisco: Jossey-Bass, 2005.

Ehrenreich, Barbara. *Blood Rites: Origins and History of the Passions of War*. New York: Henry Holt, 1997.

Ehrenreich, Barbara. *Nickel and Dimed*. New York: Metropolitan Books, 2001.

Elbow, Peter. *Embracing Contraries*. Oxford: Oxford University Press, 1993.

Elshtain, Jean Bethke. *Women and War*. New York: Basic Books, 1987.

Elshtain, Jean Bethke. *Jane Addams and the Dream of American Democracy*. New York: Basic Books, 2002.

Ennis, Robert. "A Concept of Critical Thinking," *Harvard Educational Review* 32(1), 1962: 83–111.

Epstein, Cynthia Fuchs. *Deceptive Distinctions: Sex, Gender, and the Social Order*. New Haven, CT: Yale University Press, 1988.

Farrell, John C. *Beloved Lady: A History of Jane Addams's Ideas on Reform and Peace*. Baltimore: Johns Hopkins University Press, 1967.

Farrell, J. G. *The Siege of Krishnapur*. New York: New York Review Books, 2004.

Feingold, Alan. "Sex Differences in Variability in Intellectual Abilities: A New Look at an Old Controversy," *Review of Educational Research* 62(1), 1992: 61–84.

Ferguson, Ann. "On Conceiving Motherhood and Sexuality: A Feminist Materialist Approach," in *Feminist Social Thought: A Reader*, ed. Diana Tietjens Meyers. New York: Routledge, 1997, pp. 38–63.

Ferguson, John. *War and Peace in the World's Religions*. New York: Oxford University Press, 1978.

Fineman, Martha. *The Autonomy Myth: A Theory of Dependency*. New York: New Press, 2004.

Fischman, Wendy, Solomon, Becca, Greenspan, Deborah, and Gardner, Howard. *Making Good: How Young People Cope with Moral Dilemmas at Work*. Cambridge, MA: Harvard University Press, 2004.

Flanagan, Caitlin. "How Serfdom Saved the Women's Movement," *Atlantic Monthly*, March 2004: 110.

Fogarty, Brian E. *War, Peace, and the Social Order*. Boulder, CO: Westview Press, 2000.

Forbes, Scott H. *Holistic Education: An Analysis of Its Ideas and Nature*. Brandon, VT: Foundation for Educational Renewal, 2003.

Frankl, Viktor E. *The Doctor and the Soul*. New York: Vintage Books, 1973.

Franz, Marie-Louise von. *Shadow and Evil in Fairy Tales*. Dallas: Spring, 1983.

Fraser, James. *The Golden Bough*. New York: Macmillan, 1951.

Freire, Paulo. *Pedagogy of the Oppressed*, trans. Myra Bergman Ramos. New York: Herder and Herder, 1970.

Friedan, Betty. *The Feminine Mystique*. New York: W. W. Norton, 1963.

Frost, Robert. *Complete Poems*. New York: Henry Holt, 1949, p. vi.

Galston, William. *Liberal Purposes: Goods, Virtues and Diversity in the Liberal State*. Cambridge: Cambridge University Press, 1991.

Galston, William. "Two Concepts of Liberalism," *Ethics* 105(3), 1995: 516–534.

Gardner, Martin. *The Annotated Alice: Lewis Carroll*. New York: World, 1963.

Gardner, Martin. *Mathematical Carnival*. New York: Alfred A. Knopf, 1975.

Gardner, Martin. *The Whys of a Philosophical Scrivener*. New York: Quill, 1983.

Gaylin, Willard. *Hatred: The Psychological Descent into Violence*. New York: Public Affairs, 2003.

Gilbert, Margaret. *Sociality and Responsibility*. Lanham, MD: Rowman & Littlefield, 2000.

Gilbreth, Frank B., Jr. and Carey, Ernestine Gilbreth. *Cheaper by the Dozen*. New York: Bantam Books, 1966.

Gilligan, Carol J. *In a Different Voice*. Cambridge, MA: Harvard University Press, 1982.

Gilligan, James. *Violence*. New York: G. P. Putnam's Sons, 1996.

Gilman, Charlotte Perkins. *Herland*. New York: Pantheon Books, 1979.

Girard, Rene. *Violence and the Sacred*. Baltimore: Johns Hopkins University Press, 1979.

Giroux, Henry A. *Schooling and the Struggle for Public Life*. Minneapolis: University of Minnesota, 1988.

Glendon, Mary Ann. *Rights Talk*. New York: Free Press, 1991.

Glover, Jonathan. *A Moral History of the 20th Century*. New Haven, CT: Yale University Press, 2000.

Goldensohn, Lorrie. *Dismantling Glory*. New York: Columbia University Press, 2003.

Goodman, Paul. *Growing Up Absurd*. New York: Random House, 1960.

Goodman, Paul. *Compulsory Mis-education*. New York: Horizon, 1964.

Goozner, Merrill. *The $800 Million Pill*. Berkeley: University of California Press, 2004.

Gordon, Suzanne, Benner, Patricia, and Noddings, Nel, eds. *Caregiving*. Philadelphia: University of Pennsylvania Press, 1996.

Grass, Gunter. *Crabwalk*, trans. Krishna Winston. Orlando, FL: Harcourt, 2002.

Graves, Robert. *Goodbye to All That*. London: Folio Society, 1981.

Gray, J. G. *The Warriors: Reflections on Men in Battle*. New York: HarperCollins, 1977.

Greene, Maxine. *The Dialectic of Freedom*. New York: Teachers College Press, 1988.

Griffin, David Ray. *God, Power, and Evil: A Process Theodicy*. Philadelphia: Westminster Press, 1976.

Bibliography

Griffin, David Ray. *Evil Revisited*. Albany: State University of New York Press, 1991.

Grimshaw, Jean. *Philosophy and Feminist Thinking*. Minneapolis: University of Minneapolis Press, 1986.

Grissell, Eric. *Insects and Gardens: In Pursuit of a Garden Ecology*. Portland, OR: Timber Press, 2001.

Groenhout, Ruth E. *Connected Lives: Human Nature and an Ethics of Care*. Lanham, MD: Rouman & Littlefield, 2004.

Groenhout, Ruth E. and Bower, Marya, eds. *Philosophy, Feminism, and Faith*. Bloomington: Indiana University Press, 2003.

Grubb, W. Norton, ed. *Education through Occupations in American High Schools*, vols. 1 and 2. New York: Teachers College Press, 1995.

Hacker, Andrew. "The Underworld of Work," *New York Review of Books*, Feb. 12, 2004: 38–40.

Hadamard, Jacques. *The Psychology of Invention in the Mathematical Field*. New York: Dover, 1954.

Halevi, Yossi Klein. *At the Entrance to the Garden of Eden*. New York: Perennial, 2001.

Hall, G. Stanley. *Adolescence: Its Psychology and Its Relation to Physiology, Anthropology, Sociology, Sex, Crime, Religion, and Education*, 2 vols. New York: D. Appleton, 1904.

Halpern, Diane F. *Thought and Knowledge*. Mahwah, NJ: Lawrence Erlbaum, 2003.

Harding, M. Esther. *Woman's Mysteries*. New York: Harper & Row, 1971.

Hart, B. and Risley, T. R. *Meaningful Differences in the Everyday Experience of Young American Children*. Baltimore: Brooks, 1995.

Hart, D. G. *The University Gets Religion*. Baltimore: Johns Hopkins University Press, 1999.

Head, Simon. *The New Ruthless Economy: Work and Power in the Digital Age*. Oxford: Oxford University Press, 2004.

Heath, Shirley Brice. *Ways with Words*. Cambridge: Cambridge University Press, 1983.

Hedges, Chris. "War Is a Force That Gives Us Meaning." *Amnesty Now*, Winter 2002: 10–13.

Hedges, Chris. *War Is a Force That Gives Us Meaning*. New York: Public Affairs, 2002.

Heidegger, Martin. *Basic Writings*, ed. David Farrell Krell. New York: Harper & Row, 1977.

Hellman, Hal. *Great Feuds in Science*. New York: John Wiley & Sons, 1998.

Hendra, Tony. *Father Joe*. New York: Random House, 2004.

Hick, John. *Evil and the God of Love*. New York: Macmillan, 1966.

Hitler, Adolf. *Mein Kampf*. New York: Reynal and Hichcock, 1939.

Hoffer, Eric. *The True Believer*. New York: Harper & Row, 1951.

Hulbert, Ann. *Raising America*. New York: Alfred A. Knopf, 2003.

Hume, David. *Dialogues Concerning Natural Religion*, ed. Richard Popkin. Indianapolis: Hackett, 1980.

Hume, David. *An Enquiry Concerning the Principles of Morals*. Indianapolis: Hackett, 1983.

Hutchins, Robert Maynard. *The Higher Learning in America*. New Haven, CT: Yale University Press, 1936.

Ikeda, Daisaku. *For the Sake of Peace: Seven Paths to Global Harmony*. Santa Monica, CA: Middleway Press, 2001.

Illich, Ivan I. *Deschooling Society*. New York: Harper & Row, 1971.

Jackson, John Brinckerhoff. *A Sense of Place, a Sense of Time*. New Haven, CT: Yale University Press, 1994.

Jacoby, Susan. *Freethinkers*. New York: Metropolitan Books, 2004.

James, William. *The Varieties of Religious Experience*. New York: Modern Library, 1929.

James, William. *The Principles of Psychology*. New York: Dover, 1950.

James, William. "The Moral Equivalent of War," in *The Writings of William James*, ed. John J. McDermott. New York: Random House, 1967, pp. 660–671.

Judson, Horace Freeland. *The Great Betrayal: Fraud in Science*. Orlando, FL: Harcourt Brace Jovanovich, 2004.

Juergensmeyer, Mark. *Terror in the Mind of God: The Global Rise of Religious Violence*. Berkeley: University of California Press, 2000.

Jung, Carl G. *Collected Works*, vol. 2. Princeton, NJ: Princeton University Press, 1958.

Jung, Carl G. *Answer to Job*, trans. R. F. C. Hull. Princeton, NJ: Princeton University Press, 1973.

Kahn, Peter. *The Human Relationship with Nature*. Cambridge, MA: MIT Press, 1999.

Kahneman, Daniel, Diener, Ed, and Schwartz, Norbert, eds. *Well-Being*. New York: Russell Sage Foundation, 1999.

Kane, Paula, Kenneally, James, and Kenneally, Karen, eds. *Gender Identities in American Catholicism*. Maryknoll, NY: Orbis Books, 2001.

Kant, Immanuel. *Critique of Pure Reason*, trans. F. Max Muller. Garden City, NY: Doubleday Anchor Books, 1966.

Kanter, Rosabeth Moss. *Commitment and Community: Communes and Utopias in Sociological Perspective*. Cambridge, MA: Harvard University Press, 1972.

Keller, Catherine. *From a Broken Web*. Boston: Beacon Press, 1986.

Kelman, Herbert C. and Hamilton, V. Lee. *Crimes of Obedience*. New Haven, CT: Yale University Press, 1989.

Kerber, Linda. *Toward an Intellectual History of Women*. Chapel Hill: University of North Carolina Press, 1997.

Kierkegaard, Søren. *Fear and Trembling* and *The Sickness Unto Death*, trans. Walter Lowrie. Princeton, NJ: Princeton University Press, 1941.

Kimmel, Michael S. "Clarence, William, Iron Mike, Tailhook, Senator Packwood, Spur Posse, Magic . . . and Us," in *Transforming a Rape Culture*, ed. Buchwald, Fletcher, and Roth, pp. 121–138.

Bibliography

Kingsolver, Barbara. "Small Wonder," *Peace and Freedom* 64(1), Winter 2004: 5.

Kipling, Rudyard. *The Works of Kipling*. Roslyn, NY: Black's Readers Service, n.d.

Kissen, Rita M. *The Last Closet: The Real Lives of Lesbian and Gay Teachers*. Portsmouth, NH: Heinemann, 1996.

Klaits, Joseph. *Servants of Satan*. Bloomington: Indiana University Press, 1985.

Kliebard, Herbert. *Schooled to Work: Vocationalism and the American Curriculum 1876–1946*. New York: Teachers College Press, 1999.

Knowles, John. *A Separate Peace*. New York: Macmillan, 1960.

Kohn, Alfie. *Punished by Rewards: The Trouble with Gold Stars, Incentive Plans, A's, Praise, and Other Bribes*. Boston: Houghton Mifflin, 1993.

Kohn, Alfie. "The Trouble with Character Education," in *The Construction of Children's Character*, ed. Alex Molnar. Chicago: National Society for the Study of Education, 1997, pp. 154–162.

Krakauer, Jon. *Under the Banner of Heaven*. New York: Doubleday, 2003.

Kuhse, Helga. *Caring, Nurses, Women and Ethics*. Oxford: Blackwell, 1997.

Kung, Hans. *Does God Exist?* Garden City, NY: Doubleday, 1980.

Lagemann, Ellen Condliffe, ed. *Jane Addams on Education*. New York: Teachers College Press, 1985.

Lane, Robert E. *The Loss of Happiness in Market Democracies*. New Haven, CT: Yale University Press, 2000.

Larson, Erik. *The Devil in the White City*. New York: Vintage Books, 2004.

Lauter, Estella and Rupprecht, Carol Schrier, eds. *Feminist Archetypal Theory*. Knoxville: University of Tennessee Press, 1985.

Leibniz, Gottfried W. *Theodicy*, trans. E. M. Huggard. New Haven, CT: Yale University Press, 1952.

Leming, James, Ellington, Lucien, and Porter, Kathleen, eds. *Where Did Social Studies Go Wrong?* Washington, DC: Thomas B. Fordham Foundation, 2003.

Le Shan, Lawrence. *The Psychology of War*. Chicago: Noble Press, 1992.

Levi, Primo. *The Periodic Table*, trans. Raymond Rosenthal. New York: Schocken Books, 1984.

Levi, Primo. *The Drowned and the Saved*, trans. Raymond Rosenthal. New York: Vintage, 1988.

Levin, M. "Animal Rights Evaluated," *Humanist* 37, July – August 1977: 14–15.

Levinas, Emmanuel. *The Levinas Reader*, ed. Sean Hand. Oxford: Blackwell, 1989.

Lewis, Anthony. "Un-American Activities," *New York Review of Books*, Oct. 23, 2003: 16–19.

Lewis, C. S. *The Problem of Pain*. New York: Macmillan, 1962.

Lewontin, Richard. "Dishonesty in Science," *New York Review of Books*, Nov. 18, 2004: 38–40.

Lickona, Thomas. *Educating for Character: How Our Schools Can Teach Respect and Responsibility*. New York: Bantam Books, 1991.

Lindberg, David and Numbers, Ronald L., eds. *When Science and Christianity Meet*. Chicago: University of Chicago Press, 2003.

Lindbergh, Anne Morrow. *Gift from the Sea*. New York: Random House, 1955.

Lipman, Matthew. *Thinking in Education*. Cambridge: Cambridge University Press, 1991.

Lippmann, Walter. *Public Opinion*. New York: Free Press, 1965.

Livio, Mario. *The Golden Ratio: The Story of Phi, The World's Most Astonishing Number*. New York: Broadway Books, 2002.

Lorenz, Konrad. *On Aggression*. New York: Bantam, Books, 1966.

Macdonald, Lyn, ed. *Anthem For Doomed Youth*. London: Folio Society, 2000.

Macedo, Donald. *Literacies of Power: What Americans Are Not Allowed to Know*. Boulder, CO: Westview Press, 1994.

MacIntyre, Alasdair. *After Virtue*. Notre Dame, IN: University of Notre Dame Press, 1981.

Maitland, Sara. Introduction to *The Hound and the Falcon: The Story of a Reconversion to the Catholic Faith* by Antonia White. London: Virago Press, 1992.

Martin, Jane Roland. *Reclaiming a Conversation*. New Haven, CT: Yale University Press, 1985.

Martin, Jane Roland. *Cultural Miseducation*. New York: Teachers College Press, 2002.

Martin, Michael and Monnier, Ricki, eds. *The Impossibility of God*. Amherst, NY: Prometheus Books, 2003.

Maslow, Abraham. *Motivation and Personality*. New York: Harper & Row, 1970.

Maslow, Abraham. *The Farther Reaches of Human Nature*. New York: Viking Press, 1971.

Masson, Jeffrey Moussaieff and McCarthy, Susan. *When Elephants Weep: The Emotional. Lives of Animals*. New York: Delacorte Press, 1995.

May, Larry and Hoffman, Stacey, eds. *Collective Responsibility*. Lanham, MD: Rowman & Littlefield, 1991.

McCarthy, Mary. *Memories of a Catholic Girlhood*. San Diego, CA: Harvest/Harcourt, 1985.

McPeck, John E. *Critical Thinking and Education*. Oxford: Martin Robertson, 1981.

Mead, George Herbert. *Mind, Self, and Society: From the Standpoint of a Social Behaviorist*. Chicago: University of Chicago Press, 1934.

Meier, Deborah and Wood, George, eds. *Many Children Left Behind*. Boston: Beacon Press, 2004.

Meyers, Diana T. *Self, Society, and Personal Choice*. New York: Columbia University Press, 1989.

Michel, Sonya. *Children's Interests/Mothers' Rights*. New Haven, CT: Yale University Press, 1999.

Miles, Jack. *God: A Biography*. New York: Alfred A. Knopf, 1995.

Bibliography

Miller, Ron. *Free Schools, Free People: Education and Democracy after the 1960s*. Albany: State University of New York Press, 2002.

Molnar, Alex. *Giving Kids the Business: The Commercialization of America's Schools*. Boulder, CO: Westview Press, 1996.

Morris, Simon Conway. *Life's Solution: Inevitable Humans in a Lonely Universe*. Cambridge: Cambridge University Press, 2003.

Moskos, Charles C. and Chambers, John Whiteclay II, eds. *The New Conscientious Objection*. Oxford: Oxford University Press, 1993.

Mossner, Ernest C. "Deism," in *The Encyclopedia of Philosophy*, ed. Paul Edwards. New York: Macmillan, 1967, pp. 326–336.

Nabhan, Gary Paul and Trimble, Stephen. *The Geography of Childhood: Why Children Need Wild Places*. Boston: Beacon Press, 1994.

Naimark, Norman M. *Fires of Hatred: Ethnic Cleansing in Twentieth-Century Europe*. Cambridge, MA: Harvard University Press, 2002.

Nash, Robert J. *Faith Hype and Clarity*. New York: Teachers College Press, 1999.

National Education Association. *Cardinal Principles of Secondary Education*. Washington, DC: U.S. Government Printing Office, 1918.

Nearing, Scott. *The Making of a Radical: A Political Autobiography*. White River Junction, VT: Chelsea Green, 2000.

Nearing, Scott and Nearing, Helen K. *Living the Good Life*. New York: Schocken Books, 1970.

Neill, A. S. *Summerhill*. New York: Hart, 1960.

Nelson, Richard. *The Island Within*. New York: Vintage Books, 1991.

Noble, David F. *A World without Women*. Oxford: Oxford University Press, 1992.

Noddings, Nel. *Women and Evil*. Berkeley: University of California Press, 1989.

Noddings, Nel. "Stories in Dialogue," in *Stories Lives Tell*, ed. Carol Witherell and Ned Noddings. New York: Teachers College Press, 1991, pp. 157–170.

Noddings, Nel. *The Challenge to Care in Schools*. New York: Teachers College Press, 1992.

Noddings, Nel. *Educating for Intelligent Belief or Unbelief*. New York: Teachers College Press, 1993.

Noddings, Nel. "Must We Motivate?" in *Teaching and Its Discontents*, ed. Nicholas Burbules and David Hausen. Boulder, CO: Westview Press, 1997, pp. 29–44.

Noddings, Nel. *Educating Moral People*. New York: Teachers College Press, 2002.

Noddings, Nel. *Starting at Home: Caring and Social Policy*. Berkeley: University of California Press, 2002.

Noddings, Nel. *Caring: A Feminine Approach to Ethics and Moral Education*, 2nd ed. Berkeley: University of California Press, 2003.

Noddings, Nel. *Happiness and Education*. Cambridge: Cambridge University Press, 2003.

Noddings, Nel. *The Challenge to Care in Schools*, 2nd ed. New York: Teachers College Press, 2005.

Noddings, Nel and Shore, Paul. *Awakening the Inner Eye: Intuition in Education*. New York: Teachers College Press, 1984.

Norman, Donald A. *Memory and Attention: An Introduction to Human Information Processing*. New York: John Wiley & Sons, 1969.

Norris, Kathleen. *The Cloister Walk*. New York: Riverhead Books, 1996.

Norris, Stephen R. *The Generalizability of Critical Thinking*. New York: Teachers College Press, 1992.

Ochs, Carol. *Women and Spirituality*. Totowa, NJ: Rowman and Allanheld, 1983.

Ochshorn, Judith. *The Female Experience and the Nature of the Divine*. Bloomington: Indiana University Press, 1981.

Okin, Susan Moller. *Women in Western Political Thought*. Princeton, NJ: Princeton University Press, 1979.

Orme, Nicholas. *Medieval Children*. New Haven, CT: Yale University Press, 2001.

Orwell, George. *Nineteen Eighty-Four*. New York: Harcourt, Brace and World, 1949.

Owen, David. "Bright Green Mega-City," *The New Yorker*, Oct. 18, 2004: 112.

Page, Linda Garland and Wigginton, Eliot, eds. *Aunt Arie: A Foxfive Portrait*. New York: E. P. Dutton, 1983.

Paley, Vivian Gussin. *A Child's Work*. Chicago: University of Chicago Press, 2004.

Pascal, Blaise. *Pensées*, trans. A. J. Krailsheimer. Baltimore: Penguin Books, 1966.

Patmore, Coventry. *The Angel in the House*. New York: E. P. Dutton, 1876.

Paul, Richard. *Critical Thinking: What Every Person Needs to Survive in a Rapidly Changing World*. Rohnest Park, CA: Center for Critical Thinking and Moral Critique, 1990.

Perotta, Tom. *Little Children*. New York: St. Martin's Press, 2004.

Perry, C. and Jones, G. E. "On Animal Rights," *International Journal of Applied Philosophy* 1, 1982: 39–57.

Peshkin, Alan. *God's Choice: The Total World of a Fundamentalist Christian School*. Chicago: University of Chicago Press, 1986.

Phillips, John Anthony. *Eve: The History of an Idea*. San Francisco: Harper & Row, 1984.

Plantinga, Alvin. *God, Freedom, and Evil*. Grand Rapids, MI: Erdmans, 1974.

Plato. *Republic*, trans. B. Jowett. Roslyn, NY: Walter Black, 1942.

Poincaré, Henri. "Mathematical Creation," in *The World of Mathematics*, ed. J. R. Newman. New York: Simon & Schuster, 1956, pp. 2041–2050.

Pollan, Michael. *Second Nature*. New York: Delta, 1991.

Pollan, Michael. *A Place of My Own: The Education of an Amateur Builder*. New York: Delta, 1997.

Pollan, Michael. *The Botany of Desire*. New York: Random House, 2001.

Bibliography

Pope, Denise Clark. *"Doing School": How We Are Creating a Generation of Stressed Out, Materialistic, and Miseducated Students*. New Haven, CT: Yale University Press, 2001.

Postman, Neil and Weingartner, Charles. *Teaching as a Subversive Activity*. New York: Delta, 1969.

Powers, Richard. *Prisoner's Dilemma*. New York: HarperCollins, 1988.

Putnam, Robert. "Bowling Alone: America's Declining Social Capital," *Journal of Democracy* 6, 1995: 65–78.

Rawls, John. *A Theory of Justice*. Cambridge, MA: Harvard University Press, 1971.

Reardon, Betty A. *Sexism and the War System*. New York: Teachers College Press, 1985.

Regan, Tom. *The Case for Animal Rights*. Berkeley: University of California Press, 1983.

Remarque, Erich Maria. *All Quiet on the Western Front*, trans. A. W. Wheen. New York: Fawcett Books, 1982.

Rendell, Ruth. *The Babes in the Woods*. London: Arrow Books, 2003.

Reverby, Susan. *Ordered to Care*. Cambridge: Cambridge University Press, 1987.

Rhode, Deborah L., ed. *Theoretical Perspectives on Sexual Difference*. New Haven, CT: Yale University Press, 1990.

Rich, Adrienne. *Of Woman Born*. New York: W. W. Norton, 1976.

Richardson, Robert D., Jr. *Emerson: The Mind on Fire*. Berkeley: University of California Press, 1995.

Ricoeur, Paul. *The Symbolism of Evil*. Boston: Beacon Press, 1969.

Roberts, Donald F. and Foehr, Ulla G. *Kids and Media in America*. Cambridge: Cambridge University Press, 2004.

Rogers, Carl. *Freedom to Learn*. Columbus, OH: C. E. Merrill, 1969.

Rose, Mike. *Possible Lives: The Promise of Public Education in America*. Boston: Houghton Mifflin, 1995.

Rosenbaum, Ron. *Explaining Hitler*. New York: HarperCollins, 1999.

Rossiter, Margaret. *Women Scientists in America: Struggles and Strategies to 1940*. Baltimore: Johns Hopkins University Press, 1982.

Rouner, Leroy S., ed. *The Longing for Home*. Notre Dame, IN: University of Notre Dame Press, 1996.

Ruddick, Sara. *Maternal Thinking: Towards a Politics of Peace*. Boston: Beacon Press, 1989.

Ruether, Rosemary Radford. *Sexism and God-Talk*. Boston: Beacon Press, 1983.

Ruse, Michael. *Darwin and Design: Does Evolution Have a Purpose?* Cambridge, MA: Harvard University Press, 2003.

Russell, Bertrand. *Why I Am Not a Christian, and Other Essays on Religion and Related Subjects*. New York: Simon & Schuster, 1957.

Ryan, Alan. *Bertrand Russell: A Political Life*. New York: Hill and Wang, 1988.

Rybczynski, Witold. *Home: A Short History of an Idea*. New York: Viking Press, 1986.

Rykwert, Joseph. *On Adam's House in Paradise*. Cambridge, MA: MIT Press, 1997.

Sandel, Michael. *Liberalism and the Limits of Justice*. Cambridge: Cambridge University Press, 1982.

Sartre, Jean-Paul. *Being and Nothingness*, trans. Hazel E. Barnes. New York: Washington Square Press, 1956.

Sartre, Jean-Paul. *Search for a Method*, trans. Hazel E. Barnes. New York: Vintage Books, 1968.

Saunders, Harold H. *The Other Walls*. Princeton, NJ: Princeton University Press, 1991.

Schaler, Jeffrey A., ed. *Drugs: Should We Legalize, Decriminalize or Deregulate?* Amherst, NY: Prometheus Books, 1998.

Schein, Seth L. *The Mortal Hero*. Berkeley: University of California Press, 1984.

Schor, Juliet B. *Born to Buy: The Commercialized Child and the New Consumer*. New York: Scribner, 2004.

Schrijvers, Peter. *The GI War Against Japan*. New York: New York University Press, 2002.

Sebald, W. G. *On the Natural History of Destruction*, trans. Anthea Bell. New York: Random House, 2003.

Shanks, Niall. *God, the Devil, and Darwin*. Oxford: Oxford University Press, 2004.

Shay, Jonathan. *Achilles in Vietnam: Combat Trauma and the Undoing of Character*. New York: Scribner, 1994.

Shipler, David K. *The Working Poor: Invisible in America*. New York: Alfred A. Knopf, 2004.

Sidorkin, Alexander M. *Learning Relations*. New York: Peter Lang, 2002.

Siegel, Harvey. *Educating Reason: Rationality, Critical Thinking and Education*. New York: Routledge, 1988.

Silberman, Charles. *Crisis in the Classroom: The Remaking of American Education*. New York: Random House, 1970.

Singer, Peter. *Animal Liberation*. New York: New York Review Books, 1990.

Singer, Peter. "Taking Humanism Beyond Speciesism," *Free Inquiry*, October–November 2004: 20.

Skinner, B. F. *Science and Human Behavior*. New York: Free Press, 1953.

Skinner, B. F. *Walden Two*. New York: Macmillan, 1962.

Skinner, B. F. *Beyond Freedom and Dignity*. New York: Vintage Books, 1972.

Slone, D. Jason. *Theological Incorrectness: Why Religious People Believe What They Shouldn't*. Oxford: Oxford University Press, 2004.

Smith, Alexander McCall. *The Sunday Philosophy Club*. New York: Pantheon Books, 2004.

Smith, Christian. *Soul Searching: The Religious and Spiritual Lives of American Teenagers*. Oxford: Oxford University Press, 2005.

Smith-Christopher, Daniel L., ed. *Subverting Hatred: The Challenge of Nonviolence in Religious Traditions*. Maryknoll, NY: Orbis Books, 2002.

Bibliography

Smith, Huston. *Why Religion Matters*. San Francisco: HarperCollins, 2001.

Smith, Robert Paul. *"Where did you go?" "Out" "What did you do?" "Nothing"*. New York: W. W. Norton, 1957.

Sontag, Susan. *Regarding the Pain of Others*. New York: Farrar, Straus and Giroux, 2003.

Spina, Stephanie Urso, ed. *Smoke and Mirrors*. Lanham, MD: Rowman & Littlefield, 2000.

Spock, Benjamin. *Dr. Spock's Baby and Child Care*. New York: Pocket Books, 1998.

Spock, Benjamin. *On Parenting*. New York: Pocket Books, 2001.

Spretnak, Charlene, ed. *The Politics of Women's Spirituality*. Garden City, NY: Anchor Books, 1982.

Spring, Joel. *Educating the Consumer-Citizen*. Mahwah, NJ: Lawrence Erlbaum, 2003.

Stanton, Elizabeth Cady and the Revising Committee. *The Woman's Bible*. Seattle: Ayer Press, 1974.

Stark, Rodney R. and Bainbridge, William S. *The Future of Religion*. Berkeley: University of California Press, 1985.

Steele, Claude M. "A Threat in the Air: How Stereotypes Shape Intellectual Identity and Performance," *American Psychologist*. 52, 1997: 613–629.

Stein, Sara. *Noah's Garden: Restoring the Ecology of Our Own Back Yards*. Boston: Houghton Mifflin, 1993.

Steinberg, Ted. *Down to Earth*. Oxford: Oxford University Press, 2002.

Stone, Merlin. *When God Was a Woman*. New York: Dial Press, 1976.

Suskind, Ron. *A Hope in the Unseen*. New York: Broadway Books, 1998.

Swofford, Anthony. *Jarhead*. New York: Scribner, 2003.

Tatum, James. *The Mourner's Song*. Chicago: University of Chicago Press, 2004.

Taylor, Charles. *Sources of the Self*. Cambridge, MA: Harvard University Press, 1989.

Thaxter, Celia. *An Island Garden*. Boston: Houghton Mifflin, 1988.

Thayer-Bacon, Barbara. *Transforming Critical Thinking*. New York: Teachers College Press, 2000.

Thompson, Helen B. *The Mental Traits of Sex*. Chicago: University of Chicago Press, 1903.

Thompson, Patricia. *The Accidental Theorist*. New York: Peter Lang, 2002.

Thompson, Patricia. *In Bed with Procrustes*. New York: Peter Lang, 2003.

Thompson, Patricia. *Fatal Abstractions*. New York: Peter Lang, 2004.

Thorndike, Edward L. *Education: A First Book*. New York: Macmillan, 1912.

Thornton, Stephen. J. "Silence on Gays and Lesbians in Social Studies Curriculum," *Social Education*. 67(4), 2003: 226–230.

Thornton, Stephen. J. *Toward Social Studies That Matters*. New York: Teachers College Press, 2004.

Thurber, James. *The 13 Clocks*. New York: Donald I. Fine, 1990/1957.

Tierney, Kevin. *Darrow: A Biography*. New York: Thomas Y. Crowell, 1979.

Tillich, Paul. *The Courage to Be*. New Haven, CT: Yale University Press, 1952.

True, Michael. *An Energy Field More Intense Than War*. Syracuse, NY: Syracuse University Press, 1995.

Turner, James. *Without God, Without Creed*. Baltimore: Johns Hopkins University Press, 1985.

Unamuno, Miguel De. *Tragic Sense of Life*, trans. J. E. Crawford Flitch. New York: Dover, 1954.

Unrau, Norman J. *Thoughtful Teachers, Thoughtful Learners*. Scarborough, Ontario: Pippin, 1997.

Walter, Eugene V. *Placeways: A Theory of the Human Environment*. Chapel Hill: University of North Carolina Press, 1988.

Ward, Geoffrey C. and Burns, Ken. *Not for Ourselves Alone: The Story of Elizabeth Cady Stanton and Susan B. Anthony*. New York: Alfred A. Knopf, 1999.

Watson, Marilyn. *Learning to Trust*. San Francisco: Jossey-Bass, 2003.

Weil, Simone. *Simone Weil Reader*, ed. George A. Panichas. Mt. Kisco, NY: Moyer Bell Ltd., 1977.

West, Rebecca. *Black Lamb and Grey Falcon*. New York: Penguin Books, 1994/1941.

Westbrook, Robert. *John Dewey and American Democracy*. Ithaca, NY: Cornell University Press, 1991.

Whimbey, Arthur and Lockhead, Jack. *Problem Solving and Comprehension*. Philadelphia: Franklin Institute Press, 1982.

Whitehead, Alfred North. *The Aims of Education*. New York: Free Press, 1967.

Whitman, Walt. *Poetry and Prose*. New York: Library of America, 1982.

Wiesel, Elie. *Night*, trans. Stella Rodway. New York: Hill and Wang, 1960.

Wilson, Edward O. *Biophilia*. Cambridge, MA: Harvard University Press, 1984.

Wilson, Edward O. *The Future of Life*. New York: Alfred A. Knopf, 2002.

Wisotsky, Steven. *Beyond the War on Drugs*. Buffalo: Prometheus Books, 1990.

Wissler, Clark. *Indians of the United States*. New York: Anchor Books, 1989.

Woolf, Virginia. *A Room of One's Own*. New York: Harcourt Brace, 1929.

Woolf, Virginia. *Three Guineas*. New York: Harcourt Brace, 1966.

Woolf, Virginia. *Letters*, vol. 6, ed. Nigel Nicholson. London: Hogarth Press, 1980, p. 464.

Wuthnow, Robert. *After Heaven: Spirituality in America since the 1950s*. Berkeley: University of California Press, 1998.

Yalom, Marilyn and Carstensen, Laura L., eds. *Inside the American Couple*. Berkeley: University of California Press, 2002.

Index

Abraham, God and, 264
abuse. *See* drug abuse; verbal abuse
"achievement" motivation, 16
Acquired Immune Deficiency
    Syndrome. *See* AIDS
"Adam and Eve" myth, 241–242
    evil and, 260, 263
    Ricoeur on, 263, 266
    serpent as symbolism in, 267
    women and, influence on, 267–268
    See also literature, religious
Addams, Jane, 217, 247, 276
    pacifism of, 46, 49
Adler, Mortimer, 14, 16, 221
adolescence
    belief systems during, 258
    deists during, 258
    parenting skills during, 121
    socialization during, 100
advertising, 173
    consumerism and, 173
    health industry and, 183–189
    of Nexium, 189
    political, 193–195
    in schools, 187
    self-censorship in, 175
advertising, political
    against Kerry, 194
    "liberal" as pejorative in, 195
    "Swift Boat" ads, 194
    during U.S. elections, 193–195
    See also propaganda
Aeneid (Virgil), 36
Aesop's Fables, 133

African Americans, socialization of, 99
After Heaven (Wuthnow), 277
agnostics, 255
    Darwin as, 272
AIDS (Acquired Immune Deficiency
    Syndrome), as religious
    punishment, 248
Alcott, Louisa May, 134
Alger, Horatio, 199
Alice's Adventures in Wonderland
    (Carroll), 135
    symbolism in, 135–136
Alienist, The (Carr), 186
Alighieri, Dante, 273
All Quiet on the Western Front
    (Remarque), 105
American Association of University
    Women, 283
American Legion, 175
Amery, Jean, 60
Angel in the House, The (Patmore), 128
animal rights, 162–165
animals, 147–148
    anthropomorphism of, 150
    cruelty to, 151
    ethics and, 155–160
    hunting of, 157–158
    pain and, 157, 158
    reincarnation and, 153
    religious perspectives on, 155–156
    research on, 159–160
    rights for, 162–165
    sacrifices, 152
    See also pets

Annotated Alice, The (Gardner), 135
anthropomorphism, 150
Apple, Michael, 201
Aquinas, Thomas, on women, 236
Arendt, Hannah, 85, 86
  on labor v. work, 86–87
Ariès, Philippe, 126
Aristotle
  on friendship, 103
  on women, 236
Armstrong, Karen, 272
As You Like It (Shakespeare), 127, 132
AstraZeneca, 189
  Nexium advertising by, 189
  Prilosec and, 189
atheists, 255
Auden, W. H., 93
Auerbach, Nina, 268
autonomy
  myth of, 116
  socialization and, 103–104

Babcock, Linda, 225
Bachelard, Gaston, 64, 65, 75, 204
  on homes, 67
  on household tasks, 83
  on nests, 67
Bartholomew I (Patriarch), 156
Baumrind, Diana, 123
Beauvoir, Simone de, 236
behaviorist tradition (teaching), 12
Bekoff, Marc, 150, 157
belief systems, 256–262
  for adolescents, 258
  Christianity and, 256
  hell as part of, 270–273
  humanism as, 275
  for scientists, 254
  "theological incorrectness" and, 259
  in U.S., on God, 250–251
Bellamy, Francis, 260
Benedict XVI (Pope), 280
Bentham, Jeremy, 156, 158
Berlin, Isaiah, 177
Bettelheim, Bruno, on children's
    literature, 133
biophilia, 166–169
  curiosity of, 167
  development of, 166
  human balance within, 167

Bloom, Harold, on U.S. belief systems,
    257
Brannon, Robert, 234
Brooke, Rupert, 41, 47
Buber, Martin, 47, 93, 97, 113, 141, 261
Buck, Pearl, 243, 257
Buddhism, pacifist movements and, 43
building. *See* construction
Bush, George Walker, 188, 192
Bush, Jeb, 221
Business Roundtable, 218
Butler, Samuel, 1, 3, 116

Campbell, Joseph, 268
*Cardinal Principles of Secondary
    Education*, 64
"caring" occupations, 226–228
  exploitation of, 229
  nursing, 226–227
  subservience and, 228–229
  women in, 229
Carr, Caleb, 186
Casey, Edward
  on construction, 66
  on shelters, 68
Catholic Church
  "ensoulment" in, 262
  future of, 280
  "mental reservation" and, 195
  miracle testing by, 34
  women in, 257
Catholic League of Decency, 175
Catholic Worker, The, 44, 49
Chancer, Lynn, 235
Chase, Salmon P., 259
Cheaper by the Dozen, 138
childbirth, 129
  puerperal fever during, 129
  in religion, 129
childcare
  child-centered, 139, 140, 141, 144
  parent-centered, 139, 140
  parenting skills and, 120–128
  psychology of, 122
  punishment and, 139
children
  adult communications with, 108,
    122
  concept of "self" for, 94–97
  literature for, 132–137

Index

during medieval times, 126
under poverty, 202
questioning by, importance of, 97–98
reciprocal behaviors in, 96
response behaviors in, 95
socialization for, 97–106
See also childcare
children's literature. *See* literature, children's
Chodorow, Nancy, 95
Christianity
belief systems and, 256
pacifist movements and, 43
"Pandora" myth and, 241
"theodicy" and, 261
women under, 257
Chronicle of Higher Education, 249
Chrysostom, John, 241
Churchill, Winston, 18
Cicero, 74
cities. *See* urban centers
Civil War (U.S.)
conscientious objectors during, 44
draft riots during, 44
classical tradition (teaching), 11–13
Clean Air Initiative (U.S.), 193
Clinton, Bill, 195
Cohen, Lisbeth, 172, 176
communes, as family system, 88–90
communication
adult-to-child, 108, 122
cultural differences in, 108
dialogue as, 80
family meetings and, 138–139
organic habits and, 79–80
parenting skills and, 123–124, 137–138
within social interactions, 106
communities. *See* communes; cults; movements, Kibbutz; urban centers
concept of "self"
in children, 94–97
reciprocity and, 95
confirmation, 116, 117, 141–142
in moral education, 113–114
moral interdependence and, 117
religion and, 141

conscientious objectors
during Civil War, 44
female support for, 50
Mennonites and, 43
Quakers and, 43
U.S. history of, 43–44
during Vietnam War, 44
during WWI, 44
during WWII, 44
construction
Casey on, 66
material care, 66
consumer protections, 174
consumerism, 171–176
advertising's influence on, 173
moral effects of, 174–176
"Protestant work ethic" and, 174
schools and, 171
consumers, 178
health industry spending by, 183
conversation. *See* communication
courage, 38
manliness v., 38
Covey, Stephen, 138
Cox, Archibald, 75
Crabwalk (Grass), 55, 62
"creation" science
evolution theory v., 253
God and, 253–254
critical thinking
as concept, 32–35
as domain-specific, 35
as educational aim, 32–33
formal logic and, 34
as generalizable, 33–34
philosophers on, 32
psychologists on, 32
Cronbach, Lee, 25
cults, Peoples Temple, 89
Cultural Miseducation (Martin), 206
culture
communication and, differences in, 108
conservation of, 206
parenting skills and, influence of, 124
social interactions based on, 77
socialization and, 101–103

309

Daly, Mary, 257, 267
damnation. *See* hell
Dante. *See* Alighieri, Dante
Darrow, Clarence, 18, 116
Darwin, Charles, 18, 165
    agnosticism of, 272
Day, Dorothy, 44, 270
daydreaming, 205, 206–207
    "double-mindedness" and, 207–208
Declaration of Independence (U.S.),
    163
deists, 255
    adolescent, 258
democracy. *See* liberal democracy
Descartes, René, 20, 153, 157
    on God, ontological proof of, 252
Deschooling Society (Illich), 14
Dewey, John, 21, 114, 123, 192, 198,
    216, 217, 224
    on "desire to construct," 67
    on geography, 66
    on "single-mindedness," 21
dialogue, as communication, 80
Didion, Joan, 84
    on household tasks, 83
discipline, as parenting skill, 122–123
Disney, Walt, 56
"double-mindedness," 22, 207
    daydreaming and, 207–208
drug abuse
    education about, in schools, 142, 143
    social treatment of, 186–187
drug trade, in England, 185–186

ecumenism, 275
Edison, Thomas, 18
education
    constructivism in, 284
    critical thinking and, 32–33
    cultural conservation in, 206
    goals of, 10, 23, 64
    liberal democracy in, 218
    pacifist movements and, 48
    parent's role in, 124–126
    participation in, by gender, 232
    poverty and, 202–203
    practical studies philosophy in, 217
    socioeconomic status and, 119
    specialization in, 220–221
    standardization movement in, 202

teachers' qualifications and,
    282–283
    vocational, 216–223
    for women, 81–82
    in writing, 134
    See also education, moral;
        education, vocational; schools;
        students; teachers; teaching
education, moral, 140
    confirmation as part of, 113–114
education, specialization, 220–221
education, vocational, 216–223
    academic v., 218
    criticisms of, 217
educational institutions. *See* schools
Educational Psychology (Cronbach),
    25
educators. *See* teachers
Ehrenreich, Barbara, 152
Einstein, Albert, 18
Eliot, Charles, 218
Emerson, Ralph Waldo, 114, 115, 143
"enantiodromia," 30–31
Encyclopedia of Philosophy, 258
energy cycles, study habits and, 29
England, drug trade in, 185–186
"ensoulment," in Catholic Church, 262
Epstein, Cynthia, 233
Erewhon (Butler), 1, 116
essentialism, 230
    femininity under, 232
    feminists and, 233
    in religious literature, 230–231
ethics
    animals and, 155–160
    morality v., 213
    in occupations, 211–216
    relativism in, 214
Evangelical Environmental Network,
    156
evil
    "Adam and Eve" myth and, 260, 263
    God and, 260–261
    moral, 260
    natural, 260–261, 267–268
    original sin and, 262
evolution theory, "creation" science v.,
    253
expectations, occupational, 198–204
    self-analysis as part of, 210

Index

faith. *See* belief systems
families
  communes as, 88–90
  living arrangements for,
    nontraditional, 90
  meeting schedules for, 138–139
  responsibility within, 139–140
Farrell, J. G., 185
females. *See* women
femininity
  under essentialism, 232
  sociology and, 40
  subservience and, 234
  Woolf on, 235
feminists, essentialism and, 233
Ferraro, Barbara, 131
films. *See* media
Finn, Chester, 52
Flanagan, Caitlin, 83
Fogarty, Brian, 51
Forster, E. M., 185
Frankl, Viktor, 115
Franklin, Benjamin, 258
Fraser, James, 151, 152, 159, 164
Freire, Paulo, 109
Friedan, Betty, 82
friendship
  Aristotle on, 103
  socialization and, 103
Frost, Robert, 27

Gandhi, Mahatma, 47
Gardner, Martin, 135, 137, 264
Gauss, Johann, 27
gender
  economic inequality as result of,
    225–226
  educational participation by, 232
  literature on, 233–234
  myths and, 266–270
  stereotypes, 240–241
  See also males; women
geography, Dewey on, 66
German Americans
  during WWI, 49
  during WWII, 62
Germans, propaganda against, 191
Gilligan, James, 113
Girard, Rene, 153
Giroux, Henry, 222

Glover, Jonathan, 50, 51, 54, 192
God
  Abraham and, 264
  for agnostics, 255
  for atheists, 255
  "creation" science and, 253–254
  for deists, 255
  evil and, 260–261
  existence of, 251–256
  faith v. reason about, 251–253
  Jephthah and, 264
  Kant on, 261
  as morality source, 273–274
  ontological proof of, 252
  for polytheists, 255
  Russell on, 265
  scientists belief in, 254
  surveys about, in U.S., 250–251
  teleological proof of, 252–253
  for theists, 255
"Golden Ratio," 65–66
Golden Bough, The (Fraser), 152
Goodall, Jane, 150
Goodman, Paul, 100
Goozner, Merrill, 183
grading, institutional demands for,
  16
Grahame, Kenneth, 134
Grass, Günter, 55, 59
Gray, J. G., 39
Greene, Maxine, 193
Grissell, Eric, 181
Gulf War, U.S. propaganda during, 51,
  192
Gustloff, Wilhelm, 55

habits. *See* organic habits; study habits
Hall, G. Stanley, 231
Happiness and Education (Noddings),
  161
"hardihood," 234
Hardy, Thomas, 10
hatred
  situational factors for, 246
  from socialization, 245–247
Hays Office, 175
health industry
  advertising for, 183–189
  retail spending on, 183
  scientific research for, 185

Healthy Forests Re-Forestation Act
(U.S.), 193
Hedges, Chris, 37
Heidegger, Martin, 61
on Holocaust, 61
on homelessness, 70–71
hell, belief systems and, as part of,
270–273
Hendra, Tony, 117
Henty, G. A., 185
Hitler, Adolf, 53, 54, 273
Hodge, Charles, 256
Hoffer, Eric, 55
Holocaust, Heidegger on, 61
homeless, in U.S., 70
homelessness, Heidegger on,
70–71
homes
Bachelard on, 67
"comfort" in, 78
household tasks and, 81–87
lawns as part of, 68
living conditions as part of, 76
as metaphor, 65
natural locations of, 72
organic habits and, 75–81
privacy as part of, 78, 90
same-sex couples and, 88
sharing, 87–92
as shelter, 64–71
types of, 71
in urban centers, 72
See also household tasks; nests;
shelters
homosexuality, 244–249
contemporary views on,
247–249
educational programs about,
246–247
marriage rights for, 89
religion and, 90, 246, 247–249
verbal abuse against, 244–245
Hopi tribes, 47
household tasks, 81–87
Bachelard on, 83
Didion on, 83
men's responsibility for, 82–83
by women, 81–85
human impersonators, 73, 84

humanism, 275
ecumenism and, 275
humanistic psychology, 16
Hume, David, 95, 252
on response behaviors, 95
Hussein, Saddam, propaganda use by,
191
Hussey, Patricia, 131
Hutchins, Robert Maynard, 221

Iliad (Homer), 38, 39, 51, 58
Illich, Ivan, 14
Industrial Workers of the World,
during WWI, 49

"Jabberwocky" (Lewis), 136
James, William, 25, 39, 41, 42,
234
Japan, privacy in, 78
Japanese Americans, WWII
internment of, 49
Jefferson, Thomas, 75, 258
Jephthah, God and, 264
"Job" myth, 265. *See also* literature,
religious
John Paul (Pope), 156
Jones, Jim, cults and, 89
Judaism, myths in, 265–266
Jude the Obscure (Hardy), 10
Jung, Carl, 30, 232, 261
on "enantiodromia," 30–31
justice, Rawls on, 156–157

Kant, Immanuel, 252
God as architect, 261
Kanter, Rosabeth Moss, 88
Keller, Catherine, 268
Kerry, John, 194
Kibbutz movement. *See* movements,
Kibbutz
Kierkegaard, Søren, 255, 264
Kimmel, Michael, 234
Kingsley, Charles, 134
Kingsolver, Barbara, 75
Kipling, Rudyard, 57
Kissen, Rita, 244
Klein, Jessie, 235
Knowles, John, 17
Kung, Hans, 251

Index

labor
  ancient assessments on, 85
  under Marxism, 86
  work v., 86–87
  See also household tasks
Laschever, Sara, 225
lawns
  ecological impact of, 179–181
  homes and, 68
  in U.S., demographics, 180
leaders v. followers, 54
Leibniz, Gottfried W., 273
LeQuire, Stan L., 156
Levi, Primo, 60, 77
  on WWII torture, 60
Lewis, C. S., 260
liberal democracy, in education, 218
liberalism, philosophical, 94
liberation movements. *See*
    movements, liberation
Lindbergh, Anne Morrow, 279
Lippmann, Walter, 192
listening, 110
  during social interactions, 109
literature
  on gender, 233–234
  Plato on, 133
  Rousseau on, 133
  See also literature, children's;
    literature, religious
literature, children's, 132–137
  Aesop's Fables, 133
  Bettelheim on, 133
  psychology of, 133
literature, religious
  essentialism in, 230–231
  women in, 269
Little Children (Perotta), 107
Little Women (Alcott), 134
logic, critical thinking and, 34
Looking Backward, 215
Luther, Martin, 256
Lutz, Frank, 68

MacIntyre, Alasdair, 219
MAD ("mutually assured
    destruction"), 209
magic, religion v., 151–152
Magic Mountain, The (Mann), 77

Maitland, Sara, 269
males
  biological predispositions of,
    230–236
  emotionality of, 235
  household tasks and, 82–83
manliness, 234
  courage v., 38
  "hardihood" and, 234
  See also masculinity
Mann, Thomas, 77
Marcel, Gabriel, 110
Marcuse, Herbert, 61
marriage, for homosexuals, 89
Martin, Jane, 206
Marxism, 115
  labor under, 86
masculinity, 39, 234
  four "rules" of, 234–235
  Woolf on, 235
Maslow, Abraham, 14, 15, 16, 89, 280
McCarthy, Mary, 270
media
  Hays Office influence on, 175
  moral effects from, 175
  war representations in, 37, 41
  women in, 96
memorization. *See* remembering
men. *See* males
Mennonites, conscientious objectors
    and, 43
"mental reservation," Catholic Church
    and, 195
Merck Industries, 183, 189
  Vioxx recall by, 183
Michelangelo, 27
Michulski, Joanne, 130
Miles, Jack, 237, 265
Mill, John Stuart, 274
Milne, A. A., 134
Minding Animals (Beckoff), 150
minorities
  educational opportunities for, 200
  "skipped generation" mobility for,
    200
  See also African Americans;
    Japanese Americans; Native
    Americans
Miro, Joan, 27

mnemonic devices, 25, 26
moral identity, 36
  authority and, 104
  loss of, 57–63
  during My Lai massacre, 57
  in *Nineteen Eighty-Four*, 115
moral interdependence, 117, 118
  confirmation and, 117
morality
  ethics v., 213
  female, in religion, 241–242
  from God, 273–274
  sources of, 273–277
Mormonism, polygamy within, 89, 91
Morris, Simon Conway, 253
motherhood, 128–132
  Nazi glorification of, 131
  political exploitation of, 131
  Soviet glorification of, 131
  See also childcare
motivation
  "achievement," 16
  behaviorist teaching and, 12
  in Classical tradition, 11–13
  hybrid theories of, 17
  internal, 15–16
  in Progressive tradition, 11–13
  for students, 19
  by teachers, 11–18
  theories of, for teachers, 11–14
movements, Kibbutz, 89
movements, liberation, for women,
    83–84
movements, pacifist
  Addams and, 46, 49
  Buddhism and, 43
  Christianity and, 43
  liberal education and, 48
  Native Americans as part of, 47
  Oxford Pledge and, 48
  Rankin and, 45
  in U.S., 43
  against war, 42–43
  during WWI, 49
  See also conscientious objectors
movements, standardization
    (education), 202
Mozart, Amadeus, 27
"mutually assured destruction." *See*
  MAD

My Lai massacre, 57
Myers, Diana, 98
myths, 263–266
  "Adam and Eve," 241–242, 263
  gender and, 266–270
  Jewish interpretations of, 265–266
  "Job," 265
  "Pandora," 241
  See also symbolism

Nabhan, Gary, 166
Nash, Robert, 279
National Association of
    Manufacturers, 217, 218
Native Americans
  Hopi tribes, 47
  in pacifist movements, 47
  Pueblo tribes, 47
natural world. *See* biophilia
Nazis, 53
  motherhood and, glorification of, 131
  propaganda use by, 51
Nearing, Helen, 177
Nearing, Scott, 172, 177
Neill, A. S., 12, 16, 119
Nelson, Richard, 157
nests, 67
  Bachelard on, 67
New Age spirituality, 279–280
Nexium, advertising of, 189
Night (Wiesel), 158
9/11, U.S. and, 52
Nineteen Eighty-Four (Orwell), 115
  moral identity themes in, 115
  political propaganda in, 193
No Child Left Behind Act (U.S.), 194
Noble, David, 240
Nordau, Max, 238
Norris, Kathleen, 270
nursing, as "caring" occupation,
    226–227

occupations
  "caring," 226–228
  ethical considerations in, 211–216
  expectations of, 198–204
  hierarchical view of, 200–201
  prestige as result of, 200
  See also "caring" occupations
Old Testament, 91

Index

Ordered to Care (Reverby), 229
orderliness, in study habits, 20
organic habits
   communication patterns as, 79–80
   homes and, 75–81
   linguistic, 80
Orme, Nicholas, 126, 127, 132
Orwell, George, 18, 53
Owen, David, 181
Owen, Wilfred, 47
   on patriotism, 41
Oxford Pledge, pacifist movements
   and, 48

pacifist movements. *See* movements,
   pacifist
Paideia Proposal, The (Adler), 14, 221
pain, animals and, 157, 158
Paine, Thomas, 258
Paley, Vivian, 209
"Pandora" myth, Christianity and, 241
parenting skills
   for adolescents, 121
   bad, 119
   childcare and, 120–128
   communication as part of, 123–124,
      137–138
   cultural differences' influence on,
      124
   discipline as part of, 122–123
   education in, 120–121
   education responsibilities and,
      124–126
   educational pressure and, 144–145
   expert opinions on, 124
   punishment as part of, 123
   Spock on, 124
   See also childcare
Pascal, Blaise, 254
Passage to India, A (Forster), 185
Patmore, Coventry, 128
patriotism, during war, 41
Patten, Simon, 172, 174
peace movements. *See* movements,
   pacifist
Peoples Temple, 89
Perotta, Tom, 107
Peshkin, Alan, 275
pets, 148–150
   responsibility for, 148–149

Phaedrus (Socrates), 168
Phillips, J. A., 242
philosophical liberalism. *See*
   liberalism, philosophical
places
   attachment to, 72–73
   as metaphors, 72
   naming of, 72
Plato
   on literature, 133
   on "psychagogy," 168
Poetics of Space (Bachelard), 65
Poincaré, Henri, 28
Pollan, Michael, 64, 79, 180
   construction, 65
polygamy, 91
   within Mormonism, 89, 91
   in Old Testament, 91
polytheists, 255
Pope, Denise Clark, 144, 210
Potter, Beatrix, 134
poverty, 201–202
   children under, 202
   education as antidote to, 202–203
Powers, Richard, 56
Prilosec, 189
Prisoner's Dilemma (Powers), 56
privacy
   homes and, 78, 90
   in Japan, 78
Progressive tradition, teaching, 11–13
Prohibition Act, in U.S., 186
propaganda, 50, 190–197
   against Germans, 191
   during Gulf War, by U.S., 51
   Hussein use of, 191
   Islamist, 51
   Nazis' use of, 51
   in *Nineteen Eighty-Four*, 193
   during Vietnam War, by U.S., 51
   war, 190–192
"Protestant work ethic,"
   consumerism's effect on, 174
"psychagogy," 168
psychologists, on critical thinking, 32
psychology
   of childcare, 122
   of children's literature, 133
   humanistic, 16
public opinion, 192

Public Opinion (Lippmann), 192
Pueblo tribes, 47
puerperal fever, 129
punishment
    AIDS as, 248
    childcare and, 139
    parenting skills and, 123

Quakers, conscientious objectors and,
    43

Rankin, Jeannette, 45
    pacifism of, 45
    WWI and, 45
Rawls, John, 161
    on justice, 156–157
reciprocity, 95
    in caring relationships, 95
    in children, 96
reincarnation, animals and, 153
religion
    AIDS and, as punishment, 248
    animals' role in, 155–156
    childbirth in, 129
    confirmation and, 141
    female morality in, 241–242
    history of, in U.S., 259–260
    magic v., 151–152
    reproductive rights and, 131
    responsibility under, 141
    sacrifices for, 153
    scientific proof of, 34
    See also Buddhism; Catholic Church;
        Christianity; Judaism; spirituality
Remarque, Erich Maria, 105
remembering, 24–27
    mnemonic devices for, 25, 26
    structures for, 26
    techniques for, 24–26
Rendell, Ruth, 106
reproductive rights, religious
    affiliation and, 131
research, for health industry, 185
response behaviors
    in children, 95
    Hume on, 95
responsibility
    within families, 139–140
    for pets, 148–149
    religious training and, 141

rules as form of, 112, 139
    shared, 112–118
Reverby, Susan, 227
Rich, Adrienne, 129
    on female devaluation, 96
Ricoeur, Paul, 262, 265
    on "Adam and Eve" myth, 263, 266
rights
    language of, 163, 164
    needs v., 163
    slavery and, 164
    UN Universal Declaration of Human
        Rights, 164
    See also animal rights
Rogers, Carl, 15
Roosevelt, Eleanor, 248
Rose, Mike, 203
Rousseau, Jean-Jacques, on literature,
    133
Ruddick, Sara, 40, 129
Russell, Bertrand, 209, 272, 274, 275
    on God, 265
Russia, Soviet, motherhood and,
    glorification of, 131
Rybczynski, Witold, 78

same-sex relationships. *See*
    homosexuality
Sartre, Jean-Paul, 93, 115
Schein, Seth, 38
schools
    advertising in, 187
    consumerism and, 171
    course offerings in, 23
    curriculum development in, 285–289
    drug education in, 142, 143
    environmental issues in, 68
    socialization in, 106
Schopenhauer, Arthur, on suffering,
    154–155
Schweitzer, Albert, 147, 158
science
    "creation," 253–254
    religion and, 34
    See also "creation" science
Selective Service, in U.S., end of, 44
self-discipline, for students, 20
Semmelweiss, Ignaz, 129, 185
"sense of belonging," during wartime,
    56

Index

Separate Peace, A (Knowles), 17, 18
serpent, as symbolism, 267
7 *Habits of Highly Effective Families,
  The* (Covey), 138
Shay, Jonathan, 104
shelters, 67
  Casey on, 68
  "found," 67
  as home, 64–71
  primitive, 67
  sociological study on, 69, 70
Shipler, David, 203
Shulman, Alix Kates, 84
Siegel, Harvey, 45
Siege of Krishnapur, The (Farrell), 185,
  245
Singer, Peter, 156, 159
  on "speciesism," 160
"single-mindedness," 21
Skinner, B. F., 14, 89, 116
"skipped generation" mobility, 200
slavery, rights, 164
Slone, Jason, on intuitive religious
  concepts, 259
Smith, Christian, on adolescent belief
  systems, 258
Smith, Huston, 158
Smith, Joseph, 91
Smith, Mary Rozet, 248
social interactions, 106–111
  communication within, 106
  debate as, 109
  listening during, 109
  note-taking as part of, 109
  patterns of, 76
Socialists, during WWI, U.S., 49
socialization, 105
  for adolescents, 100
  for African Americans, 99
  antisocial behaviors as result of, 111
  autonomy and, 103–104
  for children, 97–106
  cultural differences in, 101–103
  friendship as part of, 103
  hatred from, 245–247
  mutual relations as part of, 102–103
  schools' role in, 106
  structures for, 98
  of teachers, 102
  See also social interactions

sociology, femininity and, 40
Socrates, 10, 168, 289
Somerville, Mary, 240, 241
Sontag, Susan, 48, 193
Soviet Russia. *See* Russia, Soviet
"speciesism," 159, 160–165
  Singer on, 160
Speer, Albert, 51
Spellings, Margaret, 249
spirituality, 277–281
  female, 278–279
  in nature, 278
  New Age, 279–280
  skeptical, 279
  Wuthnow on, 277
Spock, Benjamin, 119, 121, 139
  on parenting skills, cultural
    differences in, 124
Spooner, W. A., 60
"Spoonerisms," 61
Spring, Joel, 172
standardization movement. *See*
  movements, standardization
Stanton, Elizabeth Cady, 231
Stein, Sara, 179, 181
Steinberg, Ted, 179
stereotypes, gender, 240–241
Stimson, Henry, 56
students
  motivation for, 19
  self-discipline for, 20
  study habits for, 19–24
  See also study habits
study habits
  conditions for, 20
  copying and, 20
  "double-mindedness" and, 22
  energy cycles and, 29
  orderliness in, 20
  "single-mindedness" and, 21
  for students, 19–24
  time-management as part of,
    74–75
  Wallas on, 28
suffering, Schopenhauer on, 154–155
Summerhill (Neill), 14
Sunday Philosophy Club, The, 173
Suskind, Ron, on minority educational
  opportunities, 200
Swofford, Anthony, 37, 48, 58, 75

symbolism
  In *Alice's Adventures in Wonderland*,
    135–136
  serpent as, 267
  women as, 237

Tale of Peter Rabbit, The (Potter), 134
Taylor, Frederick, 179
teachers
  in Classical tradition, 11–13
  colleges for, 283
  motivation by, 11–18
  multidisciplinary proficiency for,
    288
  in Progressive tradition, 11
  qualifications for, 282–283
  socialization of, 102
  See also teaching
teachers colleges, 283
  American Association of University
    Women and, 283
teaching
  behaviorist tradition, 12
  in Classical tradition, 11–13
  ideology in, 14
  motivation theories for, 11–14
  in Progressive tradition, 11
Thaxter, Celia, 168
theists, 255
"theodicy," 261
"theological incorrectness," 259
13 Clocks, The (Thurber), 137
Thomas, M. Carey, 231
Thompson, Helen, 239
Thoreau, Henry David, 177
Tillich, Paul, 38, 56
time
  perception of, 74
  sociological effects of, 75
time-management, study habits and,
    74–75
"Tommy" (Kipling), 57
"topolepsy," 168
Tuesdays With Morrie (Albom), 189
Turner, James, 274

Unamuno, Miguel, 250
United Nations, Universal Declaration
    of Human Rights, 164
United States. *See* U.S.

urban centers
  cultural importance of, 74
  ecological impact of, 181–182
  homes in, 72
U.S. (United States)
  conscientious objectors in, 43–44
  Declaration of Independence, 163
  God and, belief surveys, 250–251,
    257
  homeless in, 70
  lawns in, demographics, 180
  9/11 in, 52
  pacifist movements in, 43, 49
  Prohibition in, 186
  propaganda use by, 51
  religious history in, 259–260
  Selective Service in, end of, 44
  spirituality in, 277
  WWI propaganda by, 191
  See also African Americans; German
    Americans; Japanese Americans;
    Native Americans

Valery, Paul, 27
Van Dusen, Henry, 256
"variability hypothesis," 239
  women in, 238–240
verbal abuse, against homosexuals,
    244–245
Victoria (Queen), 61, 129
Vietnam War, 41, 99
  conscientious objectors during, 44
  moral atrocities during, 59
  My Lai massacre during, 57
  U.S. propaganda during, 51
  veteran attitudes toward, 104
Vioxx, recall of, 183, 189
Virgil, 36
vocational education. *See* education,
    vocational

Walden Two (Skinner), 14, 119
Wallas, Graham, 28
  on study processes, 28
Walter, E. V., 168, 205
war
  attractions of, 36–42
  courage and, 38
  media representations of, 37, 41
  objectification during, 38–39

pacifist movements against, 42–43
patriotism during, 41
propaganda, 190–192
rejection of, 42–48
"sense of belonging" during, 56
See also Civil War; Gulf War;
    Vietnam War; warrior tradition;
    WWI; WWII
Warner, Maria, 267
warrior tradition, 40
Washington, George, 258
Water Babies, The (Kingsley), 134
Weil, Simone, 20, 38, 58
West, Rebecca, 101
White, William Allen, 45
Whitehead, Alfred North, 120
Whitman, Walt, 222
Whyte, William H., 170
Wiesel, Elie, 72, 158
Wilhelm Gustloff (ship), 55, 62
Williams, Rowan, 111
Wilson, E. O., 156, 166
Wilson, Woodrow, 45, 46, 49, 191
    during WWI, 49
Wind in the Willows, The (Grahame),
    134
Winnie-the-Pooh (Milne), 134
Wissler, Clark, 47
With Clive in India (Henty), 186
Woman's Bible, The (Stanton), 231
women
    "Adam and Eve" myth and, effects
        on, 267–268
    Aquinas on, 236
    Aristotle on, 236
    biological predispositions of,
        230–236
    in "caring" occupations, 229
    in Catholic Church, 257
    under Christianity, 257
    conscientious objector support by,
        50
    devaluation of, 96
    education advancements of, 81–82
    emotionality of, 235
    household tasks by, 81–85
    as intellectually "inferior," 231
    liberation movement for, 83–84

media images of, 96
    morality of, in religion, 241–242
    in pacifist movements, 46–47
    in religious literature, 269
    Rich on, 96
    salary negotiations by, 225–226
    serpent and, 267
    spirituality and, 278–279
    symbolism about, 237
    in "variability hypothesis," 238–240
    in workforce, post-WWII, 81–82,
        225–230
    See also femininity; feminists
Woolf, Virginia, 40, 46, 48, 128, 193,
    237
    on masculinity/femininity, 235, 238
work
    labor v., 86–87
    women and, post-WWII, 81–82,
        225–230
World War I. *See* WWI
Wuthnow, Robert, 277
    on spirituality, in U.S., 277
WWI (World War I)
    anti-immigrant sentiment during,
        49
    conscientious objectors during, 44
    German American treatment during,
        49
    Industrial Workers of the World
        during, 49
    literature about, 41
    Rankin during, 45
    Socialists during, 49
    U.S. pacifist movement during, 49
    U.S. propaganda in, 191
    Wilson, Woodrow, during, 49
WWII (World War II)
    conscientious objectors during, 44
    German American treatment during,
        62
    Japanese American internment
        during, 49
    moral atrocities during, 59
    torture during, 60
    See also Holocaust; Nazis

Yates, Andrea, 130

284